To get Nortel Certified:

- study the material in the guide
- take the certification practice exam on the enclosed CD
- register for the official exam (920-807) at *www.prometric.com/nortel*
- pass the official exam

By passing exam 920-807, you will become a
Nortel Certified Technology Specialist (NCTS):
Unified Communications Solutions

Unified Communications Solutions

Nortel Press

Nortel Networks Inc.
4001 E. Chapel Hill-Nelson Hwy.
Research Triangle Park, NC 27709
www.nortel.com/nortelpress

Published by:

Nortel Press
Nortel Networks Inc.
4001 E. Chapel Hill-Nelson Hwy.
Research Triangle Park, NC 27709

Printed in Canada

Second Printing January 2009

Library of Congress Control Number: 2008932946

ISBN 978-0-9801074-1-8

Warning

Always refer to the procedures described in the most current documentation that are appropriate for the system and software release that you support. Failure to use the appropriate documentation can result in serious technical difficulties and damage to your system.

To access Nortel technical documentation, visit *www.nortel.com/support* or contact your local system vendor for the most current documentation releases.

Foreword

Unified Communications: A major force for business transformation

International Data Corporation (IDC) believes the demand for more efficient and productive communications will spark the next major wave of information technology (IT) and communications transformation. This trend and the technologies that support it are called Unified Communications (UC). Very simply, UC involves the integration of multiple modes of communication with key business applications. Through a single integrated interface, users can place an audio or video call, send an instant message, check a user's presence, or make a conference call. All of this functionality is integrated within applications such as e-mail, productivity suites, and other business software. This is a new frontier because what were once separate silos—information technology, communications, and application software—are coming together to deliver productivity improvements and exciting new industry value propositions.

The promise of UC has been long in coming. We have finally rounded the corner and UC is positioned to forever change the face of communications in business and consumer markets. The reality is turning out to be even better than we could have imagined, bringing us the ability to define with whom, when, and how we communicate, and allowing us to choose the preferred medium for communication within the context of the business demands.

How to navigate toward successful UC deployment

UC is a journey with incremental gains and unique paths for every organization; no one size fits all. As UC moves out of pilot projects and onto the production network, it will herald a change in IT organizational structures. IT departments are realigning themselves, breaking apart traditional domains to make way for the merging of communications and traditional IT infrastructure. As UC options continue to proliferate, so will the complexity of the network and the interactions among various types of communications.

Chief information officers, IT architects, and business managers are increasingly attempting to take a more holistic view of communications in the enterprise. As executives look for new opportunities, someone needs to study and understand how UC can transform their business. This will include understanding how to evaluate vendor options, choosing the best migration path from existing infrastructure, and evaluating the value of integrating communications with applications and processes. This UC certification study guide is designed to help IT professionals make informed decisions toward successful deployment of UC solutions.

Why UC certification credentials matter

The road to all-encompassing UC can be complex and daunting; in all cases it forces technology professionals beyond their traditional knowledge base. People who can navigate through different solution sets, return-on-investment options, communications mediums, security threat models, applications development, and business transformation are rare today. UC certifications give IT professionals the critical skills to achieve early wins and accelerate long-term success.

If this skills gap wasn't bad enough, UC deployment cannot be solved through the consolidation of everything with a single vendor. Enterprise customers have sunk IT and network investments and need to explore multivendor solutions to leverage that investment into the future.

IT and communications professionals are encouraged to pursue UC solutions certification programs. Not only do they provide the necessary education on the challenges ahead, but they also fill the skill set gaps needed to successfully deploy a UC solution and gain a competitive advantage.

Nora Freedman, Senior Analyst, Unified Communications, IDC

About IDC

IDC is the premier global provider of market intelligence, advisory services, and events for the information technology, telecommunications, and consumer technology markets. IDC helps IT professionals, business executives, and the investment community make fact-based decisions on technology purchases and business strategy. More than 1,000 IDC analysts provide global, regional, and local expertise on technology and industry opportunities and trends in over 100 countries. For more than 44 years, IDC has provided strategic insights to help our clients achieve their key business objectives. IDC is a subsidiary of IDG, the world's leading technology media, research, and events company. You can learn more about IDC by visiting *www.idc.com*.

Authors

David Kim

David Kim, B.S.E.E., is the President and Chief Security Officer for Security Evolutions, Inc. (www.securityevolutions.com), which specializes in VoIP, convergence, and SIP layered security solutions for businesses and organizations that must secure VoIP and SIP communications. He is also a Director for UC Integration, LLC (www.ucintegration.com), a Unified Communications training and consulting firm that specializes in solving unique business communication challenges with UC solutions and systems integration in VoIP, Nortel, Microsoft, and VoIP and SIP layered security solutions.

Michael Gibbs

Michael Gibbs is a network and security architect for VeriSign, Inc., where he is part of a team responsible for the overall network and security architecture of the main security product lines within VeriSign. He brings 15 years of network and security experience, with a strong background in IP network engineering, VoIP design, and security best practices, as well as hands-on experience with voice, data, networking, and security software and hardware. Previously, he was with Security Evolutions, Inc. (SEI) as their active Chief Technical Officer, where he was responsible for the overall technical management of SEI's IT security consulting services. He was also SEI's lead in the development and design of secured solutions for enterprise VoIP and SIP implementations in a layered security solution where compliancy and information security are paramount.

Bob Decker

Bob Decker, a Certified Information Systems Security Professional (CISSP), is currently the Unified Communications Practice Leader for Security Evolutions, Inc. His IT and enterprise communications experience encompasses 30 years of technical design and development, network design, technical marketing, and management. This experience includes LAN/WAN, internetworking, enterprise networks management, and IT security for voice, video, and data networking infrastructures. He continues to support Nortel channel partners in their transformation to full-service, value-added resellers of IT infrastructure solutions.

Acknowledgments

Nortel

No single person is responsible for this book; it is due to the effort of many Nortel employees, all of whom were invaluable for their individual contributions.

Authors

The author team consisting of David Kim, Bob Decker, and Michael Gibbs embarked on this project with two goals in mind. The first goal was to educate the reader on how Unified Communications can solve unique business communication challenges commonly found in businesses and organizations today. The second goal was to help the reader with how best to design, procure, and implement a successful Unified Communications solution.

We would like to thank the Nortel Press project team for providing us with this authoring opportunity. We would also like to thank our respective spouses and families for providing the author team patience and support during content writing.

Contents at a Glance

Part I: The Evolution of Messaging

Chapter 1: Introduction to Unified Communications 1

Chapter 2: Elements of Unified Communications...........................19

Chapter 3: The Impact of Convergence, VoIP, and SIP 43

Chapter 4: Current Unified Communications Landscape.............63

Part II: Solving Enterprise Business Communications Challenges

Chapter 5: Critical Business Applications and Processes 81

Chapter 6: Solving Business Challenges 109

Chapter 7: Mapping the Solution to Technology 141

Chapter 8: Building a Measurable Financial ROI with KPIs 171

Part III: Implementing Unified Communications Solutions

Chapter 9: Conducting a Unified Communications
Proof-of-Concept Pilot Project...195

Chapter 10: Creating a Unified Communications
Project Statement of Work 213

Chapter 11: Conducting Unified Communications
Systems Integration 229

Chapter 12: Applications Integration with Endpoint Devices ... 249

Part IV: Securing VoIP, SIP, and Unified Communications Solutions

Chapter 13: VoIP Threats and Vulnerabilities 265

Chapter 14: Best Practices for VoIP Security............................... 295

Chapter 15: SIP Threats and Vulnerabilities 319

Chapter 16: Best Practices for SIP Security.................................343

Chapter 17: Implementing a Multilayered VoIP
and SIP Security Solution 369

Appendix A: Answers 393

Glossary... 425

Index... 435

Table of Contents

Part I: The Evolution of Messaging

Chapter 1: Introduction to Unified Communications *1*

The human communications center 3
Unified Communications 4
    What is UC? 4
    Who is driving UC? 7
    Why UC now? 9
    Key market makers 10
    Vendor solutions 12
Knowledge Check 1-1: Introduction to Unified Communications 16
Chapter summary 18

Chapter 2: Elements of Unified Communications *19*

Converged desktop 21
Presence 24
What is presence? 25
    Presence-aware applications 29
    Instant messaging 32
    Conferencing 34
    Collaboration 36
    Fixed mobile convergence 37
Knowledge Check 2-1: Elements of Unified Communications 39
Chapter summary 41

Chapter 3: The Impact of Convergence, VoIP, and SIP *43*

Just what is convergence? 45
Infrastructure convergence 46
Protocol convergence 47
Application convergence 49
Organization convergence 50
VoIP: The foundation for SIP enablement 51
SIP: The foundation for Unified Communications 52
SIP features 53
Federations and company-to-company communications 57

Federations 58
B2B collaboration 59
Knowledge Check 3-1: The Impact of Convergence, VoIP, and SIP 60
Chapter summary..62

Chapter 4: Current Unified Communications Landscape **63**

Overview of UC vendors and offerings: Enterprise...65
Microsoft Office Communication Server 2007 66
IBM Lotus Sametime..71
Overview of UC vendors and offerings: SMB..74
Gartner Group UC Magic Quadrant..75
Assessment and overview of completeness of vision for UC enablement 77
Knowledge Check 4-1: Current Unified Communications Landscape 78
Chapter summary..80

Part II: Solving Enterprise Business Communications Challenges

Chapter 5: Critical Business Applications and Processes........................... **81**

Enterprise transformation 83
Service-oriented architecture (SOA) 84
Customer service (CS)...87
Customer relationship management (CRM) 90
Supply chain management (SCM) 93
Enterprise resource planning (ERP)..97
Sales force automation (SFA)..101
Knowledge Check 5-1: Critical Business Applications and Processes.......................104
Chapter summary..107

Chapter 6: Solving Business Challenges **109**

Unified Communications solution benefits...111
Common UC benefits 111
Integrating UC within SOA applications to solve inefficiencies 112
Solving CS business challenges with UC enablement 117
Solving customer relationship management business challenges
with UC enablement 123
Solving supply change management business challenges with UC enablement 125
Solving enterprise resource planning business challenges with UC enablement......130
Solving sales force management business challenges with UC enablement.............133
Knowledge Check 6-1: Solving Business Challenges..137
Chapter summary..140

Chapter 7: Mapping the Solution to Technology **141**

Mapping the solution to technology and UC enablement............................. 143
Mapping the solution to SOA applications and UC enablement 145
Mapping the solution to CS with CRM and UC enablement...................... 149
Mapping the solution to SCM and UC enablement...................................... 153
Mapping the solution to ERP and UC enablement...................................... 158
Mapping the solution to SFA and UC enablement....................................... 163
Knowledge Check 7-1: Mapping the Solution to Technology 167
Chapter summary 170

Chapter 8: Building a Measurable Financial ROI with KPIs **171**

The business case for UC enablement.. 173
    UC business decision makers... 173
    UC enablement business decision.. 173
    UC enablement benefits.. 174
    UC enablement cost savings 175
    UC enablement cost elements... 175
Using KPIs to measure UC enablement success 176
    SFA example KPIs and metrics.. 176
    Integration of UC enablement with business processes 177
Tracking and monitoring UC KPIs and metrics.. 178
    Example SFA UC KPIs and metrics 179
Forrester Consulting UC Business Value Tool v1.5...................................... 182
    UC Business Value Tool v1.5 positioning 183
    Total Economic Impact model 183
    Inputting data into the UC Business Value Tool v1.5 184
Building the UC enablement business case 186
    UC Business Value Tool v1.5 financial outputs 186
Knowledge Check 8-1: Building a Measurable Financial ROI with KPIs.................. 190
Chapter summary 193

Part III: Implementing Unified Communications Solutions

Chapter 9: Conducting a Unified Communications Proof-of-Concept
Pilot Project **195**

Unified Communications pilot project planning considerations 197
    Purpose of UC enablement... 198
    Cost justifying a UC project 198
Define the scope of the project... 199
    Project technical requirements and capabilities....................................... 199
    UC enablement projects have two major phases 200

UC project goals and objectives...203
    Minimizing the risk associated with a UC project 203
    Scope of defining goals and objectives...203
Align requirements, goals, and objectives with key performance
indicators and metrics...205
    Forrester Consulting Business Value Tool v1.5 KPIs and metrics 206
Develop a financial budget for the project...207
    UC project budget scope 207
Knowledge Check 9-1: Conducting a Unified Communications
Proof-of-Concept Pilot Project...209
Chapter summary...211

*Chapter 10: Creating a Unified Communications Project Statement
of Work* **213**

UC project phases, tasks, and deliverables..215
Defining the statement of work for a UC project...................................217
Major UC project milestones and checkpoints......................................220
Aligning a UC project scope to a project budget 222
Building a UC project team...223
Knowledge Check 10-1: Creating a Unified Communications
Project Statement of Work...225
Chapter summary...227

Chapter 11: Conducting Unified Communications Systems Integration **229**

Putting it all together in an enterprise UC ecosystem 231
TDM-PBX, IP-PBX, and IP Softphone system integration requirements 232
    Installation and configuration of Office Communications
    Server 2007 proxy with MCM..235
    Installation of Telephony Gateway and Services component....................235
    Remote call control...237
    Normalization...238
    SIP routing and redundancy configuration.....................................238
UC enablement with the Office Communications Server 2007 application server ...239
System integration requirements for the Office Communications
Server 2007 application server 241
Active Directory and enterprise systems integration requirements 243
Knowledge Check 11-1: Conducting Unified Communications
Systems Integration...245
Chapter summary...247

Chapter 12: Applications Integration with Endpoint Devices **249**

Endpoint device application integration 251
    Local endpoint devices 251
    Mobile endpoint devices... 251
Desktop and laptop application and system integration................................ 252
    Unified user interface.. 252
    Application and service support 253
Mobility and computing application and system integration........................ 254
    Tablets 254
    Tablets and UC... 254
    PDAs.. 254
    Smartphones.. 255
    Dual-mode devices... 255
    Mobile applications 256
Secure network access and authentication requirements 257
    Local vs. mobile UC devices 257
    Encrypting the call on mobile devices.. 257
    Encrypting the data on mobile devices 258
    Encryption on a local endpoint device 259
    Authentication on an endpoint device 259
    Registering an endpoint device 260
    Endpoint authorization... 260
Tracking and monitoring endpoint device access and security policies 260
    Monitoring end-device access... 261
    Monitoring end-device usage 261
    Tracking an endpoint's location 262
Knowledge Check 12-1: Applications Integration with Endpoint Devices.............. 263
Chapter summary 264

Part IV: Securing VoIP, SIP, and Unified Communications Solutions

Chapter 13: VoIP Threats and Vulnerabilities **265**

Introduction 267
What is a vulnerability? 268
    Hardware 269
    Software 270
    Protocol vulnerabilities.. 273
    Social engineering... 274
    Phishing.. 274
What is a threat?... 275
    Known threats 275
    Unknown threats 277

What is risk? 278
    Product solution 279
    Industry...279
    Accessibility...279
VoIP protocol vulnerabilities 280
    H.323..280
    Session Initiation Protocol (SIP) 286
    UNISTIM 289
    RTSP 289
    RTP and RTCP 289
    MGCP..290
Knowledge Check 13–1: VoIP Threats and Vulnerabilities.....................292
Chapter summary...293

Chapter 14: Best Practices for VoIP Security **295**

The need for VoIP security...297
Defining confidentiality goals and objectives for VoIP 298
    VoIP and UC confidentiality goals and objectives 299
Defining integrity goals and objectives for VoIP......................................302
    VoIP data integrity 302
    VoIP integrity security goals and objectives 303
Defining availability goals and objectives for VoIP 305
    VoIP availability security goals and objectives..................................305
Compliance and VoIP security 306
Best practices for enterprise VoIP security 308
    VoIP usage policies best practices...310
    Validation of security policies best practices 311
    Audit of software and images best practices.......................................312
Vendor solutions for VoIP security...313
Knowledge Check 14-1: Best Practices for VoIP Security 315
Chapter summary...317

Chapter 15: SIP Threats and Vulnerabilities... **319**

SIP in the enterprise IP network 321
SIP 321
What is at risk?..326
Common SIP threats 327
Common SIP vulnerabilities 328
SIP protocol vulnerabilities 337
SIP attacks 338
SIP extension into other federations 339

Knowledge Check 15-1: SIP Threats and Vulnerabilities.. 340
Chapter summary 341

Chapter 16: Best Practices for SIP Security **343**

The need for SIP security 345
Defining confidentiality goals and objectives for SIP applications 346
    Confidentiality and SIP.. 348
    SIP confidentiality goals and objectives 348
Defining integrity goals and objectives for SIP applications...................................... 352
    SIP application integrity goals and objectives... 353
Defining availability goals and objectives for SIP applications 360
Compliance and SIP security 361
Best practices for enterprise and federation SIP security... 362
    Network security best practices... 362
Knowledge Check 16–1: Best Practices for SIP Security 366
Chapter summary 367

Chapter 17: Implementing a Multilayered VoIP and SIP Security Solution **369**

Introduction 371
Designing a layered defense strategy for enterprise VoIP and SIP infrastructures.. 371
Enterprise VoIP and SIP security policy creation 373
Implementing secure federations between companies 375
VoIP and SIP security: Ensuring confidentiality, integrity, and availability 377
    Endpoint device: Cell, PDAs, wireless, and more 378
    Edge network: Branch office or remote locations 380
    Firewalls... 380
    Access network or Internet: WAN or public Internet 381
    Core backbone network: Enterprise IP backbone network 383
TDM-PBX system hardening: Securing the core voice infrastructure 384
IP-PBX and VoIP system and server hardening: Securing systems and servers....... 385
SIP application UC server hardening: Securing UC application servers 387
    Operating system security.. 387
Knowledge Check 17-1: Implementing a Multilayered VoIP
and SIP Security Solution 389
Chapter summary 391

Appendix A: Answers...**393**

Knowledge Check 1-1: Introduction to Unified Communications.............................. 394
Knowledge Check 2-1: Elements of Unified Communications.................................... 395
Knowledge Check 3-1: The Impact of Convergence, VoIP, and SIP 397

Knowledge Check 4-1: Current Unified Communications Landscape 399
Knowledge Check 5-1: Critical Business Applications and Processes.......................400
Knowledge Check 6-1: Solving Business Challenges.......................................403
Knowledge Check 7-1: Mapping the Solution to Technology 406
Knowledge Check 8-1: Building a Measurable Financial ROI with KPIs 408
Knowledge Check 9-1: Conducting a Unified Communications
Proof-of-Concept Pilot Project...411
Knowledge Check 10-1: Creating a Unified Communications
Project Statement of Work..413
Knowledge Check 11-1: Conducting Unified Communications
Systems Integration..415
Knowledge Check 12-1: Applications Integration with Endpoint Devices 417
Knowledge Check 13–1: VoIP Threats and Vulnerabilities.................................418
Knowledge Check 14-1: Best Practices for VoIP Security................................419
Knowledge Check 15-1: SIP Threats and Vulnerabilities.................................420
Knowledge Check 16–1: Best Practices for SIP Security.................................421
Knowledge Check 17-1: Implementing a Multilayered VoIP
and SIP Security Solution..422

Glossary..**425**

Index...**435**

Introduction

Unified Communications (UC) solutions removes barriers among voice, e-mail, conferencing, video, and instant messaging, allowing for instantaneous people-to-people communications. For the hyperconnected, this means reduced time to decision, increased productivity, and the ability to provide a simple and consistent user experience across all types of communications.

UC integrates business applications and processes with existing communication channels to open the door for substantial business process improvements. It represents a new way of doing business, enhancing individual, workgroup, and organizational productivity.

Successful implementation of UC requires a thorough understanding of the capabilities of UC, how business communications problems can be solved, and how best to approach and implement UC solutions from a financial investment and technology point of view. These requirements are common across any vendor's proposed solution.

Unified Communications Solutions: A Practical Business and Technology Approach provides a clear description of the evolution of messaging, UC capabilities, and how UC can improve business processes such as sales force automation and supply chain management. The guide also explains how key performance indicators can be mapped to a financial return-on-investment model, how to implement UC solutions using a proof-of-concept pilot, and important deployment considerations such as securing VoIP and SIP protocols for UC applications.

Acknowledging that a large number of organizations are still in the planning stages for wide-scale UC deployment and need individuals skilled in UC solutions, Nortel created a vendor-neutral professional certification, *Nortel Certified Technology Specialist (NCTS): Unified Communications Solutions (920-807)*, to help the industry move forward in deploying UC solutions.

Because UC touches many different elements within IT, professionals working in IT, telecommunications, networking, desktop application, and local area networking will gain a valuable understanding of UC by studying for and successfully completing the *NCTS Unified Communications Solutions* certification exam.

Objectives

At the end of each part of this book, you will be able to:

Part I: The Evolution of Messaging

• describe key terms and definitions used in Unified Communications (UC)

• understand the evolution of messaging from voice mail to unified messaging to Unified Communications and its integration with business applications

• identify vendors participating in the UC marketplace

• compare features and functions and distinguish between unified messaging and UC

Part II: Solving Enterprise Business Communications Challenges

• match a list of UC features and functions and map them to the specific business communications challenges they solve

• understand the impact of convergence and how Session Initiation Protocol (SIP)-enabled applications like UC lead to the convergence of applications

• identify the business value UC deployment can bring to customer service, customer relationship management, supply chain management, enterprise resource planning, and sales force automation

• describe how service-oriented architecture (SOA) coupled with UC can streamline processes and reduce human latency

• identify key performance indicator (KPI) metrics that can be mapped to a financial return on investment (ROI) model

Part III: Implementing Unified Communications Solutions

• scope a UC proof-of-concept pilot project with measurable KPIs and a financial ROI model

• understand best practices for UC system integration configurations and implementations regarding heterogeneous voice communications infrastructures

• understand what applications, features, and functions are supported on endpoint devices, personal digital assistants (PDAs), and cell phones

Part IV: Securing VoIP, SIP, and Unified Communications Solutions

• identify Voice over Internet Protocol (VoIP) and SIP risks, threats, and vulnerabilities

• understand how to implement VoIP best practices for security in an IP infrastructure

• understand how to implement SIP best practices for security and specifically for endpoint devices and PDAs that may be transporting private customer data and information

• describe how to implement a layered security solution to ensure the confidentiality, integrity, and availability of VoIP and SIP-enabled applications like UC and endpoint and PDA devices

Nortel

Nortel is a recognized leader in delivering communications capabilities that make the promise of Business Made Simple a reality for its customers. Nortel's next-generation technologies, for both service provider and enterprise networks, support multimedia and business-critical applications. Nortel's technologies are designed to help eliminate today's barriers to efficiency, speed, and performance by simplifying networks and connecting people to the information they need, when they need it.

With more than a century of experience in shaping the evolution of communications, Nortel continues its tradition of innovation today by providing secure solutions that ignite and power global commerce while helping solve the world's greatest challenges.

Nortel's leading portfolio of solutions spanning packet, optical, wireless, and voice technologies are at the very foundation of the world's economy, powering global commerce and delivering innovative network capabilities to connect rural and underdeveloped regions.

Working together with its customers in 150 countries, Nortel is improving the human experience by fundamentally changing how the world works and how people communicate, creating unique capabilities for business, education, entertainment, and security through reliable data and voice technologies.

Drawing on its fundamental understanding of the network—both voice and data—Nortel secures computing, network applications, and end-user environments while maintaining five 9s of reliability.[1] Nortel helps governments, businesses, and individuals stay ahead of threats including hacker intrusion, worms, denial of service attacks, and identity theft, and by delivering enhanced network management capabilities.

Whether supporting billions of transactions by a financial institution, providing vital information services for health care, or helping education heighten learning experiences through the most advanced technologies, Nortel solutions are at work wherever reliable data and voice communications are most critical.

For more information about Nortel, go to *www.nortel.com*.

---

1.   Reported customer availability metrics across Nortel's popular products exceed 99.999 percent, as of August 2004.

Intended Audience

This book is designed for individuals who wish to gain a strong understanding of UC and how to implement UC solutions.

> **Note** Exam skills and objectives are subject to change without prior notice and at the sole discretions of Nortel. Please visit *www.nortel.com/certification* for the most current exam information.

Prerequisite Knowledge

It is recommended that individuals who read this book have an understanding of Internet Protocol (IP) fundamentals (basic networking, IP Suite, and the basics of routing) and VoIP, but this knowledge is not required to understand and appreciate the concepts presented in this book.

How to Use This Book

This book is meant to be used as a study guide for understanding UC and how to successfully implement a UC solution. The guide will help prepare you for the Nortel Certified Technology Specialist (NCTS): Unified Communications Solutions certification exam 920-807.

Although the best attempt has been made to provide the most current information, this text is only as current as the moment it is printed. As those who work in technology are aware, information is constantly changing. Therefore, be sure to visit *www.nortel.com* for the most current UC information, and visit *www.nortel.com/certification* for the most current list of certification exam objectives. Please visit *www.nortel.com/nortelpress* for the most current information related to the Unified Communications Solutions guide.

Additional UC information can be found on the *www.innovativecommunicationsalliance.com* Web site jointly hosted by Nortel and Microsoft.

Chapter Layout

Each chapter begins with a brief description of the concepts presented in the chapter and how they connect to VoIP.

Chapter Topics identify the specific topics within the chapter.

Chapter Goals list the objectives of the chapter and what specific information should be gained on completion of the chapter.

Key Terms list the specific terms within the chapter and the page where the terms are introduced.

> **Note** Notes provide specific information related to topics being discussed that are important to understand when working with the topic.

> Sidebars provide additional information or case studies related to the topic.

Knowledge Check presents multiple-choice questions reviewing the topics just discussed. These questions help to identify topics that may need to be reviewed to be able to demonstrate a complete understanding of the chapter. Answers for Knowledge Check questions are found in Appendix A.

Chapter Summary briefly discusses the main topics of the chapter just presented.

About the CD-ROM

The CD-ROM that comes with this book contains links to sites and applications that can assist when planning and evaluating UC projects.

Additionally, a sample Certification Exam is found on the CD-ROM, which can help in the preparation for the Nortel Certified Technology Specialist (NCTS): Unified Communications Solutions certification exam 920-807.

Nortel Technical Training and Talent Assurance Service

The demand for learning services is on the rise. Among the primary concerns that businesses face today are how to determine what level of training is appropriate for each core job function and what is the best way to optimize the costs and time spent on learning.

Take advantage of Nortel end-to-end Technical Training and knowledge-based services to easily educate your employees on networking solutions, the convergence points between wired and wireless networks, applications and infrastructure, and carriers and enterprises. By better equipping employees in the field, you'll increase operations efficiencies.

Nortel Technical Training

Nortel Knowledge Services and its authorized education partners offer a wide variety of eLearning and classroom training options:

• "Self-paced eLearning-Web and CD-ROM-based eLearning.

• "Instructor-led eLearning (Facilitated and Hands-in eLearning)-Facilitated eLearning provides real-time access to an instructor/subject matter expert (SME) from the location of your choice. Hands-in eLearning provides real-time access to an instructor/SME from the location of your choice, but also allows customers to complete hands-in exercises on Nortel networking equipment from their own location.

• "Instructor-led Training-Instructor-led Training is a traditional classroom training option. In most cases, this training delivery method provides customers with access to Nortel equipment so they can complete hands-on exercises. Most courses can be completed at a Nortel facility or the customer's location.

Custom training options are also available. Visit www.nortel.com/training to access detailed course descriptions, curriculum paths, a list of Nortel's global training centers and more.

Talent Assurance Service

In many businesses today, one-size-fits-all learning solutions are developed for employees. Unfortunately this approach is ineffective and results in excessive costs and unneeded duplication. To succeed, factors such as the specific requirements for each role, geography and experience levels must be considered. To move the business forward, a customized enterprise talent development strategy must be put in place, subsequent actions must be taken to up-skill employees at each job function and business metrics must be maintained to ensure business objectives are met. The Talent Assurance Service delivers this and more.

Nortel is a global leader in delivering end-to-end knowledge based services to customers and partners. By taking advantage of the service, Nortel will partner with you to complete a thorough analysis of your learning needs. A subsequent detailed talent strategy will highlight the most effective and cost-friendly learning options for your business at each job function to ensure you achieve the desired results. Nortel will be in close communication with you throughout the process, and a Nortel Talent Assurance Manager will help you implement the plan across multiple activities.

To learn more, visit *www.nortel.com/tas*.

Nortel Professional Certification

Nortel Professional Certification provides the best method to prove your command of current technologies and Nortel products. These certification exams are developed to validate mastery of critical competencies as you design, develop, implement, and support communications solutions.

Nortel has seven certification designations:

Nortel Certified Technology Specialist (NCTS)

This designation is technology focused. It certifies that the successful candidate can apply an entry level of technical proficiency required to engineer or support a converged network solution in support of a customer's business requirements.

Nortel Certified Technology Expert (NCTE)

This designation is technology focused. It certifies that the successful candidate can apply an intermediate to advanced level of technical proficiency required to plan, design, engineer, or support a converged network solution. It builds on the Nortel Certified Technology Specialist level competencies.

Nortel Certified Support Specialist (NCSS)

This designation certifies that the successful candidate can apply an entry level of technical proficiency required to install, configure, administer, maintain, and troubleshoot a Nortel solution or product. Support Specialist certifications for Application Development certify that the successful candidate can apply an entry level of technical proficiency required to write and debug applications for a Nortel solution. Support Specialist certifications for Database Administration certify that the successful candidate can apply an entry level of technical proficiency required to administer a database for a Nortel solution.

Nortel Certified Support Expert (NCSE)

This designation certifies that the successful candidate can apply an intermediate to advanced level of technical proficiency required to configure, administer, maintain, and troubleshoot complex Nortel solutions and products. It builds on the Nortel Certified Support Specialist level competencies and focuses on advanced solution support, which may involve multiple products and interworking functionalities.

Nortel Certified Design Specialist (NCDS)

This designation certifies that the successful candidate can apply an entry level of technical proficiency required to plan, design, or engineer a solution in support of a customer's business requirements using Nortel products.

Nortel Certified Design Expert (NCDE)

This designation certifies that the successful candidate can apply an intermediate to advanced level of technical proficiency required to plan, design, or engineer a solution using multiple Nortel products. It builds on the Nortel Certified Design Specialist level competencies and focuses on advanced solution engineering and may involve multiple products and interworking functionalities.

Nortel Certified Architect (NCA)

The highest level of certification, the Nortel Certified Architect represents a highly advanced level of technical design and analytical expertise for complex Nortel solutions.

To get the most current information regarding Nortel Professional Certifications, visit *www.nortel.com/certification*.

About Nortel Press

Nortel Press is a Nortel authorized publisher, developing self-study guides on the networking subjects that are shaping the future of business communications. The guides are designed for IT professionals, individuals supporting and maintaining Nortel product solutions, and participants in the Nortel Technology Solutions Academy.

All Nortel Press guides are developed by Nortel subject matter experts in conjunction with leaders in networking technology, who have the knowledge and experience to keep readers ahead of the technology curve. The guides complement a robust portfolio of Nortel Learning Services and help prepare individuals for professional certifications. To learn more, visit *www.nortel.com/nortelpress*.

Contacting Nortel Press

Nortel can be reached at 1-800-466-7835.

Nortel Press can be reached at:

Mail:

Nortel Networks Inc.
4001 E. Chapel Hill-Nelson Hwy.
Mailstop: D17/03/0F1
Research Triangle Park, NC 27709

E-mail:

ntpress@nortel.com

Preparing for the Exam

The following steps provide a guide on how to use this guide to help you achieve your certification goals:

1. Read this textbook.

2. Review each chapter once more. Pay special attention to your notes and any information you highlighted. Complete the Knowledge Checks again. Pay special attention to any questions that you answered incorrectly. Make sure you understand why answer choices are correct or incorrect.

3. Read the scenario and answer options carefully. Eliminate distracters (words or phrases that are irrelevant or technically inaccurate).

4. Some questions instruct you to select more than one correct answer. Make sure to double-check the number of answers you select. For example, if instructed to supply two answers, do not supply three.

1: Introduction to Unified Communications

Humans have been looking for ways to improve interpersonal communications from the beginning of time. This is nowhere more obvious than in business, where companies have spent millions of dollars on technologies that ensure no incoming voice calls go unanswered and that a person is available to communicate with the caller as soon as possible. Of course, this need for improved communication must be balanced with the return on investment (ROI) for businesses. In addition, new modes of communication must be adaptable to current business processes.

Many modern communications tools have existed in parallel for more than a quarter-century, with relatively little substantive change. E-mail and voice mail provide the same functionality as they did when introduced in the 1980s. Voice and data communications convergence happened in the backbone network at the infrastructure level, but added no value to the activity. Even packet-based voice has simply been a replacement for circuit-based voice. However, Unified Communications (UC) solutions are about to revolutionize the way people interact and the way business gets done.

Chapter 1 Topics

In this chapter, you will learn:
- the basic terms used in UC

- what UC is and what it is not

- how UC differs from Unified Messaging (UM)

- the companies involved in the UC market

- the benefits of investing in UC technologies at this point in time

- why enterprise application vendors are adding UC functions to their applications

Introduction to Unified Communications

Chapter 1 Goals

Upon completion of this chapter, you will be able to:

- explain the basic terms used in UC

- provide a basic definition of UC

- define the technology evolutions that are facilitating the emergence of UC

- identify the current market leaders and explain their position in the market

- explain why now is a good time to implement UC solutions

Key Terms

Coadaptation	8	Unified Communications (UC)	4
Communications channel	5	Unified Messaging (UM)	3
Converged desktop	13	Voice mail	3
Private Branch Exchange (PBX)	7		

The human communications center

In many businesses, executives and knowledge workers use multiple communications methods, ranging from an office telephone extension, a desktop and notebook computer, and a company-supplied mobile phone to a home office phone, a home office fax, a home computer, and a personal mobile phone. Modern workers likely have both business and personal e-mail accounts and instant messaging services. Figure 1-1 shows the wide variety of communication devices and mediums available to individuals and businesses.

FIGURE 1-1: USER COMMUNICATIONS DEVICES.

Although these devices provide new opportunities to reach a particular individual, they are not linked; the user must check each device for messages. For example, each telephone may have its own voice mail system or answering machine. Voice mail does not provide real-time contact, even when using an improved system that flags priority calls or flashes a light on the handset to indicate a waiting message.

The need for real-time contact drove the development of Unified Messaging (UM). UM delivers voice mail, e-mail, and fax messages into a common e-mail mailbox. Many UM implementations include the caller ID of a voice mail or fax in the subject line, and the systems indicate whether the message is voice, fax, or e-mail. Some UM systems can read messages to the user if messages are being retrieved by phone. Newer versions of UM offer extended services such as calendar management, schedule retrieval, and updating over the voice network.

UM helped streamline the message retrieval process by showing the calling number, which allowed the end user to prioritize responses. It allowed remote message retrieval, minimizing the time spent retrieving messages. However, UM does not resolve the need for real-time communications, and it cannot ensure that calls are directed to the appropriate available individual. Modern professionals need more than UM alone can provide. UM solutions are still ideal for communications that do not require real-time contact, but they should be integrated into a larger UC enablement to ensure that real-time people-to-people communications are handled appropriately.

Unified Communications

UC is a solution that integrates all communications devices and channels into a single uniform interface. Not only does UC incorporate existing communications methods, it allows the user to decide how to activate or use each channel. For example, UC-enabled applications treat a phone number or an e-mail address as a data element for which it executes specific and relevant actions.

Another benefit of UC is that it does not require Voice over Internet Protocol (VoIP) implementation across the enterprise to return benefits to every user. Gateways can bridge between information technology (IT) applications and voice systems to deliver basic functionality within the organization. Although migration to a fully converged voice and data network is ultimately the most cost-effective solution, the migration can be performed in stages as relevant project ROI justifies the expense.

UC is not a specific technology, but an application foundation; therefore, ensuring secure operations is key to continued success with UC. The security issue is so critical that the final chapters of this book will help you to develop a comprehensive awareness of the security challenges inherent in multimodal communication. As more business processes become interlaced with UC, security failures threaten more of the organization's systems and data. Building an appropriate and robust security plan is a critical part of deploying UC.

What is UC?

There are many definitions of UC. This book uses the following definition:

Unified Communications is an application foundation that enhances individual, workgroup, and organizational productivity by enabling and facilitating the integrated control and management of communications channels, networks, systems, and business applications.

Application foundation is included in this definition because UC is more than a technology. It represents a new way of doing business, where communications channels are tightly integrated with business processes. UC allows management to be aware of daily activities without imposing new reporting requirements on the supported resources.

UC has particular appeal to executives because it integrates business applications with existing communication channels, making substantial business process improvements easier. As UC evolves, productivity will be enhanced by UC interfaces to popular enterprise applications like SAP, PeopleSoft, Oracle Financials, and others. UC elements are already integrated into products offered by Microsoft, IBM, and other major software providers. If your organization has significant investment in enterprise-level software, your vendor may already offer UC-enabled solutions.

Throughout this book, key UC elements are introduced and discussed in detail. The following list contains basic definitions of the elements covered in future chapters:

- **Communications channel**—A connection between the initiating and terminating ends of a circuit, established to exchange information in real time.

- **Converged client**—A device from which communications can be initiated, terminated, or both, for a wide variety of communications channels.

- **Directory services**—A standardized way to access and maintain a structured repository that contains relevant information about authorized users and network resources within a business unit.

- **Presence**—A standard way to provide the current status of registered clients to third-party interrogations. Figure 1-2 shows an example of presence within Microsoft Office Outlook. The sender's status and schedule are visible, as are communications channels through which the individual can be reached.

FIGURE 1-2: PRESENCE AS VIEWED IN MICROSOFT OFFICE OUTLOOK.

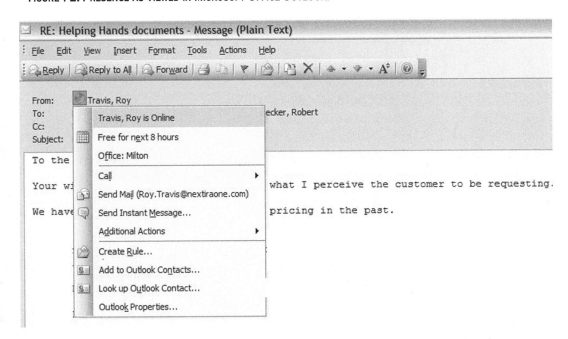

- **Instant messaging**—A form of real-time communications between two or more persons, using typed text. Figure 1-3 shows an example of instant messaging done within the Microsoft Outlook presence pane. From the instant message pane, the user can initiate a video session, start a voice conversation, or even set up shared folders to support real-time collaboration.

FIGURE 1-3: INSTANT MESSAGING IN MICROSOFT OFFICE OUTLOOK.

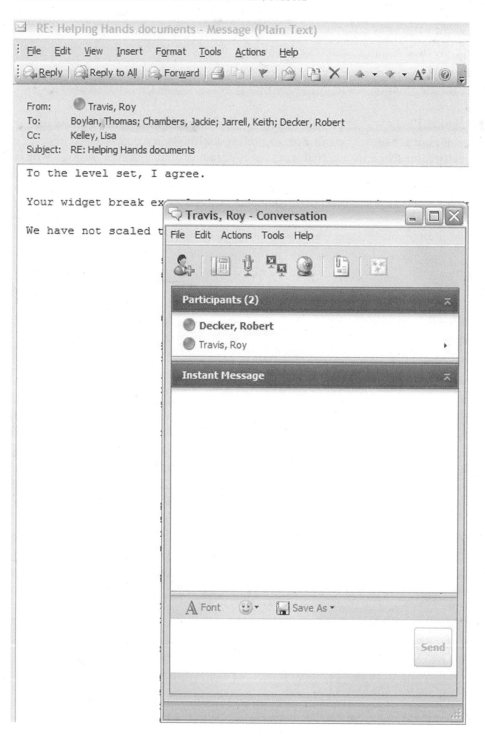

• **Smart tag**—A user-configured data identifier. Smart tags provide common relevance, context, and automation to data, regardless of where the data is being used. Figure 1-4 shows an example of a Name smart tag in Microsoft Word 2003. The individual's presence status is visible; the user can initiate contact from within the application, if desired.

FIGURE 1-4: SMART TAG VIEWED IN MICROSOFT WORD 2003.

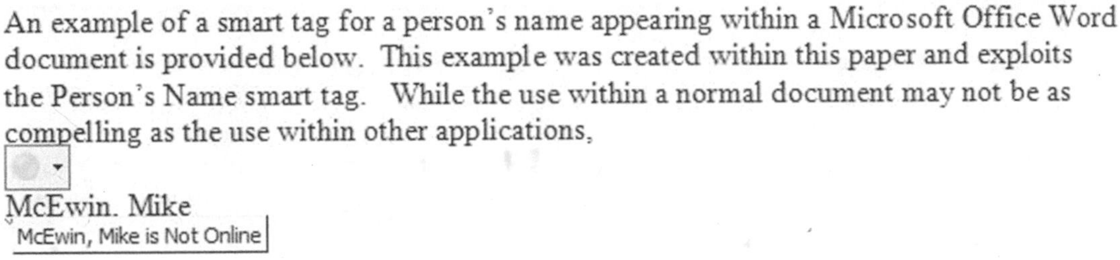

An example of a smart tag for a person's name appearing within a Microsoft Office Word document is provided below. This example was created within this paper and exploits the Person's Name smart tag. While the use within a normal document may not be as compelling as the use within other applications.

McEwin. Mike

McEwin, Mike is Not Online

• **Conferencing**—Real-time communications involving more than two parties.

• **Collaboration**—Synchronized use of automated resources that allows simultaneous modification and updating of work products.

• **Federation**—Formation of a larger user community by linking the directories of two or more entities.

Who is driving UC?

Over the past 10 to 15 years, the communications industry has been under constant consumer pressure to change. Mobile communications now drive the market, requiring traditional telecommunications companies to acquire wireless companies to expand their market share. At the same time, suppliers to the communications industry have transitioned from proprietary hardware and software solutions to standards-based solutions. Suppliers have adopted common development environments that encourage interoperability between solutions, reducing development time and cost. Although this transition has attracted many startups, Cisco is the only organization that has established a significant presence in the enterprise market previously dominated by companies like Nortel and Avaya. At the same time, traditional market leaders have transformed themselves to meet market demand and continue to hold a strategic advantage.

Nortel, Avaya, and Cisco have one thing in common: They are supplying the same applications that were available in the Private Branch Exchange (PBX) market, but have modified the underlying infrastructure. All three companies introduced new collaboration and multimedia applications with moderate success. Nortel introduced the Multimedia Communications Server (MCS) family of products and slowly evolved that family to deliver a remarkable set of advanced capabilities, while other voice vendors introduced competitive solutions for their customer base.

The market regarded these solutions as evolutionary, seeing them only as enhancements or replacements for traditional voice services. These applications could not meet enterprise investment hurdles and ROI requirements. Customers wanted products that were integrated at the individual user's desktop, where they would be most effective.

While the communications industry was exploring new technology, IT organizations needed to meet management demands for improved employee productivity and decreased costs. Platform providers were barraged with increasing demand for standards-compliant solutions ranging from directory services that offered common authorization for application access, to stronger e-mail security methods and improved business productivity tools. Several standards initiatives, including H.323 and various other communications protocols, worked to meet this demand, but could not rapidly provide the quality of service demanded by enterprise users.

Microsoft and IBM/Lotus, dominant forces in enterprise desktop productivity software, introduced new applications that began to address their customers' demands. Some of these applications resembled solutions offered by traditional telecommunications suppliers. Applications like Microsoft Live Communications Server and IBM Lotus Sametime became popular ways for employees to collaborate at the desktop level. Some desktop clients, like Microsoft Office Communicator, even began to incorporate voice and video communications.

In 2007, Microsoft introduced a UM module for Exchange Server 2007. This module offered functions normally provided by traditional telecommunications providers, including integrated voice recognition and automated attendant features. Because Microsoft integrated these features into their market-leading desktop client, they simplified end-user training and integrated administration tasks. Microsoft thus delivered one of the primary advantages of convergence: the effective consolidation of support staff.

As important as the Exchange 2007 UM module was, the way in which the services were delivered was equally important. Microsoft embraced the Session Initiation Protocol (SIP) to integrate its solution with the telecommunications industry's products. Because some traditional telephony companies did not yet have the more modern protocols implemented, Microsoft also partnered with companies who could provide low-cost gateways that bridged to older voice platforms. This decision meant that proprietary interface definitions were no longer a roadblock to adopting the technology.

While networking and communications vendors already offered presence solutions, the Microsoft solution provided previously unavailable integration with the Microsoft Office suite of programs. Figure 1-5 shows Windows Live Messenger, in which a user can use several modes of communication, including instant messaging, voice, video, and file exchange. The user can also see which mode of communication is available at a given time for each contact. Users and contacts benefit from a single client that can manage all of these communications channels; knowing whether a person is available, through the presence indicator, helps the user communicate more efficiently.

Although Microsoft could provide the much-needed integration of applications and presence capability, they still needed a way to fuse their UM solution with legacy communications equipment and applications. In July 2006, Microsoft and Nortel announced the Innovative Communications Alliance (ICA). This alliance provided credibility for Microsoft's entry into the communications applications market. It also proved that Nortel understood the changing market and was taking a leadership position to ensure promised applications would meet the availability, reliability, and performance characteristics that traditional voice customers expected.

Microsoft's Office Communications Server 2007 and the native integration, provided by Nortel's Communications Server 1000 release 5.0, with Microsoft's Exchange Server 2007 UM module are clear evidence that successful coadaptation has promoted faster market change that benefits customers of both companies. Each company continues to develop its own products, while cooperating to ensure that elements of those products integrate effectively to deliver a better customer experience.

FIGURE 1-5: PRESENCE AS VIEWED IN WINDOWS LIVE MESSENGER

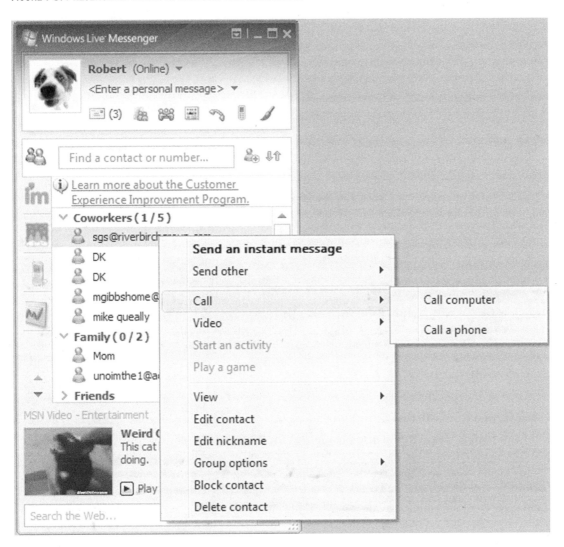

Why UC now?

Many businesses are working to enhance their customers' experience. Most enterprise-sized organizations have invested millions to create call centers that ensure customers can reach a real person with minimal delay. Some call centers use online chat services, or accept e-mail messages that are handled with the same processes used for real-time voice and chat sessions.

Despite the investments in these specialized resources, customers continue to be dissatisfied with customer service experiences. For example, the individual with specific knowledge or power to resolve the customer's problem might not be available. The customer cannot develop affinity with an impersonal call center if the same service agent is not available each time support is required. From the customer's perspective, it is reasonable to expect that the right person should be immediately available when a call is placed, or that the person answering can bring in the right resources to resolve the issue.

Delays in responding to critical business demands can result in financial consequences, whether the demands originate with a customer, a supplier, or from any other source. In addition, the workforce is increasingly mobile, no longer working in a traditional office building. Although there are many advantages to a location- and time-independent workforce, this shift requires new solutions to maintain timely communications and to support collaboration. Traditional telecommunications solutions no longer serve these needs.

Organizations often need to decrease their workforce to meet financial objectives. The demand for increased productivity due to a reduced workforce means that workers must find new ways to meet the challenge of increased communications while still meeting internal goals. One partial solution is a central repository that contains messages from all communications channels and can be accessed from the desktop or remotely. Alternative ways to interact with the repository in real time have a profound impact because this ability eliminates repetitive message-handling tasks. As more business processes result in real-time transaction completion, the more time becomes available to manage additional transactions.

The standards-based central repository has another advantage; it is an ideal framework for a communications continuity plan. Because one underlying element of this foundation is directory services, which are geographically distributable by design, services can readily be recovered at an alternate site. Ongoing business operations can be managed with minimal disruption when clients are configured to register with both a primary and secondary directory server, and when the organization contracts with carriers to reroute incoming calls to an alternate destination.

Key market makers

Industry analysts regularly identify leaders in the UC market. For example, Gartner Research produces annual reports on many technology market sectors. In 2005, Gartner placed Nortel, Siemens, and Alcatel in their Magic Quadrant, which indicates those companies' visionary status combined with perceived exceptional ability to execute that vision. In 2007, Gartner placed Nortel, Alcatel-Lucent, and Microsoft in that quadrant.

Nortel entered the UC market with its internally developed MCS product family, a highly scalable solution delivered on industry-standard servers. Teleconferencing capabilities were especially strong on this platform; in fact, large distributed enterprises purchased this system solely to replace third-party teleconferencing services. The Nortel solution also offered effective integration with the enterprise's telephony system. Although Nortel's technology was feature-rich and robust, it used its own client and directory services that did not integrate with common desktop productivity tools.

Meanwhile, Microsoft began to support instant messaging in the Live Communications Server 2005 product. Some Microsoft customers were also developing low-end integrated voice response deployments on Microsoft Speech Server, but it was not an easy replacement for proprietary products from other vendors. Microsoft Exchange Server could integrate with other vendors' voice mail systems if the right UM solution was in place, but it was a complicated process. In late 2005, Microsoft announced the Exchange Server UM module; at about the same time, they released Live Communications Server's Service Pack 1 (SP 1), which permitted integration between Office Communicator 2005 and traditional phone systems using a traditional telecommunications standard, Computer Supports Telecommunications Applications III (CSTA III).

There were many advantages to implementing Live Communications Server SP 1. For example, it offered an automated process for the phone system to provide dynamic status information through a desktop client. The client also provided pop-up notifications for incoming calls, including caller information if the caller was in the user's contacts database; the user could then decide whether to answer the desktop phone, answer with the desktop client, or forward the call to another device.

Although Microsoft implemented only a small subset of the CSTA III standard's capabilities (shown in Table 1-1), it was sufficient to catch the interest of traditional communications system vendors. Microsoft also brought their solution into traditional IT space by modifying the Active Directory schema to include phone information for the end user, thus establishing a central point through which authentication services could be delivered for voice telephony.

TABLE 1-1: SERVICES DEFINED IN THE CSTA III STANDARD.

Type of Service	Example of Service
• Call control	• Making call, answering call
• Call associated services	• Sending user data
• Logical device services	• Do not disturb, forwarding
• Physical device services	• Writing to device display
• Capability exchange services	• Client feature discovery
• Snapshot services	• Query existing calls
• Monitor event services	• Subscribe to event reports
• Voice services	• For listener, dual tone multifrequency (DTMF), prompts
• Utility services	• Routing, media attachment, data collection, accounting

Microsoft's expansion into UC products established a credible bridge between traditional telecommunications and enterprise IT. Microsoft offered an interoperable solution that provided smooth migration for users and vendors. Microsoft's willingness to embrace and incorporate telecommunications standards provided a catalyst for the market to take action.

Enterprise telecommunications managers tend to purchase solutions from vendors known for carrier-grade voice solutions, a list that does not include Microsoft. Similarly, enterprise IT managers tend to purchase products from vendors known for high-quality, business-critical solutions, a list that does not include Nortel or Avaya. Although cooperation between industry leaders may eventually lead to a new wave of consolidation across the industries, Nortel's cooperation with Microsoft has brought new perspective to the telecommunications manufacturers.

Vendor solutions

For UC to succeed, companies that influence the market must embrace the changing technology. Enterprise IT application developers must deliver communications-aware applications that exploit UC infrastructure capabilities. Telecommunications product companies must continue to collaborate with leading enterprise IT infrastructure vendors, like Microsoft and IBM, to expand the richness of interdependent operations. Communications service providers must embrace tighter integration with enterprise IT solutions to enable critical presence and connectivity elements. Although these technology investments are well underway, success ultimately depends on enterprise IT and the IT consulting services industry developing the skills necessary to deliver the business process improvements being touted by UC evangelists.

Enterprise application initiatives

To demonstrate the potential influence of UC, it is important to understand the perspective of enterprise application providers. Engaging application vendors in a UC initiative will ensure continued business process improvement and increased ROI for customers.

In 2006, Microsoft and SAP introduced Duet, a jointly developed product that integrates many mySAP reporting functions into Microsoft Office Outlook (see Figure 1-6). Linking this enterprise application to Office elements lets users apply existing Office features, such as smart tags, to the SAP application without impacting the core application system.

FIGURE 1-6: SAMPLE DUET APPLICATION WITHIN MICROSOFT OUTLOOK.

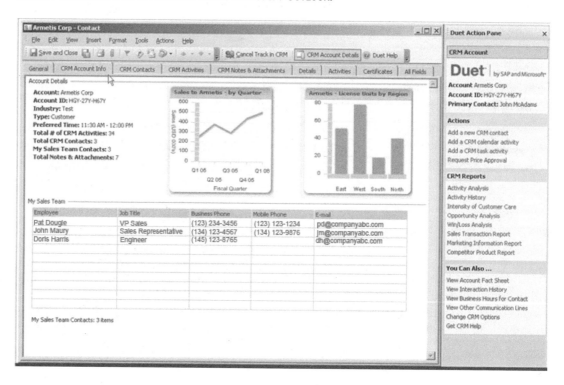

Imagine that a sales agent receives an e-mail report that identifies the sales contacts scheduled for that day. The report is built in an Office document template, with the customer's name, address, and phone number included as elements within the report. With smart tags turned on, the agent sees a list of contact options, based on information in the contact's entry in the customer management database. Without exiting the report, the agent can view presence information and determine the customer's availability; if the customer is unavailable, the agent can wait to contact that customer until later in the day, thereby saving the time required to initiate the contact and leave a message, and saving the customer the task of checking messages and returning the call. This streamlined operation provides a significant business advantage over companies that do not implement this technology. Most important, this solution is not unrealistic; even if only using commercially available solutions, IT can deliver these process improvements with minimal customization.

In October 2007, SAP participated in the Microsoft launch of Office Communications Server 2007. The companies jointly announced their intent to integrate Duet closely with the new server platform, which would enable click-to-communicate functionality for supported users. The two companies predicted more than 100 million users would have this capability over the next three years.

PeopleSoft and Oracle's E-Business Suite also support Microsoft Windows desktop interfaces. These applications permit users to publish reports or results as Excel spreadsheets, PDF documents, PowerPoint charts, or InfoPath forms. Any data appearing in the published report can be marked with a smart tag. If the user is enabled for converged desktop functions, appropriate actions can then be defined for a name or telephone number entry. In the field's smart tag option box, the user can select a contact method for the target person, using instant messaging, telephone, e-mail, or other communication channels.

As large enterprise software vendors embrace UC integration, other producers will join the initiative. This increasing engagement will further encourage development of additional solutions that will drive growth for the entire market.

Telecommunications product manufacturers

Through the ICA, Nortel and Microsoft continue to cooperate to enrich solutions for their customers. Nortel's Communications Server 1000 product line incorporates native SIP integration with Microsoft Office Exchange Server 2007 UM. Nortel delivers converged desktop features that integrate Communications Server 1000 with Microsoft Live Communications Server 2005 SP 1. This provides PBX-like services to personal computers attached to the corporate network, and enables improved user control of the communications environment. Other features allow users to forward incoming calls to other numbers or devices and to use a desktop client to identify contacts in a global directory and initiate a telephone call from a PBX-enabled digital phone or the desktop client itself.

Nortel also offers the MCS family of products. This SIP-based group of products leverages industry-standard server technology to provide full multimedia communications support, such as video conferencing, telephony conferencing, and instant messaging. Features of the converged desktop are available to users supported by this system. This is Nortel's platform of choice for integration with IBM Lotus Sametime.

Nortel also delivers features, such as Universal Wireless Extensions, that extend traditional phone system features to a user's mobile phone. This allows the wireless phone, regardless of its carrier-assigned number, to be defined as an extension on the communications server. This allows the user to publicize only an office phone number, and not the private mobile number. The enterprise can extend previously defined access policies and dialing plans to mobile phones. It also permits the capture of call detail records to provide an audit trail in support of compliance reporting requirements. In addition, the feature extends advanced PBX functionality to the wireless phone.

Although Avaya does not have an alliance with an enterprise desktop software partner like Nortel has with Microsoft, it also offers a product that addresses this market, called Unified Communications Standard Edition. Avaya provides a similar wireless support feature, called Extension to Cellular, and includes an Avaya one-X Mobile application for the end-user device.

UC product companies are working toward native SIP integration with IT infrastructure solutions. Although this will provide no extra functionality to the end user, it will decrease complexity and lower operating costs. Expanding the use of SIP will also allow third-party developers to further extend the market by providing niche solutions.

IT infrastructure companies

Microsoft has taken a leading position in the software industry in developing product integration to support UC. Microsoft's alliance with Nortel allows Microsoft to incorporate enterprise-class features into Microsoft products where they make sense, and to leverage products from Nortel and other vendors to deliver other features where the technology requires traditional communications expertise.

IBM Lotus Sametime Unified Telephony will deliver comparable functionality. IBM has successfully partnered with leading telecommunications product suppliers to ensure interoperability.

IBM and Microsoft clearly dominate the enterprise desktop, a key element in delivering the benefits to be derived from UC. It is imperative that these two companies continue to work cooperatively with enterprise application developers and telecommunications product manufacturers to continue building UC acceptance in the market.

Service provider initiatives

The technical architecture associated with UC solutions enables companies to host some elements of the solution internally, and contract externally for other elements. Additionally, most companies do not have the breadth of coverage that can be delivered by service providers. There are other services that cannot be addressed internally, even by enterprise-sized organizations.

Core network routing services will become increasingly critical to support robust business continuity programs. For example, dynamic rerouting of an enterprise's calls to alternate locations is a key service increasingly offered by carriers. Services that link modified business practices and applications to the communications infrastructure will shift enterprise thinking about how service outages should be managed.

Carriers are also incorporating other UC services, such as providing presence information for a mobile phone as if it were an extension on an office phone system. If the target party is taking a call on the mobile phone, the presence indicator in the caller's application will indicate that the target is on another call. Carriers can differentiate their services by providing UC features, like presence, that offer real value to customers.

As UC initiatives expand, carriers will host applications and deliver UC services as an extension to the telephony services they have traditionally provided. Voice delivery via SIP has established a credible market. Enhancing those services will allow companies without the resources of the largest enterprises to benefit from the business process improvements enabled by UC.

Enterprise IT consulting companies

High-priority business initiatives must be part of the assessment when organizations consider new technology investments. Value-added resellers and network integrators can assist with UC technology integration; however, they do not have the skills required to assist in process reengineering. If UC adoption is to be swift, resources must be available to exploit the technology. Most enterprises will rely on industry consultants to drive UC implementations. Most large consulting providers have established UC-specific programs, some of which recommend specific product solutions and others that work with clients to enhance existing business processes with a UC foundational element.

A successful UC project requires resources who understand that existing business processes must be modified to incorporate UC elements and drive success. Even if outside consultants are brought in to manage the implementation, organization employees must be involved in the planning and implementation process. This increases the likely success of the UC enablement.

Knowledge Check 1-1: Introduction to Unified Communications

Answer the following questions. Answers to these Knowledge Check questions are located in *Appendix A: Answers to Knowledge Check Questions.*

1. Which of the following is NOT a key capability of UC?

    a. Paging services

    b. Instant messaging

    c. Presence notification

    d. Multimedia conferencing

2. Which are the two companies that formed the ICA?

    a. Nortel and SAP

    b. SAP and Microsoft

    c. Oracle and Microsoft

    d. Nortel and Microsoft

3. What activity will drive business success for UC?

    a. Lower IT operating expense

    b. New, inexpensive IP phones

    c. Convergence of data and voice networks

    d. Streamlining of business processes involving human interaction

4. Which of the following is a key element of UC?

    a. Networks

    b. Business applications

    c. Communications channels

    d. All of the above

5. Which market influencers will be critical to the adoption of UC?

    a. System integrators

    b. Enterprise voice vendors

    c. Enterprise IT organization

    d. Enterprise application vendors

    e. All of the above

6. UC is focused on real-time communications.

   a. True

   b. False

7. UC will eliminate the need for e-mail and voice mail.

   a. True

   b. False

8. UC allows users more control of their communications channels.

   a. True

   b. False

Chapter summary

UC is much more than a technology initiative. UC eliminates the artificial organizational boundary between computing and communications. It removes artificial constraints created by silos of automation and the resulting lack of readily available information.

Much like the transition from typewriters and manual ledgers to computer-based tools enhanced business productivity, businesses that incorporate foundational elements of UC will gain a significant productivity advantage over their competition. Key knowledge workers, selected professionals (such as the sales force), and executives will benefit from early adoption of UC elements. Once initial or project programs with extremely high ROI begin delivering the promised productivity gains, the process changes will rapidly integrate across the entire enterprise.

2: Elements of Unified Communications

Unified Communications (UC) focuses on integrating the voice infrastructure with data applications so that communications become an integral component of business applications and processes. This chapter describes the basic applications that underlie UC. These building blocks include converged desktop, collaboration, instant messaging (IM), presence, and conferencing. Pure message applications, such as voice mail and e-mail, are not included in this chapter.

In Chapter 1, "Introduction to Unified Communications," you learned that Voice over Internet Protocol (VoIP) technology is not required to implement UC. However, if VoIP is not implemented, gateways must be used to bridge business computing and digital communications. The telecommunications industry has developed standards that facilitate delivery of cost-effective technology transition. Session Initiation Protocol (SIP) support is the building block for VoIP, and is the standard used to provide the required intersystem command and control.

Chapter 2 Topics

In this chapter, you will learn:

- the key applications included in the foundation for UC

- the call flow between voice and data applications

- the role of gateways in connecting voice and data networks and public and private networks

- the uses of the converged desktop and the functions it provides to the user

- the definition of presence, how presence status can be reported, and what status transitions can occur

- the technical environment required to support conferencing and the basic functions of conferencing

- the collaboration environment and the applications minimally required to be supported

- the functionality delivered by fixed mobile convergence and why carriers must be engaged to complete the UC ecosystem

Chapter 2 Goals

Upon completion of this chapter, you will be able to:

- describe the key applications that form the foundation for UC

- describe the control flow between voice and data applications

- identify the role of gateways in delivering converged desktop functions

- explain which basic functions are enabled by a converged desktop

- describe the operations associated with presence

- describe the technical environment required to support conferencing

- describe the basic elements of a collaboration environment

- describe the functionality delivered by fixed mobile convergence

Key Terms

Collaboration	24
Conferencing	34
Co-Web browsing	36
Fixed mobile convergence	37
Gateway	23
Public Switched Telephone Network (PSTN)	23
Remote device control	37
View sharing	36

2

Elements of Unified
Communications

Converged desktop

Many attempts have been made to replace the desktop phone. The latest UC efforts twin the desktop phone to the desktop computer, allowing the devices to work together to enhance user control of all communications paths that the user has with other individuals or groups.

Business desktops and applications are saturated with contact information for peers, customers, family members, service providers, and many others. According to Nortel primary market research, most employees with a desktop phone also have either a desktop or notebook computer. Even though these devices coexist on the physical desktop, little has been done to help them work cooperatively.

Whenever a phone call is made, the user must look up the number in a contacts file or directory, and then enter the number manually on the telephone. When a call is received, the user may screen the number if caller ID services are enabled and the phone has a visual display. If the call needs to be forwarded, there is no way to know whether the transfer recipient is available until the transfer is actually attempted. These issues can be solved with UC-enabled technologies.

The applications underlying UC are not new to the industry. This technology has been the foundational element of contact centers for many years. Unfortunately, standards evolution focused on VoIP, and desktop convergence was of only moderate interest and limited to call center agents. Call center agents are typically categorized by skill sets. Calls are routed to agents based on their defined skills, and on who is currently available to take a call.

If information flow can be routed based on skills in a contact center, the same concept can be used to align structured business processes with call flow scenarios. Skills-based routing eliminates many opportunities for error in communications. It reduces, and potentially eliminates, time-consuming activities. It allows an individual to give out one number but receive calls on any device, as necessary to meet current business requirements. It also permits the user to control a desktop phone remotely, after logging on to the enterprise network or taking advantage of fixed mobile integration.

As shown in Figure 2-1, communication services provide the interface between voice and data infrastructures and between clients and applications. These communication services understand the inherent capabilities of each environment, the legacy protocols that allowed them to operate, and the new protocols that allow them to cooperate.

FIGURE 2-1: CONVERGED DESKTOP BLOCK DIAGRAM.

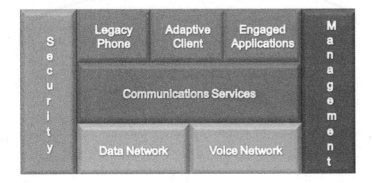

Elements of Unified Communications — 2

The following list describes the key elements required to ensure the successful operation of a converged desktop and to create new opportunities for productivity enhancement:

- SIP is a control-signaling protocol used to create, modify, and terminate sessions with one or more participants. Sessions can include VoIP calls, multimedia distribution, and multimedia conferences.

- Computer Supported Telecommunications Applications III (CSTA III) standardizes a powerful and flexible set of application services that observe and control voice and nonvoice media calls and non-call-related features. A subset of CSTA call control functionality, First Party Call Control, bridges the gap for SIP user agents. If a traditional Private Branch Exchange (PBX) is not part of the integration scenario, CSTA will probably not be part of the required solution.

- User agent CSTA (uaCSTA) describes transporting CSTA Extensible Markup Language (XML) messages over a SIP session. User agent CSTA leverages SIP mechanisms to provide a rich set of extensible features, similar to those described in this section, to support applications in the enterprise environment. In the scenario described below, the uaCSTA is implemented by a proxy server situated in front of a PBX and acting as the SIP user agent. The Nortel Communications Server 1000 (CS1000) integration with Microsoft Live Communications Server software uses the Multimedia Communications Manager (MCM) as the uaCSTA.

The converged desktop feature set gives users more control over their integrated environment, while retaining necessary management control to ensure compliance with access policies. The company can elect to deploy these capabilities for a select group of employees without impacting traditional services provided to all other employees.

Figure 2-2 shows the Nortel Multimedia Communications Server (MCS) providing integration for IBM Lotus Domino Server software, IBM Lotus Sametime Server software, the user desktop, the user legacy telephone, and the Nortel CS1000. Working with IBM, Nortel developed this tightly integrated solution to ensure consistent offerings, whether the client is running a Microsoft-based or IBM-based productivity desktop.

FIGURE 2-2: NORTEL MCS 5100 WITH IBM LOTUS DOMINO SERVER SOFTWARE.

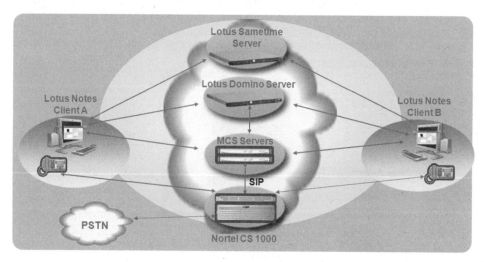

Elements of Unified Communications 2

> **Note** The user's PBX extension(s) must be properly configured to allow all identified operations to function as designed.

UC-enabled voice telephony call control capabilities, integrated at the user desktop with the Microsoft Office Communicator client software, include the following:

- **Make Call**—From the PC client, users can initiate a call from a selected voice telephony device, whether it is the PC or a PBX-supported extension. If the PC is used as the voice client, SIP is used between the desktop client, and a SIP gateway is connected to the Public Switched Telephone Network (PSTN). If the PBX extension is used as the voice client, SIP is used for call control between the desktop client and a PBX.

- **Answer Call**—Users can answer incoming calls on the PBX extension by clicking an Accept Call pop-up window. If the calling party is in the user's contacts file, the identity of the caller is also shown in the pop-up window. As shown in Figure 2-3, the user can take the call on a predefined number such as the desktop phone, the PC client, or a mobile phone, or deflect the call to an alternate phone number. If the user is using a handsfree headset with the desktop phone, it is not necessary to pick up the handset or press any buttons on the phone to answer the call.

FIGURE 2-3: NORTEL CONVERGED DESKTOP ACCEPT CALL POP-UP WINDOW.

- **Deflect Call**—Users can transfer a ringing call to a designated number. The number to which the call is deflected might be part of the local PBX, another location's phone system, a mobile phone, or any other number.

- **Conference Call**—Users can connect additional parties to form an ad hoc conference call, using the PC client. The service puts an active call on hold and creates another active call to another called party. When the user clicks the Add button in the PC client's call window, the held call and currently active call are joined. The joined call might consist of more than two parties, thus permitting multiparty conference calls to be assembled as necessary to meet business requirements.

- **Transfer Call**—Users can place a call on hold and then transfer the call to another number. Transfers can either be announced or executed blindly by clicking the appropriate transfer button on the PC client.

- **Call Forwarding**—Using the PC client, the user can configure incoming calls to be forwarded directly to an alternate number.

- **Clear Connection**—The user can terminate the call by clicking the PC client's Hang Up button whether or not the PC client was the call recipient, or can use any call termination feature of the telephone if the call was received on the desktop telephone.

- **Hold Call**—A user can place an active call on hold on the active device by selecting the Hold button on the PC client.

- **Generate Digits**—Some calls require additional digits to be entered after the initial connection. The Generate Digits feature allows the user to use a 12-button keyboard image to enter the required numbers. The user may also use the numeric keypad on the PC client keyboard to enter additional digits.

Over time, key product vendors and independent software vendors will expand the set of available functions. For example, a European integrator, Geomant, developed a message waiting indicator (MWI) application before Microsoft Exchange Server Unified Messaging (UM) software was widely available. The Geomant MWI was launched successfully in conjunction with the release of Microsoft Exchange Server 2007, and is a strong example of the extensibility facilitated by adoption of SIP as the call control plane for this technology.

UC offers a new frontier for specialized software companies to complement the infrastructure provided by the major market competitors. Entrepreneurs will quickly identify an opportunity to deliver a small application that further enhances the user's communication experience. The affected tasks might be miniscule in nature but, when combined with the services already available, could deliver significant productivity gains. This is especially true when evaluating real-world applications.

Although these functions are interesting, they do not drive significant productivity enhancement. Making voice technology more efficient might save 15 to 30 minutes per day for the casual business user, and might improve customer satisfaction ratings by a point or two. Revenue enhancement and productivity improvement will not be improved to the degree that generates a return on investment (ROI) significant enough to alert the CFO. However, when these small services are combined with other underlying technologies, such as presence and collaboration, and the services are facilitated across the extranet, productivity could improve by an order of magnitude.

Presence

Adding call control to the desktop client reduces some inefficiency and eliminates some errors associated with manually entering numbers and using the telephone's touch pad, but it does not address the problem of knowing whether someone is available prior to attempting a call.

As anyone who uses Internet-based instant messaging knows, it is a positive and time-saving experience to see the status flag indicate that the user is available for someone who is needed for a conversation. Why call and leave voice mail for someone who is already on the phone?

Why call in hopes the person will answer, even if the status flag indicates the call target is busy or away? Why call and leave a message if the status flag indicates the recipient is in a meeting and detailed information indicates that the meeting will last the whole day?

Figure 2-4 shows a user's instant messaging client. Many channels of communication are managed by this client because they are compatible with a wide variety of clients deployed for the front end of UC.

FIGURE 2-4: MICROSOFT WINDOWS LIVE MESSENGER EXAMPLE.

The power of presence extends well beyond instant messaging. It is this extension beyond a stand-alone client that supercharges employee productivity and promotes streamlining business processes.

What is presence?

Presence is an indication of a person's availability to communicate with others. Presence awareness is a person's knowledge of whether another person is available on a communications channel. In traditional voice systems, if a call forwards to voice mail, the caller may infer that the targeted recipient is away, on the phone, or busy. These traditional systems were designed to allow an individual to use a different voice mail message when away from the desk rather than on the phone; unfortunately, most users do not leave multiple messages for callers. If the system defaults are applied, the caller might receive erroneous presence information, such as a message indicating that the person is away when that is not the case.

The personalities of presence, as first defined in Request for Comments (RFC) 2778, include the following:

- **Presentity**—An entity described by presence information. This term usually refers to a human. Presence indicates the presentity's availability and willingness to communicate by a defined set of communications services.

- **Watcher**—Information requestors that receive presence information for the presence service.

- **Fetcher**—A watcher that requests the current value of some presentity's presence information from the presence service.

- **Subscriber**—A watcher that requests notification from the presence service when some presentity's future presence information changes.

- **Poller**—A special kind of fetcher that retrieves presence on a regular basis.

The Common Profile for Instant Messaging (CPIM), first defined in RFC 3860 in 2004, provides a common addressing scheme for IM and presence. CPIM specifies that IM addresses must conform to the format of the mailto: Uniform Resource Identifier (URI), as defined in RFC 2368. The mailto: uniform resource locator (URL) scheme designates the Internet mailing address of an individual or service. RFC 2368 extended the mailto: definition to allow setting mail header fields and the message body: for example, im:user123@companyabc.com.

In addition to standardizing the addressing scheme, CPIM specifies the common format required for instant messages and presence. Although applications might support additional formats, any system with content that travels across the border between services must conform to the format specified in this standard. CPIM also defines the behavior required of gateways that relay the messages between services.

Where CPIM defined a standard profile for IM and presence, the Extensible Messaging and Presence Protocol (XMPP), first defined in RFC 3920 in 2004, defines the protocol used to stream XML elements to exchange messages and presence information in close to real time.

XMPP-compliant message elements for presence can include subject, body, or thread. Subject contains human-readable character data that specifies the topic of the message. Body contains the human-readable character content of the message. Thread contains machine-readable content specifying an identifier used for tracking all messages between the parties. The type attribute in a presence message will be one of the following:

- **unavailable**—The entity is no longer available for communication.

- **subscribe**—The sender wishes to subscribe to the recipient's presence.

- **subscribed**—The sender has allowed the recipient to subscribe.

- **unsubscribe**—The sender is unsubscribing from another entity's presence to which the sender had previously subscribed.

- **probe**—The sender requests the status of an entity's current presence. This message type should be generated by only a presence server on behalf of a user.

- **error**—An error has occurred in processing or delivery of a presence message.

Individuals may subscribe to another person's presence and receive notifications when that status changes. When a person's presence status changes, all users who have subscribed to that user's presence information will receive notification of that person's presence change. Presence states are Active, Connected, Unavailable, and Unknown. Presence status notes provide information and level of detail about presence states. Table 2-1 provides a summary of presence states with associated presence status notes as implemented in the Nortel MCS 5100.

TABLE 2-1: MCS 5100 PRESENCE STATE AND PRESENCE STATUS NOTES

Presence Status	Presence Status Notes
Active	For the Active state, the Presence Manager and client support automated determination of the state and the appropriate note from the following list: • Available: The user is actively using one or more clients such as the Multimedia PC, Multimedia Web, or a Nortel IP phone 2002, 2004, or 2007. • On the phone: The user is on a call.
Connected	Users can select from the following list of predefined notes, or they can create a custom note consisting of up to 32 characters. • Away: The user is connected but is away from the Presence Manager and client support. • Out to lunch: The user is connected but is out to lunch. • Be right back: The user is connected but is temporarily away. User-defined notes are saved at the clients, not in the network. Caching applies only to notes entered at that client location. Only the last five notes entered are saved. Custom notes appear at the end of the list of available notes, after the predefined values.
Unavailable	Users can select from the following list of predefined notes, or they can create a custom note consisting of up to 32 characters. • Busy: The user is not available to engage on any communications channel. • On vacation: The user is on vacation and unavailable. • Offline: The user is described by the system as offline. Watchers cannot distinguish this status from that of a user who is not registered to the network. The user might configure this state explicitly, or the Presence Manager might detect that the user is logged off all clients.
Unknown	This is an error condition indicator used because the Presence Manager cannot determine the presence status. This can occur if: • An administrator banned the user from watching users in a particular domain (for example, the executive officers of a company). • The subscription exceeds the service package limit. • The contact address was incorrectly entered. • The user is banned from watching the other user's status by the other user.

2 | Elements of Unified Communications

With real-time communication, Online, Busy, or On the Phone status is articulated automatically. A converged desktop tells the server when a user's status should indicate On the Phone, whether that individual is on a PBX-attached digital phone, a mobile device supported by a PBX universal extension, or a VoIP call. In some implementations, this notification can be provided by mobile devices even when the mobile device is not supported by a PBX universal extension. The benefit of using SIP for message control is that new software can provide gateways to integrate systems that were previously stand-alone. Points of integration can be provided by service providers, third-party brokers, industry organizations, or independent software vendors. The industry standards are sufficiently well-designed to allow rapid adoption as demand grows.

Presence state transition notifications are sent to subscribers as indicated in Table 2-2. This table shows the impact that a change in any number of communications channels can have on a user's presence state.

TABLE 2-2: MCS 5100 PRESENCE STATE TRANSITIONS

Presence State Transitions	Presence State Transition Notes
From Unavailable to Unavailable	The user previously manually selected an option that displayed the user as unavailable. This selection persists across both client and server restart and failure.
From Unavailable to Connected	The user was previously in the Unavailable state because the user logged off the last client device and then logged on to the system with an IP phone 2002, 2004, or 2007 only. The user selected these states manually.
From Connected to Unavailable	The user is logged off the last registered client device. The user manually selected the Unavailable state.
From Connected to Connected	The user manually selected a different Connected note to display.
From Connected to Active	The user is logged on to a multimedia PC client or multimedia Web client and did not use the mouse and keyboard for a prolonged period, but is now using the PC.

The user is logged on to an IP phone (2002, 2004, or 2007), multimedia PC client, or multimedia Web client, and either places or answers a call.

The user previously selected the Connected state, continues to use the keyboard or mouse on the multimedia PC client or multimedia Web client, or places or answers a call with any client. Forty-five seconds after configuring the state to Connected, the user is still actively using the client. |

From Active to Unavailable	The user logs off the last client device.
	The user manually selects an option to display the Unavailable state.
From Active to Connected-Inactive	The user is logged on to a multimedia PC client or multimedia Web client, and no keyboard or mouse activity is detected for a predetermined amount of time.

Presence-aware applications

Presence awareness is useful when it is available only in a stand-alone communications client, such as IM. When UC extends beyond the specialized client to being embedded in business and productivity applications, it becomes the catalyst for change. Microsoft has included presence-awareness capability in most Microsoft Office productivity tools. Many enterprise software vendors, such as SAP and Oracle, have provided flexible ways to present output reports by using Microsoft Office productivity tools, and those reports inherit the presence-awareness capabilities provided with the tools.

The following examples describe existing presence-aware applications.

Microsoft Office Outlook 2005 messaging and collaboration client is a presence-aware application. Figure 2-5 shows a user who is reviewing incoming mail and who has opened a message from Adrienne. When the user's cursor passes over the presence icon (indicated by the ▪[1] symbol), the drop-down box opens and displays Adrienne's status. The user can now initiate contact with Adrienne so that pending business can be addressed immediately. Because this user is converged desktop–enabled, the contact options include the ability to place a call to Adrienne, using any available numbers for her; these numbers are pulled either from the user's contacts or from the corporate Active Directory directory service.

Microsoft Outlook is a communications product and should therefore be expected to have these capabilities; but these features can also be found in noncommunications software. Figures 2-6 and 2-7 provide an example of the contact information as it is seen within Word 2003. Figure 2-6 shows the ▪ symbol, which appears because the name smart tag is active for the document. When the cursor passes over the contact symbol, the named individual's current status is immediately displayed. If the user wants to contact Mike to discuss the document, the user can click the presence icon to display the options available for reaching Mike, as shown in Figure 2-7. One of those communications channels can be initiated from within Word.

2

Elements of Unified
Communications

---

1. Screenshot of presence icon in Microsoft Outlook.

FIGURE 2-5: MICROSOFT OFFICE OUTLOOK MESSAGING AND COLLABORATION CLIENT PRESENCE AWARENESS.

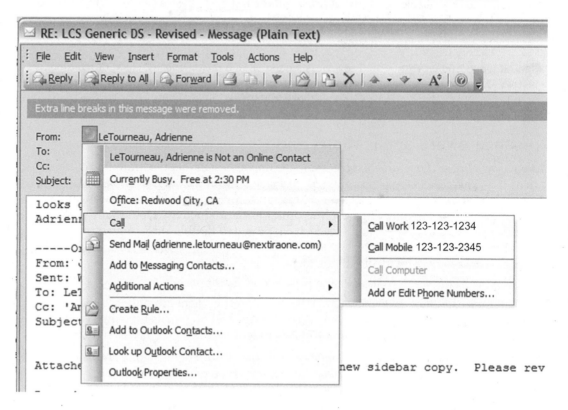

FIGURE 2-6: MICROSOFT OFFICE WORD CONTACT-AWARENESS APPLICATION.

An example of a smart tag for a person's name appearing within a Microsoft Office Word document is provided below. This example was created within this paper and exploits the Person's Name smart tag. While the use within a normal document may not be as compelling as the use within other applications,

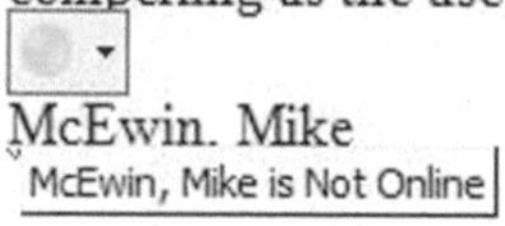

McEwin. Mike
McEwin, Mike is Not Online

FIGURE 2-7: MICROSOFT OFFICE WORD CONTACT EXPANSION APPLICATION.

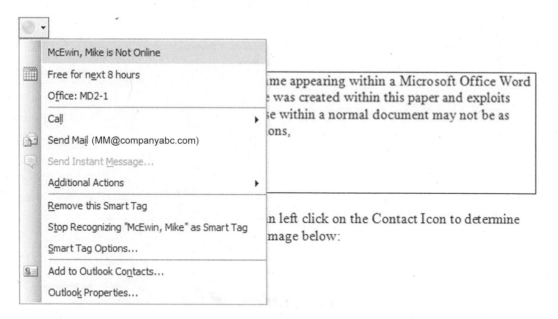

McEwin, Mike is Not Online

Free for next 8 hours

Office: MD2-1

Call ▸

Send Mail (MM@companyabc.com)

Send Instant Message...

Additional Actions ▸

Remove this Smart Tag

Stop Recognizing "McEwin, Mike" as Smart Tag

Smart Tag Options...

Add to Outlook Contacts...

Outlook Properties...

me appearing within a Microsoft Office Word was created within this paper and exploits se within a normal document may not be as ons,

n left click on the Contact Icon to determine mage below:

Other productivity applications, such as Microsoft Excel spreadsheet software, Outlook messaging and collaboration client, Microsoft Access database software, and Microsoft PowerPoint presentation graphics software can be smart tag–enabled, thereby inheriting presence awareness and converged desktop capabilities.

These UC-enabled applications are a good starting point for improving productivity. However, with this approach, each individual works on his or her own copy of the document, and documents are still distributed as e-mail attachments.

To minimize the proliferation of multiple copies of working documents, some of the communications capabilities should be enabled in a document management system. Figure 2-8 shows an example of the contact awareness enabled in Microsoft SharePoint Portal Server. Although SharePoint Portal Server does more than manage content, this feature adds presence awareness and supports converged desktop functionality that significantly enhances the value to the enterprise.

Content management capabilities that simplify management and control of electronic content deliver many business benefits. Visible presence status for all contributors to a document enables rapid resolution of any issues. It is easier to enforce enterprise content policy because only one copy of master documents must be maintained. Owners and contributors for policies are easily identified and can be contacted efficiently to address any questions.

Corporate policies and standards documents should be managed within the content management system. In this case, all users have access to the latest version of a document rather than printed copies of varying dates, so there is reduced risk of inadvertently conforming to the wrong version of a policy or standard. Improved conformity with policy reduces time spent on unproductive activities and empowers staff to function efficiently.

FIGURE 2-8: MICROSOFT SHAREPOINT PORTAL SERVER PRESENCE AWARENESS.

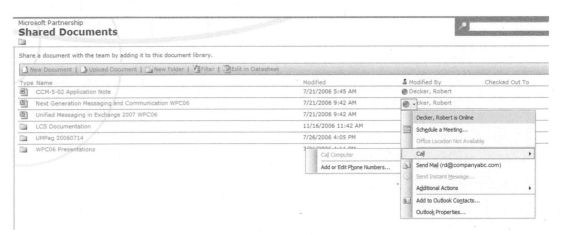

As developers continue to enhance the presence awareness embedded in enterprise applications and as integrated communications continue to evolve, enterprises will have increasing opportunity to evolve their business processes. Functions that require significant amounts of human interaction, such as sales and purchasing, will be most likely to benefit from this technology.

Instant messaging

The IM communications channel was originally defined to deliver small, simple messages immediately to online users. Over time, developers have enhanced IM clients to support dynamic transfer to a voice call, sharing a document, sharing video, and other functions, but the fundamental elements remain unchanged. The formal definition, originally described in RFC 2778, is that the Instant Message Service accepts and delivers instant messages addressed to instant inboxes.

An instant inbox is the receptacle for instant messages. Its address is usually the same as the information included in presence information. Certain presence status indicators indicate whether IMs will be accepted by that inbox. The following list describes the key terms of IM language:

- **Principal**—The people, groups, and software that use the system as a means of coordination and communications.

- **Communication means**—A method through which communication can take place. An IM service is one example of a communication means.

- **Contact address**—A specific point of contact through some communication means. An instant inbox address is the contact address for an IM service.

- **Delivery rules**—The constraints on how an IM service delivers received messages to the instant inbox. These rules are manipulated by the inbox user agent of the principal that controls the inbox.

- **Inbox user agent**—The means by which the principal manipulates instant inboxes controlled by that principal. The manipulation includes fetching messages and setting delivery rules.

- **Instant inbox**—The receptacle for instant messages intended for a principal.

- **Instant inbox address**—The address that indicates how a principal can receive an IM in his or her inbox. The presence status and this address are sufficient to determine whether the principal appears ready to accept the incoming IM. In some systems, the inbox can receive the IM even if the principal's inbox indicates an Unavailable status. The sender is informed of the status, and the inbox retains the message until the principal is next available on the system.

- **Instant message**—The small content to be delivered to a principal's inbox.

- **Instant message protocol**—The definition of the messages that can be exchanged between a sender user agent and an IM service.

- **Instant message service**—The software that accepts and delivers instant messages.

As described earlier in this chapter, CPIM was needed to resolve limited interoperability between the various IM solutions that were in place in 2004 and that were unable to communicate outside their community. Subscribers to one Internet service provider (ISP) were unable to use IM with users of a competing ISP. CPIM defined common semantics and data formats for IM to facilitate the creation of gateways between IM services. However, this interoperability brought up a large set of security issues that are addressed in later chapters of this book.

The specification recommends that the following message types be included in the IM message:

- **chat**—The message is sent in the context of a one-to-one chat conversation. Compliant clients should also provide maintenance of a conversation history.

- **error**—A previous message sent by the user has resulted in an error condition. Compliant clients should also provide information relative to the nature of the error.

- **groupchat**—The message is sent in the context of a multiuser chat environment. Compliant clients should support many-to-many chat between the parties, including delivery of a roster and maintenance of a conversation history.

- **headline**—The message is most likely generated by an automated service that pushes (broadcasts) content such as market data, news, sports, and so on.

- **normal**—The message behaves similarly to chat but does not maintain a conversation history.

The rapid adoption of IM and text messaging for leisure activity, especially among teens and young adults, ensures availability of resources capable of using the same technologies as they are integrated into enterprise operations. According to Gartner, Inc., 95 percent of employees will use IM as their tool of choice for voice, video, and chat by 2013.[2]

---

2. Sean Michael Kerner, "Gartner: Instant Messaging Reigns Supreme," CIO Update 27 June 2008 <http://www.cioupdate.com/research/article.php/3685781

Conferencing

With the exception of the ad hoc conferencing capability discussed in the section titled "Converged Desktop" earlier in this chapter, most interest has centered on person-to-person communications. One of the best ROI applications delivered by UC is the ability to replace commercial teleconference services with internally delivered multimedia conferencing capabilities.

Many traditional PBXs support voice conferencing, and some enterprises have leveraged these capabilities to minimize the use of external services. However, administration of the internal services was generally restricted to a small number of personnel, and many professionals considered voice conferencing to be difficult to coordinate. Therefore, many professionals continued to use external services, and the internal service was used only by a limited number of staff.

SIP-based conferencing is presence-aware, simple to administer, and multimedia capable. Simple administration enables users to view presence information and create ad hoc conferences as they are necessary. Multimedia-capable conferencing enables users to share common views of materials and reduce confusion in real time, thereby minimizing the number of discussions required to reach decisions.

Guidelines for building interoperable SIP conferencing applications are described in RFC 4245, "High-Level Requirements for Tightly Coupled SIP Conferencing," published in 2005. As SIP's interoperability with traditional PBXs is combined with the interoperable and highly scalable solutions that conform to RFC 4245, a robust, cost-effective, premise-based conferencing solution will be delivered. Although scalable conferencing solutions existed well before the publication of RFC 4245, UC focuses on the standardization of profiles and protocols to ensure interoperability.

A SIP conference is an association of SIP user agents with a central focus, where the focus has direct peer-wise relationships with the participants. The focus is a SIP user agent that can host conferences, including creation, maintenance, and manipulation, using SIP call control means and potentially using other non-SIP means. The conference focus can be implemented either by a participant or by a separate application server. In addition to the limited set of features that can be delivered by a client-based focus, a dedicated conference server can deliver simultaneous conferences, large scalable conferences, reserved conferences, and managed conferences. A compliant product can support any subset of the services defined in RFC 4245. The capabilities defined in RFC 4245 are outlined in Table 2-3.

TABLE 2-3: BASIC CONFERENCING SYSTEM REQUIREMENTS

Discovery	Supports the automated discovery of a SIP conferencing server. Identifies the address of record, particular conference properties, and current state.
Conference creation	Creates and specifies properties for ad hoc and reserved conferences. (The conferences initiated from the converged desktop are compliant with the ad hoc definitions.)

Conference termination	Requires a user agent to be able to terminate all connections from a conference. Termination can include the capability of a conference with only two participants to revert to a basic SIP point-to-point session and release the conferencing resources.
Participant manipulation	Requires the conference focus to be able to invite and disconnect participants from a conference. A focus must be able to join another session to an active conference. A user agent must be able to connect to the request joining a conference even if not previously invited to attend. A user agent must be able to connect with and join a third party to the conference. When appropriate, a focus must maintain participant anonymity. A client can support anonymous conferencing.
Conference state information	Requires the focus to maintain a database that tracks various aspects of the conference. Some of the elements to be tracked include participant information, current chair, media sessions, and so on. Any change in a participant's state should add a new snapshot of the conference to the database.
Focus role migration	Requires a means for the current focus to delegate that role to another participant. This must include a means for a participant to request control.
Sidebar conferences	Requires a means for a participant to create a sidebar conversation with another participant or with another client that is not a current participant of the conference.
Cascading of conferences	Requires an efficient means of distributing both signaling and media for the conference; it is not necessary for the same means to be used for both.
Conference coordination	Conferencing solution must allow multiple concurrent channels of communication to be active for the participants.

Additional RFCs provide more detailed definition for the elements appearing in Table 2-3. These elements may be developed by different organizations, so it is critical that they interoperate.

RFCs 4240 and 5022 define the Media Server Control Markup Language (MSCML). This language provides a means of delivering enhanced conferencing applications, such as sizing and resizing, in-conference interactive voice response (IVR) operations, and conference event recording. The IVR specification includes collecting dual-tone multifrequency (DTMF) digits and playing and recording multimedia content.

SIP-compliant conferencing capabilities are a key building block of UC. New applications will continue to emerge, further enhancing premise-based services.

Collaboration

Collaboration tools are not a new concept. Many specific applications, such as distance learning, existed in some form well before the explosion of the Web. The integration of these tools with the evolved channels of communication facilitated by the growth of the Web will further enhance the ability to collaborate in real time.

> **Note** Nortel defines collaboration as the seamless integration of voice, video, Web-based meeting delivery, virtual classroom training, e-learning delivery, and business process.

Collaboration involves multiple individuals working together to deliver a common output. Historically, this has been accomplished either by a meeting in which all parties participate or through multiple teleconferences and distributions of interim documents for review. Significant costs and delays are associated with both approaches. In a real-time world, neither of these approaches is adequate. Although document management systems help with compliance, document tracking, and accountability, document management does not provide the basic collaborative tools necessary to facilitate group interaction.

All the applications discussed up to this point can be considered part of the collaboration solution. UC, when implemented properly, provides the necessary resources to organize real-time ad hoc collaboration without routing multiple copies of documents or depending on manual revision control. UC provides the means of managing the communications channels under a common umbrella to ensure that the most appropriate resources are available to produce group product efficiently.

Draft Session Description Protocol (SDP) extensions are being considered to address rich collaboration applications that can complete the multimedia sessions already discussed. These applications include view sharing with remote manipulation, co-Web browsing, and file transfer. Existing legacy applications address each of these areas; however, most of those solutions predate SDP specifications and do not have the interoperability characteristics expected in a heterogeneous environment.

View sharing with remote manipulation

Many collaboration activities require that users be able to view one participant's computer desktop and be able to manipulate that desktop as if they were the local user. Many legacy applications providing this function operate in one-to-one mode and do not support group activities. Other legacy applications that extend this capability to one-to-many operations do so using proprietary solutions unique to a single computing platform.

The following list describes functions that must be supported for view sharing with remote manipulation:

- **Whiteboard**—The whiteboard function enables participants to share a common whiteboard image and use tools such as virtual pens and erasers. This service allows the developed images to be saved and printed.

- **View sharing**—View sharing enables one participant to share a video display image with the other participants in a collaboration session. This does not require the other participants to have the same application running, because only the video image is shared.

- **Remote device control**—Remote device control enables a remote participant to use his or her local mouse, keyboard, and pointing devices to control an application being presented in view sharing.

Co-Web browsing

Co-Web browsing enables participants in a multimedia conference to visit the same Web pages in near real time. Although some solutions might perform this by sharing one user's desktop with another user, as described for view sharing with remote manipulation, this approach does not consider other capabilities that might be important. If one participant is using a personal digital assistant (PDA) and the other is using a personal computer, the incompatible presentation capabilities might render the content useless to one of the users. More important, the remote user would not be able to save information to the favorites list, record the history of pages visited, acquire cookies, save bookmarks, and so on. Other issues with font size, color scheme, or even familiarity with the particular Web browser being used might impact the value of the collaboration for one of the users.

A better option is to share the URL of the page and allow each participant to be responsible for independently rendering the content on his or her respective browser. This approach eliminates issues relative to device-specific capabilities and individual user preferences. This also allows each participant to keep the history, bookmarks, and cookies on his or her own platform for future use.

The objective of this application in a collaboration environment is for the URL to be shared automatically and to avoid cut-and-paste activities or mistyping of a verbally communicated URL. The co-Web browsing application shares the URL with the remote client and instructs the client to open the reference URL. As additional links are traversed by the controlling participant, those links are shared by the attendees, so the relative pages are the same even though the rendered content might be somewhat different.

File Transfer

This feature enables a local user to offer a file to a remote user. The offer can include a preview icon if the file is an image or video. The remote user may accept or reject the transfer. Although there are many ways to transfer files, having this capability within the same client as the other applications making up the collaboration environment makes the process more efficient and less resource-consuming.

Fixed mobile convergence

A major objective of UC is to enable anytime, anywhere access to any type of content from any device. Fixed mobile convergence (FMC) integrates voice, video, text, and data communications into a seamless communications environment between desktop and mobile devices, using cellular and wireless local area network (WLAN) access.

IP Multimedia Subsystem (IMS) technology is at the heart of FMC. At its base level, IMS attempts to define an all Internet Protocol (IP)–based wireless network that replaces the historically disparate elements transporting voice, data, video, and control signaling. IMS integrates existing voice, video, messaging, and data capabilities over a single IP network, thus bringing the power of Internet technology to mobile users and enabling the creation and deployment of IP-based multimedia services for next-generation wireless networks.

Due to its simplicity, its full compatibility, and its interworking potential with the Internet community, SIP has been selected as the enabling protocol for IMS session control. This is important because the entire development community is already familiar with SIP, and this protocol will be available to deliver enhanced applications for FMC. In addition, any existing SIP application can be adapted to the IMS environment.

Knowledge Check 2-1: Elements of Unified Communications

Answer the following questions. Answers to these Knowledge Check questions are located in *Appendix A: Answers to Knowledge Check Questions*.

1. Which of the following is a standard presence status?

    a. Active

    b. Connected

    c. On the phone

    d. All of the above

2. When a user is logged on to a multimedia PC client or multimedia Web client, and no keyboard or mouse activity is detected for a predetermined amount of time, which presence state transition occurs?

    a. From Available to Unavailable

    b. From Connected to Unavailable

    c. From Unavailable to Connected

    d. From Active to Connected-Inactive

3. Which type of IM message is NOT included in the Internet Engineering Task Force (IETF) specification?

    a. Chat

    b. Trailer

    c. Normal

    d. Headline

    e. Groupchat

4. Which of the following is NOT a basic conferencing system requirement?

    a. Sidebar

    b. Discovery

    c. Video transmission

    d. Conference creations

    e. Conference termination

    f. Participant manipulation

5. Which of the following is expected to be supported for view sharing with remote control?

   a. Whiteboard

   b. View sharing

   c. Remote device control

   d. All of the above

6. Which collaboration type enables near real-time viewing of the same Web pages?

   a. Desktop sharing

   b. Co-Web browsing

   c. Application sharing

   d. Remote device control

7. UC increases user control of the user's voice environment.

   a. True

   b. False

8. A single-mode wireless device is supported with fixed mobile convergence.

   a. True

   b. False

9. No PBX configuration changes are required to support remote desktop operations with traditional digital phones.

   a. True

   b. False

10. Which of the following is NOT a personality of presence?

   a. Poller

   b. Stalker

   c. Fetcher

   d. Watcher

   e. Presentity

   f. Subscriber

Chapter summary

The transportation of VoIP has been a reality for more than 30 years. Cost-effective application of the technology has been delivered for more than 10 years. The convergence of voice and data communications infrastructures, the convergence of wireline and wireless communications infrastructures, and the creation of communications-aware applications are the beginning of the next major shift in enterprise productivity.

UC empowers end users with control of their communications environment. Converging control of the desktop phone into the desktop PC enables more intelligence to surround voice calls. Putting the desktop phone onto the corporate network and extending those resources to the user, even when the user is out of the office, reduces overall time spent coordinating activities and makes more time available for productive work.

The selection of SIP and SDP as common building blocks for all aspects of UC ensures the rapid evolution of applications to drive business success.

3: The Impact of Convergence, VoIP, and SIP

The convergence of voice and data networks began with the birth of the data communications industry in the late 1960s. Companies needed a way to provide access to their computers from a remote location. Engineers developed technology that allowed data transmission to share the voice telephone circuits of the day. Data was transformed to traverse the 64-kilobit bandwidth available in a single telephony system circuit.

Demand for faster communication speeds pushed development in voice and data communications technologies along diverse technology paths. Data communications developed in two channels: proprietary research completed by the major computer manufacturers, and research funded by the United States Defense Advanced Research Projects Agency (DARPA). Through the 1970s and early 1980s, development of voice and data infrastructure continued along parallel paths. Toward the end of the 1980s, demand for data networking capacity was growing at an exponential rate and showed no signs of slowing. Based on customer demand, primarily generated by the long-haul carriers, leading vendors began to create solutions that allowed voice traffic to be transported over the rapidly evolving data infrastructure.

This shift could be described as a "reconvergence" of voice and data communications. The research done during this transformation enables availability of the multimedia applications driving businesses today. Convergence on the data infrastructure is the key to delivering Unified Communications (UC).

Chapter 3 Topics

In this chapter, you will learn:

- the process that led to the divergence and reconvergence of voice and data infrastructure

- the process that allowed the transformation of voice from circuit-switched technology and protocols to packet format

- the transformation of enterprise applications from islands of computing to integrated environments

- the key differences between an IP-PBX and an IP-enabled PBX

- the reasons why Session Initiation Protocol (SIP) is a key enabling protocol for UC

- the basic operation of SIP and how specific aspects of the protocol are adaptable to newly emerging technology

- how SIP can be leveraged to create enterprise federations that cross organizational boundaries and support a multicompany ecosystem

- the benefits of business-to-business (B2B) collaboration

Chapter 3 Goals

Upon completion of this chapter, you will be able to:

- describe the convergence factors that enabled the development of UC

- understand the meaning of infrastructure convergence

- understand the meaning of protocol convergence

- understand the meaning of application convergence

- understand the differences between Voice over Internet Protocol (VoIP) and SIP enablement of Private Branch Exchange (PBX) systems

- understand the important role SIP plays in enabling UC applications

- understand the basic operation of SIP

- understand the value and importance of enterprise federations

- understand the value and importance of B2B collaboration

Key Terms

Application convergence 49

Infrastructure convergence 46

Organization convergence 50

Protocol convergence 47

The Impact of Convergence, VoIP, and SIP

3

Just what is convergence?

Convergence is a word increasingly used across both industry and technology. For more than 30 years, the auto industry has held a biennial convergence conference in Detroit. An organization in Minnesota that promotes science fiction and fantasy interests recently celebrated the tenth anniversary of its convergence conference. The Mathematical Association of America publishes an e-zine that uses a unique spelling of convergence as its title. In 2008, a Google search for *convergence* resulted in nearly 3.5 million hits, although the same engine returned only 2.8 million results for Session Initiation Protocol (SIP).

In the communications technology industry, *convergence* was first used to describe combining voice and data networks to reduce the cost of information transport. When first deployed, *data communications* meant the conversion of digital signals to analog to allow transport across the voice network. Ultimately, the channelization and speed constraints of the voice network resulted in the carriers building data networks that ran parallel to the voice network. These networks evolved from X.25 to Frame Relay. The cost of maintaining redundant networks drove the telecommunications industry to converge their long-distance networks. The technology used to deliver the initial carrier convergence found its way to enterprises, where the thirst for data capacity was escalating rapidly.

As convergence has evolved, it has come to mean different things to different people in the industry. Figure 3-1 shows the typical penetration path of convergence within an enterprise. The corporation only truly begins to benefit as the progressions flow out of the network infrastructure. In this chapter, you will learn about the areas in which UC is facilitating further convergence of technology, people, organizations, and corporate policy.

FIGURE 3-1: STAGES OF CONVERGENCE.

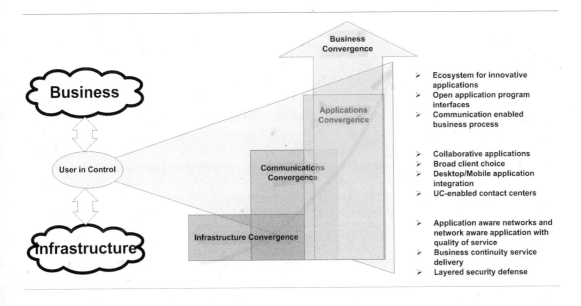

3 The Impact of Convergence, VoIP, and SIP

Infrastructure convergence

Many people think that voice and data convergence emerged with the introduction of VoIP technology. In reality, convergence has been evolving ever since data was first transported between two sites using modem technology.

The carrier infrastructure is where diverse communications technologies, such as voice, video, and data, began to converge. In North America in the 1960s, Lucent and Nortel delivered multiplexing products that allowed carriers to maximize throughput on their circuits. The voice networks transported data in the same 64-kilobit channels that were used to transport a single voice conversation. Multiplexing allowed multiple input paths to be grouped into a single transport trunk by managing inactivity periods effectively.

In the 1980s, several technology suppliers (including Timeplex, General Datacom, and Larscom) created Time-Division Multiplexing (TDM) equipment that allowed enterprises to transport channelized isochronous (voice and video) and data traffic over one or more circuits leased from their carrier between their various sites, both domestically and internationally. This first step toward convergence allowed customers to consolidate what had previously been redundant links and terminating equipment between their facilities.

In their original form, multiplexors used a static number of channels operating at constant bandwidth per channel. Although this reduced the number of links between facilities, it resulted in some channels being congested while other channels were nearly idle. Multiplexing technology was complex and required more support resources rather than fewer; however, it could be justified based on the cost trade-off for circuits and equipment. As technology evolved, the industry became rife with proprietary protocols that locked customers into a specific vendor's products, even when better products were available from a third party.

At the same time the wide area communications market was expanding, local area networking emerged to support data communications within a given location. This new communications method was incompatible with the wiring implemented for telephones. Enterprises had to install an additional type of wiring at each workstation where a personal computer would be located. The cost of maintaining separate infrastructure for voice and data created increasing demand for convergence.

In 1995, the American National Standards Institute (ANSI) published *ANSI/TIA/EIA-568A*, better known as the specifications for Cat 5 cabling. Vendors for both data and voice products were involved in development of the standard, and promised support in new products. Cat 5 became the cable of choice for local area network (LAN) workstations and telephone sets, allowing enterprises to simplify infrastructure wiring and better manage maintenance costs. This transition also facilitated an organizational change for enterprises that elected to cross-train their voice and data technicians and share workloads.

Although this activity occurred in the commercial communications and computing space, academia and the government were also exploring the technologies that eventually emerged as the Internet. In 1985, Transmission Control Protocol and Internet Protocol (TCP/IP) was selected as the data communications transport protocol standard for the U.S. Department of Defense (DOD), the U.S. National Bureau of Standards, and the U.S. Department of Commerce. In fact, the U.S. DOD had adopted TCP/IP as its standard by 1978, after only four years of development.

At the same time, IBM partnered with ROLM in 1984 and ultimately acquired the telephone equipment manufacturer. This foretold the convergence of the voice and data infrastructure, even though IBM later sold ROLM's voice technologies component to Siemens.

By the late 1980s, the Internet had emerged as a generally accepted means of interconnecting computers, particularly for electronic mail, file transfer, and electronic bulletin boards. Personal computers rapidly replaced terminals as the preferred way of connecting people with computers. Ethernet LANs were becoming predominant for connecting workstations with the computers that supplied the enterprise applications, whether they were minicomputers or mainframes.

The Internet's evolution included drafts of standards for many forms of communication. In 1996, the International Telecommunication Union's (ITU) H.323 standard was adopted as the standard for audio and video communications. At this point, VoIP began to emerge as a practical solution to rising international phone service charges. Many startups began to sell products that were initially called IP-PBX solutions. Even Nortel and Lucent created internal projects to develop IP-PBXs for small businesses.

In 1998, two compelling acquisitions changed the voice infrastructure environment. Cisco acquired Selsius Systems, Inc., a leading supplier of network PBX systems for high-quality telephony over IP networks. In June of that same year, Nortel Networks acquired Bay Networks, a leader in the worldwide data networking market. These two actions put Cisco, the data networking leader, and Nortel, a digital network infrastructure industry leader, in direct competition for the enterprise voice market and set a clear direction toward converged voice and data infrastructure for the entire voice communications industry.

The carrier network continued to evolve, with extensive deployment of fiber infrastructure to meet the demand for bandwidth created by the rapid growth of the World Wide Web. Fiber can use Multi-Protocol Layer Switching (MPLS), which allows packet transport throughout the entire network, from the individual workstation through the LAN and then through the wide area network (WAN). Labeling packets to indicate priority handling, where required, allows effective delivery of any media, whether voice, video, or data.

Protocol convergence

Even though telephone systems throughout the world interoperate based on a well-defined set of standards, the voice telephony market had minimal local site interoperability standards prior to the emerging trend toward VoIP. Each vendor's digital voice communications protocol, used to connect telephones with the PBX, was proprietary and rarely licensed to others. Although this closed architecture allowed a particular vendor to efficiently deliver enhanced capabilities and earn customer loyalty, it inhibited interoperability across platforms and discouraged third-party entry in the market.

This does not mean that there were no defined standards. The Q Signaling (QSIG) protocol and Digital Private Network Signaling System (DPNSS) are defined standards for PBX interoperability. QSIG is used by many third-party voice add-on software producers to interface their products with proprietary PBXs.

Audio Messaging Interchange Specification analog (AMIS-A) provides a mechanism to transfer messages between different voice messaging systems. This specification uses the existing voice network to execute a call and uses digits, similar to a user entering digits on a keypad, to identify the target mailbox and any authentication information. It then plays the message to the target system.

Signaling System 7 (SS7) has been used to control voice calls since it was defined by AT&T in 1975 and deployed worldwide in 1981. One feature of this protocol suite was that it separated call control and signaling from the user's audio flow. This eliminated a security problem by removing the end user's access to control signaling.

It is critical to understand these preexisting standard protocols to enhance the success of any effort to deliver a converged solution. These protocols will likely exist in parallel with any evolving standards because most of the world, whether IP-enabled or not, will continue to use the traditional voice infrastructure. Investment in the existing infrastructure is simply too great to abandon.

The evolution to a packet transport infrastructure required the development of complementary application layer protocols for multimedia content. To fill this need, H.323 and SIP were defined in 1996. H.323 originated in the ITU and leveraged telephony standards; SIP originated with the Internet Engineering Task Force (IETF) and leveraged all prior Internet-related works.

At the same time, wireless networks were experiencing an equally important evolution. Mobile intelligent devices, such as the RIM BlackBerry and Palm Treo smartphones, were capable of receiving e-mail with large attachments and performing various other PC-type activities. These devices created demand for more bandwidth than previous-generation cellular phones required. An increasingly mobile workforce created demand for wireless LAN access from virtually anywhere at any time. Wireless fidelity (Wi-Fi) wireless local area networks (WLANs) rapidly emerged, providing access services to the public. Enterprises began to deploy wireless services in parallel with their wired LANs.

Intelligent mobile devices were enhanced to include voice and video communications capabilities. Enterprises began to demand products that could work with internal LANs when the user was in the building, and work with carrier networks when the user left the building. Moreover, enterprises wanted a smooth transition from inside to outside so that connections would not be lost when migrating between networks.

Mobile carriers worked with major suppliers to define requirements for an advanced set of applications that would enable continued market growth. The Third Generation Partnership Project (3GPP/3GPP2) was a collaboration of standards bodies chartered with responsibility for maintaining the Global System for Mobile Communications (GSM) Technical Specifications and Technical Reports. 3GPP defined IP Multimedia Services (IMS) to enable all-IP person-to-person and person-to-content communications in a variety of modes. This has resulted in delivery of voice, text, pictures, and video, in any combination and in a highly personalized way, on a wireless device. The IMS specification has become the core of next-generation mobile communications and is heavily dependent on the SIP protocol.

SIP is a relatively simple ASCII-based protocol that uses request–response dialogues to establish communication among components in the network. User agents in a SIP network are identified by unique IP addresses, which are constructed much like e-mail addresses. The SIP address uses the format *sip:user123@companyabc.com,* where *user123* is the user ID and *companyabc.com* is the registrar server where user123's requests can be delivered.

SIP's simplicity allowed it to be embraced for all forms of communications. The text orientation and address structure made it easily adaptable for end-user applications. SIP has become the core of next-generation applications, including mobility, fixed mobile convergence, and UC.

Application convergence

The original deployment of computers within enterprises resulted in unique applications in each business for all core functions. Over time, businesses realized that the applications required to operate a company are essentially the same, regardless of the core market the company serves. Payroll system works in the same way for almost everyone, with a few unique specifications for the particular company. Most accounting systems are the same and have few variances, primarily because they must comply with many government regulations. Manufacturing resource planning system requirements are essentially the same, regardless of the product being manufactured. Because core applications are so similar, the software industry developed solutions that could be purchased rather than custom-built for each client.

All applications provide access control. Companies want to grant application access only to authorized users. Originally, each application defined user IDs and passwords to control access. Unfortunately, there were no standards for this requirement, so end users had different logon information for each application to which they had access.

Further complicating matters, each application had a unique user interface. Users had to learn different command structures to interact with each application. Product suppliers worked to provide a uniform operating environment for their applications; however, those environments were generally proprietary to a given manufacturer's equipment or a given software company's applications.

The World Wide Web initially evolved as an entirely new set of applications disconnected from business-critical systems. Over time, the Web browser has become the de facto standard for presentation to end users. Whether users connect to the enterprise through the Internet or by way of an intranet, they experience the same look and feel for all applications.

Although the ability to access systems either locally or remotely brought greater flexibility to the end user, the network logon was a source of frustration because it added another step to the process, even though it enhanced security. As directory services became more prominent, this issue was addressed. Directory services, commonly deployed in Novell environments, provided a single repository to track a user's privileges. Lightweight Directory Access Protocol (LDAP) became the industry standard around which heterogeneous enterprise IT organizations could deploy common access control services.

LDAP services are a series of transactions that allow applications to validate the authorization level an individual may have for gaining access. Based on organizational requirements, what a given person may be able to do from within the corporate network might vary from what that individual can do with that same application from a remote location. What a person may do from 8 A.M. to 5 P.M. might vary from what that same individual may be able to do with the same application after hours. The key benefit to the enterprise is the ability to protect vital information assets adequately, while simplifying user training and complexity and delivering improved productivity. Although directory services could be considered a key infrastructure convergence element, its full advantages are not realized until all enterprise applications are modified to exploit the capabilities fully. This includes emerging communications applications.

Just as the browser has evolved for the business applications interface, the desktop productivity environment, whether Microsoft Office or IBM Lotus, has become the standard interface for almost all applications with which a user interacts on a daily basis. Enterprise application vendors deliver output through standard word processing and spreadsheet templates, enabling end users to customize reports rapidly to meet specific requirements.

The convergence of the user presentation layer of applications with browser and productivity tools allows developers to focus on product functionality. This permits applications to evolve more rapidly, to meet changing business requirements. The advantage is that users get new functionality while continuing to work with tested human interaction tools, thereby minimizing delays due to training.

For UC to succeed, it must continue to leverage these environments. Although the industry is introducing new ways of communicating, such as instant messaging and click to call, it does so through integration with the well-known user environment, thus reducing the impact of change.

Although convergence of the infrastructure and protocols is critical, convergence does not make a significant contribution to the business until applications are fully exploited. Organizational process improvements and workload redistribution are driven by application convergence, which offers an opportunity to streamline corporate policy.

Organization convergence

Although downsizing, right-sizing, flattening the organization, and other euphemisms have been popular for many years and some organizational realignment has occurred, much of the change has been in administration and management with little change at the business process level. Computers have automated some tasks, but they are historically used as transaction processing engines that allow fewer people do to the same work.

Infrastructure has already led to the convergence of telecommunications and IT organizations. Although this is good for the administrative budget, it has not contributed much to change in the rest of the organization.

By properly implementing UC and exploiting technologies primarily developed for call centers, such as skills-based routing, companies can modify their customer support business processes. In the name of customer satisfaction, contact centers have been built, streamlined, staffed, restaffed, outsourced, and in-sourced. What customers really want, however, is to talk with someone who can actually address the problem about which they are calling. Who better to do this than the person directly responsible for the product being discussed? Who better to take a corrective action than the person who created the problem or the one who can directly initiate an improvement?

Organizations can eliminate the need for an altogether separate organization by adding one additional technical person to compensate for time that may be spent by others engaged in interactions with customers. Although this may be more costly than adding a contact center technician, it will be a significant benefit to the overall budget. More important, it will deliver customer services that are unparalleled in today's environment.

Many service providers today offer this kind of service to their top enterprise accounts, or as an optional, more expensive, premium service level. They use alternative phone numbers to facilitate alternative call routing. Implementing these processes incurs incremental cost to the organization, resulting in its premium customers delivering lower overall sales margin performance.

If these services are so desirable that they are provided to the most preferred customers, this should be the ultimate objective for every customer so that incremental costs can be eliminated and overall customer satisfaction can be improved. Later chapters of this book introduce other areas in which UC leads to organizational, process, and people convergence.

VoIP: The foundation for SIP enablement

Voice over packet technology has evolved over many years. Early experimentation with full-duplex voice communications over low-bandwidth connections was a particularly important element in the evolution of the Internet. Experimentation with voice over packet protocols began as early as 1973 with the introduction of RFC 741 for Network Voice Protocol (NVP).

Early deployment of NVP led to improved understanding of the many elements required to ensure high-quality, secure communications. The following list describes some elements of the original NVP specification:

- recovery of loss of any message without catastrophic effects (this requirement results in message identities [IDs] to ensure proper delivery and sequencing of traffic)

- design that prevents a system from tying up the resources of another system unnecessarily

- avoidance of end-to-end retransmission

- separation of control signals from data traffic

- separation of vocoding-dependent parts from vocoding-independent parts

- adaptation to the dynamic network performance

- optimal performance, for instance, guaranteed required bandwidth and minimized maximum delay

- independence from lower level protocols

These design considerations were incorporated more than 20 years later, in both the H.323 and SIP specifications. Although the original NVP specification focused almost entirely on technical requirements, the SIP specification is focused toward user enablement. RFC 2543 identified five facets of establishing and terminating multimedia communications:

- **User location**—Determination of the end system to be used for communication

- **User capabilities**—Determination of the media and media parameters to be used

- **User availability**—Determination of the willingness of the called party to engage in communications

- **Call setup**—"Ringing," establishment of call parameters at both the called and the calling party

- **Call handling**—Methods that include transfer and termination of calls

The SIP specification reflects the evolved understanding that a user is not a static resource that always demonstrates the same capabilities. In other words, the SIP specification allows the user to be identified independently of the type of client that may be used for communications, and negotiates the user's capabilities at the time a session is initiated.

The SIP specification acknowledges that voice is only one of several different multimedia elements and ensures the ability to embrace all modes of communicating properly. This allows SIP to support video calls in the same way that voice calls are supported.

This discussion is not complete without a basic understanding of the differences between VoIP and SIP enablement of PBX systems. VoIP implementation transports the control and media streams in packets and removes the circuit switch from the call path of a conversation. If two clients know that each other exists and the call is person-to-person, there is no requirement for any server between the two points.

SIP enablement of a PBX allows the PBX to use SIP for control signaling with other devices and even with some SIP phones that might be interoperating with that PBX. SIP enablement allows VoIP clients and traditional circuit switch devices to communicate without requiring that all users replace their traditional phones with IP appliances. Given the investment companies have made in traditional circuit-switched products, the extensive requirements to upgrade the LAN infrastructure to deliver quality VoIP, and the end-user training required for any phone system change, SIP enablement of the existing voice infrastructure will prove to be much more cost effective for most enterprises. As the traditional platforms evolve to interoperate in a UC environment, a greater return on the historical voice investment of these companies will be possible.

Although it is not a good strategy to invest in new circuit-switched technology if an investment decision must be made, continuing to use a hybrid SIP-enabled PBX will not prove to be a business obstruction.

SIP: The foundation for Unified Communications

Because SIP provides user transparency from hardware and media, it provides the flexibility required to deliver communications effectively anywhere, anytime, to any device. SIP is an application layer protocol; so it operates above all the other infrastructure but is not directly dependent on any single element that makes up that infrastructure.

SIP invitations carry session descriptions that support the users negotiating the attributes of the particular interaction. Each interaction is a unique pairing of two or more parties, using an agreed-on set of attributes relevant for that communication only. During one session, one user might want to interact only over a traditional desktop telephone through the PBX, whereas for the next session that same user might elect to interact through his or her desktop client or cell phone. Clearly, the attributes that are negotiated for each of these environments will be substantially different; however, SIP allows these sessions to be conducted in a meaningful manner.

Most communications protocols rely on establishing a connection between a client and a remote server: for example, a client–server architecture. When a phone is dialed, it interacts with a phone switch and tells the phone switch what it wants to do. For the most part, the phone switch does the work and is engaged throughout the connection with the called party.

Provided that call routing is properly supported by directory servers, SIP sessions are peer-to-peer in nature. User A can submit a call invitation to user B and, if the addressing information is resolved through normal address resolution procedures, no other servers need to be engaged during the session.

Of course, this is the most basic of interactions and provides no level of oversight or centralized management. This is similar to a business in which no Web proxy server is used for end users who view external Web sites. Proxy servers are a defined element of the SIP specification and allow organizations to administer and ensure compliance with corporate policies effectively.

Not every call is between two like clients. One client may be a desktop telephone and the other a mobile phone. The SIP specification provides for the deployment of gateways that can act on behalf of users to bridge two incompatible technologies. An enterprise that has deployed a VoIP solution uses a gateway to connect its IP phones to the Public Switched Telephone Network (PSTN). Other gateways support interaction with mobile phones, fax machines, and any number of other devices that may evolve in the future.

SIP is the enabling technology behind a range of applications and services, some of which are already in service and others that will become available in the near future. More importantly, it is a flexible protocol designed to adapt to technologies that have yet to be created. It is this flexible design that makes SIP the ideal enabler of UC solutions.

SIP features

SIP is an application layer control protocol that can initiate sessions as well as invite members to sessions that have been advertised and established by other means. These sessions include multimedia conferences, distance learning, Internet telephony, instant messaging, and similar applications. SIP transparently supports name mapping and redirection services, allowing the implementation of Integrated Services Digital Network (ISDN) and Intelligent Network telephony subscriber services. These facilities also enable personal mobility.

Personal mobility unleashes services such as hot desking (having the same extension number/SIP address regardless of the individual's physical location), presence, and find me/follow me. The objective is to simplify and control the personal experience, supporting features such as picture caller ID, dynamic call handling, and personal call management. Personal mobility allows end users to receive and send calls from any location, on any device, at any time, while maintaining the same identity to the network based on a unique personal identity.

Along with personal mobility, SIP can be used to initiate multiparty calls (conferences) using a multipoint control unit (MCU) or fully meshed interconnection instead of multicast. Internet telephony gateways that connect PSTN parties can also use SIP to set up calls between them.

One important aspect of SIP is that it can be used in conjunction with other call setup signaling protocols. SIP can be used to determine that a desired party is available via H.323, obtain the H.245 gateway and user address, and use H.225 to establish a call. In the case of a PSTN user, SIP can determine the phone number to be called and suggest the Internet-to-PSTN gateway to be used.

The following list describes the many roles that comprise the SIP environment, as originally defined in RFC 2543 and updated in RFC 3261:

- **Back-to-back user agent (B2BUA)**—A logical entity that receives a request and processes it as a user agent server (UAS). To determine how the request should be answered, it acts as a user agent client (UAC) and generates requests. It maintains dialogue state and must participate in all requests sent on the dialogues it has established.

- **Proxy server**—An intermediary program that acts as both server and client for the purpose of making requests on behalf of other clients.

- **Redirect server**—A server that accepts a SIP request even though it is not the target address, then forwards the message to the intended address. It neither accepts calls nor initiates its own SIP requests.

- **Registrar server**—A server that accepts register requests and places information it receives from those requests into the location service for the domain it handles. (This works like the home location register service for a mobile phone, which registers between cells as it moves.)

- **User agent client (UAC)**—An end-user application that initiates a SIP request.

- **User agent server (UAS)**—A server application that contacts the user when a SIP request is received and that accepts, rejects, or redirects the request.

A SIP message is either a request from a client to a server or a response from a server to a client. The format of both types of messages consists of a *start-line*, one or more *header fields*, an *empty line* that indicates the end of the header fields, and an optional *message-body*.

SIP requests use a Request Line for a start line. A Request Line contains a method name, a target address, and the SIP protocol version, separated by a single space character. The methods that might be included in this message are:

- **Register**—For registering contact information with a Registrar

- **Invite**—For initializing the session with the user or service to which the message is being addressed

- **Ack**—For acknowledging receipt of a message

- **Cancel**—For canceling a request sent by a client

- **Bye**—For terminating an established session

- **Options**—For querying servers about their capabilities

SIP responses use a Status Line as their start line. A Status Line consists of the protocol version, followed by a numeric Status Code and its associated textual phrase. The Status Code is a three-digit integer result code that indicates the outcome of an attempt to understand and satisfy a request.

SIP allows six possible values for the first digit of the Status Code. The currently defined codes are:

1xx:. **Provisional**—Request received, continuing to process the request

2xx:. **Success**—Action successfully received, understood, and accepted

3xx:. **Redirection**—Further action necessary to complete the request

4xx:. **Client error**—Request contains bad syntax or cannot be fulfilled by the target server

5xx:. **Server error**—Target server failed to fulfill an apparently valid request

6xx:. **Global failure**—Request cannot be fulfilled at any server

Although there are many important aspects of the SIP protocol, registration is a key element in making it all work. If a user wants to initiate a session with another user, SIP must discover the current host(s) at which the destination user is reachable.

Users can move between SIP endpoints (soft client, PBX-attached phone, mobile phone, and so on), and they may be addressable by multiple names. SIP deals with this complexity by distinguishing between an address of record (AOR) and contact addresses.

An AOR is a SIP Uniform Resource Identifier (URI) that points to a domain with a location service. A contact address is an IP address or Domain Name System (DNS) name for a SIP device.

SIP registration expires unless refreshed. At periodic intervals, SIP devices send REGISTER requests to inform the SIP of the device's current contact address. The SIP Registrar associates the AOR in the REGISTER message with the contact address. The SIP Registrar writes the binding to a database, called the location service. The location service contains a list of bindings of AORs to zero or to more contact addresses. The location service and routing tables are used by a SIP proxy or a SIP redirect server for AOR-to-contact-address resolution.

Basic SIP signaling paths are reflected in Figure 3-2, which shows the SIP call flow. This shows SIP only as a traditional voice communications replacement tool. The real power of SIP is realized when value-added applications are converged into the communications model to deliver new business functions and processes. An enhanced model is reflected in Figure 3-3, SIP with applications.

The important aspect of Figure 3-3 is the interface between the communications server and the engaged applications. Although this is still relatively simple in the overall scheme of expectations for SIP and integration with enterprise applications, it clearly shows how this integration might be accomplished. Later chapters of this text explore specific application opportunities.

3

The Impact of
Convergence, VoIP,
and SIP

FIGURE 3-2: SIP CONNECTIVITY MODEL IN A NORTEL CS 1000 ENVIRONMENT.

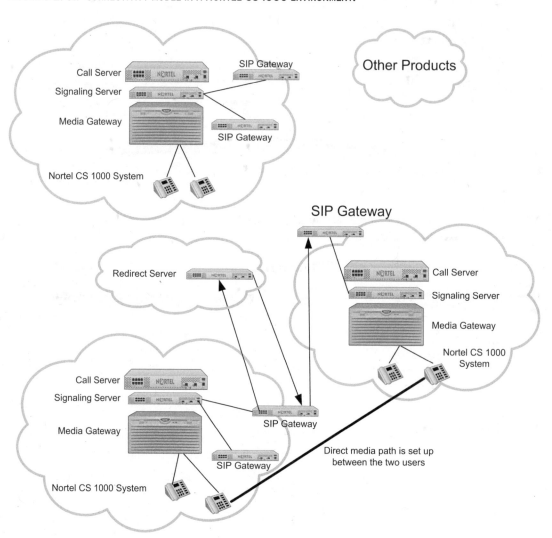

FIGURE 3-3: SIP ADVANCED CONNECTIVITY MODEL IN A NORTEL CONTACT CENTER ENVIRONMENT.

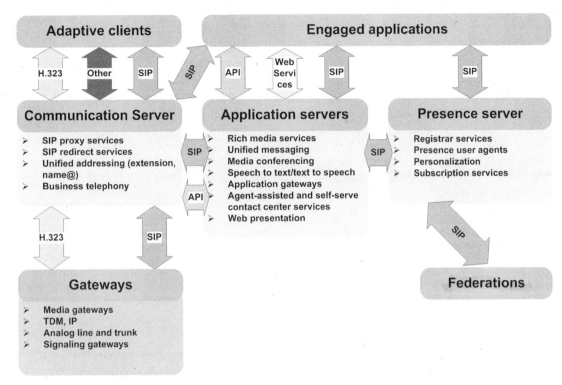

Federations and company-to-company communications

Since the late 1980s, an enormous body of work has been created describing new forms of organization. Terms such as *virtual corporation* and *virtual community* have become commonplace in discussing the business and socioeconomic strategies that can prepare companies to compete in the 21st century. This literature suggests that companies will outsource a majority of their functions so they can be flexible in responding to changing market demands, and that a specialized ecosystem of small companies will develop to deliver specific functions to major companies.

Electronic Data Interchange (EDI), the intercompany application-to-application exchange of data in standard format, is an early example of a virtual corporation-like activity. For a given set of partners, a limited number of transactions recur continuously. When applications communicate those transactions without human intervention, accuracy increases and therefore operating efficiency is improved for both parties. However, implementing application-to-application relationships is highly complex, and network infrastructure carries a high cost. Therefore, almost every implementation must minimize the number of business partners.

Before two companies establish an EDI relationship, there must be a great deal of collaboration among several groups in both organizations. Anyone involved in one of these intercompany activities is well aware of the delays involved in coordinating meetings of the right individuals and waiting for approvals after those meetings have been conducted.

The Web's emergence somewhat lowered the infrastructure cost of these relationships, but did not reduce the level of effort required to integrate the transactions. Some of the new communications channels began to be exploited by a subset of the organizations, but they were not embraced as a corporate practice. The need to ensure information security compliance led many IT organizations to block the new channels from being used by individuals inside their companies.

Even though enterprises did not embrace the new communications channels, individuals became accustomed to using those tools outside the corporation and began to demand IT support resources. The need to reach people anytime, anywhere led to the deployment of bidirectional text messaging tools such as the BlackBerry smartphone. This created a new demand on IT organizations to synchronize these devices with corporate mail systems.

Ultimately, IT organizations deployed secure instant messaging solutions to support internal communications. Because both internal and external users need to communicate effectively, IT organizations began to bridge their internal instant messaging (IM) systems with commercial service providers such as MSN and AOL. Although this solved part of the emerging communications problem, it did not provide a direct business-to-business IM connection.

Federations

Identity federations are multiorganizational infrastructures that enable enhanced communications while respecting privacy and the security of shared identity information. Federated IM networks allow communications across different IM clients and platforms, similar to the way e-mail allows people to send and receive mail regardless of the mail client they happen to use. Federation between businesses allows users in one organization to perceive the presence of users in the other.

The key element of federation that most IT organizations are concerned about is the requirement to maintain an open directory that allows other IM networks to send messages to their users. Although the voice community has been allowing this federated communication for many years, the IT community is not accustomed to having its directory exposed for external purposes.

As implemented today, IM supports two methods of server federation: white list federation and open federation. A white list, the preferred approach for the enterprise, is a specific list of servers with which the enterprise permits users to communicate. Open federation allows the enterprise users to communicate with any other IM server that allows open federation without explicit definition. With open federation, the IM server performs a DNS lookup instead of referencing the white list to identify other servers with which it can communicate.

The protocol used to support open federation is the Extensible Messaging and Presence Protocol (XMPP). The protocol initially provided for near real-time, extensible IM and presence information. As its name indicates, it was built to be extensible, and other features such as VoIP and file transfer signaling have been added.

Security issues relative to federation behavior are addressed by using Transport Layer Security (TLS). TLS protocol allows client–server applications to communicate in a way that is designed to prevent eavesdropping, tampering, or message forgery.

It is very important for the corporate security teams to gain confidence in the effectiveness of TLS for federation access during the early phase of collaboration through IM. IM clients are the launch point for content sharing and e-commerce, both of which go well beyond the simple act of communicating.

B2B collaboration

In the past, B2B collaboration meant passing files through e-mail and holding conference calls to review changes made by either party. Emerging UC tools greatly enhance B2B collaboration by providing whiteboards, application sharing, and other tools that permit near real-time decision making. These tools, combined with a robust content management system, provide effective solutions to the technical problems that plagued early B2B marketplaces.

Solving technical issues will not alleviate corporate cultural resistance to the changes that are enabled by the technology. They will not resolve archaic compliance legislation. However, the latest solutions allow professionals to collaborate from their desks, using tools they can easily master with minimal training. Using the latest UC tools, there is no need to have a third party coordinate and schedule conference calls. Most of the tools support an on-demand conferencing capability that any team member can use to bring resources together virtually to address a critical issue quickly. The user simply accesses the system to schedule the meeting, provides the meeting access information to the participants, and manages the meeting as it progresses. Most of the tools even permit recording the voice stream to ensure retention for compliance, if required.

Knowledge Check 3-1: The Impact of Convergence, VoIP, and SIP

Answer the following questions. Answers to these Knowledge Check questions are located in *Appendix A: Answers to Knowledge Check Questions*.

1. Convergence as it applies to UC includes which of the following?

    a. Protocol convergence

    b. Application convergence

    c. Infrastructure convergence

    d. All of the above

2. In what year was the original specification of VoIP published?

    a. 1998

    b. 1988

    c. 1978

    d. 1968

3. In what year was TCP/IP officially named the transport protocol for major U.S. government agencies such as the DOD?

    a. 2005

    b. 1995

    c. 1985

    d. 1975

4. What was the first specification published for voice over packet protocol?

    a. SIP

    b. NVP

    c. H.323

5. What is the primary function of LDAP?

    a. Access control

    b. Load balancing

    c. Performance reporting

    d. Packet assembly/disassembly

6. SIP is a relatively new, experimental protocol.

   a. True

   b. False

7. SIP is an ASCII-based protocol.

   a. True

   b. False

8. H.323 is a more mature protocol than SIP.

   a. True

   b. False

9. PBX systems must be completely replaced to effectively deploy UC solutions.

   a. True

   b. False

10. Personal mobility allows a user to do which of the following?

   a. Send calls from any location

   b. Receive calls from any location

   c. Send or receive calls on a wide variety of devices

   d. Present only one contact phone number regardless of the number of devices with which that user might communicate

   e. All of the above

Chapter summary

Companies that wish to compete successfully in the 21st century must move rapidly beyond projects that focus only on the convergence of technology infrastructure and protocols. It is the convergence of applications and people, and of processes and organizations, that will deliver the results needed to survive in the global economy.

The evolution of SIP has resulted in standards-based, cost-effective, interoperable tools to implement the B2B solutions only imagined when the first marketplaces emerged in the 1990s. Rising above the transaction-oriented B2B exchanges reminiscent of EDI, and embracing federation with partners, is the best way to ensure that the potential of UC is realized.

4: Current Unified Communications Landscape

In the early stages of the Unified Communications (UC) market, some interesting products were introduced. As with many new products, these offerings predated the availability of accepted industry standards, and existing technologies did not facilitate easy integration. Although some of these products were spectacular, they were typical first-generation products that were somewhat ahead of their time. Evolutionary cycles often have one or two thought leaders who introduce concept products to the market to evaluate what real requirements might exist. These first efforts are like the concept cars that automotive manufacturers showcase at international shows but never bring to market, even though they contribute significantly to changing the market over time.

Products currently on the market, or soon to be released, provide a solid foundation on which many value-added features will be delivered for many years to come. Because these products comply with industry standards, it is possible for little-known companies to introduce extensions that will change the way professionals perform tasks, similar to the impact the personal computer has had for knowledge workers.

This chapter introduces current vendors and offerings for both the enterprise and small business markets. It also explains which offerings are expected to be premise-based and which will be successfully delivered as services by traditional carriers, as well as by potential new entrants.

Chapter 4 Topics

In this chapter, you will learn:

- what applications are currently available on the market

- why Microsoft Office Communications Server 2007 and IBM Lotus Sametime are market-leading software products and what features they offer

- how Microsoft Office Communications Server 2007 and IBM Lotus Sametime can solve unique communications challenges when integrated closely with communications platforms

- the offerings targeted to small and medium-size businesses as opposed to those intended for enterprises

- the analysts' perspective of the product vendors

- the long-term vision for the evolution of UC solutions

Chapter 4 Goals

Upon completion of this chapter, you will be able to:

* define the product offerings in the UC market

* differentiate between single-function applications and integrated solutions

* differentiate between solutions relevant to the small and medium-size business market and the enterprise UC market

* understand the analysts' view of the UC market

* describe the vision that each of the leading vendors demonstrates for UC

Key Terms

Active Directory directory services 65

Communications-aware application 66

Disaster recovery plan (DRP)   68

Innovative Communications
    Alliance (ICA)   69

Location and presence status   65

Unified Communications
    asa service   74

4

Current Unified Communications Landscape

Overview of UC vendors and offerings: Enterprise

Every discussion of vendors and offerings in the UC market should start with the solutions offered by the leaders in desktop productivity tools and personal communications devices. This is especially true because personal communications are at the heart of UC. Although not all UC applications run through the desktop, the replication of desktop tasks in other forms leads to acceptance of these solutions and paves the way for major changes that should be expected.

It is critical to consider solutions from leading suppliers of personal voice communications products because the communications infrastructure will undergo the most significant shift as a result of UC. Although not all UC applications involve voice communications, newly evolving communications channels such as instant messaging will facilitate the integration of communications into day-to-day business processes.

The next step is to evaluate solutions that will be significantly transformed by the UC market. The technologies now being introduced in UC products have been deployed in contact center solutions for many years. As these technologies are further refined, and new functions are incorporated, these products will migrate into leadership roles in UC.

In the enterprise desktop productivity tools market, two solutions have dominated for many years: Microsoft Office and IBM Lotus Notes. The same two vendors also dominate the e-mail client market. Although non-real-time communications such as e-mail are not the objective of UC, or even a key element, this market distribution dictates that any successful UC solution must integrate in some way with these solutions.

In addition to the other leadership areas, Active Directory directory services has become a market-leading enterprise directory services software product. Enterprise directory services are a key area for UC because they provide a common repository for identity and access control information.

With the overwhelming penetration of Microsoft and IBM software, it is reasonable to assume that any solution in the enterprise market must work with the market-leading platforms to have a credible future. It is just as important for desktop solution providers to integrate with the industry leaders in enterprise communications solutions. Although desktop productivity software providers could work independently to create end-to-end UC solutions, they would likely meet stiff resistance from owners of the classic voice applications as companies try to maximize their return on investment (ROI) of installed assets. Because Nortel, Avaya, Cisco, and Siemens dominate certain aspects of the enterprise communications market, new entrants in the solutions space must find a way to leverage industry-standard approaches rather than focus on a single vendor's proprietary technologies.

Although much can be accomplished by communications and desktop productivity suppliers on the customer's premises, any viable UC solution must integrate in the off-premise, carrier-supplied services market. For instance, access to location and presence status for mobile users will likely involve integration with mobile carriers. Failing to include carrier-based clients in an overall UC solution will result in a solution that does not meet customer expectations and is generally unsuccessful in the market.

Of course, the desktop is a valid client scenario only when the user actually uses a personal computer as the client. The user might need to interface with many clients to access content.

4

Current Unified
Communications
Landscape

Any solution must support a broad range of access methodologies and client devices to provide consistently available, everywhere access to every type of content required from UC.

The following list describes the four major requirements for a viable UC solution:

- Integrate with leading desktop productivity tools, including Microsoft Office, Microsoft Exchange Server, and IBM Lotus software suites.

- Integrate desktop tools with the existing voice infrastructure within the enterprise, whether that environment is strictly Voice over Internet protocol (VoIP) or traditional Time-Division Multiplexing (TDM)–based technology.

- Integrate easily with carrier-provided services, especially those intended for the mobile enterprise market.

- Render content for a wide variety of client devices that can be used by any user at any time.

Many products are available in the UC market. Many of these products satisfy component requirements but only a few attempt to cover the entire solution space as it is understood today.

In this chapter, two complete solutions for the enterprise market are described. These two companies have sufficient market presence to satisfy enterprise concerns about the viability of a new technology, and they have sufficient presence to attract developers who will add new functionality to UC. Existing enterprise software vendors know how to integrate with their classic products and can rapidly develop new applications that make those applications more communications aware. As more communications-aware applications become available, business process integration will proceed more smoothly.

Only one solution for the small- to medium-size business (SMB) market is described in this chapter. This is primarily because the two enterprise solutions have entry-level options that can address this market for all but the smallest companies. Smaller companies are encouraged to investigate server suppliers to obtain the most complete solution at a competitive price.

The only product marketed to the SMB market comes through the cooperation of Nortel and IBM. Nortel delivers a software communications solution and UC bundle specifically created for this market. IBM built a special server product to host the solution and, where enhanced UC features are required, can compete with the Lotus Sametime entry bundle.

Microsoft Office Communication Server 2007

The best place to begin evaluating existing solutions is with the market leaders. Microsoft began to pursue enterprise UC solutions with the introduction of Live Communications Server 2005 Service Pack 1 and Office Communicator 2005. These products delivered secure instant messaging to the enterprise, enabling staff in the workplace to use tools commonly used outside of work. Those tools also encouraged federations that enabled the enterprise environment to integrate with the leading residential services providers, such as Yahoo! and AOL. Live Communications Server 2005 was extremely successful because Microsoft provided a telecommunications industry standards-based interface that enabled the product to work with the leading communications vendors' voice solutions (after those voice vendors incorporated the small changes required for interoperability).

Office Communications Server 2007 enhanced the services initially delivered in Live Communications Server 2005. Although Office Communications Server 2007 is proposed as a potential stand-alone voice services platform, it does have a few missing elements, such as emergency services. Office Communications Server 2007 should be implemented as a planned migration path to a complete VoIP environment. Companies that adopt it will likely empower key personnel with UC capabilities, while maintaining a Private Branch Exchange (PBX) system for most of their staff population. Over time, as more applications are UC enabled, additional staff will migrate to the UC platform as their primary voice application server. Eventually, the lines between the voice platform and the UC infrastructure will have blurred to the point that a casual observer cannot identify a difference in the environment.

The following list identifies the elements of Office Communications Server 2007 that give it a dominant position in the market:

- **Instant messaging and presence for internal users**–These abilities enable users within the enterprise to subscribe to each other, be notified of changes in presence state, and send each other short instant messages.

- **On-premise Web conferencing**—This feature enables users both inside and outside the enterprise firewall to create and join real-time Web conferences hosted on the enterprise's internal servers.

- **Multimedia conferencing (audio/video)**—This feature supports multipoint links by which multiple users participate in the same exchange, using real-time audio, video, and data communications.

- **Address book**—The address book provides global user information from Active Directory to subscribing clients.

- **Archiving and call detail records (CDRs)**—These features generate and provide retention of instant messaging (IM), VoIP, and meeting usage statistics.

- **External user access**—External access enables users outside the corporate firewall to share data and media with users inside the corporate firewall.

- **Federation**—This feature allows users authenticated for access on one domain to participate in on-premise conferencing on a trusted partner domain without specifically logging on to the federated partner's domain.

- **Public IM connectivity**—This connectivity connects the internal IM users with the top public IM service providers (MSN, AOL, and Yahoo!) while using enterprise-grade encryption and optional logging features.

- **Multimedia conferencing with external users**—This service enables users outside the corporate firewall to participate in multimedia conferences.

- **IM and presence through a browser-based client**–These abilities provide access to IM and presence services through a Web-based client as an alternative to Microsoft Office Communicator, and offer additional device independence.

- **Enterprise Voice**—This service enables users to place a call by clicking a Microsoft Outlook or Office Communicator contact name. Users receive incoming calls simultaneously on all their registered user endpoints. The user chooses how to answer a call.

When considering Office Communications Server 2007 for voice communications in place of a PBX, the enterprise must also consider the services on which it relies for its traditional voice communications. For instance, if the enterprise uses voice mail, auto attendant, subscriber access, or all three, Office Communications Server 2007 will require Microsoft Exchange Server 2007 Unified Messaging. With this function enabled, users use subscriber access to their individual mailboxes to retrieve e-mail, voice messages, contacts, and calendaring information.

There are two platforms for Office Communications Server 2007: Standard edition and Enterprise edition. The Enterprise edition provides highly reliable services that also complement an organization's disaster recovery plan (DRP). This is especially true for multisite organizations in which a backup data center is already part of the IT infrastructure. A sample Office Communications Server 2007 Enterprise edition configuration is shown in Figure 4–1.

FIGURE 4-1: MICROSOFT OFFICE COMMUNICATIONS SERVER 2007 ENTERPRISE EDITION WITH NORTEL CS 1000.

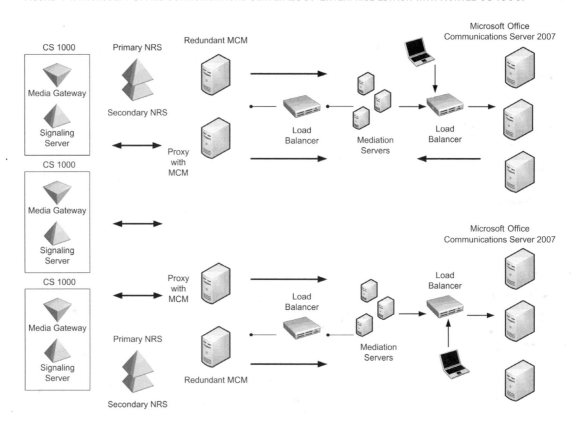

Current Unified Communications Landscape
4

Office Communications Server 2007 can be configured in many ways, depending on the desired features and service levels. In the configuration shown in Figure 4-1, any enterprise customer can communicate with any other enterprise customer, whether they are solely supported as an Internet Protocol (IP) phone on Office Communications Server 2007, as a digital extension on CS 1000, or any combination thereof. From a hardware perspective, Office Communications Server 2007 can run completely on a single server; however, multiple servers are required where greater scale, geographical distribution, or high availability is required.

Nortel was the first communications vendor to integrate tightly with Office Communications Server 2007. Microsoft and Nortel are partners in the Innovative Communications Alliance (ICA), which was formed specifically to promote delivery of improved UC applications and drive market expansion. Having these two industry leaders cooperating and developing applications together ensures that those solutions embrace the leading desktop environment while delivering carrier-class availability, reliability, and scalability.

The client-side application for the Microsoft UC offerings is Office Communicator 2007. Office Communicator is the primary tool for presence and directory information, IM, telephone calls, and audio and video conferencing. This solutions element integrates the communications experience into the Microsoft Office systems and beyond to enterprise applications. Figure 4–2 shows a snapshot of the Office Communicator 2007 client.

FIGURE 4-2: MICROSOFT OFFICE COMMUNICATOR 2007.

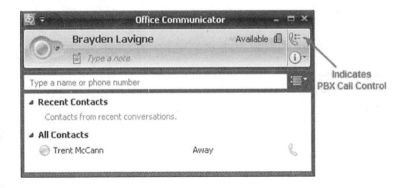

With Office Communicator Mobile 2007, these tools are available on any device running Windows Mobile software. For a user to truly have the everywhere, anytime connectivity required of a UC application, services must be deliverable from the carriers. Figure 4-3 shows a snapshot of the Communicator contacts list. Devices using Windows Mobile software can take advantage of all the features available in Office Communicator.

In addition to the desktop client and support for devices using Windows Mobile software-based devices, Microsoft, Nortel, and other vendors are introducing purpose-built handsets that integrate with Office Communications Server 2007, such as the LG-Nortel IP Phone 8500 series. This might seem unnecessary in a UC environment; however, many users, including many chief financial officers (CFOs), prefer handsets to talking through a universal serial bus (USB) headset or other PC-based appliance.

4

Current Unified Communications Landscape

FIGURE 4-3: WINDOWS MOBILE SOFTWARE DEVICE RUNNING OFFICE COMMUNICATOR MOBILE.

This discussion of the Microsoft UC solution has focused on Microsoft Windows–based platforms. However, Microsoft Communicator Web Access, shown in Figure 4-4, offers true platform independence for access to the services provided by Office Communications Server 2007. Users already familiar with Office Communicator 2007 do not have to learn a new user interface, because the look, feel, and key functionalities of Communicator Web Access are similar to those in the Windows-based clients. However, the Web client does not have all the functionality of Microsoft Office Communicator; its focus is on IM and presence.

FIGURE 4-4: MICROSOFT OFFICE COMMUNICATOR WEB ACCESS (2007 RELEASE).

With wide acceptance for the many Microsoft software development kits, many vendors currently provide and develop applications that can easily be integrated with Office Communications Server 2007, Office Communicator 2007, and Windows Mobile. This encourages rapid development of new UC-capable applications and rapid expansion of the market.

IBM Lotus Sametime

Lotus Sametime offers integrated IM, VoIP, video chats, and Web conferencing with the security features that enterprises expect. Unlike Office Communications Server 2007, the IBM solution supports a wide variety of server operating systems (Microsoft Windows Server 2000 and 2003, IBM AIX, Sun Solaris, IBM i5/OS, and Linux Red Hat and Novell's SUSE) and supports a wide variety of desktop client's operating Systems (Microsoft Windows, AIX, Linux, and Macintosh OS), as well as mobile clients, including Microsoft Windows Mobile, RIM BlackBerry, and Symbian OS, including Sony Ericsson and Nokia eSeries devices.

Lotus Sametime Standard capabilities include the following:

- enterprise instant messaging and presence, enabling management of multiple IM sessions from within the same window
- rich text, time stamps, spell check, and emoticons, improving the business acumen of IM and enabling effective compliance administration
- multiway chat, enhancing collaboration capabilities
- VoIP within the enterprise and point-to-point video, taking advantage of Session Initiation Protocol (SIP)
- integration with desktop productivity applications such as Microsoft Office, Microsoft Outlook/Microsoft Exchange, and Lotus Notes
- optional file transfer, enabling point-to-point file transfer within an active IM session
- integrated chat histories, enabling more effective compliance administration
- location awareness, enabling the user to specify geographic location to allow subscribers to understand communication options
- contact list with type-ahead and search to find individual contacts and initiate sessions rapidly
- contact business cards to define contact options more effectively and to integrate with click-to-contact features
- managed interoperability with supported public IM networks to maximize individual communities of interest
- Web conferencing to support on-demand and scheduled collaboration activities
- integration with supported audio, video, and telephony systems, enabling highly scalable conferencing capabilities
- security using 128-bit encryption for data privacy authentication of users against LDAPs or IBM Lotus Domino Servers

4

Current Unified
Communications
Landscape

Lotus Sametime can be integrated with Active Directory successfully to ensure ease of integration in the enterprise market where customers are already using that directory service. Lotus Sametime can be supported on multiple platforms and is not exclusively tied to Active Directory for directory services. LDAP Directory support includes IBM Tivoli Directory Server, IBM Lotus Domino, Microsoft Active Directory 2000 and 2003, and Sun Java Directory Server.

This provides flexibility to users who have heterogeneous environments.

Lotus Sametime software is also designed to provide flexibility and choice for enterprises, IBM Business Partners and other developers to extend Lotus Sametime software's native functionality.

Lotus Sametime software includes comprehensive software development toolkits (SDKs) to embed realtime capabilities, including presence, IM and telephony capabilities, into business applications such as e-commerce sites, portals, help desks, and enterprise applications such as salesforce automation. Vendors can use the Lotus Sametime Telephony Conferencing Service Provider Interface (TCSPI) toolkit to integrate with a wide variety of SIP or legacy PBXs, audio conferencing bridges, and videoconferencing solutions.

Figure 4-5 shows a snapshot of the Connect client associated with Lotus Sametime.

FIGURE 4-5: LOTUS SAMETIME CONNECT CLIENT.

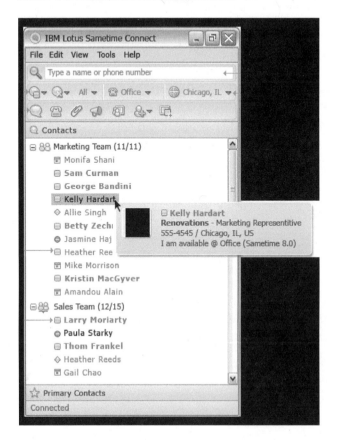

Alliances with leading communications suppliers, such as Nortel, enable Lotus Sametime users to integrate click-to-call capabilities whether those individuals are available through SIP or through traditional switched telephony sources. Nortel Agile Communication Environment for Lotus Notes and Lotus Sametime is a unique solution that leverages underlying communications infrastructure and works ubiquitously across multiple vendors' telephony and infrastructure equipment to deliver UC capabilities quickly and simply. Also, because the solution works with the existing infrastructure, there is no need to buy new equipment; current investments are protected. The Nortel multimedia client for Lotus Notes is shown in Figure 4-6.

IBM has historically excelled at building a strong partner community that provides solutions for every aspect of business. IBM also provides a large number of tools that simplify integration efforts and allow rapid development of productivity-enhancing tools.

FIGURE 4-6: NORTEL MULTIMEDIA CLIENT FOR LOTUS NOTES.

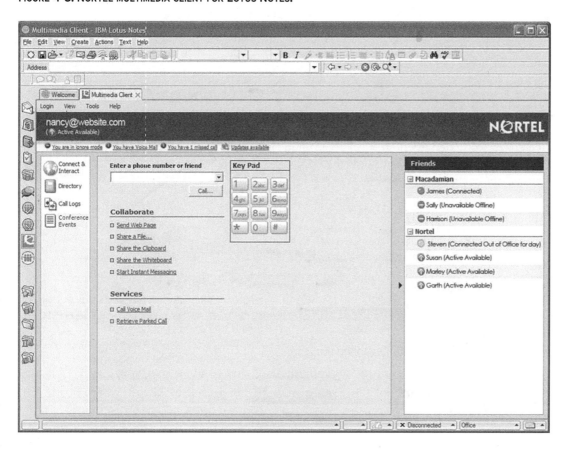

Overview of UC vendors and offerings: SMB

The SMB UC market is being addressed along diverse paths. Most of the solutions currently available require replacement of the SMBs' existing voice systems. When replacing existing technology, the SMB should consider vendors who provide a bundled solution that leverages all the traditional voice applications and also delivers UC functionality.

Enterprise-solution vendors position their products to address the medium-sized solutions market. Both Microsoft and IBM have entry versions of their software offerings that provide basic UC functionality, including conferencing capabilities. The challenge for these companies is to find an SMB-class telephony system with which their products can integrate.

SMBs wondering how to acquire UC capabilities with less capital investment and lower risk might want to work with service providers who are leveraging their market presence to deliver Unified Communications as a Service (UCAAS). UCAAS has the potential to serve the SMB market well, if carriers can deliver support services effectively at the customer premises. For the carriers to meet the requirements at the customer premises, they must build a virtual support organization that incorporates third-party resellers and service partners. This approach will be particularly successful in accounts for which the carriers already deliver IP Centrex services.

The third path to the SMB market is through niche, purpose-built products that address the customer's entire communications needs. One such product is Nortel's Software Communication System (SCS) 500. This product is designed to address the needs of SMBs with 30 to 500 office professionals. It is a SIP-based solution that leverages the simplicity of open-source code delivered on specially built industry standard servers. By deploying a platform based on open source code, the application can be integrated easily with other business applications to provide additional flexibility and functionality.

The IP voice system includes:

- a communications server that routes and authenticates calls

- a configuration server that provides the Web browser–based interface for a centralized, in-house way to administer managed user devices

- a media server that provides voice mail and auto attendant services

- a robust, enterprise-grade voice mail system that supports message retrieval by telephone or a personal Web portal. (E-mail forwarding of the voice mail message as a .wav file is also supported.)

Additional components of the SCS 500 include:

- gateways to connect to digital and analog trunks, phones, and fax machines

- session border controllers that allow users to use the Internet to make calls from outside the corporate network

Although the UC elements of this solution are not as extensive as the services provided in the enterprise environment, they do provide some of the basic elements. Companies wishing to deploy a more extensive UC capability can integrate SCS with Lotus Sametime. SCS 500 includes the following UC elements:

- address book with detailed call history and the ability to import Outlook contacts; supports click-to-call from Outlook, Lotus Sametime, and Lotus Notes contacts

- presence with optional privacy rules and notification alerts

- individual and group IM capabilities

- voice conferencing for ad hoc and multiparty connections with recording available; plug-ins for Outlook and Lotus Sametime facilitate participation in voice conferences

- video conferencing for ad hoc connections and up to four participants with recording available

- find me/follow me to support connecting to subscribers anytime, everywhere

- personal auto assistant to enable users with mailbox customization to add caller prompts such as press 1 to leave voice mail, press 2 to reach my cell phone, and similar prompts

A major advantage of the SCS 500 is the ease with which it can be installed and configured. Estimates indicate that the system can be configured for 100 users in 10 to 20 minutes. Figure 4-7 shows the PC soft phone used with the SCS 500. Note the video images that are displayed on the left side of the figure and the contact area displayed on the right.

FIGURE 4-7: NORTEL SCS 500 SOFT PHONE.

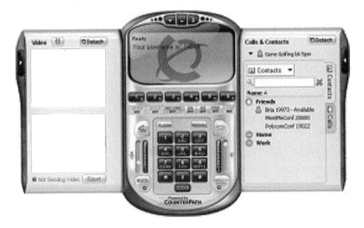

Other telephony vendors, such as Avaya, Siemens, NEC, Alcatel, and more, have also created specific bundles to address the SMB market. Most of these purpose-built solutions require replacement of the existing core voice technology to migrate to the UC environment. SMBs are advised to work with knowledgeable resellers to find a solution that best fits their business.

Gartner Group UC Magic Quadrant

For many years, the analyst firm Gartner has advised corporate IT leadership on IT initiatives. The Magic Quadrant (MQ) analysis plots the intersection of a vendor's "completeness of vision" for a given solution with that vendor's "ability to execute." For each vendor, this point lies in one of four graphic quadrants: Leaders, Challengers, Visionaries, and Niche Players. Although the MQ is two-dimensional and could be misunderstood, Gartner also produces detailed analysis that fully explains the rationale behind its placement of each vendor on the chart. The combination of the chart location and the detailed analysis makes the MQ an effective tool for IT leadership.

Gartner believes that the greatest value of UC is the reduction of human latency in business processes.[1] Human latency is all the things that inhibit progress on tasks:

- telephone tag
- delays responding to voice mail and e-mail
- difficulty scheduling meetings when all required resources are available
- difficulty engaging the right person in a customer interaction
- difficulty contacting necessary resources at a supplier organization
- any other activity for which human interaction is required and delays occur

This perspective on UC's value supports the idea that it is not the technology that delivers the ROI for UC, but the convergence of applications and people, and of processes and organizations.

In the 2007 MQ report, Gartner describes the UC market and technologies as being at an early stage of maturity. Gartner also indicates that adoption of the solutions remains slow, and provides several reasons for market reluctance to move. Gartner predicted that many barriers would slowly be resolved and that, in 2008, UC would enter mainstream adoption globally.

Some vendors have been in the Leaders quadrant since Gartner began reporting on this market segment. Although not unknown, it is unusual for a vendor to be in the Leaders quadrant both in the developmental stages of a market and when that technology reaches maturity. It is also unusual for a competitor in a legacy aspect of a technology to be in the Leaders quadrant simultaneously in an emerging competition to that technology. Over the past 20 years, the standard pattern has been for start-ups to drive early adoption markets, only to be acquired by a legacy leader as the market approaches maturity.

Nortel and Alcatel defy many of the expectations common in the technology markets, because they have also been leaders in the traditional voice market. These two vendors have married proprietary technology with emerging standards-based platforms to deliver solutions that enable customers to migrate at the rate most beneficial to their businesses, without requiring customers to make monolithic technology compromises that impact their entire workforce.

Gartner's claims about market maturation are supported by the emergence and position of Microsoft and IBM on the UC MQ chart. However, customers are most reassured that many of the vendors in the Leaders quadrant have learned how to partner effectively to deliver even better solutions than one could do on its own. Nortel's cooperation with Microsoft in the Innovative Communications Alliance (ICA), and Nortel's cooperation with IBM to deliver enhanced solutions for both the enterprise market with Lotus Sametime integration and the SCS 500 co-marketing programs with IBM System i demonstrate that Nortel truly understands the market requirements and is committed to ensuring that its solutions enable customers to realize the potential of UC.

1. Lassman, Jay, and Costello, Rich, *Magic Quadrant for Corporate Telephony in North America, 2007*, Gartner RAS Core Research Note G00150386, 8 August 2007.

Assessment and overview of completeness of vision for UC enablement

The enabling technologies of UC have reached a mature stage in which real standards are developed and understood. Compliant applications are on their second, third, or even fourth release. The major participants in the communications and enterprise IT markets have created an ecosystem to deliver a complete set of complementary products. Creative entrepreneurs have begun to deliver add-on capabilities that further enhance the solutions delivered by the market leaders.

It remains to be seen whether customers can apply the technology and transform their businesses. This is a line-of-business issue, not a corporate IT issue. The growth of this market will parallel that of unified messaging if the chief information officer (CIO) or IT director develops an ROI model that will convince the CFO that UC is a good investment.

Large business consultants and IT services firms have created specialty practices focused on effective deployment of UC. This is very much like combining the practices that focus on contact center deployment and business process reengineering.

One of the reasons this book focuses so heavily on solutions that integrate with existing voice platforms is that these solutions encourage pilot testing in small groups, where the most benefit can be achieved most quickly. UC enablement of a mobile sales force can have a direct impact on sales volumes. UC enablement of a service organization can directly impact customer satisfaction and reduce retention expenses. UC enablement of a development organization can reduce development time, get products to market more quickly, and accelerate ROI.

4

Current Unified Communications Landscape

Knowledge Check 4-1: Current Unified Communications Landscape

Answer the following questions. Answers to these Knowledge Check questions are located in *Appendix A: Answers to Knowledge Check Questions.*

1. Which two products dominate the enterprise productivity tools market?

    a. Lotus Notes and Yahoo! Mail

    b. Yahoo! Mail and Microsoft Office

    c. Lotus Notes and Microsoft Office

    d. Microsoft Office and Adobe Acrobat Reader

2. Which feature(s) are required to enable PBXs to work cooperatively in a UC ecosystem?

    a. Twinning

    b. Call forwarding

    c. Remote call control

    d. All of the above

3. Which of the following products is designed specifically for the SMB market?

    a. Lotus Sametime

    b. Nortel Software Communication System

    c. Microsoft Office Communications Server 2007

4. Which of the following vendors has appeared most frequently in the Leaders quadrant of the Gartner Magic Quadrant for UC?

    a. IBM

    b. Nortel

    c. Oracle

    d. Microsoft

5. Which of the following is a limited capability of Microsoft Office Communications Server 2007?

    a. Conferencing

    b. Emergency services

    c. Presence management

    d. None of the above

6. Microsoft Office Communications Server 2007 can be used to build federations between enterprises.

   a. True

   b. False

7. The greatest value of UC is the reduction of human latency in business processes.

   a. True

   b. False

8. UC solutions can dynamically provide phone presence status without integrating with enterprise PBXs.

   a. True

   b. False

9. Carriers can effectively deploy UCAAS without having a presence at the customer presence.

   a. True

   b. False

10. Which of the following is not a UC requirement?

   a. Voice mail

   b. Presence management

   c. Telephony remote control

   d. Audio/video conferencing

Chapter summary

Industry-leading suppliers with strong channel partners, who can assist customers with implementation, can deliver full-featured UC solutions. These solutions are built by companies that understand the need to adopt and adhere to industry standards, thereby allowing rapid development of new features and capabilities by their own engineers and by third parties.

These companies understand the benefit of building a new ecosystem that incorporates a bridge to older technologies, which allows customers to evolve into new solutions according to their business requirements. They have large channel partner organizations that have already been trained to install and configure the new solutions properly.

The technology is the easy part. It is incumbent upon the customers to adapt the technology to modify their business operations.

4

Current Unified Communications Landscape

5: Critical Business Applications and Processes

Today's small-, medium-, and enterprise-sized organizations face a multitude of operational and financial challenges. These challenges are often created by inefficient processes and work flows. Isolated and disparate information technology (IT) systems, as well as databases that restrict information sharing, might also be part of the problem. If these challenges are not resolved, an organization may be unable to change its internal processes, grow revenue, expand product and service offerings, or enhance operational effectiveness.

This chapter describes a number of critical business applications and processes that might apply to your particular business challenges.

Chapter 5 Topics

In this chapter, you will learn:

- why enterprise transformation is an important first step in solving process inefficiencies

- what service-oriented architecture (SOA) is, and what challenges must be overcome to deploy its application

- how customer service (CS) can be used to drive customer acquisition, create customer loyalty, and increase revenue potential

- how customer relationship management (CRM) can deliver enhanced customer service

- how supply chain management (SCM) can be used within supply chain infrastructures to reduce cycle time

- how enterprise resource planning (ERP) can provide real-time access to accurate financial information

- how sales force automation (SFA) can increase deal flow, revenue, and profitability

Chapter 5 Goals

Upon completion of this chapter, you will be able to:

- list common challenges that must be resolved to increase revenue and profitability, and to create a unique competitive advantage

- describe commonly found challenges in software architectures, CS, CRM, SCM, ERP, and SFA

- identify key goals and objectives for SOA, CS, CRM, SCM, ERP, and SFA implementations to resolve common challenges

Key Terms

Applications-aware network	90	Enterprise resource planning (ERP)	84
Business process reengineering	83	Enterprise transformation	83
Customer acquisition	87	Multimodal communications	89
Customer relationship management (CRM)	84	Network-aware applications	90
Customer retention	86	Sales force automation (SFA)	84
Customer service (CS)	84	Supply chain management (SCM)	84

Enterprise transformation

Organizations of all types are often unable to make timely decisions due to inaccurate or unavailable information. To solve this challenge, organizations must replace inefficient processes with new streamlined processes and new software applications. The process of identifying streamlined business processes and mapping them to new software applications and IT solutions is called enterprise transformation. This process is used by organizations that want to achieve or improve a competitive advantage.

Enterprise transformation is similar to business process reengineering, which involves an analysis of current business processes and the applications that support those processes used to streamline people-to-people communications. When process improvements are identified and incorporated within new applications and Unified Communications (UC) enablement, real-time communications between individuals, workgroups, and key decision makers are enhanced. This improves both internal business communications and external communications with customers and partners. Figure 5-1 shows how streamlined business processes can be aligned with technology.

FIGURE 5-1: ENTERPRISE TRANSFORMATION.

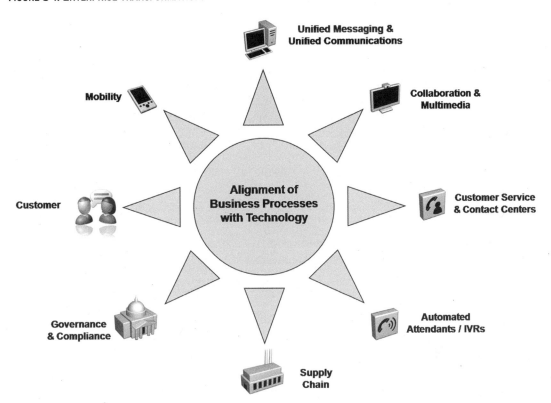

Organizations of all sizes can benefit from enterprise transformation. For example, enterprise transformation examines current processes, their supporting applications, and communications. Understanding how information is accessed and used for key decision making is also part of this analysis. This enterprise transformation study shows how the organization makes key decisions, which has a direct impact on the financial performance of the organization. In many cases, building streamlined processes mapped to effective applications, systems, and information sharing requires that the existing process be redesigned and the existing application be rebuilt to work more effectively. Critical business applications and processes include the following:

- service-oriented architecture (SOA)

- customer service (CS)

- customer relationship management (CRM)

- supply chain management (SCM)

- enterprise resource planning (ERP)

- sales force automation (SFA)

Service-oriented architecture (SOA)

Business challenges are often identified at the core of an organization's infrastructure. As an organization (of any size) expands its product and service offerings, it becomes less able to manage rapid operational changes efficiently. These changes include back-office operations; market dynamics; increased competition; and interaction with customers, suppliers, manufacturers, and distributors. In addition, the applications that support these processes are often not easily modified. These challenges can make it difficult to achieve the following goals and objectives shared by most organizations:

- increasing shareholder value through revenue growth, increased profitability, and greater operational efficiency

- maintaining a competitive advantage through business flexibility, agility, and time to market

- maximizing productivity and efficiency through real-time collaboration and providing access to customer information for enhanced customer service

- creating an invulnerable operation through implementation of proper security controls, risk management processes, and business continuity

- streamlining operational processes through reuse of software applications

To meet these goals and objectives, an organization must develop and implement applications that support new streamlined processes. These applications must define and embed easier ways to communicate each new process's information flow. They must also provide employees, partners, and customers with real-time access to that information flow. Enterprise transformation is a critical step toward a successful SOA software solution built as part of the core design. By removing manual elements from the process, SOA helps to diminish—or even eliminate—human delays in critical decision making. This is done by replacing manual processes with automated rule sets, and by implementing strategic thinking and migration strategies from legacy software applications. This new software architecture allows organizations to adapt quickly to changing conditions and dynamics to maintain a competitive advantage.

Figure 5-2 shows how an organization might implement SOA-based software applications and streamlined processes to improve customer service.

FIGURE 5-2: SOA SOLUTIONS CAN DELIVER CUSTOMER SERVICE.

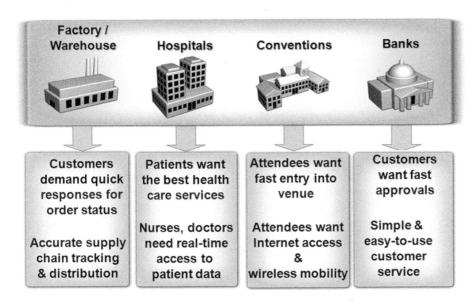

Large enterprises use SOA to improve effectiveness and efficiency in employee and customer service, even in the face of the various information silos and disparate process flows that may exist. SOA allows organizations to achieve the functionality depicted in Figure 5-2 and push this information to employees or customers when asked. This level of functionality requires enterprise transformation analysis, including the rearchitecting of existing software applications to include embedded UC enablement. The actual business process must be integrated with production IT systems, databases, and customer information. Organizations can then provide real-time access to information and customer data when an individual needs it, reducing human latency.

> **Note** Some types of organizations will not find SOA to be beneficial. In particular, small- to medium-sized organizations that use off-the-shelf software solutions may not need custom-developed and supported SOA software applications.

SOA, with embedded UC functionality, provides streamlined process flows and access to corporate and customer information in real time. Together, SOA and UC bring this information to employees and customers to provide a positive customer experience. In turn, this generates high-value customer satisfaction and customer retention. To connect the right people with the right information at the right time, SOA applications integrated with UC enablement must incorporate three foundational elements:

- **People-to-people communications**—Individuals, workgroups, collaboration teams, customers, and the entire organization involved in a function.

- **Processes**—The workflows or steps that must be taken to execute a function or task.

- **Information**—The specific data pertinent to a function or task.

By incorporating people-to-people communications, processes, and information into new SOA-enabled software applications (see Figure 5-3), an organization can create value. SOA-based applications combine streamlined processes and a need to communicate in real time with real-time access to information and data provided through UC enablement.

FIGURE 5-3: SOA-BASED APPLICATIONS INCORPORATE PEOPLE-TO-PEOPLE COMMUNICATIONS, PROCESSES, AND INFORMATION.

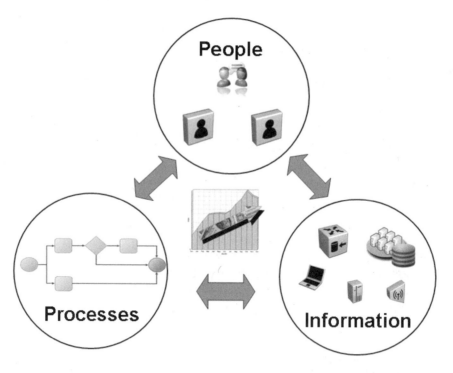

There are many benefits when using SOA applications and software components that incorporate people-to-people communications, processes, and information. They can be reused, modified quickly, and ultimately mapped to a streamlined process supported by an IT solution. Linking the business process flow to data from various IT systems and databases provides real-time access to information. For example, SOA applications can be delivered through Web Services technology, which can be used for intranets (employee communications), extranets (supplier and partner communications), and customer-facing Web sites (self-serve access to information). Getting the right information to the right person, process, or application is a major communication challenge for many organizations. SOA applications and their reusability incorporate people-to-people communications, processes, and real-time information dissemination to solve current communication inefficiencies.

Customer service (CS)

Customer service is a critical challenge for many organizations. Many organizations focus on acquiring new customers while also working to retain existing customers. SOA software components, combined with embedded UC enablement, provide enhanced solutions to the customer service challenge. To fulfill a customer service plan, organizations must incorporate people-to-people communications both internally and externally, simplify processes, and permit access to real-time customer information.

The following list describes some common customer service challenges:

• **Increasing shareholder value through revenue growth and operational efficiency**— Customer acquisition and retention affects financial performance.

• **Mapping customer satisfaction to an overall customer service delivery strategy**—Monitor, measure, and track customer satisfaction data to see how it relates to customer retention and repeat business.

• **Enhancing customer service delivery through multiple modes of communication**— Multimodal communication between the organization and its customers supports customer service and communications delivery. Provide multiple tools, ranging from preferred customer service agents to self-service options, to enhance customer service. To minimize operational costs, align customer service options to the type and value of customer.

• **Increasing contact center effectiveness**—First-call resolution of customer concerns requires automated routing and servicing. Through caller ID and CRM data, customer service agents have real-time access to customer information. CRM data can include call history that provides real-time updates to the customer's profile. If the customer service agent cannot answer or resolve the customer's problem, a UC-enabled contact center that has real-time access to the right person is critical.

• **Increasing contact center efficiency**—The contact center will become more efficient when the right customer service delivery method is aligned to the specific type of customer.

IT systems are designed to support specific applications and the requirements of the data owners. Traditional IT organizations react to internal customer requirements based on existing corporate IT policies, standards, procedures, and other organizational influences. In some cases, this approach led to disparate and disconnected IT systems and databases within a single organization, leaving pockets of information inaccessible to other systems. Client–server applications and customer databases proliferated throughout the enterprise, making it difficult to provide enhanced customer service delivery because customer information was not accessible.

SOA uses a modularized component-based IT infrastructure to bring order to the chaos of disparate and disconnected client–server databases and information management. Figure 5-4 shows the inefficiencies created when customer data is not stored in a systematic manner.

5 | Critical Business Applications and Processes

FIGURE 5-4: CUSTOMER DATA IS EVERYWHERE AND ACCESS IS INEFFICIENT.

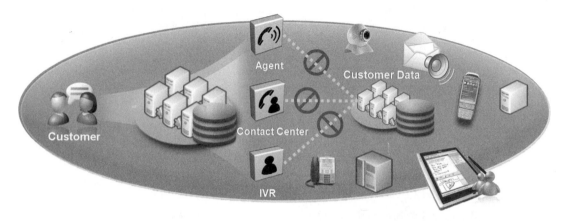

Properly designed and implemented SOA applications, paired with real-time access to customer information, can enhance customer service delivery (see Figure 5-5). When UC functionality, such as instant messaging or audio/video conferencing, is embedded in Web sites, customers have real-time access to customer service agents. Customer inquiries and problem resolution are supported by UC with real-time presence and availability. Customer service agents need real-time access to customer information and data through back-end CRM systems to provide first-call response handling and real-time answers to customer inquiries. These efficiencies can ultimately drive customer satisfaction and retention.

FIGURE 5-5: ACCESS TO CUSTOMER DATA MUST BE EFFICIENT.

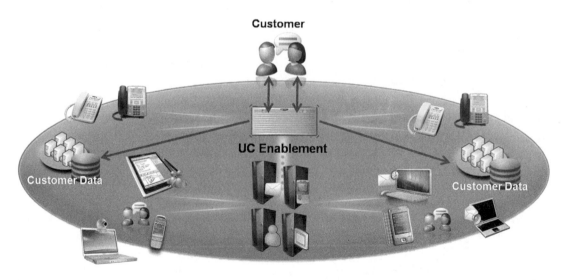

Organizations can build a multimodal customer service contact center that combines SOA applications to provide people-to-people communications, processes, information, Voice over Internet Protocol (VoIP), and UC. The contact center can support enhanced customer service

5

Critical Business
Applications and
Processes

delivery solutions through preferred agents, self-service Web sites, or automated attendants. Such a center can differentiate an organization from its competitors and provide it with a competitive advantage. The technological foundation of this design supports next-generation VoIP and UC-enabled contact tools that support multimodal communications with customers, suppliers, and partners.

The key to success for any organization is a customer service-focused strategy based on acquiring and retaining customers. The foundation for a customer service-focused strategy is shown in Figure 5-6.

FIGURE 5-6: CUSTOMER SERVICE-FOCUSED STRATEGY.

The following list describes the basic elements of building a customer-focused strategy:

- **Customer service strategy**—To implement a customer service strategy, the organization may need a complete transformation that includes employees, IT systems, customer databases, and data that supports customer service delivery.

- **SOA framework**—An SOA framework creates a flexible and agile organization that builds and links software applications with people-to-people communications, processes, and information dissemination. A modularized software environment, with reusable components, consolidates disparate IT systems, applications, and databases. Self-service and UC-enabled Web delivery are typical elements of an SOA customer service delivery solution.

- **Extend SOA to people**—UC enablement can provide real-time access to key people or subject matter experts, and can quickly provide customer information. This is a critical foundation for enhanced customer service delivery.

- **Convergence**—UC and real-time information dissemination requires a properly designed and implemented Internet Protocol (IP) data networking infrastructure. Network convergence must support network-aware applications and applications-aware networks with quality of service (QoS) prioritized end-to-end IP traffic delivery.

- **Unified Communications**—UC supports real-time people-to-people communication with direct integration of UC elements within applications and processes. UC features and functions include real-time presence and availability, IM chat, audio and video conferencing, and real-time collaboration.

The foundation for improved customer satisfaction and retention is a customer service-focused strategy that offers both customer service effectiveness and efficiency. This approach can affect an organization's financial performance. Customer acquisition, linked with customer retention, generates new revenue and gross profit margin.

Customer relationship management (CRM)

CRM is a process that describes how the organization provides service and support to customers, based on accessibility to customer information, purchasing history, buying patterns, and other customer care processes. Acquiring and retaining customers are critical components in an organization's success. Although it sounds simple, CRM helps the organization acquire and retain customers by building on existing customer relationships. After acquiring a customer, it is critical to build a relationship to support continued success. This, in turn, creates repeat business, revenue, and gross profit margin.

CRM systems and databases typically contain critical customer information. Sales, marketing, and customer service representatives require real-time access to this information. Analysis of customer purchasing behavior patterns, additional revenue streams, push-marketing strategies, and preferred agent customer service support strategies will lead to unique service opportunities for each customer. This drives the customer's experience to a higher level of satisfaction. In addition, sales and marketing professionals can analyze the customer database for buying characteristics that will provide helpful information to the sales, marketing, and customer service departments.

Customer service can provide a competitive advantage through the successful implementation of a CRM infrastructure combined with a customer service-focused strategy. When UC is integrated into CRM infrastructures that support sales, marketing, and customer service, the organization can deliver real-time information and immediate response to customer inquiries and problems. Figure 5-7 shows how CRM can help consolidate customer-specific information when it is implemented at the core of the customer service delivery strategy.

FIGURE 5-7: CUSTOMER RELATIONSHIP MANAGEMENT.

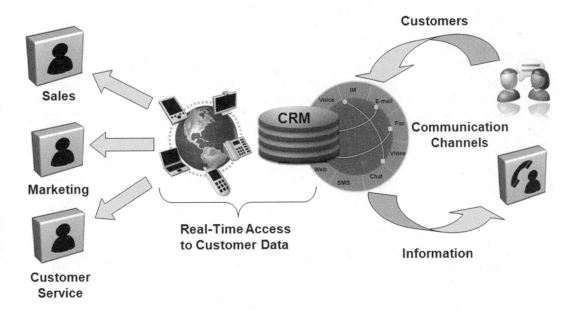

The following list describes how CRM applications and tools can benefit an organization:

- CRM warehouses customer information and buying patterns, resulting in enhanced customer service, which can drive revenue.
- CRM builds customer loyalty, resulting in customer retention.
- CRM drives high-value returns from customers, resulting in continued business with the organization.
- CRM provides opportunities to create an enhanced customer service delivery strategy uniquely targeted to high-value, long-term customers.

To manage customer relationships effectively, a CRM system is required. CRM requires collection and analysis of purchasing patterns and behaviors. This information is necessary to develop and build new marketing campaigns and programs, as well as to customize incentives for sales professionals. In addition, customer purchasing history and buying pattern analysis can shape new customer acquisition and retention strategies. You can support an investment in UC-enabled customer service multimodal contact centers by demonstrating additional opportunities for customer acquisition and retention.

New customers are acquired through existing customer service agents and multimodal contact centers. Direct mail, advertising, and marketing campaigns, combined with inside sales and telemarketing, provide channels to obtain new customers. The most expensive way to acquire new customers is to rely completely on outside or inside sales professionals. Maximize organizational resources by using existing customer service agents, coupled with various sales and marketing campaigns, to help identify new customers.

Create an enhanced customer service delivery strategy to retain the customers you already have. High-value customers should receive high-value services, whereas low-value customers can be directed to self-service and automated services. Figure 5-8 shows how an organization might handle high-value versus low-value customers. By aligning less expensive customer service delivery with low-value customers, an organization can realign expensive resources to provide high-value customer service delivery. When organizations have limited numbers of high-value customer service agents and subject matter experts, UC-enabled real-time access to these individuals becomes a critical customer service delivery tool. Without UC enablement, organizations cannot adequately support first-call response handling and problem resolution.

FIGURE 5-8: HIGH-VALUE VERSUS LOW-VALUE CUSTOMER SERVICE.

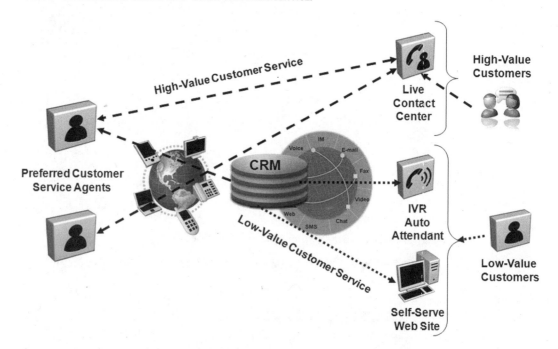

By analyzing a customer's lifetime value, organizations can financially model and track that customer's impact to the bottom line. Review purchases, top-line revenue, and gross profit margin per customer order to build customer retention strategies based on accurate purchasing history and buying patterns.

CRM helps support the overall customer service delivery strategy. Without a CRM application and consolidated customer information database, customer service agents cannot provide first-call response handling. Many organizations must confront the challenge that access to customer information and data requires expertise from individuals or groups within the organization. UC can solve this challenge by providing efficient real-time access to available experts and customer service agents. This is a critical element in building customer loyalty and retention.

Supply chain management (SCM)

Today's manufacturing and distribution organizations face many challenges that directly affect financial performance and customer satisfaction.

The following list describes some common challenges that organizations face within the SCM environment:

- lack of continuity in the organization's overall SCM strategy
- lack of communication between the organization's operational systems and SCM
- lack of support from the organization's chief financial officer (CFO) for SCM
- lack of communication between the organization's suppliers and distributors about sourcing and procurement with SCM
- lack of ability to solve logistics issues quickly due to human latency and inability to reach key decision makers within SCM
- lack of consistent purchasing and shipping of raw materials and supplies, as well as delivery of customer products and services with SCM

To overcome these challenges, many organizations hire outside consulting firms to assess the current supply chain and distribution network infrastructure and recommend efficiency improvements and cost savings. Incorporating enterprise transformation into SCM process analysis can help identify ways to obtain critical supply chain information and disseminate that information to decision makers.

> **Note**
>
> Imagine a supply chain in which a factory is dependent on raw material deliveries for just-in-time (JIT) manufacturing, and the primary supplier has a workforce strike or supply shortage that prevents delivery of its raw materials. Should additional raw materials be purchased at a higher cost, or should manufacturing be delayed and customer delivery dates be postponed? Answering these questions requires real-time access to key decision makers via presence, availability, and IM chat, coupled with real-time collaboration with business managers and customers.
>
> Similarly, if increased fuel costs affect the cost of a product due to drastically increased shipping and handling costs, critical business decisions based on financial factors require real-time access to the CFO and sales management. In particular, this is the case when profitability may be affected unless the increased shipping and handling charges are passed on to the customer.

Solving SCM communication challenges, whether internal or external to the supply chain, requires a careful analysis of inbound and outbound customer service transmissions throughout the organization. UC implementation throughout the supply chain provides real-time access to people, information, and answers that ultimately contribute to customer service and financial returns.

SCM involves managing the procurement systems that acquire raw materials and supplies in the manufacturing process. This includes a streamlined distribution system that transports

5

Critical Business
Applications and
Processes

goods to the consumer in a timely and economical fashion. The following list describes the core elements of every SCM infrastructure:

- **Delivery, fulfillment, and logistics**—The process by which the organization delivers its goods and services to the customer.

- **Manufacturing**—Any manufacturing or development process undertaken to create the product.

- **Operations**—Tracking, monitoring, and reporting on financial transactions and purchases, including realized cost savings from supply chain and operational efficiencies.

- **Sourcing**—The procurement and purchase of raw materials and supplies to support the manufacturing process.

Figure 5-9 shows a basic SCM infrastructure composed of these core elements.

FIGURE 5-9: SCM STRUCTURE.

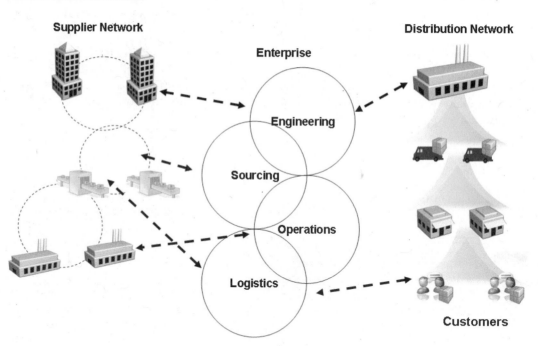

There are many challenges involving SCM infrastructures. The amount of information and data that flows through the supply chain infrastructure can further complicate these challenges. SCM flows can be divided into three main categories:

- **Product flow**—Supplies, manufacturing, and distribution.

- **Information flow**—SCM data from sales, ordering, procurement, inventory, manufacturing, distribution, payment, customer delivery, and customer service.

- **Money flow**—Sales orders, delivery, fulfillment, shipping costs, credit card transaction processing, invoices and accounts receivable, automated clearinghouse (ACH) wire transfers, return merchandise authorizations, credits, and other financial concerns.

Product flow within SCM encompasses the activities associated with the purchase and movement of goods. This includes movement of raw materials and supplies from the supplier to the manufacturer, then to the distributor, and ultimately to the customer. Return merchandise authorizations and credits are also included in this process.

• Information flow within SCM encompasses the information passed from one business process to the next within the supply chain work flow. All information pertaining to the sales order, supplies, manufacturing, distribution, delivery, and customer service is part of the SCM information flow. Part of the overall challenge is ensuring access to information flow at all points in the SCM infrastructure. SCM information flow is critical for manufacturing organizations. It affects sales and order entry, supply requirements, manufacturing production schedules, and the distribution and delivery of the final product to the customer.

• Money flow within SCM encompasses everything pertaining to the financial aspect of the organization. This includes transactions, costs, purchases, invoicing, sales orders, customer credit terms, and payment schedules, as well as consignment and title ownership arrangements.

• Figure 5-10 shows the three common flows of data within an SCM environment. Real-time access to product, information, and money flow data specific to a customer order is critical for enhanced customer service delivery.

FIGURE 5-10: SCM FLOW.

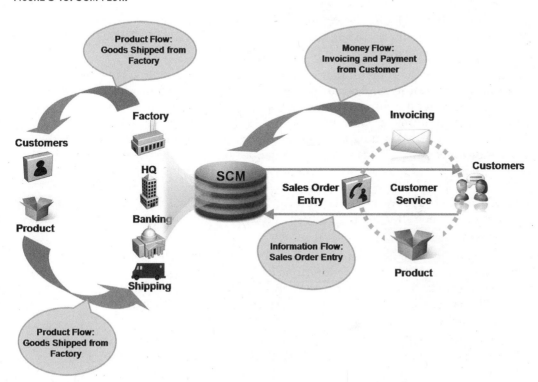

Many organizations face the challenge of tracking increased operating costs accurately, particularly as they relate to the cost of goods sold for a manufactured product. If accurate financial information is not available, a CFO may find it difficult to make decisions based on financial factors. Organizations lose competitive advantage in such situations. Many CFOs and business managers make decisions based on financial return-on-investment (ROI) models or cost–benefit analysis. One way to obtain greater efficiency and cost savings within the SCM environment is through the buyer–supplier relationship.

To lower expenditures, an organization must find new ways to lower operating costs. Some options include streamlined processes, eliminating human latency, and simplified decision making. Using UC enablement to integrate information flow, product flow, and money flow allows key decisions to be made in real time. The following list describes some SCM areas that can help to lower operational costs and the cost of goods sold to customers.

- **Improving existing supply chains for more efficient processes and lowering raw material and supply costs**—By process mapping and flowcharting current supply chain links, organizations can identify inefficiencies and resolve them with enterprise transformation and streamlined processes.

- **Recognizing the critical role of cycle time reduction throughout the supply chain**—Time and empty shelf space are critical factors in an organization's profitability. JIT manufacturing requires JIT supply ordering, JIT inventory control, and streamlined procurement processes with suppliers. Elimination of manual processes and human latency when making business decisions is crucial.

- **Reengineering supply chain logistics for operational improvements and streamlined business processes**—If there are non-value-added activities in logistics, they should be streamlined or eliminated.

- **Establishing supply chain performance benchmarks to set expectations regarding real-time tracking, monitoring, and reporting for continuous, on-demand analysis**—After a baseline definition for the current SCM infrastructure is identified, implementing the proper metrics and key performance indicators (KPIs) provides performance monitoring and reporting to resolve SCM issues. SCM KPIs and metric reporting are crucial tools for the organization's CFO. The CFO can affect the organization's financial performance and success through continuous fine-tuning and refinement of the supply chain process and costs. SCM, coupled with the distribution network, creates an end-to-end supply and delivery chain that supports multiple processes. Enterprise transformation analysis and key SCM internal function streamlining generally produce improvement in financial performance.

Without accurate financial information, it is difficult to determine the value of SCM to an organization. Proper tracking and identification of cost and expense elements associated with the end-to-end supply chain can improve supply, distribution, delivery, and logistics efficiency. Human latency in decision making can be eliminated with appropriate cost controls and operational policies that use predefined and automated rule sets.

Figure 5-11 shows how SCM can lower operational costs to improve financial performance. This, in turn, can result in greater customer satisfaction and customer retention. These steps are all part of the organization's customer service-focused strategy.

FIGURE 5-11: BUSINESS VALUE OF SCM.

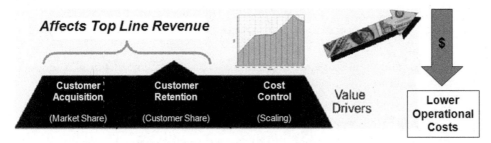

- Lowering supply chain costs results in lower "costs of goods sold"

- Lowering "costs of goods sold" means more gross profit margin (GPM) or cost savings can be shared along the value chain with the end-user customer

- Lowering delivery/fulfillment/logistics costs result in lower overall product costs given that shipping & handling is reduced

- Tracking and monitoring these costs savings and revenue/GPM increases is critical to cost justify UC enablement in SCM

The goal of SCM, from a value perspective, is to identify and lower operational costs throughout the supply chain. This analysis, combined with enterprise transformation, provides an organization with real-time access to information as it is identified. It also provides the organization with real-time access to key decision makers when emergency supply chain issues must be resolved.

Enterprise resource planning (ERP)

Today's enterprise organizations depend on a single core financial system that integrates common accounting applications. Examples of these applications include general ledger, accounts receivable, accounts payable, and SCM. Without proper financial hooks and integration between the various money flows in and out of the organization, it is impossible to achieve optimal financial performance. Many critical decisions about particular customers require real-time access to financial data. This data includes financial statistics pertinent to the customer, the customer's order, and the impact or penalties that might arise from potential delays due to problems in service-level agreements. This real-time access is not only important for enhanced customer service delivery, but is necessary to provide management with information required to make critical decisions.

The following list includes challenges, typically found within ERP and financial systems, that prevent key decisions from being made in real time:

- disparate IT systems, applications, and customer data

- lack of coordination among related departments, applications, processes, and functions

- inefficient cycle times for processes that introduce human latency in making critical decisions

- inability to access and view real-time financials and procurement, accounts receivable, and accounts payable information to make sound decisions

- business processes and functions that are not integrated into a single ERP or financial system accessible to key managers throughout the organization

ERP includes the software applications and tools used to manage enterprise data. ERP systems help organizations deal with supply chain, receiving, inventory management, customer order management, production planning, shipping, accounting, human resource management, and other common functions within large enterprises. Many ERP software tools and applications are built around financial systems that have general ledger, accounts payable, and accounts receivable as software modules. These software modules interface with the organization's ERP financial system infrastructure.

ERP systems typically provide a consolidated, enterprise-wide information sharing infrastructure that incorporates enterprise financials, human resources, manufacturing, logistics, and sales and marketing functions. The following list describes elements of a typical deployment and implementation of an ERP financial system:

- An ERP system is used to consolidate an organization's information and data (supply chain, inventory management, shipping, accounting, human resource management, and other factors).

- An ERP system is used as a consolidated business software application to automate and integrate processes. Information can be accessed in real time when needed.

- An ERP system is used to integrate enterprise-wide information, both financial and nonfinancial.

- An ERP system is used to provide a consolidated, enterprise-wide database in which all financial transactions are entered, processed, monitored, and reported. Decisions can be made in real time with proper access to up-to-date financial information and reports.

- An ERP system is used to incorporate best practices, which are the best and most efficient ways to perform given processes. ERP systems can align an associated cost element to a specific best practice business process.

Leading ERP software vendors include SAP, Oracle, and BEA. These vendors build ERP application suites composed of software modules that support particular business functions, such as human resources, accounting, and sales order entry. Enterprise-wide business functions and processes, such as sales order processing, purchasing, production planning, financial accounting, management accounting, and human resources are examples of how ERP software modules can integrate major business functions within a single ERP framework.

ERP software modules are fully integrated under a common umbrella and can generally be purchased and customized one module at a time. This makes a phased migration and implementation plan possible for many organizations.

5

Critical Business
Applications and
Processes

ERP systems replace the disparate, isolated IT systems, applications, and databases that house accurate financial information about business processes and functions. With full integration and financial metrics embedded within ERP software modules (see Figure 5-12), an enterprise can access accurate and real-time financial data about the organization. Decisions can therefore be made based on accurate financial priorities, and cost–benefit analysis can be assessed based on profitability or financial loss.

FIGURE 5-12: CONSOLIDATION OF FINANCIALS WITHIN A SINGLE ERP SYSTEM.

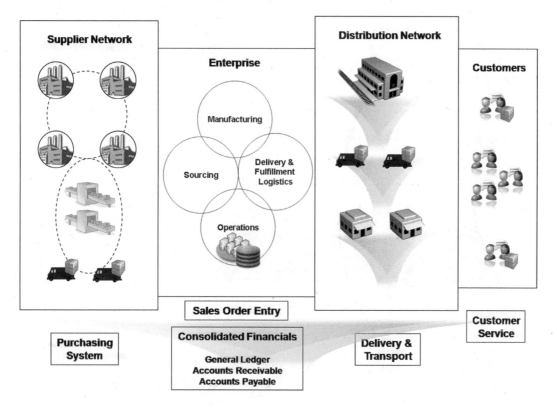

ERP systems can be a substantial investment for an organization. Because of the financial burden, many organizations transfer their disparate IT systems, applications, and solutions toward a consolidated ERP infrastructure in a migratory fashion: one software module at a time. Organizations invest from tens of thousands to millions of dollars in ERP software, software modules, and systems integration support. Because of the size of the investment, ERP is not considered suitable for small- to medium-sized organizations.

In some cases, ERP systems replace archaic enterprise IT systems, applications, and databases. This is particularly the case when the old applications cannot easily integrate or share information and data. ERP tools and applications can be aligned to financial ROI if the goal is to achieve lower operational costs through greater process efficiencies, shortened cycle times, and automated business functions. Because ERP systems can be financially tracked, the value of an investment in ERP can be easily monitored.

5

Critical Business
Applications and
Processes

When ERP is used to manage financials and metrics, it is critical to design accurate processes because decisions will be made based on the generated financial metrics. UC-enabled ERP information can deliver real-time financial information to key decision makers. UC also provides a conduit for real-time access to that key decision maker, in the event that person is not at his or her desk. ERP systems provide an integrated approach by establishing a common set of applications and software modules that support the organization's operations and processes.

The true value of ERP is the integration of all business functions and processes within a common financial system. This consolidation provides key decision makers with the necessary financial information in one location, so that sound decisions can be made. ERP cost savings and benefits can be tracked, particularly as process efficiencies improve operational functions. A key driver for ERP is the measured impact of lower operational costs through greater effectiveness and efficiency. The actual financial ROI is obtained through tracked process cost efficiencies and improvements. Figure 5-13 shows the business value of ERP systems and how they can affect operational efficiency.

FIGURE 5-13: BUSINESS VALUE OF ERP: EFFICIENT OPERATIONS.

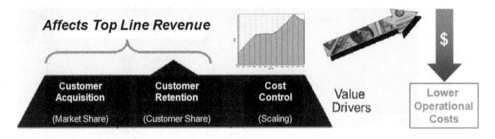

- ERP can bring lower operating costs through streamlined and integrated business processes

- ERP can streamline processes and eliminate delays and human intervention or approval processes through automated business rule sets

- ERP can provide access to real-time financials, providing executive management with the data needed to make on-the-fly business decisions

ERP systems provide a consolidated view of the organization's financial health by providing access to real-time financials. Implementing KPIs and metrics for executives helps achieve or maintain a competitive market advantage. A unified view of internal operations, such as cost of goods sold and sales, general, and administrative (SG&A) overhead, is critical to tracking financial performance. UC, coupled with ERP information dissemination, provides managers with the information they need in real time to make sound decisions.

Sales force automation (SFA)

Organizations that link their outside and inside sales forces with back-office systems have many challenges to overcome. Improvements that streamline the sales cycle can be identified by analyzing current sales and order entry processes. These improvements require real-time access to key presales information, speed in preparation, and efficient methods to deliver a customer proposal.

The following list describes challenges that organizations encounter within SFA functions and processes:

- disparate IT systems, applications, and customer data

- lack of coordination among related business departments, applications, processes, and functions

- inefficient cycle times for sales processes, tasks, and activities leading up to the closed deal and purchase order from the customer

- inability to access and view a customer's real-time account information, purchasing history, order status, financials, and profitability

- processes and functions that are not integrated into a single ERP or financial system that can be accessed by key managers throughout the organization

SFA is comprised of software applications and tools that are used in a presales process that leads to a closed deal and purchase order from the customer. SFA systems typically integrate CRM and contact management, and establish sales lead tracking functionality. Elements of an SFA sales infrastructure can include the following:

- real-time communications supported during the presales cycle

- customer contact management and tracking

- sales forecasting per customer and for all customers of a single sales representative

- back-office sales order entry system

- proposal generation system and templates

- sales order tracking, monitoring, and management

- product and solution knowledge and access to key subject matter experts

- collaborative communications and real-time communications with subject matter experts

- specific solutions that solve the customer's unique challenges and problems

To use enterprise transformation in the sales cycle, organizations must analyze their current presales, sales, and order entry processes. This analysis will identify manual processes, along with human latency bottlenecks and cumbersome tasks. SFA solutions can then be designed to streamline these inefficient processes and provide real-time access to presales support specialists.

UC-enabled SFA provides the value proposition of real-time access to information and key presales subject matter experts. Sales organizations can close deals more quickly through streamlined sales tasks and processes, better response to customer inquiries, and efficient real-time internal and external communications. By reducing the sales cycle time, an organization will generate more revenue and gross profit margin.

Streamlining the sales order entry process is a key SFA benefit. UC enablement brings real-time communications and information dissemination to the presales process. Automated sales order entry processes will eliminate paperwork and reduce cycle time, particularly when secure e-forms and Web-enabled applications are integrated. Figure 5-14 shows a streamlined sales order entry process.

FIGURE 5-14: STREAMLINING THE SALES ORDER ENTRY PROCESS.

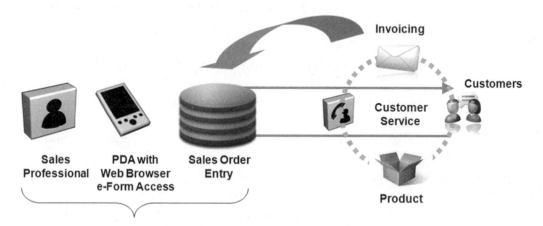

- Reducing sales process cycle time
- Elimination of manual tasks and paperwork
- Sales orders can be entered from any browser (IP mobile device, PDAs) securely
- Sales professionals can track sales order from any browser securely
- Linkage to ERP system provides unified view into customer order

Sales managers and executive management want to track real-time financials and, more important, real-time sales figures (see Figure 5-15). ERP systems track cost elements throughout the entire organization. This includes accurate reports used to track revenue, cost of goods sold, expenses, and gross profit margin. These cost elements are then linked to general ledger accounting functions that track and report every financial transaction and movement throughout the business, accurately and in real time. This includes sales orders, revenue, cost of goods sold, and gross profit margin reporting.

Sales managers and executives can get accurate sales revenue figures from UC-enabled linkage between SFA systems and applications. This provides access to real-time financials, particularly revenue, gross profit margin, sales quota tracking, and sales forecasting. This is critical for sales professionals, sales managers, and executives who need a real-time snapshot of revenue and gross profit margin figures to make sound decisions.

FIGURE 5-15: TRACKING REAL-TIME FINANCIALS AND SALES FIGURES.

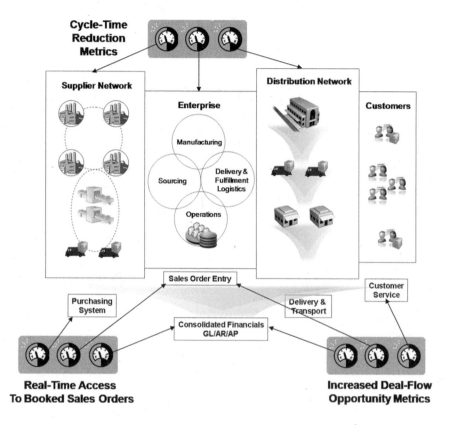

Organizations also face challenges in the integration of presales, sales, postsales, and customer service functions and processes. When SFA is incorporated within an ERP infrastructure, the organization can leverage sales order entry information with enhanced customer service delivery for high-value customers. This requires the sales order entry system to be integrated and consolidated with a back-end CRM. It also requires a multimedia contact center infrastructure where UC provides real-time access to key sales management and subject matter experts, as well as real-time access to customer order entry and shipping status information.

Real-time access to customer account and sales order information can be obtained from the organization's sales order entry system or back-end CRM system. With access to this information, both sales professionals and customer service agents can provide consistent presales and postsales customer service functions, fostering customer loyalty and retention.

Sales professionals involved in presales activities with a customer can have specific customer calls routed directly to them from the UC-enabled multimedia contact center. This is particularly important if the customer calls the contact center directly, but the sales professional is the single point of contact for all customer communications leading to a closed deal.

Knowledge Check 5-1: Critical Business Applications and Processes

Answer the following questions. Answers to these Knowledge Check questions are located in *Appendix A: Answers to Knowledge Check Questions*.

1. Enterprise transformation is similar to business process reengineering.

   a. True

   b. False

2. Enterprise transformation integrates which of the following? (Choose two.)

   a. People-to-people communications

   b. Enhanced customer service delivery

   c. Streamlined business processes and work flows

3. Which of the following challenges can be solved by SOA implementations?

   a. Flexibility to change operations based on changing dynamics

   b. Inability to share and access customer data in different repositories

   c. Communications with disparate IT systems, applications, and databases

   d. Inability to reuse software applications in a simple and cost-effective manner

   e. All of the above

4. SOA solutions are typically delivered as middleware software applications.

   a. True

   b. False

5. Organizations that implement a customer service–focused strategy can create a competitive differentiator.

   a. True

   b. False

6. Which of the following is NOT a common customer service challenge that organizations must overcome?

   a. Increasing contact center effectiveness

   b. Increasing contact center operating costs

   c. Mapping customer satisfaction to an overall customer service delivery strategy

   d. Enhancing customer service delivery through multiple modes of communication

   e. All of the above

7. CRM solves which of the following business challenges?

   a. Sales process inefficiencies

   b. Access to real-time financials

   c. Manual sales order entry processing

   d. Analysis of customer purchasing history and buying patterns

   e. None of the above

8. Enhanced customer service delivery requires a back-end CRM application and system, providing customer service agents with real-time access to customer information.

   a. True

   b. False

9. SCM challenges are related to which of the following?

   a. Cycle time reduction

   b. Lowering operational costs

   c. Implementing JIT inventory

   d. Implementing JIT manufacturing

   e. All of the above

10. CFOs track operational costs in the supply chain for which of the following reasons?

    a. To track cost of goods sold

    b. To determine when price increases may be needed

    c. Because they lack confidence in financial reporting information provided

    d. Both A and B

    e. None of the above

11. ERP systems are best suited for small- to medium-sized businesses.

    a. True

    b. False

12. Which challenge is the most important when trying to incorporate ERP systems into critical decision making?

   a. Access to real-time financials

   b. Inability to generate and obtain accurate financial reporting

   c. Inability to make sound business decisions based on financial priorities

   d. Inability to obtain financial cost elements and financial performance throughout the enterprise

   e. None of the above

13. Sales force automation is most concerned with shrinking which of the following?

   a. Cost of goods sold

   b. Size of the sales force

   c. Sales order data entry time

   d. Sales cycle time from start to close

   e. None of the above

14. Sales professionals typically have which of the following challenges to overcome?

   a. Time

   b. Inability to access sales order entry system remotely

   c. Real-time access to sales management for approvals on discounts

   d. Real-time access to subject matter experts and technical specialists during presales

   e. All of the above

Chapter summary

In this chapter, you learned about several business applications and processes and the challenges they bring to organizations. You learned that enterprise transformation is similar to process reengineering, in that streamlined processes and workflows replace inefficient ones with people-to-people communications. An organization can transform how it communicates and makes critical decisions by aligning streamlined processes with UC enablement such as real-time presence and availability, instant message chat, audio and video conferencing, and real-time collaboration.

SOA, CS, CRM, SCM, ERP, and SFA bring specific challenges that can be solved with streamlined processes and embedded UC solutions.

6: Solving Business Challenges

One of the many daily challenges an enterprise business faces is how to stay in the mind of the consumer. Before you can solve this, or any, business challenge, you must first identify the problem and then correct the inefficiencies that cause it. In previous chapters, you learned about enterprise transformation, which examines where best to streamline and how to reduce decision-making time. Unified Communications (UC) brings a variety of solutions and benefits that can help you with enterprise transformation. In this chapter, you will learn more about the advantages of UC and how to integrate it within business applications and processes. The chapter concludes with examples of real-world solutions incorporating enterprise transformation and UC enablement.

Chapter 6 Topics

In this chapter, you will learn:

- the benefits UC solutions can provide

- how service-oriented architecture (SOA) brings business value

- how customer service (CS) can lead a customer-focused business strategy

- how customer relationship management (CRM) can enhance customer service delivery

- how streamlined processes and elimination of human decision making within supply chain management (SCM) can reduce cycle time

- how enterprise resource planning (ERP) can provide real-time access to financials for critical business decision making

- how sales force automation (SFA) can increase deal flow, revenue, and profitability

Chapter 6 Goals

Upon completion of this chapter, you will be able to:

• identify and describe UC solution benefits

• describe solutions, business challenges, and processes in SOA, CS, CRM, SCM, ERP, and SFA describe how SOA, CS, CRM, SCM, ERP, and SFA, integrated with UC enablement, can solve unique business challenges and problems

Key Terms

Cost of goods sold	114	Hyperconnected	120
Customer experience management	115	Just-in-time (JIT) inventory	114
Cycle time	114	Just-in-time (JIT) manufacturing	114
Delivery, fulfillment, and logistics	114	Low-value customers	118
Distribution network	126	Operations	115
Federation	128	SIP-enabled application	118
Generation Y or Echo Generation	120	Supplier network	126
High-value customers	112		

Unified Communications solution benefits

Chapter 5, "Critical Business Applications and Processes," presented a variety of business challenges and processes, including SOA, CS, CRM, SCM, ERP, and SFA. Previous chapters also introduced enterprise transformation, a process used to analyze and assess current communication processes. Enterprise transformation also identifies areas where streamlining, coupled with convergence and UC, can enhance overall efficiency. This analysis leads to solutions that can be established and integrated with UC enablement. Once integrated, the true benefits of UC can be realized.

Common UC benefits

The following list provides examples of UC benefits, compiled from the Nortel and Microsoft UC Business Value Tool developed by Forrester Research (2007). These benefits include, but are not limited to:

- **Reduced real estate requirements and costs through remote telecommuting and mobile workers**—As workers become more flexible and mobile, the need for dedicated office space becomes less critical. With telecommuting, mobility, presence, remote messaging, Voice over Internet Protocol (VoIP), audio and video conferencing, and use of Internet Protocol (IP) soft phones, organizations can minimize real estate and office leasing requirements.

- **Reduced internal organization traveling for meetings**—With full audio and video conferencing capabilities, including collaboration, businesses can conduct productive face-to-face meetings without expending travel and entertainment expenses or time.

- **Employee retention is improved because workers are given greater flexibility in telecommuting with real-time access to key employees for critical business decision making**—Presence, instant messaging, mobility, and flexibility to work from home or other places all contribute to employee satisfaction and retention, which in turn results in greater cost savings to the organization.

- **Reduced training expenses**—On-site Web conferencing capabilities with full collaboration allow organizations to deliver distance learning programs to employees. Training, printing, and travel costs can be minimized. With full audio and video recording and playback capabilities, employees can train on their own when and where it is most convenient for them.

- **Shortened sales cycles**—SFA, coupled with UC enablement, provides real-time presales support, communication with subject matter experts, and access to critical answers in support of customer proposals. This can also reduce the time it takes to answer customer queries and develop sales proposals.

- **Reduced time to complete projects**—With enhanced communications and real-time access to key employees and subject matter experts, project team member productivity is improved.

- **Improved resolution of customer inquiries and issues**—Enhancing communications between customer service agents and key subject matter experts allows organizations to develop CS-focused strategies where preferred agents can provide first-call problem resolution. UC enablement can support real-time access to high-value CS resources.

• **Customer experience and retention**—Enhanced communications between high-value customers and their high-value customer service agents enhances the overall customer experience, ultimately boosting retention. This improves revenue, profitability, and future financial returns. Presence, availability, instant messaging (IM), chat, short message service (SMS) text messaging, and real-time access to key resources all contribute to the overall customer experience and satisfaction.

Integrating UC within SOA applications to solve inefficiencies

When multimodal forms of communication are combined, there are many opportunities to improve processes. For example, desktop features and functions are now integrated into cell phones and personal digital assistants (PDAs). The standard desktop phone has grown to support more than just telephony features. Such integration is made easier with a standardized signaling protocol, Session Initiation Protocol (SIP).

FIGURE 6-1: TODAY'S MULTIMODAL BUSINESS COMMUNICATION OPTIONS.

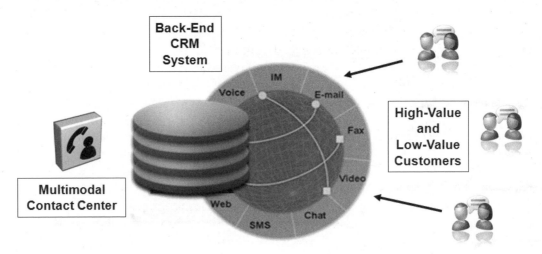

By combining different communication features and functionality through SIP, the enterprise business can identify new opportunities. An enterprise business can benefit from a VoIP and UC solution that combines its communications into a much smaller footprint. Given the multiple modes of business communications shown in Figure 6-1, an SOA can break the different processes into smaller components, which permits rapid reuse of existing software and code in newer applications. In service-oriented businesses, such as health care and law enforcement, this decrease in deployment time could literally be the difference between life and death. Consider the following examples of SOA software applications integrated with UC functionality in very different implementations.

What if you worked for a health care organization?

What if it was possible to enhance patient care services by providing the right medical expert with the right information when it was needed most? What if you could minimize errors in medical diagnosis and treatments by eliminating human latency in life-threatening situations? Can UC support secure, real-time medical and patient care services and save lives?

In 2006, the Yale School of Medicine estimated that there is a 14.9 percent chance of medical error when there are human delays in medical information dissemination and real-time access to medical experts is not available. As documented previously by the Yale School of Medicine, as many as 44,000 to 98,000 deaths per year in the United States alone can be attributed at some level to preventable medical error. How can we enhance real-time communications to deliver enhanced patient care services?

Doctors, nurses, and medical professionals need the following real-time communications capabilities to offer enhanced patient care services:
- access to accurate patient health care information and status
- access to medical specialists, medical experts, and surgical teams for collaboration
- seamless integration with IT for self-service Web-delivered patient services, and for patient care information delivery

SOA, embedded with SIP-enabled UC applications, combines multimodal people-to-people communications to streamline business processes and disseminate information in real time to those who need it most. Consider an SOA and UC-enabled application, such as presence, in the hospitality, hotel, and entertainment industries, where enhanced customer service delivery can contribute to the overall customer experience and retention.

What if you worked in the hospitality and hotel services industry?

A business traveler logs on to a favorite hotel's Web site to make a reservation. The customer's profile is loaded onto the Web site, complete with the traveler's previously recorded preferences. When the reservation is made, all of the customer's unique requirements and requests are automatically logged into the reservation.

A confirmation is sent via any multimodal form of communication desired. The traveler's personalized requests for that reservation and confirmation can be e-mailed to a business e-mail address and also sent via SMS text messaging. In the confirmation e-mail, the hotel provides not only confirmation for the reservation, but an access code for authentication on arrival at the hotel as well. The traveler already has a frequent customer card that has a preprogrammed smart radio frequency identification (RFID) chip.

On arrival at the hotel, the traveler bypasses the registration desk, inserts the frequent customer card with embedded RFID chip into the VIP self-service check-in kiosk, and enters the access code. The hotel room number appears on the kiosk screen. This provides the business traveler with direct access to the hotel room using the frequent customer card as the hotel room key, activated to work only on the room number displayed on the self-service kiosk.

Upon entry into the room, the RFID chip sends a profile to the room's location sensors. The profile tailors the room to the business traveler's liking, changing Internet access restrictions, television stations, and environmental controls. VoIP and UC calls are directed to the traveler's laptop via the Internet and no calls are forwarded through the hotel's telecommunications system. VIP hotel customer service with UC is linked to the customer's hotel room phone at the push of a button, providing real-time access to VIP customer service agents.

In this hotel, SOA software applications are integrated with enhanced customer service delivery and UC to improve the online reservation process for savvy customers. This self-service mode of communications streamlines the entire reservation and check-in process. Such enhanced customer service delivery drives a positive customer experience.

UC solution benefits can also be found in enhanced process flow efficiency and real-time communications throughout the SCM infrastructure. Operational efficiency can be streamlined by automating and linking sales order entry, purchasing, just-in-time (JIT) inventory, and JIT manufacturing processes. Through detailed analysis of current processes and the elimination of manual tasks and human decision making, a system based on policies and decision criteria can streamline processes and reduce sales cycle time. Product sales and manufacturing business follow a linear sequence of steps that typically encompass the following:

- **The sale and closing of the deals**—Before a contract is signed, several tasks must be completed: crafting the executive summary, proposal, and statement of work; mapping the solution to IT and UC; accumulating the costs for the overall solution, including parts, labor, service, maintenance, and ongoing support.

- **Obtaining a customer purchase order or contract**—The customer's purchasing department must generate a purchase order or requisition to allocate funds for the acquisition.

- **Sales order entry system**—Customer orders must be entered into the system and scheduled for manufacturing.

- **JIT inventory and purchasing triggered by sales order entry**—Sales order systems maximize manufacturing schedules based on product delivery requirements and number of orders.

- **JIT manufacturing triggered by manufacturing production schedules**—Sales orders are normally scheduled according to manufacturing schedules specific to resource availability. JIT manufacturing maximizes the use of raw materials and labor requirements needed for the manufacturing of the product.

- **Manufacturing of products**—Manufacturing contributes to the cost of goods sold because of production scheduling and labor pool requirements that must support the manufacturing process. The lower the labor required and cost to manufacture, the lower the cost of goods sold.

- **Delivery, fulfillment, and logistics of products through distribution or direct to customer**—Once the product has been manufactured and assembled, it must be packaged and warehoused prior to staging and shipping. At this stage, final quality assurance and invoice or bill of lading information is added.

- **Invoicing and payment processing**—Depending on the payment terms of the purchase order and actual sales commitment, the invoice for the finished product is sent to the customer with predefined payment terms once the product is shipped.

- **Post-sale and ongoing customer service**—The organization may wish to implement a complete post-sale customer experience management strategy.

These processes are common in modern manufacturing operations. Many of these steps introduce human latency and delay, because most of these processes are manual and human decision making is required. This delay can be reduced as more of these steps are automated or streamlined through a faster and easier communications solution.

What if you could streamline sales order entry with JIT inventory/purchasing and JIT manufacturing?

Imagine a UC-linked sales professional with real-time access to presales support specialists and subject matter experts, all with a single goal in mind: solving the customer's business challenges. Couple that with streamlined and integrated processes that allow the sales professional to enter sales order information via a remote, secured browser connection on a laptop or PDA, thus accelerating order placement and processing.

By streamlining and automating manual processes, SCM infrastructures can benefit from UC enablement by providing the real-time access to key business managers. Organizations have a competitive advantage when they transform manual processes into fully automated ones.

Not only are you shortening the order lead time for the customer, but you can offer rapid JIT inventory and manufacturing, maximizing efficiency and ultimately reducing cost. Speeding up sales, manufacturing, and delivery increases revenue and gross profit margins. Not only can SOA solve these challenges, it can create a competitive advantage for organizations that implement SOA-based software applications embedded with UC functionality.

These examples of SOA software application and streamlined business process integration have something in common: the integration of people-to-people communications with access to information in real time, coupled with streamlined processes. Together, these elements can result in tremendous value to the organization. This value can create a competitive advantage, particularly if that value is embedded in a strategy that focuses on customer service. In these examples, SOA software applications were built to serve the customer in a self-service, automated, or preferred/VIP customer service capacity. This value is depicted in Figure 6-2.

Typical IT software architectures are based on a suite of enterprise software applications. SOA is an entirely new way to develop software, based on modularized components that can be reused in different processes. A typical IT software architecture might look like the one shown in Figure 6-3. Common software architectures are supported by software modules, and each module performs a unique task or function within the overall operations of the organization.

FIGURE 6-2: SOA APPLICATION BUSINESS VALUE.

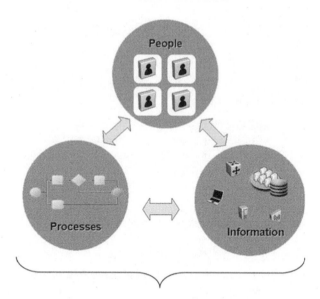

SOA Combines People,
Processes & Information Access

FIGURE 6-3: COMMON IT SOFTWARE ARCHITECTURES.

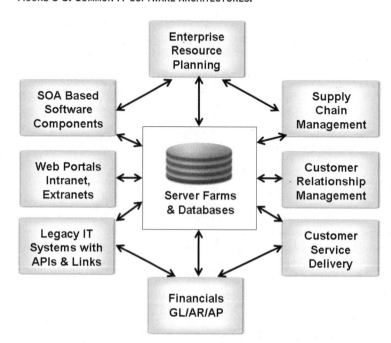

SOA is a style of software architecture that employs loosely coupled interoperating modules, as opposed to customized interfaces that interoperate between proprietary products. SOA applications and modules are predominantly built for Web service delivery where security, access, and interaction with a business application or process are handled through Web front-ends. SOA provides a completely open and flexible development capability, allowing components to mix and match features and functions. Building communications-enabled applications allows the features and functions of UC to be embedded within the software delivery itself. Business value is enhanced by coupling SOA-based software applications with a strategy that focuses on customer service. Examples of this include the following:

- **IM chat, audio, or video conferencing capability providing live customer service communication on a Web site**—Many Web sites offer visitors the option to interact with a live customer service agent, providing enhanced customer service delivery through self-service browsing combined with live audio, video, and IM chat.

- **Online food ordering with real-time delivery and notification service**—Imagine ordering pizza or a gourmet meal online by simply perusing a menu on the restaurant's Web site, purchasing the meal with your credit card in a secure manner, and then having that meal delivered to your door. With UC embedded in a delivery notification application, the system can trigger an e-mail or SMS text message to the customer's e-mail or cell phone indicating when the driver left the restaurant with the order. An automated delivery notification system provides updates to the customer in 10- or 15-minute increments or at a predefined notification alert frequency to the customer's e-mail or SMS text message device.

- **IM chat, audio, or video conferencing capability at a banking or financial institution ATM kiosk**—Instead of being limited to traditional ATM menu options, UC-enabled ATM kiosks offer the customer full audio and video communications with a banking customer service representative. Full-service banking can now provide enhanced customer service capabilities beyond what the traditional ATM can support. Embedding UC within ATM menu selections allows fully integrated, real-time access to customer service and customer banking information.

Today's organizations demand new ways to lower operational costs and eliminate manual processes that introduce human latency. When workers are not at their desks, real-time access to key decision makers is still critical for organizational efficiency. Combine SOA software applications with streamlined processes and UC enablement, and you will have an organization with an advantage over its competitors. UC enablement allows critical decision making to occur in real time.

Solving CS business challenges with UC enablement

The previous section described how SOA-based software applications, coupled with a strategy focused on customer service, can provide an organization with a competitive advantage. Building a competitive advantage in and around CS requires analyzing who the customers are and how best to service them. This analysis will help businesses build and map the best customer service delivery strategy with its customers.

An SOA software framework that integrates customer service applications (self-service Web sites, integration of customer service with CRM applications, VIP preferred agents, etc.) is the key to building a strategy specific to customer support and service. With convergence technologies such as VoIP and SIP-enabled applications, you can implement customer service delivery that supports the multiple modes of communication that your customers want to use. By deploying a UC infrastructure within the SOA, an enterprise business can accurately direct high-valued services to customers who can afford them, supporting only low-valued services for low-valued customers. This focus on directing the proper services to the right customers is critical, given that resources and resource allocation is cost sensitive.

> **Note** When defining a customer service delivery strategy, organizations generally align the least expensive customer service delivery to low-value customers and the most expensive customer service delivery to high-value customers. For example, very important person (VIP) or preferred customer service agents can be aligned to VIP or high-value customers. Self-service customer Web sites and automated attendants are typically built to deal with the masses of low-value customers.

Gartner Group has identified average industry-standard cost elements for different customer service communication channels, as shown in Figure 6–4. The key is not the actual number, but the differences between the numbers where organizations must collectively design, select, and implement customer service delivery strategies.

FIGURE 6-4: AVERAGE CUSTOMER SERVICE CONNECTION COSTS.

Average customer service channel costs:

- Live Agent $4.50
- IVR $1.85
- Web $ .65
- Email $2.50
- Chat $7.50
- Collaboration $5.50

Customer service business challenges are issues for many organizations, as described earlier. Today, organizations that strive to create focused customer service strategies will need to embrace the following elements:

- **Customer acquisition**—Acquiring new customers and revenue streams.

- **Customer retention**—Achieving additional profitability from repeat business and purchases.

- **Differentiated services for high-value customers**—Aligning your best resources in the most economical manner to provide customer support for high-value customers.

- **Reducing operational costs for low-value customers**—Using automated attendants, interactive voice response (IVR) systems, and Web-enabled portals to provide simplified self-service capabilities at reduced costs.

- **First response problem or inquiry resolution**—Providing real-time access to customer information (CRM back-end systems and databases) integrated with UC-enabled contact centers, customer service agents, subject matter experts, and high-value customer support personnel.

- **Too many channels of communications**—Simplifying and defining how customers should contact them and communicating these options to the customer.

- **Customer service performance and quality monitoring**—Improving customer service delivery through performance monitoring and continuous training of customer service agents.

- **Customer satisfaction**—Defining what customer satisfaction means to the business and its customers. With these definitions as a guideline, an enterprise can build customer satisfaction into the business's customer service delivery strategy.

Applying these elements to a customer service delivery UC deployment will impact customer satisfaction, acquisition, and retention. The process starts with defining the organization's objectives for customer experience management. Customer experience management is an analysis of how and what that organization defines as being part of its customer's experience.

Today's customer is changing rapidly. Organizations must first understand who their customers are and profile them. They must also learn the modes of communication their customers like to use and assess how best to service each customer, particularly high-value customers versus low-value customers. Figure 6-5 depicts today's customers and why it's important to map the best customer service delivery to the type of customer. Understanding how these customers prefer to communicate is part of the customer experience management challenge.

FIGURE 6-5: CUSTOMER EXPERIENCE MANAGEMENT.

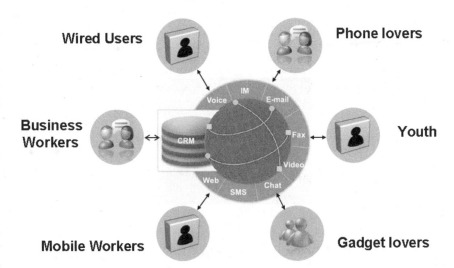

Whether the organization's interest is sales or service, the customer is paramount. However, the needs and expectations of customers change rapidly. For example, consider the features available on today's cell phones: real-time SMS text messaging, IM chat, presence and availability, full Web browsing, and more. The Internet has made the business and nonbusiness world a virtual environment, with most people now spending more time on the World Wide Web than watching television. As more devices are connected, a hyperconnected, virtual environment is created. The implications touch every area of communications, especially those between a business and its customers. The move to a virtually connected environment has become a fast-moving directive in more and more businesses. The rapidity is partially due to customer needs, and partially to a change in the workforce. In the United States, for example, the *Y-Generation* or *Echo Generation* represents a changing consumer profile:

- **Individuals between the ages of 12 and 30**—This generation will become future business managers and executives.

- **Multimedia and technologically savvy**—People born between 1978 and 1996 grew up with the Internet, cable TV, cell phones, video games, and other technological gadgetry.

- **Communicates using multiple modes of communications**—Today's consumers are not only technologically savvy, but can communicate via multiple modes of communication. Organizations that support multimodal communications can align high-value and low-value customer service solutions to solve customer service delivery challenges.

These points characterize a changing consumer profile where VoIP and SIP-enabled communications are commonplace within a business. UC integration will change the workplace culture for each employee. The transformation will continue as Y-Generation employees become directors, vice presidents, and C-level executives.

What if your organization could do the following:

- create and deliver a breakthrough customer experience

- stand out among the increasingly large number of products and services offered

- communicate and collaborate effortlessly in real time

- provide your product or service faster and more efficiently

- continue to adapt to changing business dynamics in a flexible and agile manner

Organizations that sell products and services in a competitive landscape differentiate themselves through their customer service delivery strategy. A good customer service delivery strategy will create customer loyalty. Creating a breakthrough customer experience requires:

- Fostering vital, richer customer collaboration using audio and video for real-time business decision making.

- Changing the competitive landscape for enhanced customer service delivery using UC.

- Maximizing operational efficiency, effectiveness, and profits by transforming business communications. Additional profits can be used to develop the business-to-customer communications strategy.

- Streamlining communications to shorten delivery time to the customer. A faster response supports customer retention.

Customer service delivery strategies require customer-focused innovation and solutions to differentiate an organization from its competition. The following elements should be considered and incorporated within the strategy:

- building customer retention
- crafting customer acquisition
- calculating customer lifetime value
- providing real-time access to customer data
- improving profitability per customer
- tracking customer satisfaction and loyalty

Implementing an enhanced customer service delivery strategy requires a combination of several of the solutions depicted in Figure 6-6. Mapping customer service delivery solutions to technology may encompass any of the following:

- **Multimodal contact center**—Real-time business communications between customer service and customers using any device such as phone, Web, IM chat, SMS text, audio and video conferencing, e-mail, or fax.
- **Speech and self-service**—Welcome greetings, always-on automated self-service, and simple and easy-to-access customer information.
- **Unified messaging**—Voice, fax, and e-mail integrated into a single mailbox accessible via phone, PC, PDA, or IP-connected device.
- **Multimedia audio and video conferencing**—Always-on multimedia audio and video conferencing to increase employee mobility.
- **Collaboration**—Electronic whiteboards, presence and availability, MeetMe audio and video conferencing, and unified messaging used to communicate in real time with colleagues and project team members.
- **UC**—Real-time access to key subject matter experts, with preferred or VIP customer service agents supported through UC enablement.

The high-value customer base requires a simple way to communicate with specialized customer service agents at any time, and from anywhere in the world. With UC and real-time presence and availability information, this access can be provided in real time, offering an enhanced customer service delivery strategy. This is shown in Figure 6-7. Treating high-value customers uniquely can create a customer service delivery differentiator. Providing self-service customer service delivery can also provide customers with real-time access to their customer information through their preferred communication channel.

Today's organizations must find new ways to differentiate themselves, particularly where products and services from similar companies are readily available. Implementing and enhancing a customer service delivery strategy requires careful analysis of economics coupled with customer acquisition, retention, and loyalty strategies. By segmenting customers into high-value versus low-value customers, organizations can allocate expensive resources more appropriately.

FIGURE 6-6: CUSTOMER SERVICE DIFFERENTIATORS.

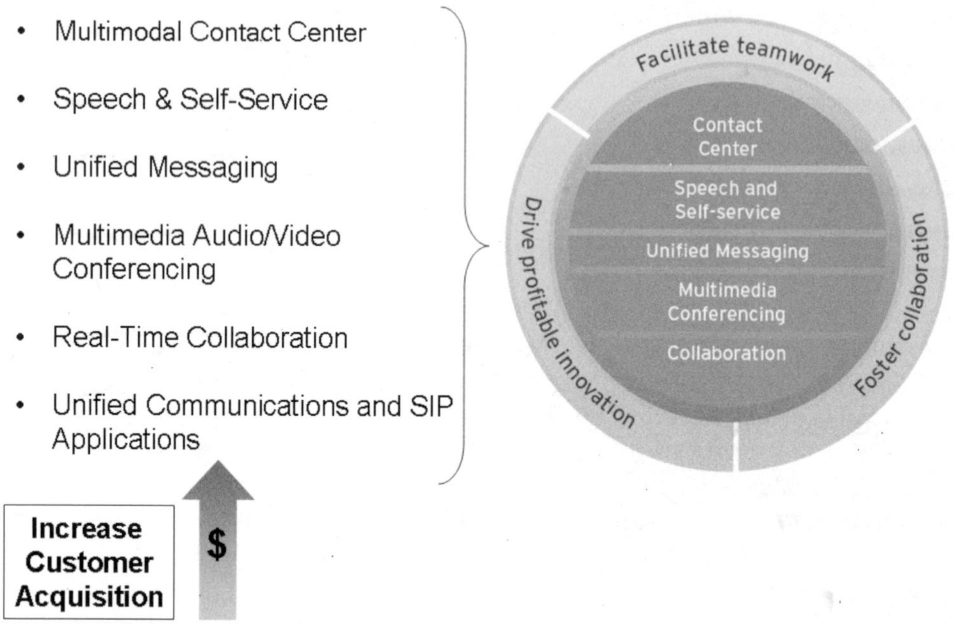

Multimodal Contact Center
Speech & Self-Service
Unified Messaging
Multimedia Audio/Video Conferencing
Real-Time Collaboration
Unified Communications and SIP Applications
Increase Customer Acquisition
$
Facilitate teamwork
Foster collaboration
Drive profitable innovation
Contact Center
Speech and Self-service
Unified Messaging
Multimedia Conferencing
Collaboration

FIGURE 6-7: ENHANCED CUSTOMER SERVICE DELIVERY.

High-Value Customer
Low-Value Customer
Preferred VIP Customer Service Agent
CRM
Voice
IM
E-mail
Fax
Video
Chat
SMS
Web
IVR Auto Attendant
Self-Serve Website

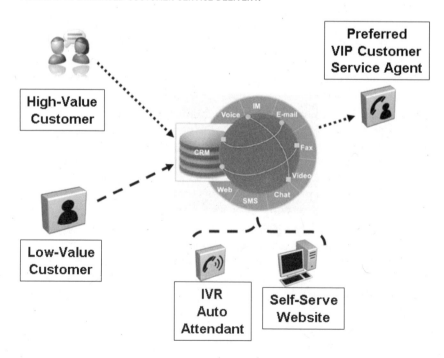

Solving customer relationship management business challenges with UC enablement

CRM is the key to managing an organization's customers and the relationship with those customers. Many organizations utilize a CRM application that stores historical information about customers, including a complete list of purchases. By analyzing and comparing customer purchasing history, organizations can identify their high-value and low-value customers, and develop specific strategies to transform low-value customers into high-value customers.

Considering the challenges that can be solved through a focused customer-service business strategy coupled with a back-end CRM application; the possibilities for enhanced customer service delivery are endless. Imagine what integrating UC with customer service delivery can provide for high-value customers when real-time, first-response problem resolution can be delivered consistently. When customer service agents have real-time access to customer information, delays in providing answers to customers can also be reduced.

The following list shows the key business benefits that CRM applications and deployments can provide for organizations:

- lowers cost of recruiting customers through strengthened customer loyalty and retention strategies

- allows organizations to focus attention on high-value customers and provide preferred and customized services

- reduces sales costs when conducting push marketing campaigns, when selling to the existing customer base, and when internal resources assist with inside sales and telemarketing

- provides the foundation for long-term customer lifetime value profitability

- increases customer retention and loyalty through "customized" services

The benefits of CRM deployments, coupled with an enhanced customer service strategy, can be measured by analyzing financial performance. This analysis should focus on customer acquisition and retention. Organizations that have both customer acquisition and retention strategies can improve their revenue and profitability. Because CRM applications are directly related to revenue and profits, many organizations can financially justify the implementation of these applications. CRM applications can also be paired with UC applications to gain additional benefits.

Properly implemented, these CRM applications can provide the following solutions and benefits for organizations:

- **Drive revenue**—Create and execute a targeted customer acquisition and retention strategy.

- **Improve customer loyalty**—Data mine customer history and create customized service delivery capabilities for high-value customers.

- **Lower operational costs**—Create, simplify, and target smaller marketing plans and campaigns based on data mining intelligence and customer buying behavior.

- **Provide real-time access to customer data**—Force a mapping and work flow analysis of customer data, where it goes, and where it resides.

- **Support an enhanced customer service delivery strategy**—Integrate a back-end CRM application and solution with UC enablement.

CRM applications and solutions provide the necessary infrastructure to allow various departments within an organization to conduct data mining and analysis of customer-buying patterns and behaviors. Figure 6-8 shows enhanced customer service delivery based on analysis of existing customer data.

FIGURE 6-8: ENHANCED CUSTOMER SERVICE DELIVERY.

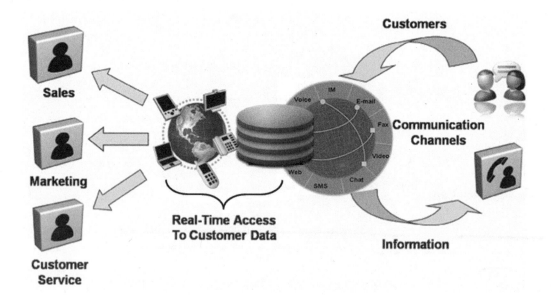

There are many benefits of using a CRM application to learn more about your customer base. Sales organizations can better understand the product and services mix and volume that their customers currently purchase. Sales and marketing campaigns can be targeted to low-value customers in an effort to increase sales and revenue. Marketing organizations thrive on a better understanding of the customer base's demographics and who purchases what products and services and where. Customer service organizations can benefit from CRM intelligence used categorize customer types based on revenue and profitability, allowing the business to distinguish between high-value and low-value customers. CRM applications and reporting allow sales executives, marketing personnel, and customer service managers to develop and align a strategy for customer service that focuses on a unique set of customer types.

CRM data is typically introduced into a cyclical process where organizations can continuously collect, analyze, and assess customer information, purchasing patterns, and buying behavior. Purchasing, inventory management, SCM, and financial planning requirements can be analyzed by managers who need to make critical business decisions based on historical data and trends. A typical CRM process includes the four steps shown in Figure 6-9.

FIGURE 6-9: CRM AS A PROCESS.

1. Knowledge Discovery

2. Marketing Planning

3. Customer Interaction

4. Analysis & Refinement

CRM, coupled with customer service delivery strategies, can help drive top line revenue and, ultimately, shareholder value. This is depicted in Figure 6-10, where the value drivers of a CRM and customer service delivery strategy are linked to financial performance and metrics.

FIGURE 6-10: CRM AND CUSTOMER SERVICE BUSINESS VALUE.

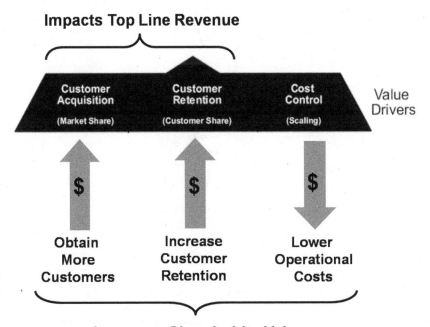

Solving supply change management business challenges with UC enablement

Earlier in this chapter, you learned the business value of SCM and how lowering the cost of goods sold can impact revenue and profitability. As fuel costs increase, shipping expenses will erode an organization's profitability unless they are passed on to the customer. In this case,

SCM can directly impact profitability. It is critical for organizations to track, monitor, and understand their supply chain costs in real time.

It is critical to measure the performance of SCM and its impact on internal and external business processes that affect the cost of goods sold to evaluate the SCM solution's overall performance. By tracking and monitoring key performance indicators (KPIs) and metrics, supply chain managers can make critical business decisions in real time, especially when suppliers or distributors have delivery problems. This is shown in Figure 6-11.

FIGURE 6-11: SCM PROCESSES AND KPIS.

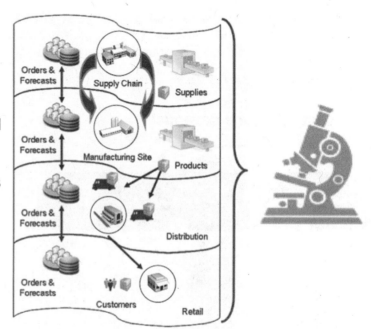

- Product Volume
- Sales Orders
- Market Share
- Cost of Goods Sold
- Quality Control
- Inventory Holdings
- Delivery Schedules
- Cycle Times
- Assets Utilized
- Responsiveness
- Customer Service

SCM and its processes extend beyond the physical organization. Organizations typically build long-term relationships with vendors or suppliers that have been preselected as business partners. Many business ecosystems must be built among the purchaser, the supplier, and the distributor or shipper.

Within the supplier network, UC enablement can support both real-time presence and real-time collaboration between purchasers and suppliers in times of crisis. Time sensitivity and advance purchasing in real time are critical to maintaining JIT inventory and JIT manufacturing production schedules. UC enablement between purchaser and supplier is critical, especially with emergency sales orders that must be fulfilled. Nurturing these relationships with suppliers and partners will contribute to lower supply costs and prioritization when requesting raw materials.

Within the distribution network, delivery, fulfillment, logistics, and shipping typically require extensive tracking, monitoring, and reporting in real time. This is critical to ensure that products and goods are delivered to customers in the most efficient and cost-effective manner. Monitoring these transactions and relationships will result in the lowest possible shipping and handling costs for product delivery. When shipping and handling costs are passed on to the customer, this increases the final product price. When shipping and handling costs are absorbed by the manufacturer, it is critical to know those costs in real time so that they are included in the price during the initial sale.

Finally, an SCM ecosystem must be built based on a customer service strategy where SCM, CRM, and customer service delivery work hand-in-hand to deliver real-time customer information. This could be for an order or shipment, or for a sales and marketing campaign to drive additional revenue and profitability. When the SCM infrastructure can be linked to a CRM application, customer service delivery can be enhanced by providing real-time access to order status. Tracking and linking high-value customer orders separately from low-value customer orders is important when attempting to deliver enhanced customer service delivery solutions.

Figure 6-12 shows the linkage among SCM infrastructure and the supplier network, distribution network, and customer service delivery.

FIGURE 6-12: SCM EXTENDS BEYOND THE ORGANIZATION.

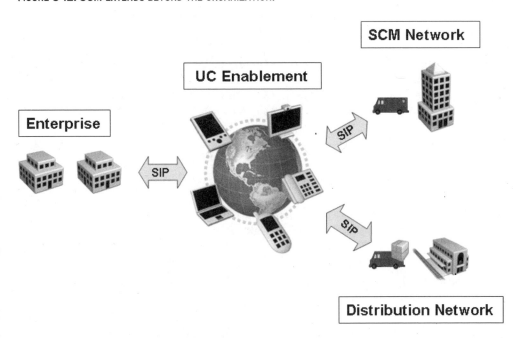

SCM extends to both the supplier network and the distribution network. Because SCM infrastructures are dependent on business partners, real-time communications must also extend to these business partners. This requires linking IP networks together and opening federations between organizations. VoIP and SIP protocols must extend and pass through firewalls. This allows UC and real-time applications like presence and availability, IM chat, collaboration, and audio and video conferencing to be supported from one desktop or PDA to another desktop or PDA. UC enablement solves the human latency business challenge and allows organizations to make critical business decisions in real time. Extending federations allows partners to communicate in real time with one another.

To extend UC enablement beyond the organization, policies must be defined to allow VoIP and SIP protocols to pass through each organization's secured IP networks and firewalls. Federation policy definitions and security solutions must be incorporated into both organizations' security infrastructure, as depicted in Figure 6-13.

FIGURE 6-13: EXTENDING THE UC FEDERATION.

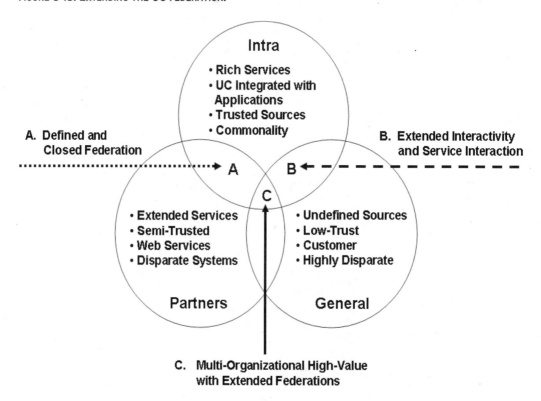

C. Multi-Organizational High-Value
    with Extended Federations

SCM ecosystems are ideally suited for Web-enabled and online VoIP, convergence, and UC enablement. These ecosystems are particularly suitable due to the time-sensitive nature of purchasing products and raw materials and to the need for on-time delivery of finished products to the customer.

Many organizations nurture and build long-term partnerships and multiyear purchasing agreements based on predefined business rule sets, such as pricing structures and market fluctuations. These business relationships can foster lower supply costs, long-term negotiated pricing discounts, and deeper integration between business processes and software interfaces. The more you use SCM processes to automate, streamline, and eliminate human latency, the greater the cost savings and long-term potential benefits. This requires relationship management and real-time communications when problems arise in the supply or distribution network. Real-time collaboration with multiple suppliers or distributors can help solve supply and delivery problems that must be identified quickly and resolved in real time. UC is ideally suited to solve this business communication challenge. Figure 6-14 shows how UC can be extended to suppliers and distributors.

FIGURE 6-14: EXTENDING UC ENABLEMENT TO SUPPLIERS AND DISTRIBUTORS.

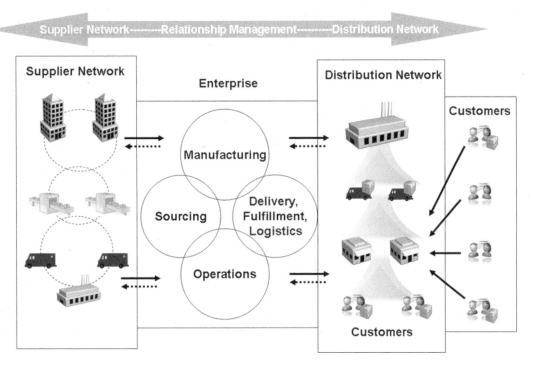

Time is a critical success factor for a successful SCM solution. Organizations must be able to build a competitive advantage on the basis of time. There are many inefficient processes within SCM that can contribute to lost time: missed service orders from sales ordering, supply ordering, manufacturing production scheduling, quality control, inventory, distribution, delivery, fulfillment and logistics, and final sale to the customer, where payment is then collected. These inefficiencies can be controlled through a well-balanced process cycle time strategy.

Cycle time is the measured amount of time required to complete a specific business process, and human intervention is often a major contributory factor. All SCM business processes and functions should have cycle time analyzed for potential reduction and streamlining. Reducing process cycle time can help solve many enterprise SCM infrastructure business challenges. The following list summarizes the time value of money within SCM infrastructures:

Time to market—The amount of time from marketing to sale to finished product and delivery to the marketplace.

Time to sale—The amount of time required to conduct an actual sale, obtain a customer purchase order or requisition, and book the order into the business's sales order entry system.

Time to obtain supplies—The amount of time to acquire supplies and goods for JIT inventory and purchasing to support JIT manufacturing.

Time to manufacture—The amount of time required to produce the product: typically aligned with JIT inventory.

Time in inventory and shipping—The amount of time the product sits in inventory or on a shelf in a warehouse, prior to being shipped to the customer.

Time latency must be reduced where possible to create a competitive advantage and to lower operational costs. Human latency and business decision-making latency are best approached with UC enablement and real-time access to key SCM business managers. The importance of time and cycle time reduction is shown in Figure 6-15.

FIGURE 6-15: IMPORTANCE OF TIME TO SCM INFRASTRUCTURES.

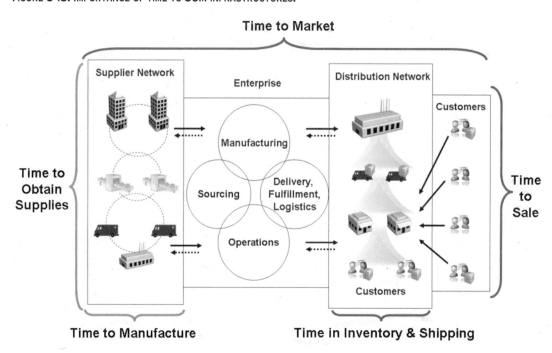

Solving enterprise resource planning business challenges with UC enablement

Earlier, you learned that ERP systems can provide accurate real-time access to financials for key business managers. With real-time access to sales order entry information and SCM information, managers can change the priority of manufacturing production cycles. This might be based on raw materials and supplies information, revenue and profitability of the order, or whether an order is from a high-value or a low-value customer. Real-time access to key managers and subject matter experts means that decisions can be made collaboratively with other managers providing input in real time, all through UC enablement. If this information were not readily available, it would be difficult for a manager to make prioritized decisions.

ERP can provide the entire organization with accurate and timely information that shows how the organization is operating. With predefined KPIs or metrics, managers can access real-time metrics and assess how the company is currently operating, particularly from a financial perspective.

ERP systems provide the following solutions for organizations:

- integration of business process with financial systems to perform real-time tracking and access to information and data

- integration of real-time financial data and flow of financial transactions throughout the organization's functions, departments, and processes

- streamlined operational processes mapped to financials (Accounting General Ledger (G/L), Accounts Receivable (AR), Accounts Payable (AP)) so that the actual cost of goods sold for an order can be tracked and monitored throughout the SCM infrastructure

- real-time access to financial information that supports critical decision making, particularly when high-value customer orders are involved

Figure 6-16 depicts an enterprise ERP system with software modules supporting different functions. KPIs and real-time financials are readily accessible to those in executive management responsible for making critical decisions.

Leading ERP software vendors generally build modularized ERP applications that support the major functional areas of an organization. ERP software modules integrate the major functions within a single ERP framework, such as sales order entry, purchasing, production planning, financial accounting, management accounting, and human resources. ERP software modules are fully integrated under a common umbrella and can typically be purchased and customized one module at a time, offering a phased migration and implementation plan.

ERP systems replace the disparate IT systems that have evolved within legacy IT infrastructures. These legacy systems require application program interfaces (APIs) and software interfaces to extract data from the systems. With full integration and financial metrics embedded within ERP software modules, a business can rapidly access its accurate and real-time financial data. Sound decisions can be made based on financial priorities, analysis of profitability, and high-value versus low-value customer orders.

Organizations benefit from implementing an ERP system because they can identify and track costs associated with specific processes. If you can track cost elements for each process, you can better identify necessary improvements. There are only two ways to increase gross profit margin: increase the selling price, or lower the costs of goods sold. Enterprises can lower the cost of goods sold by lowering their operational, supply, and manufacturing costs. Tracking, monitoring, and reporting on operational costs and costs of goods sold in real time become critical ERP KPIs. With accurate financial data, managers equipped with UC enablement can identify which managers are available to assist in critical decision making.

FIGURE 6-16: CONSOLIDATED ERP SYSTEM WITH SOFTWARE MODULES.

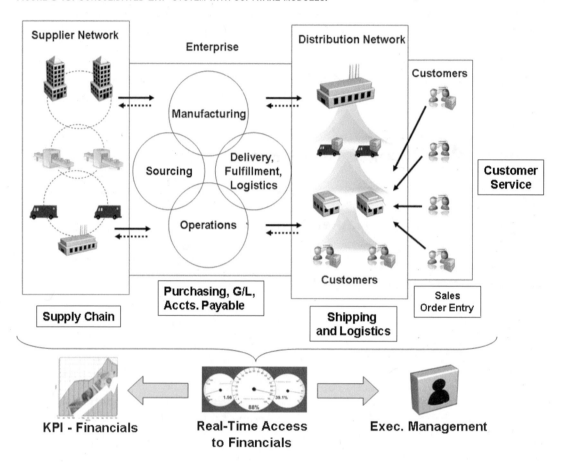

ERP systems that have a unified view into key processes can be used to create a competitive advantage. This starts with the successful implementation of an ERP system and can achieve the following goals:

- maximizing throughput of information to those who need it now

- minimizing downtime to customers, suppliers, and distributors with real-time communications and UC enablement

- pushing decision making down to the lowest appropriate level or through automated business rule sets to minimize human latency in decision making

- providing real-time access to critical information and other managers to make decisions based on financial priorities

- integrating information throughout the supply chain so cost of goods sold can be tracked in real time as conditions change

- reducing cycle time and lowering operational costs through streamlined processes and integration of UC solutions between the organization and its suppliers and distributors

The following list presents some KPIs for ERP implementation success:

- quickened information response time, particularly financial information

- increased interaction across the enterprise through real-time collaboration and decision making

- improved order management and sales cycle by integrating sales order entry systems with back-end financials and real-time costs of goods sold information

- decreased financial close cycle through SFA and integrated sales order entry systems

- improved and enhanced customer service delivery by having customer service agents UC-enabled with access to SCM, CRM, and ERP financials specific to a customer or customer order

- improved on-time delivery through real-time tracking and monitoring of SCM distribution and delivery of finished products

- improved interaction with SCM process and infrastructures, allowing customer service agents to have real-time information about a customer order

- reduced operational costs through streamlined processes and automated decision making based on predefined rule sets

- integrated sales order entry system with JIT inventory, purchasing, and manufacturing

ERP is a critical component to an organization's overall strategy. In essence, ERP is the infrastructure that allows an organization to implement its business plan. Competitive advantage is all about speed, responsiveness, revenue, and profitability. UC enablement brings real-time access to people and critical decision making, using ERP systems and financials as the source of information.

Solving sales force management business challenges with UC enablement

With SFA, the solution to solving the human latency challenge is found by enabling UC within the inside, outside, and presales support organization. Sales professionals are on the front line, meeting customer requirements and solving their challenges. Depending on the product or service that is sold, sales professionals may be heavily dependent on subject matter experts or other technical support specialists to provide real-time answers to customer questions.

Solving the SFA challenge starts with enterprise transformation analysis of current sales functions and processes. Streamlining the sales and order entry process requires assessment of both external and internal processes, as shown in Figure 6-17.

FIGURE 6-17: SFA EXAMINES BOTH EXTERNAL AND INTERNAL PROCESSES.

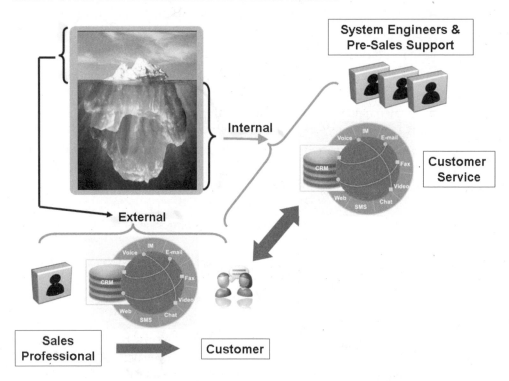

Sales professionals have unique goals and objectives. SFA goals and objectives should be defined and articulated by sales professionals as part of the overall process of streamlining sales functions and processes. Examples of SFA goals from a sales professional's perspective, and the challenges that they solve, include the following:

- Eliminate manual sales order entry processes in favor of e-forms for secure, remote, or browser-accessible sales order entry (cycle time reduction).

- Automate sales order reporting for sales management (cycle time reduction).

- Provide real-time access to customer data and information, enhancing customer service delivery (customer loyalty and retention).

- Improve sales staff training with SFA tools and applications and streamlined processes to improve morale and motivate staff to sell and close more (sales staff retention, saves on hiring and retraining).

- Enhance communications and collaboration among sales, subject matter experts, technical solution specialists, sales overlays teams, and support personnel (productivity enhancements supported by UC enablement).

- Minimize administrative time during periods of low sales, providing greater deal flow volume per salesperson (increased revenue and profitability through greater deal flow).

Sales managers often have different goals and objectives than the general sales staff for SFA and reporting. Sales managers are typically concerned with the following:

• Gathering call sheets from various salespeople and tabulating the results. With SFA, sales managers can track in real time current revenue, profit, and forecasted deal flow (cycle time reduction).

• Analyzing and tracking sales activity reports, information requests, orders booked, and other sales information, allowing the sales manager to respond directly with advice, in-stock verifications, and discount authorizations. This gives management more hands-on control of the sales process if they wish to use it (productivity enhancement and cycle time reduction).

• Automating approvals and discounts based on predefined rule sets and metrics (cycle time reduction).

Sales organizations are typically supported by marketing campaigns and programs targeted to specific customer types. Sales order information that is incorporated into back-end CRM applications provides marketing organizations with the information to create and build unique marketing, focused for specific customer types. Data mining customer sales orders provides vital information to marketing organizations, allowing them to do the following:

• understand the economic structure of their organization

• identify segments within different markets and demographics

• distinguish between high-value and low-value customers

• understand competitors and their products and solutions when deals or sales orders are lost

• base future product development and product enhancements on feedback from customers and changing requirements

• develop marketing strategies for each product line using the marketing mix variables of price, product, distribution, and promotion

• coordinate the sales function with other parts of the promotional mix such as advertising, sales promotion, and public relations

• create a sustainable competitive advantage through continuous life cycle product marketing and sales execution

Integrating SFA with ERP systems and applications provides a complete financial picture for booked and closed sales orders. This integration also helps forecast sales orders and allows sales management to make sound decisions based on financial priorities. SFA is typically a function within ERP infrastructures and can be purchased or integrated as a software module within the ERP platform. SFA, coupled with UC, can solve many customer, supplier, partner, and sales management business communication challenges. The consolidation of customer, SFA, and ERP data provides organizations with a powerful SFA, ERP, and customer service delivery solution for all customers from presales to postsales, as shown in Figure 6-18.

FIGURE 6-18: SFA AND REAL-TIME ACCESS TO CUSTOMER DATA.

- SFA_UC can provide real-time access to customer, supplier, distributor, and financial information.

- SFA_UC can be integrated with ERP sales order entry, SCM, and back-end CRM systems providing sales professionals with real-time access to customer data and information.

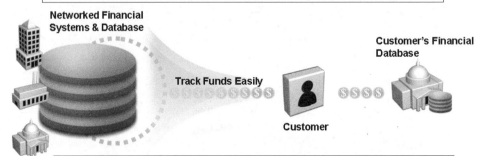

Networked Financial
Systems & Database

Track Funds Easily

Customer's Financial
Database

Customer

- SFA_UC can also provide sales professionals with real-time access to key subject matter experts and pre-sales support specialists.

- SFA_UC also links sales managers with sales professionals when inquiries must be supported in real-time.

SFA with UC enablement can be implemented both externally between sales professionals and customers, and internally between sales professionals and subject matter experts or technical solutions specialists. Reduced cycle time and reduced overall sales cycle time results in increased revenue faster, allowing more sales and deals to be pursued by sales professionals.

Knowledge Check 6-1: Solving Business Challenges

Answer the following questions. Answers to these Knowledge Check questions are located in *Appendix A: Answers to Knowledge Check Questions.*

1. Which of the following is not a potential benefit of UC enablement?

   a. Reduced real estate costs

   b. Reduced training expenses

   c. Cycle time reduction in decision making

   d. Real-time collaboration with team members

   e. Increased complexity of IT and decreased productivity

2. How can UC enablement enhance customer loyalty?

   a. By providing real-time access to sales professionals

   b. By offering lower cost customer service delivery solutions

   c. By providing presence and availability and IM chat functionality on a Web site

   d. All of the above

   e. None of the above

3. SOA is a new way to develop and deliver software applications and solutions based on software modules that are reusable.

   a. True

   b. False

4. SOA combines people-to-people communications, processes, and which of the following?

   a. Information

   b. Software modules

   c. Cost of goods sold

   d. Application programming interfaces (APIs)

   e. None of the above

5. An organization can implement an enhanced customer service delivery strategy by doing which of the following?

   a. Implementing a back-end CRM application and system

   b. Distinguishing between high-value versus low-value customers

   c. Diverting high-value customers to preferred or VIP customer service agents

   d. Diverting low-value customers to self-service Web sites and automated attendants

   e. All of the above

6. Investments in customer service solutions and technologies can be cost justified with a financial return on investment analysis.

   a. True

   b. False

7. CRM applications data warehouse which of the following?

   a. Real-time financials

   b. Current product inventory levels

   c. Manufacturing production schedules

   d. Customer purchasing history information

   e. None of the above

8. If an organization does not have a back-end CRM application or system, it cannot build an enhanced customer service strategy.

   a. True

   b. False

9. In SCM, which of the following KPIs or metrics is focused on elimination of human delay or latency in business decision making?

   a. Cost of supplies

   b. Cycle time reduction

   c. Lower cost of goods sold

   d. Cost of distribution and shipping

   e. None of the above

10. When communicating using VoIP and UC with your business partners, suppliers, and distributors, you must do which of the following?

   a. Define a security policy to allow VoIP and SIP protocols through both organization's IP firewalls

   b. Identify who and what endpoint devices will be allowed to communicate using UC solutions

   c. Extend the federation beyond your organization to allow VoIP and SIP protocols to permeate firewalls

   d. Enable UC applications such as presence and availability, IM chat, audio and video conferencing, and collaboration

   e. All of the above

11. ERP systems provide real-time access to accurate financial information for business managers to do what?

   a. Plan for fiscal year budgeting

   b. Analyze annual profits and losses

   c. Analyze annual growth in relation to overhead

   d. Determine revenue growth from previous fiscal year

   e. Make critical business decisions based on financial priorities and impact

12. ERP systems do not provide granular financial cost elements or information about a business function or process.

   a. True

   b. False

13. Shrinking the sales cycle can generate revenue and profit faster for an organization.

   a. True

   b. False

14. Which of the following provides a UC productivity enhancement for sales professionals?

   a. CRM applications integrated with customer service

   b. Manual data entry into the sales order entry system back at the branch office

   c. Manual, case-by-case approvals from sales managers for customer discounts

   d. Real-time access to presales support specialists, subject matter experts, and technical specialists via presence, availability, IM chat, and collaboration

   e. None of the above

Chapter summary

Organizations have many business application and process challenges. These challenges must first be identified and assessed through enterprise transformation analysis. The results of this analysis will identify specific areas for function and process improvement. Solutions that provide UC enablement and real-time access to key decision makers offer answers to your specific business challenges.

SOA, CS, CRM, SCM, ERP, and SFA each offer opportunities to reduce human latency and decision making. Through UC enablement, organizations can virtually connect internal employees and external business partners, suppliers, and distributors through the extension of the communications federation. UC enablement offers organizations the opportunity to enhance productivity, communicate in real time, and create a unique competitive advantage.

7: Mapping the Solution to Technology

In previous chapters, you learned about business applications, business processes, and the challenges that arise while growing profitability and maintaining a competitive advantage. Solving these challenges requires multiple approaches, including enterprise transformation, streamlined processes, an overall people-to-people communications system with embedded Unified Communications (UC) functions, and an information dissemination plan. Solving these challenges has many benefits, such as real-time access to key decision makers and lowered operational costs through implementation of audio and video conferencing and collaboration. In this chapter, you will learn how to map these solutions to technology and UC enablement.

Chapter 7 Topics

In this chapter, you will learn:

- how to map service-oriented architecture (SOA) solutions with convergence technologies and UC enablement

- how to map customer service (CS) solutions with convergence technologies, multimodal contact centers, and UC enablement for enhanced CS delivery

- how to map customer relationship management (CRM) with a CS-focused delivery strategy to provide real-time access to customer information

- how to map supply chain management (SCM) productivity enhancements with convergence technologies and UC enablement to reduce cycle time

- how to map enterprise resource planning (ERP) to convergence technologies and UC enablement for real-time access to financials and decision making

- how to map sales force automation (SFA) to internal and external communications and back-office systems for real-time presales responsiveness and streamlined order entry

Chapter 7 Goals

Upon completion of this chapter, you will be able to:

- describe how to map processes and applications to convergence technologies and UC enablement

- recommend solutions for SOA, CS, CRM, SCM, ERP, and SFA that incorporate convergence and UC enablement

- map UC benefits to productivity-enhancing solutions that enhance productivity or lower operational costs

Key Terms

Functional requirement 144

Mapping the requirements to
  a solution 144

Profit and loss (P&L) 159

Securities and Exchange
  Commission (SEC) 158

Statement of work (SOW) 145

Technical requirements 143

UC enablement 143

Mapping the solution to technology and UC enablement

In the previous chapter, you learned about the following applications, processes, and technologies:

- **Service-oriented architecture (SOA)**—Modular and reusable software applications that incorporate people-to-people communications, processes, and information dissemination into a specific business application and solution.

- **Customer service (CS)**—A multimodal contact center with integrated UC functions that provides an enhanced customer service delivery solution to support both high- and low-value customers.

- **Customer relationship management (CRM)**—Customer service enhancement with back-end integration of customer information, purchasing history, and buying patterns to support intelligent customer data mining and information analysis with real-time access.

- **Supply chain management (SCM)**—UC enablement integrated into processes and decision making to reduce cycle time and increase operational efficiency throughout the supply chain and distribution channels.

- **Enterprise resource planning (ERP)**—An enterprise-wide financial system integrated with UC enablement that enables critical business decisions to be made based on financial priorities.

- **Sales force automation (SFA)**—Integration of internal and external presales and real-time communications through UC enablement in an effort to shorten the sales cycle and generate revenue faster.

The following examples demonstrate how to map solutions to technology and UC enablement in a variety of business settings. Figure 7-1 shows how solutions are mapped to technologies by defining required functional and technical requirements and identifying technological alternatives.

FIGURE 7-1: SOLVING BUSINESS CHALLENGES.

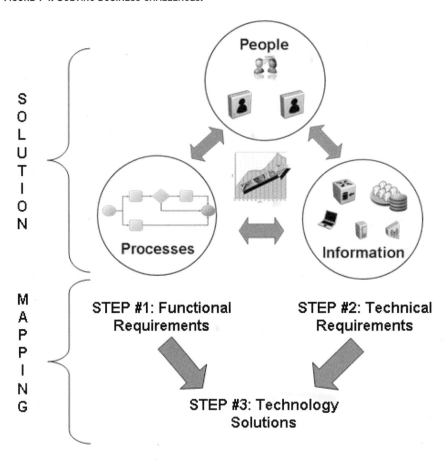

The process of mapping solutions to technology and UC enablement typically begins with the following steps:

- **Step 1: Define functional requirements**—People-to-people communications, streamlined processes (enterprise transformation analysis results), and information dissemination (real-time access to information).

- **Step 2: Define technical requirements**—Technical requirements and solutions that support the identified functional requirements.

- **Step 3: Map the requirements to technology solutions**—Specific technology elements and their costs, such as hardware, software, network, security, and UC software licenses

After functional and technical requirements have been mapped to technology solutions, the UC project is defined with the following steps:

- **Step 4: Create the statement of work**—The statement of work (SOW) defines specific tasks, deliverables, and scope for the UC project. In addition, the SOW identifies critical factors for a successful UC deployment.

- **Step 5: Implement the systems integration**—Perform tasks that lead to the deliverables defined in the SOW.

- **Step 6: Track and monitor the key performance indicators (KPIs) aligned to a financial return on investment (ROI) model**—Measure the project's overall success with metrics that track, monitor, and justify the financial investment for a UC project.

The business applications and process examples in this chapter illustrate how requirements are defined and mapped to technology solutions. In subsequent chapters, the examples show how UC projects are implemented. These UC project implementation steps are presented in detail to help ensure the success of UC projects in your organization. For example, sample SOW documents and UC project plans offer solutions and tips for a successful UC deployment. In Chapter 8, "Building a Measurable Financial ROI with KPIs," you will learn about the Forrester Consulting UC Business Value Tool v1.5 and how it can be used to build a financial ROI model to justify UC enablement for an organization.

Mapping the solution to SOA applications and UC enablement

SOA applications, integrated with UC enablement, can enhance patient care delivery in hospitals, operating rooms, emergency rooms, and trauma centers. Because these processes have life-and-death implications, it is important to streamline them.

Patient care delivery becomes more efficient when people-to-people communication, new streamlined processes, and real-time access to patient care information are mapped to specific solutions. In this enhanced patient care services model, mapping the solution begins by identifying SOA applications that streamline and automate manual processes, and mapping the functional requirements of doctors, nurses, specialists, and administrative personnel to the streamlined processes. Table 7-1 shows a sample functional requirements matrix for this environment.

TABLE 7-1: ENHANCED PATIENT CARE DELIVERY FUNCTIONAL REQUIREMENTS MATRIX.

	People-to-People Communications	Streamlined Processes	Real-Time Access to Information
Patients	Easy access to loved ones	Local/LD access	No
Relatives	Easy access to patient	Direct inward dialing (DID) access	No
Head Nurse	Real-time access to nurses	Mobile access to patient records	Yes

Floor Nurses	Real-time access to head nurse, lab, doctors, specialists	Mobile access to patient records	Yes
Doctor – On Duty	Real-time access to head nurse, lab, specialists, doctors	Mobile access to patient records	Yes
Doctor – Primary Care	Non-real-time access to nurses, specialists, doctors	Easy access to patient records	No
Specialists – On Duty	Real-time access to head nurse, lab, specialists, doctors	Mobile access, trauma, and emergency room procedures	Yes
Specialists – Off Duty	Non-real-time access to patient records	Postsurgical assessment and prognosis	No
Patient Intake and Release, Insurance Claims Processing	Fast and simple patient registration and intake/release	Self-service Web sites and kiosks and elimination of redundant data entry	Yes, for patient intake/release and claims processing

Table 7-1 shows some functional requirements for SOA applications with UC enablement. These requirements focus on real-time communications and access to patient information. Enhancing patient care services delivery requires that current processes and procedures be analyzed. SOA applications, coupled with UC enablement, can automate much of each identified process. This may include secure browser access to patient medical records, automatic retrieval of patient laboratory data, pop-up screens indicating patient allergies to medicines, and patient services checklists with embedded rule sets that require human intervention for screen closure. Streamlining and simplifying patient intake and release services, eliminating redundant data entry, and streamlining health care insurance claim processing all contribute to an enhanced patient care delivery service.

These functional requirements must be translated into technical requirements that encompass hardware, software, and systems integration tasks and deliverables as part of the overall solution. Table 7-2 shows how the functional requirements of patient care delivery might be mapped to technical requirements.

TABLE 7-2: ENHANCED PATIENT CARE DELIVERY FUNCTIONAL TO TECHNICAL REQUIREMENTS MAPPING.

	People-to-People Communications	Streamlined Processes	Real-Time Access to Information
Patients	Access to dial tone, VoIP, PSTN	Local/LD access	No
Relatives	Easy access to patient room by DID	DID access	No
Head Nurse	IP mobility, real-time presence, IM chat, text/MMS message, e-mail, collaboration	Mobile access to patient records and SOA services	From nurse stations, Wi-Fi PDAs or tablets, secure WLAN, and browser access
Floor Nurses	IP mobility, real-time presence, IM chat, text/MMS message, e-mail, voice	Mobile access to patient records and SOA services	From nurse stations, Wi-Fi PDAs or tablets, secure WLAN, and browser access
Doctor – On Duty	IP mobility, real-time presence, IM chat, text/MMS message, conference, collaboration	Mobile access to patient records and SOA services	By Wi-Fi PDAs or tablets, secure WLAN, browser access
Doctor – Primary Physician	E-mail, unified messaging, non-real-time communications	Easy access to patient records and SOA services	No
Specialists – On Duty	IP mobility, real-time presence, IM chat, text/MMS message, conference, collaboration	Simplified trauma procedures for lifesaving real-time collaboration	By Wi-Fi PDAs or tablets, secure WLAN, browser access to patient records
Specialists – Off Duty	Audio/video conferencing, e-mail, collaboration	Easy access to patient records	No
Patient Intake and Release, Insurance Claims Processing	Self-service and patient intake/release services	Elimination of redundant data entry and electronic verification of insurance coverage	By browser or self-service kiosks for patient intake/release processing

After the enhanced patient care delivery services solution has been mapped, the next step is to identify alternative technology solutions. Table 7-3 shows how alternative technology solutions can be derived from technical requirements.

TABLE 7-3: ENHANCED PATIENT CARE DELIVERY ALTERNATIVE TECHNOLOGY SOLUTIONS.

	People-to-People Communications	Streamlined Processes	Real-Time Access to Information
Patients	PBX/VoIP system with patient COS/ TAGR standardized configurations	Local/LD access	No
Relatives	DID access direct to patient room	DID access	No
Head Nurse	802.11b/g/I WLAN, IP mobile phones, browser access by UC-enabled PDAs, WLAN tablets	SOA application integration of UC and patient record system	Authenticated and encrypted browser access to patient privacy data
Floor Nurses	802.11b/g/i WLAN, IP mobile phones, browser access by UC-enabled PDAs, WLAN tablets	SOA application integration of UC and patient record system	Authenticated and encrypted browser access to patient privacy data
Doctor – On Duty	802.11b/g/i WLAN, IP mobile phones, browser access by UC-enabled PDAs, WLAN tablets	SOA application integration of UC and patient record system	Authenticated and encrypted browser access to patient privacy data
Doctor – Primary Physician	E-mail, unified messaging, non-real-time communications	Scheduled collaborative patient care analysis	No
Specialists – On Duty	802.11b/g/I WLAN, IP mobile phones, browser access by UC-enabled PDAs, WLAN tablets	SOA application integration of UC, emergency room, collaboration	Authenticated and encrypted browser access to patient privacy data
Specialists – Off Duty	Audio/video conferencing, e-mail, collaboration	Collaborative patient care analysis	No
Patient Intake and Release, Insurance Claims Processing	IVR – auto attendant, real-time Web access to patient registration system, online health insurance access	SOA services and integration of UC for real-time access to customer service	Authenticated and encrypted browser access to patient in/ out forms

This example demonstrates how functional and technical requirements can be incorporated into SOA application and process services delivery solutions for enhanced patient care delivery. SOA applications integrated with UC enablement can give medical personnel real-time access to critical patient care information, thus enhancing patient care services and reducing human latency in medical care.

> **Note**
>
> In the health care provider industry, UC-enabled SOA applications can solve the challenges of human delay and latency in patient care. This solution can become a significant customer retention tool by improving people-to-people communications, streamlining processes, and providing real-time access to patient information. This solution also enhances patient care and customer service delivery for real-time people-to-people communications. Patients rely on trust and open dialogue with their physicians and demand quick responsiveness when receiving medical services and processing medical insurance claims.

Mapping the solution to CS with CRM and UC enablement

The next example shows how to use UC-enabled SOA applications to build an enhanced customer service delivery strategy with differentiated services. The hotel and hospitality industry is highly competitive, and offers many brands and styles for both vacation and business travelers. Customer service can be significantly enhanced by solving the human and technology latency challenges of check-in and checkout. The most efficient solution to this challenge requires SOA applications integrated with back-end CRM systems, reservation systems, and Web Services delivery.

Another way to enhance customer service delivery is to extract high-value customer travel profile information from the CRM system. SOA-enabled reservation applications can use customer profile information to customize the guest's preferences into a streamlined and automated reservation confirmation that incorporates the customer's predefined preferences for reservation confirmation e-mails, real-time text messages, and IM chat.

SOA-enabled applications integrate people-to-people communications with streamlined processes to deliver real-time reservation information. They can also provide value-added information, such as directions to the hotel sent automatically to a mobile device upon confirmation that the traveler's flight has landed. This can drive customer loyalty and retention, and, ultimately, long-term revenue and profitability.

> SOA-enabled applications can provide up-to-the-second confirmations, instructions, and emergency update messages from the moment a traveler's flight lands. Solving the standing-in-line latency challenge for vacation and business travelers results in long-term customer retention, loyalty, and repeat business, as well as increased revenue and profitability for the hotel company.

Table 7-4 shows functional requirements for the hotel and hospitality industry. In this example, enhanced customer service delivery, coupled with a CRM system, differentiates high-value from low-value customers. CRM systems also help to monitor customer loyalty and retention, based on customer lifetime value and purchasing history.

TABLE 7-4: ENHANCED TRAVELER CUSTOMER SERVICE DELIVERY FUNCTIONAL REQUIREMENTS MATRIX.

	People-to-People Communications	Streamlined Processes	Real-Time Access to Information
Vacation Traveler (High-Value)	Easy-to-use customer service via toll-free number and Web	Self-service features on both toll-free number and Web	Yes, customer reservations, account information
Business Traveler (High-Value)	Immediate access to live customer service agent, 24-hour access to account through Web	Automated traveler profile mapping, enhanced check-in/out services	Online access to account and frequent-traveler information
Customer Service Toll-Free Number Access	UC-enabled contact center, differentiated services for high-value vs. low-value customers	Self-service interactive voice response (IVR), automated attendant	Reservations and CRM data
Online Customer Service – Web Site with VoIP, IM Chat, E-mail	UC-enabled contact center, real-time access to preferred agents via VoIP or IM chat through Web	Online room preference and hotel services requests, in advance, concierge e-mails	Real-time access to reservations, CRM data, hotel frequent-traveler information
Hotel Registration Front Desk Clerk	Real-time access to manager on duty, maintenance, room service, housekeeping, and security personnel	Streamlined hotel back-office procedures, high-value concierge services	Real-time access to reservations, CRM data, hotel frequent traveler information, concierge services
Hotel Manager on Duty	Real-time access to front desk, maintenance, room service, housekeeping, and security personnel	Streamlined hotel back-office procedures	Real-time access to reservations, CRM data, hotel frequent traveler information, concierge services

When an SOA solution is used to separate high-value and low-value travel customers, it is important to identify customers who have both vacation and business travel profiles. These are the highest value customers, because they have the strongest brand loyalty. Most business travelers use the same brand of hotel for vacation travel to maximize frequent traveler awards points. Providing targeted customer services to these customers will contribute to customer loyalty and retention, which leads to long-term revenue and profitability.

Tracking high-value customer lifetime value can be managed with enhanced customer service delivery through UC-enabled SOA applications. Travelers want secure access to self-service Web applications, and real-time access to high-value customer service agents when needed. Table 7-5 shows how SOA software solutions and UC enablement can be mapped to requirements within an enhanced customer service delivery strategy to help solve the hotel and hospitality industry's customer service challenge.

TABLE 7-5: ENHANCED TRAVELER CUSTOMER SERVICE DELIVERY FUNCTIONS MAPPED TO TECHNICAL REQUIREMENTS.

	People-to-People Communications	Streamlined Processes	Real-Time Access to Information
Vacation Traveler (High-Value)	IVR, auto attendant, skills-based routing, real-time preferred agents, presence, IM chat, collaboration	Access to enhanced reservation system, self-service account functionality	Customer account and reservation information; last-minute frequent flyer reward submittals
Business Traveler (High-Value)	IVR, auto attendant, skills-based routing, real-time preferred agents, presence, IM chat, collaboration	Real-time access to preferred agents, reservation system, self-service account	Customer account and reservation information, last-minute award program submittals
Customer Service Toll-Free Number Access	UC-enabled contact center, real-time presence, IM chat, preferred agents, text/MMS message, e-mail, collaboration	Real-time access to CRM and customer data delivered by SOA services, preferred agents	CRM and customer profile information, account and reservation information
Online Customer Service – Web Site with VoIP, IM Chat, E-mail	UC-enabled contact center, real-time presence, IM chat, preferred agents, text/MMS message, e-mail, collaboration	Real-time access to CRM and customer data delivered by SOA services, preferred agents	CRM and customer profile information, account and reservation information

7 | Mapping the Solution to Technology

Hotel Registration Front Desk Clerk	IP mobility, real-time presence, IM chat, text/MMS message, conference, collaboration	Real-time access to hotel back-office systems by secure browser	CRM and customer profile information, account and reservation information
Hotel Manager on Duty	IP mobility, real-time presence, IM chat, text/MMS message, conference, collaboration	Real-time access to hotel back-office systems by secure browser	CRM and customer profile information and hotel back-office systems

Once the enhanced traveler customer service delivery strategy is formulated, functional and technical requirements can be mapped to technology solutions. Typically, high-value customers are mapped to more expensive customer service delivery strategies, and low-value customers are paired with less expensive strategies. To do so, identify alternative technology solutions and determine the UC systems integration tasks and deliverables. Table 7-6 shows how the following alternative technology solutions can be derived.

TABLE 7-6: ENHANCED TRAVELER CUSTOMER SERVICE DELIVERY ALTERNATIVE TECHNOLOGY SOLUTIONS.

	People-to-People Communications	Streamlined Processes	Real-Time Access to Information
Vacation Traveler (High-Value)	Toll-free number access, differentiated services, IVR, auto attendant, real-time access with UC enablement	Easy access to reservation and frequent traveler information	Reservations, account information, and travel awards submittals
Business Traveler (High-Value)	Toll-free number preferred agent access, real-time Web access with UC enablement	Reservation system, CRM and frequent traveler program fully integrated	Preferred agents, personal account, and reservation information
Customer Service Toll-Free Number Access	Multimodal contact center with UC enablement and differentiated services	SOA integration of CRM and customer profile data with automated services	Preferred agents, personal account, and reservation information

Online Customer Service - Web Site with VoIP, IM Chat, E-mail	Multimodal contact center with UC enablement, real-time: presence, preferred agent, IM chat, text message, collaboration	SOA integration of CRM and customer profile data with automated services	Preferred agents, personal account, and reservation information
Hotel Registration Front Desk Clerk	802.11b/g/i WLAN, IP mobile phones, browser access through UC-enabled PDAs, cell phones	SOA integration of reservation and CRM systems with UC enablement	Preferred agents, personal account, and reservation information
Hotel Manager on Duty	802.11b/g/i WLAN, IP mobile phones, browser access through UC-enabled PDAs, cell phones	SOA integration of hotel back-office systems with UC enablement	Hotel back-office systems and real-time access to 24/7 operational personnel

7 | Mapping the Solution to Technology

Note

Hotel and hospitality organizations can create a competitive advantage by implementing differentiated customer service through SOA, CRM, and enhanced CS delivery strategies. This strategy requires distinguishing between high- and low-value customer services. Technologically aware high-value customers may receive real-time access to information and travel updates, whereas low-value customers are directed to low-value self-service IVRs, automated attendants, and offshore contact centers. Both vacation and business travelers want fast, effortless access to reservations and confirmations to avoid waiting in lines.

Mapping the solution to SCM and UC enablement

SCM is another area where functional requirements can be mapped to technology solutions. Cycle time reduction and automated business rule sets, coupled with UC enablement, can streamline processes related to order entry, inventorying, and purchasing. Real-time access to key decision makers can be provided by embedding UC-enabled SOA software into supply chain infrastructures. Cycle time and red flags can be tracked when the supply chain infrastructure is completely automated from sales order entry to manufacturing.

To shrink the end-to-end cycle time, analyze the current method used to streamline processes, eliminate manual tasks, and automate current human decision making. Workflows can always be improved, especially if the sequence of events is dependent on a previous step or a human decision. Automate any step or decision that can be performed with rule sets and software. Real-time access to key managers can be provided through UC enablement when unique situations arise. The following list describes some technology solutions that can reduce cycle time and enhance productivity:

- shrink the sales cycle, from presales to a purchase order booked into the sales order system
- implement rules with predefined spending limits for each supplier so purchases for raw materials can be automatically triggered from the sales order entry system
- integrate SOA applications with Web Services delivery for secure, real-time browser access to the organization's procurement systems and to real-time supply chain tracking
- integrate the sales order entry system with the purchasing system to streamline just-in-time (JIT) inventory and manufacturing scheduling
- extend the UC federation to suppliers and shipping companies for real-time presence, availability, and IM chat for emergency situations
- connect key executives and managers for real-time presence, availability, IM chat, and collaboration for emergency issue resolution through UC

In the manufacturing and retail industry, streamlined processes and lowered operating costs are the keys to success. For example, purchasing decisions can be automated to place orders with preapproved vendors when inventory systems reach a certain level. This eliminates the need for human intervention, manual purchase requisitioning, and paperwork.

Dramatic increases in fuel costs have led distribution channels and trucking companies to raise rates for manufacturers and retailers. This directly affects the costs of goods sold and gross profit margins. Manufacturers and retailers can lower operating costs and minimize latency in supply chain distribution by identifying alternative ways to distribute their goods. This is critical for survival as transportation costs continue to rise. By mapping communications to streamlined processes and real-time supply chain information, critical decisions can be made based on financial priorities, thereby lowering operating costs.

Business leaders must be interviewed to determine functional requirements before mapping SOA applications, streamlining processes, or configuring UC enablement. Requirements are usually identified through questionnaire responses and interviews with key supply chain personnel. Table 7-7 shows some functional requirements that include SOA application services and UC enablement.

TABLE 7-7: MANUFACTURING AND RETAIL SCM FUNCTIONAL REQUIREMENTS MATRIX.

	People-to-People Communications	Streamlined Processes	Real-Time Access to Information
Customer	Customer service and self-service order tracking via IVR, auto attendant, Web	Order tracking linked to self-service IVR and Web application	Customer order and shipping information
Sales Professional (Account Rep)	Real-time access to customer: presence, availability, text message, IM chat, voice	Sales order entry triggers purchase for materials based on inventory	Order status, ship date, and other related information
Presales Support (Sales Overlay)	Real-time access to managers and suppliers: presence, availability, text message, IM chat, voice, collaboration	SOA integrated business rule sets and purchasing approval limits	Raw materials inventory, ship and receive dates
Presales Technical Support (Sales Engineer)	Real-time access with purchasing managers and manufacturing scheduler	Policies and rule sets for automated purchasing limits	Inventory, purchases, ship and receive dates
Sales Management (Manager or Director)	Real-time access with inventory manager, VP - Sales, VP - Operations	Advanced notice for manufacturing scheduling	Sales order entry, inventory and manufacturing, production schedule
Corporate VP - Sales	Real-time access with manufacturing scheduler, VP - Customer Service	E-mail notification for critical issues for high-value customers	Accurate financial information

The organization's supply chain infrastructure may force counterproductive business processes and information silos. For example, an information flow gap is easily created if sales order information is not integrated with inventory, purchasing, and advance manufacturing production scheduling. This, in turn, creates raw material and supply issues and affects overall productivity. To solve this problem, rule sets can be implemented to make decisions automatically or with minimal human intervention. However, supply chain challenges may still require real-time communication with other executives to fulfill financial priorities.

Table 7-8 shows ways in which SOA applications, convergence technologies, and UC enablement solutions can solve SCM challenges.

TABLE 7-8: MANUFACTURING AND RETAIL SCM FUNCTIONAL TO TECHNICAL REQUIREMENTS MAPPING.

	People-to-People Communications	Streamlined Processes	Real-Time Access to Information
Customer (Retail Store, Consumer, Other Businesses)	IVR, auto attendant, Web order tracking, real-time: preferred agents, presence, IM chat	Integration of real-time order tracking with SOA-enabled Web Services	Customer account, order tracking system
Account Representative	UC enablement: federation expansion to customers, presence, text message, audio/video conference, IM chat, collaboration	Integration between order tracking system and CRM system	Customer account, order tracking system, CRM
JIT – Purchasing Manager	UC enablement: federation expansion to suppliers, presence, availability, text message, audio/video conference, IM chat, collaboration	SOA application integration between inventory and purchasing systems	Customer order status, inventory, purchasing, manufacturing, production schedule
JIT – Inventory Manager	UC enablement: presence, availability, text message, audio/video conference, IM chat, collaboration	SOA application integration of inventory and purchasing systems	Customer order status, inventory, purchasing, manufacturing, production schedule
JIT – Manufacturing Production Scheduler	UC enablement: IP mobility, presence, availability, text message, audio/video conference, IM chat, collaboration	SOA application integration of inventory, purchasing, and manufacturing scheduling systems	Customer order status, inventory, purchasing, manufacturing, production schedule
VP/COO – Operations	UC enablement: IP mobility, presence, IM chat, text message, audio/video conference, collaboration	Access to operations and production backlogs and production cycles	Inventory, purchasing, manufacturing, production backlog schedule
VP – Sales	UC enablement: presence, availability, text message, audio/video conference, IM chat, collaboration	Access to customer order status and backlog reports	Customer order status and tracking backlog reports and financial impact

In this example, mapping requirements to solutions requires convergence technology as part of the overall cycle time reduction strategy. The next step is to identify alternative technology solutions and determine UC systems integration tasks. Table 7-9 shows how alternative technology solutions can be derived from the mapping shown in Table 7-8.

TABLE 7-9: MANUFACTURING AND RETAIL SCM TECHNOLOGY SOLUTION MAPPING.

	People-to-People Communications	Streamlined Processes	Real-Time Access to Information
Customer (Retail Store, Consumer, Other Businesses)	Toll-free number access, differentiated services, self-service IVR, auto attendant, and automated order status e-mails	Easy access to order status and ship date information	Customer order status, tracking and ship date
Account Representative	IP mobility, PDAs, and cell phones with UC enablement and browser	Remote browser access to order status tracking and CRM system	Customer order status, tracking and ship date, SCM and manufacturing issues, CRM system
JIT – Purchasing Manager	IP mobile phone, 802.11 b/g/I WLAN, PDA or cell phone with UC enablement	SOA integration of inventory, purchasing production schedule	Sales order, inventory, purchasing information, production schedule
JIT – Inventory Manager	IP mobile phone, 802.11 b/g/I WLAN, PDA or cell phone with UC enablement	SOA integration of inventory, purchasing production schedule	Sales order, inventory, purchasing information, production schedule
JIT – Manufacturing Production Scheduler	IP mobile phone, 802.11 b/g/I WLAN, PDA or cell phone with UC enablement	SOA integration of inventory, purchasing manufacturing, production scheduling system	Customer order status, tracking and ship date, SCM and manufacturing issues
VP/COO – Operations	IP mobile phone, 802.11 b/g/I WLAN, PDA or cell phone with UC enablement	SOA integration of inventory, purchasing manufacturing, production scheduling system	Customer order status, tracking and ship date, SCM and manufacturing issues
VP/CFO – Finance & Sales	IP mobile phone, 802.11 b/g/I WLAN, PDA or cell phone with UC enablement	Access to customer order status and backlog reports	Customer order status, tracking and ship date, SCM and manufacturing issues, CRM system

7

Mapping the Solution to Technology

> | Note | In the manufacturing and retail industry, maintaining competitive advantage is a priority. This is especially true in changing market conditions, such as rising fuel costs. Manufacturing businesses depend on integrated processes between sales orders, purchasing, JIT inventory, and manufacturing information to produce, ship, and sell products in the most cost effective manner. Organizations that extend their UC federation to suppliers and partners can build competitive advantages by implementing UC-enabled SOA applications. Real-time access to raw material suppliers can make a difference in maintaining a first-to-market advantage. |

Mapping the solution to ERP and UC enablement

Managers who make financial decisions require access to real-time financial information. This is easily enabled with ERP software systems built around common accounting practices, which typically provide a consolidated general ledger, accounts payable, accounts receivable, and interdepartmental cost centers, as well as cost element tracking. These systems are often modular, reducing implementation cost because only the necessary tools need to be installed.

Cost-element tracking provides a way to monitor financial flows to and from the organization. With real-time access to accurate financial data, managers can make sound decisions. Integrating real-time access to ERP financial information with UC enablement offers a competitive advantage by allowing decisions to be made based on financial priorities, instead of operational priorities.

> For-profit businesses that are publicly traded in the United States must follow standardized accounting practices that provide accurate financial reporting. These practices must comply with the Securities and Exchange Commission's (SEC) stringent rules and regulations. Businesses dependent on real-time access to accurate financials typically require ERP systems to manage data related to revenue, gross profit margin, and sales, general, and administrative (SG&A) overhead. When financial information is available in real time, managers can make decisions based on financial analysis. Mapping people-to-people communications with real-time access to financial information helps organizations become more nimble through sound business decisions.

Business leaders must be interviewed to determine functional requirements before mapping ERP applications, streamlining processes, or configuring UC enablement. Requirements are usually identified through questionnaire responses and interviews with key personnel. Table 7-10 shows some examples of the functional requirements of key managers and executives.

TABLE 7-10: ERP FUNCTIONAL REQUIREMENTS MATRIX.

	People-to-People Communications	Streamlined Processes	Real-Time Access to Information
Departmental Manager	Departmental workers, division leader, Director – Finance	Integration of departmental expenses, budgets, and financials	Departmental profit and loss (P&L) KPIs, departmental cost centers, budgets
Division or Business Unit Leader – General Manager	Departmental managers, Director – Finance, Division CFO	Integration of departmental and business unit financials	Division/business unit P&L KPIs, division cost centers, budgets
Division or Business Unit – Director of Finance	Division leaders, Division CFO	Integration of departmental and business unit financials	Division/business unit P&L KPIs, division cost centers, budgets
Division or Business Unit – CFO	Director – Finance, Corporate VP – Finance/CFO	Integration of business unit and corporate financials	Division/business unit P&L KPIs, division cost centers, budgets
Corporate VP – Finance/CFO	Division CFO, Corporate COO, and CEO	Integration of business unit and corporate financials	Corporate and business unit P&L KPIs, cost centers, budgets
Corporate VP – Operations/COO	Division CFO, Corporate CFO, CEO	Integration of business unit and corporate financials	Corporate and business unit P&L KPIs, cost centers, budgets
Corporate CEO	Division CFO, Corporate COO, CFO	Integration of business unit and corporate financials	Corporate and business unit P&L KPIs, cost centers, budgets

Depending on the organization's ERP system and related software deployed within the financial infrastructure, even full integration between cost elements and accurate financials may still leave gaps. Full integration means that interfaces are already built within ERP software modules, such as human resources, sales order entry, and inventory and purchasing. These cost centers are then mapped to the general ledger, accounts payable, and accounts receivable software modules.

However, if the ERP system extends deeply into individual departments, business units, and corporate holdings, accurate financials can be realized. ERP systems can give organizations a competitive edge by aligning all financial inputs with outputs, to provide a real-time snapshot of the organization's financial performance. Accounting and financial software modules can be built according to the organization's particular department and business unit structure, thus permitting accurate and timely financial reporting.

Table 7-11 shows how ERP functional requirements can be mapped to technical requirements. This is how ERP financial applications, convergence technologies, and UC enablement can solve the challenge of real-time access to financial information.

TABLE 7-11: ERP FUNCTIONAL TO TECHNICAL MATRIX.

	People-to-People Communications	Streamlined Processes	Real-Time Access to Information
Departmental Manager	IP mobility, presence, text message, audio/video conference, IM chat, collaboration	Integrated ERP financial modules	Browser-accessible departmental KPI financial dashboard
Division or Business Unit Leader - General Manager	IP mobility, presence, text message, audio/video conference, IM chat, collaboration	Integrated ERP financial modules	Division/business unit P&L KPIs, division cost centers, budgets, financial dashboard
Division or Business Unit - Director of Finance	IP mobility, presence, text message, audio/video conference, IM chat, collaboration	Integration of departmental and business unit financials	Division/business unit P&L KPIs, division cost centers, budgets, financial dashboard
Division or Business Unit - CFO	IP mobility, text message, audio/video conference, IM chat, collaboration, executive level presence and availability	Integration of business unit and corporate financials	Division/business unit P&L KPIs, division cost centers, budgets, financial dashboard
Corporate VP - Finance/CFO	IP mobility, text message, audio/video conference, IM chat, collaboration, executive level presence and availability	Integration of business unit and corporate financials	Corporate and business unit P&L KPIs, cost centers, budgets, financial dashboard

Corporate VP – Operations/COO	IP mobility, text message, audio/video conference, IM chat, collaboration, executive level presence and availability	Integration of business unit and corporate financials	Corporate and business unit P&L KPIs, cost centers, budgets, financial dashboard
Corporate CEO	IP mobility, text message, audio/video conference, IM chat, collaboration, executive level presence and availability	Integration of business unit and corporate financials	Corporate and business unit P&L KPIs, cost centers, budgets, financial dashboard

In this example, departmental and business unit financials are the responsibility of the departmental managers and the business unit CFO. Hierarchical P&L responsibility and accountability aligns corporate goals and objectives with individual business units and departments. P&L statements are reviewed in every financial quarter, including strategies to increase revenue and profitability as well as recommendations to lower operating costs. At the corporate level, individual business units provide P&L financials to the corporate CFO, who consolidates all data into the corporate P&L, income statement, and balance sheet. Real-time access to accurate financials from departmental managers, business unit leaders, and CFOs is also necessary when red flags or financial deficiencies appear. Table 7-12 shows some alternative technology solutions derived from the ERP technical requirements.

TABLE 7-12: EXAMPLE OF ERP TECHNOLOGY SOLUTION MAPPING.

	People-to-People Communications	Streamlined Processes	Real-Time Access to Information
Departmental Manager	802.11 b/g/i WLAN, IP mobile phone, PDAs, cell phones, and computers with UC enablement	Browser-accessible departmental P&L financials	Departmental KPI financial metrics and departmental financial dashboard
Division or Business Unit Leader – General Manager	802.11 b/g/i WLAN, IP mobile phone, PDAs, cell phones, and computers with UC enablement	Secure browser-accessible business unit P&L metrics, financial dashboard	Business unit KPI financial P&L metrics, financial dashboard

Division or Business Unit – Director of Finance	802.11 b/g/i WLAN, IP mobile phone, PDAs, cell phones, and desktop computers with UC enablement	Secure browser-accessible business unit P&L metrics, financial dashboard	Business unit KPI financial P&L metrics, financial dashboard
Division or Business Unit – CFO	VoIP, PDAs, cell phones, and desktop computers with UC enablement	Secure browser-accessible business unit P&L metrics, financial dashboard	Business unit KPI financial P&L metrics, financial dashboard
Corporate VP – Finance/CFO	VoIP, PDAs, cell phones, and desktop computers with UC enablement executive level presence and availability	Secure browser-accessible corporate P&L metrics, financial dashboard	Corporate-wide KPI financial P&L metrics, executive level financial dashboard
Corporate VP – Operations/COO	VoIP, PDAs, cell phones, and desktop computers with UC enablement, executive level presence and availability	Secure browser-accessible corporate P&L metrics, financial dashboard	Corporate-wide KPI financial P&L metrics, executive level financial dashboard
Corporate CEO	VoIP, PDAs, cell phones, and desktop computers with UC enablement, executive level presence and availability	Secure browser-accessible corporate P&L metrics, financial dashboard	Corporate-wide KPI financial P&L metrics, executive level financial dashboard

Note

ERP financial systems provide organizations with an accurate overview of financial inputs and outputs across the entire enterprise. Real-time access to financials allows managers and executives to make sound decisions based on which business units are profitable and which are not. Real-time access also reveals which departments and business units have increasing SG&A overhead, and which P&Ls need immediate attention. This provides the organization with a competitive advantage by identifying and reacting more quickly to changing financial conditions.

Mapping the solution to SFA and UC enablement

Sales force automation (SFA) is another area that benefits from technology solutions mapped to existing requirements. Real-time access to presales support personnel and CRM purchasing information can provide a competitive edge for time-sensitive Request for Proposal (RFP) response and submittal. SFA can encompass both internal and external communications to sales team members and customers. Table 7-13 shows some common SFA functional requirements to integrate real-time communications with streamlined processes.

TABLE 7-13: SFA FUNCTIONAL REQUIREMENTS MATRIX.

	People-to-People Communications	Streamlined Processes	Real-Time Access to Information
Customer	Contact center and self-service order tracking through IVR, auto attendant, Web	Order tracking linked to self-service IVR and Web application	Customer order and shipping information
Sales Professional (Account Rep)	Real-time access to customer: presence, text message, IM chat, audio/video conference, collaboration	Secure and swift remote sales order entry	Order status, ship date, and other related information
Presales Support (Sales Overlay)	Real-time access to sales team: presence, text message, IM chat, audio/video conference, collaboration	Easy system configuration upload into order entry system	Vendor product specialists, solution tools, white papers
Presales Technical Support (Sales Engineer)	Real-time access to sales team: presence, text message, IM chat, audio/video conference, collaboration	Easy system configuration upload into order entry system	Vendor product engineers, solution tools, white papers
Sales Management (Manager or Director)	Real-time access to sales team and internal sales operations	Seamless integration between sales order entry and CRM	Sales order entry, sales forecasting, and CRM system
Corporate VP - Sales	Real-time access to sales managers and internal sales operations	Real-time access to accurate financial data	Accurate sales and financial information

7 | Mapping the Solution to Technology

Modern enhanced SFA solutions include real-time access to sales order entry systems through a secure browser with UC enablement. This provides real-time presence and availability during the sales process through short message service (SMS) text messaging, IM chat, audio/video conferencing, and full collaboration services. It is critical to provide real-time responsiveness to customers as a deal is being closed. SFA, combined with streamlined sales order entry and monitoring through a back-end CRM system, provides sales professionals with intelligence for a strategic sale. Mapping these functional requirements to UC enablement provides clear benefits because sales orders can quickly be input and retrieved remotely. Table 7-14 shows some ways in which functional requirements can be mapped to technological solutions.

TABLE 7-14: SFA FUNCTIONAL TO TECHNICAL REQUIREMENTS MATRIX.

	People-to-People Communications	Streamlined Processes	Real-Time Access to Information
Customer	Multimodal contact center, self-service IVR, auto attendant, Web	Secure Web access to order status tracking system	Order status, ship date, and other related information
Sales Professional (Account Rep)	IP mobility, presence, text message, audio/video conference, IM chat, collaboration	Fast and secure sales order entry by Web browser	Sales order entry, order status, ship date, and other related information
Presales Support (Sales Overlay)	IP mobility, presence, text message, audio/video conference, IM chat, collaboration	Rapid product and solution configurations	Product and solutions design information
Presales Technical Support (Sales Engineer)	IP mobility, presence, text message, audio/video conference, IM chat, collaboration	Rapid engineering and design for presale solutions	Engineering specs and design parameters
Sales Management (Manager or Director)	IP mobility, presence, text message, audio/video conference, IM chat, collaboration	Integration of sales order entry with CRM, sales forecasting	Sales order entry, P&L KPIs and reports, financial dashboard
Corporate VP - Sales	IP mobility, presence, text message, audio/video conference, IM chat, collaboration	Integration of sales order entry with ERP and corporate financials	P&L KPIs and reports, financial dashboard

In this example, sales professionals and management work quickly to book and close orders. It is critical to close deals in a timely manner, including all required paperwork, to maximize revenue. This is the sales professional or account representative's primary responsibility.

SFA solves the cycle time reduction challenge that faces many outside sales organizations that require support from a back-office sales operations team. Some organizations have archaic sales order entry systems that require a significant amount of time to manually enter information. When human-intensive sales processes are transformed and coupled with UC enablement, the sales team will see immediate improvement in sales cycle time. Table 7-15 shows how SFA technical requirements can be mapped to convergence technologies and UC enablement solutions.

TABLE 7-15: EXAMPLE OF SFA TECHNOLOGY SOLUTION MAPPING.

	People-to-People Communications	Streamlined Processes	Real-Time Access to Information
Customer	Toll-free number access, differentiated services, self-service IVR, auto attendant, and automated order status e-mails	Secure Web access to order status tracking system	Order status, ship date, and other related information
Sales Professional (Account Rep)	IP mobile phone, PDAs, cell phones, and computers with UC enablement	Fast and secure sales order entry through Web browser, collaboration	Sales order entry, order status, ship date, and other related information
Presales Support (Sales Overlay)	802.11 b/g/i WLAN, VoIP, PDAs, cell phones, and desktop computers with UC enablement	Rapid product and solution configurations via collaboration	Customer requirements and solution design information
Presales Technical Support (Sales Engineer)	IP mobile phone, PDAs, cell phones, and computers with UC enablement	Rapid engineering and design through collaboration	Customer requirements and solution design information
Sales Management (Manager or Director)	IP mobile phone, PDAs, cell phones, and computers with UC enablement; sales management presence	Browser-accessible CRM, sales forecasting, and collaboration	Sales order entry, P&L KPIs and reports, financial dashboard
Corporate VP - Sales	IP mobile phone, PDAs, cell phones, and computers with UC enablement; sales management presence	Browser-accessible ERP and corporate financials and collaboration	P&L KPIs and reports, financial dashboard

Note SFA can affect revenue and profitability by solving the sales cycle time reduction challenge. The more time saved in sales order processing and closing deals, the faster the organization generates revenue and profit. If a sales professional could close one additional deal each year and generate more revenue and gross profit margin, the financial cost for UC enabling that sales professional is easily justified. Organizations can analyze existing financials, combined with KPIs and a financial ROI model, to gain the confidence to conduct a UC pilot project and provide real-time communication solutions to time-sensitive sales professionals.

Knowledge Check 7-1: Mapping the Solution to Technology

Answer the following questions. Answers to these Knowledge Check questions are located in *Appendix A: Answers to Knowledge Check Questions*.

1. UC enablement encompasses all these functions except which of the following?

   a. Collaboration

   b. Unified messaging

   c. Presence and availability

   d. IM chat, voice, text messaging

   e. Audio and video conferencing

2. Cycle time reduction is a benefit provided by UC enablement in many business applications and processes.

   a. True

   b. False

3. What is the proper sequence of events for solving business challenges with convergence and UC enablement solutions?

   a. Functional requirements, identify business challenge, technical requirements

   b. Technical requirements, functional requirements, technology solutions mapping

   c. Functional requirements, technical requirements, technology solutions mapping

   d. Identify product and services solutions, functional requirements, technical requirements

   e. None of the above

4. SOA applications integrate people-to-people communications with new streamlined processes but cannot access data in real time.

   a. True

   b. False

5. Enhanced customer service delivery strategies typically include which of the following?

   a. Offshore contact center service agents

   b. Multimodal UC-enabled contact center

   c. Preferred VIP agents servicing high-value VIP customers

   d. Differentiated services for high-value versus low-value customers

   e. All of the above

6. Which of the following UC enablement functions can best shrink project time when multiple project team members are involved?

   a. SMS text messaging

   b. IM chat conversations

   c. Real-time collaboration

   d. Real-time presence and availability

   e. Audio conferencing and video conferencing

7. In SCM, which of the following can affect the cost of goods sold using technology and UC enablement?

   a. Providing an enhanced customer service delivery strategy

   b. Streamlining sales order entry, inventory, and purchasing processes

   c. Implementing quality assurance procedures that require human inspection and sign-off approval

   d. Negotiating more favorable costs in real time with suppliers to fulfill an emergency rush order for a high-value customer

   e. None of the above

8. CRM applications can provide sales professionals with valuable customer purchasing history information and discounts offered previously. This is of no value to the sales professional, and slows down the sales cycle.

   a. True

   b. False

9. ERP financial systems provide business unit and corporate financial managers with the information they need to make sound decisions based on financial priorities.

   a. True

   b. False

10. In SFA, UC enablement can be implemented internally for presales support personnel and externally for customers. Which of the following should not be implemented when using SFA externally with customers?

   a. Real-time collaboration to answer customer inquiries

   b. Real-time access to technical or subject matter experts

   c. Opening and extending UC federations between companies

   d. Presence and availability between sales representatives direct to the customer

   e. Presence and availability to all presales support team members direct to the customer

11. Why is SOA application integration, coupled with UC enablement, more effective?

   a. SOA incorporates people-to-people communications in the application itself.

   b. SOA, integrated with UC enablement, embeds UC functionality within the process itself.

   c. SOA integrates streamlined processes with real-time information access, and UC functionality can deliver it.

   d. SOA Web Services delivery is simple and easy through a browser, and real-time UC communications can be embedded in the Web site.

   e. All of the above.

12. Financial KPIs and metrics can be extracted from ERP systems in the form of a real-time financial dashboard for business managers and financial executives.

   a. True

   b. False

7 | Mapping the Solution to Technology

Chapter summary

In this chapter, you learned how to map solutions to challenges through SOA application deployments, convergence technologies, and UC enablement. This process makes the technology and its cost elements less important, because more emphasis is placed on how UC enablement will support real-time access and information dissemination. Application and process challenges can be solved through enterprise transformation analysis, streamlining processes, and replacing human decision making with automated rule sets.

Organizations implement technology solutions in many ways. They may elect to incorporate requirements and solutions into a formal RFP, Request for Quote (RFQ), or SOW documents for direct purchase from SOA application developers and UC solution providers. Deciding whether to pursue a UC pilot project includes tracking KPIs aligned to a financial ROI model. This process is described in later chapters.

8: Building a Measurable Financial ROI with KPIs

Every change has an associated cost. Therefore, before deciding to implement a Unified Communications (UC) solution, it is important to determine whether the cost can be justified. Return on investment (ROI) can be assessed by identifying measurable benefits or key performance indicators (KPIs) that contribute to the business case.

Chapter 8 Topics

In this chapter, you will learn:

- why it is important to build a business case for UC enablement

- how KPIs can be used to measure UC implementation success

- how to track and monitor UC KPIs by defining quantifiable metrics

- how to use the Forrester Consulting UC Business Value Tool v1.5, a commissioned study conducted by Forrester Consulting on behalf of Nortel

- how to map business drivers, KPIs, and UC implementation metrics with a financial ROI model

Chapter 8 Goals

Upon completion of this chapter, you will be able to:

- incorporate KPIs and a financial ROI analysis in a UC enablement project

- recommend whether to pursue a UC enablement project, based on the KPIs and the financial ROI analysis

- make sound decisions regarding when and how to implement a UC solution, based on KPIs and financial ROI analysis results

Key Terms

Capital expenditures (CAPEX)	173	Net present value (NPV)	188
Customer satisfaction (CSAT)	176	Operational expenditures (OPEX)	173
Employee satisfaction (ESAT)	176	Return on investment (ROI)	171
Internal rate of return (IRR)	188	Total cost of ownership (TCO)	174

Building a Measurable Financial ROI with KPIs

8

The business case for UC enablement

In previous chapters, you learned about UC enablement: the deployment of UC applications, features, and functions in a production business environment. UC deployment can benefit small, medium, and large enterprises in every vertical industry that wants to enhance productivity and lower operating costs, whether in the public or private sector. UC enablement provides greater operational efficiency, which can directly affect revenue, profitability, and the cost of goods sold.

Organizations must justify the cost of investment in new technology by building a business case whenever capital expenditures (CAPEX) or operational expenditures (OPEX) are incurred. Many organizations pursue UC proof-of-concept pilot projects as a way to analyze the financial ROI of UC enablement with defined KPIs to track project success. This approach minimizes the risk associated with a potentially unsuccessful UC deployment.

UC business decision makers

Although decision makers may intuitively be aware of UC's benefits and features, they must still build a business case for internal review to justify the cost of investment in new technology. This is particularly true in situations where the UC decision will involve a group of people across multiple departments and business functions. Individuals involved in the UC business decision may include the following:

- **CIO**–Chief information officer
- **CFO**–Chief financial officer
- **General manager**–Line of business (sales, supply chain, customer service, operations, finance, training, and other areas)
- **Director**–Telecommunications and voice services
- **Director**–Data networking and security
- **Director**–Applications and desktop software

A UC deployment decision typically encompasses a broad range of information technology (IT) and non-IT areas, particularly if it occurs in and around service-oriented architecture (SOA), customer service (CS), customer relationship management (CRM), supply chain management (SCM), enterprise resource planning (ERP), or sales force automation (SFA) functions.

UC enablement business decision

Many organizations divide UC enablement decisions into two areas: a strategic application for the entire organization and an infrastructure vendor for select areas of the organization. In many organizations, the senior-level people that decide on UC application deployment are often different from the people who select the infrastructure vendor.

CIOs face the challenge of structuring the organization to support convergence projects. This is a concern because UC enablement projects generally involve all IT infrastructure disciplines. This concern leads many organizations to run a UC proof-of-concept pilot project before rolling UC out to the entire organization. UC requires the entire IT organization to work cooperatively toward a common goal, regardless of the vendor selected.

UC enablement benefits

UC enablement provides many benefits to an organization. Top-level decision makers will be convinced of UC's value by increases in revenue, profitability, and customer lifetime value. Through proper KPIs aligned to financial metrics and a measurable financial ROI, UC can be mapped to financial metrics.

Organizations that understand the benefits of UC enablement base the investment decision on new business value as well as on cost savings. The following list describes some fundamental business drivers for UC enablement:

- **Total cost of ownership (TCO)**—UC enablement integrates converged voice and data networks with desktop applications to reduce expenses previously associated with technology silos.

- **Productivity enhancement**—Features such as presence, click-to-call, and instant messaging save time for both individuals and workgroups, resulting in increased productivity across the organization. However, you must define a metric to express saved employee time in financial terms; for example, organizations that provide services associate costs and revenues with hours worked.

- **Optimized business processes**—Person-to-person communication delays within business processes, such as reaching decision makers or subject matter experts, can be reduced or eliminated through UC enablement. Measurable process improvements can be mapped to an organization's financial metrics. This area provides the most significant benefit of UC enablement.

Figure 8-1 shows the three-tiered business value driver pyramid. UC business drivers are aligned to KPIs or metrics that measure the performance and success of UC enablement.

FIGURE 8-1: BUSINESS VALUE DRIVERS FOR UC TCO.

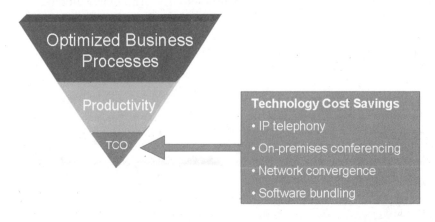

UC enablement cost savings

When organizations examine the TCO savings potential, the following cost savings should be analyzed:

- Telephony and long-distance costs can be reduced when voice conversations are transmitted as Voice over Internet Protocol (VoIP) through the IP data network. Include telecommunication expenses and costs from the previous year.

- Audio and video conference costs can be reduced or eliminated with an on-premise audio and video conferencing infrastructure. Include audio and video conferencing costs (circuit costs, equipment, maintenance and support, software licenses, and so on) from the previous year.

- Training costs can be reduced or eliminated with the convergence of networks, servers, and endpoint devices by providing users with a common UC interface on all devices, thus simplifying end-user deployment and acceptance. Include training costs from the previous year.

- Hardware IT maintenance and support costs can be reduced through implementation of software-based UC solutions. Identify IT assets that no longer require maintenance and support.

- Enterprise software licensing bundling costs can be reduced or eliminated, depending on the enterprise site licensing and the organization. Determine whether the organization already has reduced-fee, or even free, access to UC server and desktop software licenses.

UC enablement cost elements

In addition to identifying the potential cost savings listed in the previous section, it is important to capture all cost elements that contribute to the overall UC enablement investment, whether for a UC pilot project or a full implementation. The following list contains examples of common cost elements:

- Server costs, local area network (LAN) switch costs for VoIP and UC server farms, rack space power, and disaster recovery systems.

- Server and desktop operating system, UC server software, and UC desktop software licensing, maintenance, and support costs. (Desktop operating system and UC client costs are typically paid for by organizations.)

- Initial systems integration tasks and deliverables, outsource costs, and UC systems integrator costs.

- Ongoing system administration, maintenance and support costs, and costs to support and maintain UC servers, applications, and end users.

- Wide area network (WAN) bandwidth to support UC communications, audio conferencing, video conferencing, collaboration IP traffic through the LAN and WAN, incremental costs to support UC, remote VoIP systems, and UC communication servers.

Building an internal UC business case requires capturing true cost savings and accurate cost elements for the UC infrastructure. Although specific outcomes cannot be guaranteed with any financial ROI, a UC pilot project implemented with KPIs and metrics aligned to a financial ROI model provides a roadmap to track and monitor a UC implementation. KPIs and metrics that can be tied to financial performance are a critical component of the UC business case.

Using KPIs to measure UC enablement success

It is easy to see how various UC features can increase communication efficiency. For example, presence improves the odds of completing a communication exchange on the first attempt. A first contact through instant messaging (IM) chat might lead to a voice call and then to an audio/video conference or online collaboration with key project team members. Improved communication leads to individual, workgroup, and enterprise productivity, which in turn can drive employee satisfaction (ESAT) and customer satisfaction (CSAT).

Although it is a challenge to map time savings and productivity enhancements to a financial benefit, some organizations have succeeded in doing so. They can implement these enhancements by comparing a UC proof-of-concept pilot project office with a non-UC-enabled office of similar size. Later in this chapter, this approach is illustrated through a UC-enabled SFA implementation.

Cycle time is the KPI most often used to analyze and quantify productivity enhancements associated with UC enablement. If it is not possible to measure cycle time in real time, measure its benchmarks and compare KPIs to previous fiscal periods of operation for a metric to track UC enablement success.

SFA example KPIs and metrics

Although it is difficult to measure the intangible benefits of human productivity and enhanced real-time communications, it is still possible to measure KPIs and metrics. A KPI is an element that can be measured both before and after UC enablement, and the values compared to determine success or failure. The following list contains examples of SFA KPIs and performance metrics, which can be aligned to a financial ROI model with revenue, profitability, and lower operating costs:

- **Sales cycle time**—Sales organizations that use sales contact systems and back-end CRM applications can track a sale from lead to purchase order by tracing timestamps entered into the order entry or contact systems. Sales managers can compare pre-UC and post-UC sales numbers to track, monitor, and report on trends and improved sales cycle time closure.

- **First-call problem resolution in customer inquiries during presales cycle**—Real-time responsiveness to technical questions during the presales cycle is critical. Managers can compare sales deals made without UC enablement to deals that use UC enablement to contact subject matter experts and technical specialists in response to customer inquiries during the sales process.

- **Total number of sales per month/quarter**—SFA with UC enablement allows sales professionals to be more efficient, meet more appointments, and close more deals, thus producing positive results.

- **Total/average revenue and gross profit margin per sales professional per month/quarter—** Increasing the total number of sales through UC enablement can result in increased revenue and profitability metrics. These can be tied to a financial ROI model and compared to sales figures for non-UC-enabled sales offices of comparable size.

- **Improved on-time delivery of products or services—**Streamlining the sales process includes accurate order entry and on-time delivery of products and services. These metrics can be used to compare the pre-UC environment with the post-UC-enabled environment.

- **Sales professional ESAT and retention—**Managers can use an SFA UC pilot project to measure employee retention, comparing a non-UC-enabled sales office with a UC-enabled sales office of similar size. Sales professionals with the tools, support, and resources to solve customer challenges and to close deals stay with an organization longer. Project metrics can be used to compare retention of UC-enabled sales professionals to non-UC-enabled sales professionals.

Figure 8-2 shows that productivity enhancements are a clear business value driver for UC enablement in any type of organization. This is particularly true with for-profit organizations. Productivity enhancements, although difficult to capture with real-time KPIs and metrics, can be derived from measurable KPIs such as the ones described earlier for SFA. By comparing non-UC-enabled environments with UC-enabled ones, organizations can gather enough data to decide whether to expand the UC proof-of-concept pilot project. The key for many organizations is to map the KPIs to financial metrics and then to a financial ROI model. This allows business managers to analyze the financial impact of an investment in UC technology solutions.

FIGURE 8-2: BUSINESS VALUE DRIVERS FOR UC PRODUCTIVITY.

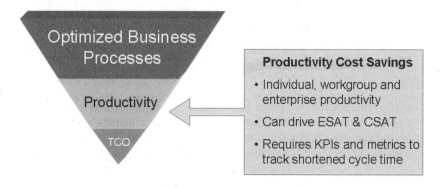

Integration of UC enablement with business processes

When UC enablement is integrated with business processes, it is possible to realize the full benefits of solving people-to-people communication challenges. Many business operations and processes have their own associated cost elements. Tracking and monitoring these cost elements provides the basis for a high ROI from UC enablement in certain situations and environments. This high ROI generates increased interest in UC deployment in various processes and functions of an organization.

Financial metrics can be assigned to certain KPIs because they represent a financial cost savings element. Figure 8-3 shows some of these UC cost-saving and measurable KPIs obtained from the Forrester Consulting Nortel and Microsoft UC Business Value Tool v1.5, a commissioned study conducted by Forrester Consulting on behalf of Nortel.

FIGURE 8-3: BUSINESS VALUE DRIVERS FOR UC, OPTIMIZED BUSINESS PROCESSES.

> **Note**
>
> Every organization must identify its own unique KPIs and metrics, particularly if those metrics can be aligned to a financial ROI model that shows cost savings, cost elements, revenue generation, and profitability directly attributable to UC enablement. As long as a KPI can be measured (time, customer satisfaction, financial savings, financial gains, etc.), it can be used for tracking and monitoring.
>
> Organizations can also analyze the impact of UC enablement by conducting a UC proof-of-concept pilot project that compares a non-UC-enabled department or sales office to a UC-enabled department or sales office of equal size. This comparison allows management to track and monitor KPIs and metrics as they relate to UC enablement benefits, cost savings, cost elements, and financial returns from the UC pilot project.

Tracking and monitoring UC KPIs and metrics

Each business value driver that supports UC enablement has its own KPIs. In most cases, these KPIs can be mapped to a specific financial metric for reporting and analysis. KPI and metric tracking and monitoring is a critical part of any UC proof-of-concept pilot project.

Example SFA UC KPIs and metrics

The following list provides examples of KPIs and metrics that can be tracked for various benefits of UC enablement:

- **Reduced real estate costs**
  - **UC driver**—Instead of opening new offices, open virtual offices by equipping remote workers with UC tools. Increase the number of home-based workers to support existing sites.
  - **Financial impact**—This direct cost contributes to sales, general, and administrative (SG&A) overhead. Savings from real estate and overhead costs contribute directly to bottom-line profitability.
  - **Tracking and monitoring**—Real estate costs and office space lease reductions can be tracked and monitored on a per-office basis as that office transitions to a mobile workforce.
  - **KPIs**—For a UC-enabled office, define a KPI that correlates cost savings in office real estate and overhead costs to UC-enabled workers. For example, if that office is a sales office, track real estate financial savings as a result of SFA and UC enablement and correlate it to sales performance metrics.
  - **Metrics**—Calculate the cost per square foot per employee for both a non-UC-enabled and a UC-enabled office. Use this financial metric for sound real estate reduction planning, once validated.
- **Reduced travel expenses for meetings and training programs**
  - **UC driver**—Replace some internal face-to-face meetings with virtual meetings. Teams can collaborate across multiple locations from the desktop, delivering training directly to the desktop with UC tools.
  - **Financial impact**—This direct cost contributes to SG&A overhead. Travel savings generated by virtual collaborative meetings and training contribute directly to profitability.
  - **Tracking and monitoring**—Track and monitor travel and entertainment expenses on a per-employee and per-office basis.
  - **KPIs**—Audio and video conferencing used for real-time collaboration or training almost eliminates the need for face-to-face meetings and travel. Accurate travel and expense costs can be derived from records of previous business trips. The value of replacing business trips with UC enablement can be forecasted and incorporated into the financial ROI model and analysis.
  - **Metrics**—Use the previous year's travel and entertainment budget to determine the average cost per business trip per employee, multiplied by the total number of business trips or training days required per month and per year, and use this number as a metric. Compare the metric for both a UC-enabled and a non-UC-enabled office and worker. You can also compare virtual meetings held with UC-enabled tools to face-to-face meetings that incur travel and entertainment expenditures.

8 | Building a Measurable Financial ROI with KPIs

- **Shortened sales cycles**
  - **UC driver**—UC tools provide enhanced project team collaboration during proposal generation and modification, as well as improved real-time access to support resources and approvers to drive proposal closure.
  - **Financial impact**—The time value of money means that the faster sales orders are generated, the faster revenue and profits are collected. This contributes to the overall financial performance of the organization.
  - **Tracking and monitoring**—With SFA, sales cycles can be tracked and monitored using the sales contact and sales order entry systems. Sales managers can track and monitor sales activities and average sales cycle time.
  - **KPIs**—Average sales cycle times for differently sized sales orders can be defined as benchmarks or KPIs for a UC-enabled sales professional and a non-UC-enabled sales professional.
  - **Metrics**—The average sales cycle time for small, medium, and large sales orders can be compared between a UC-enabled sales professional and a non-UC-enabled sales professional. The UC-enabled sales professional should be more productive, providing more time to sell and generate revenue and profit. UC-enabled and non-UC-enabled sales orders per sales professional can also be analyzed and compared.

- **Reduced time to complete projects**
  - **UC driver**—UC tools enable faster information sharing and interteam communication, as well as improved real-time access to decision makers, thus reducing project delays.
  - **Financial impact**—When dealing with professional services companies, billable worker-hours for a fixed-fee consulting engagement affect profitability and job costing. Completing the project early and under budget, as a result of UC-enabled enhanced productivity, directly affects that project's profitability.
  - **Tracking and monitoring**—Billable consultants track hours and monitor billable usage on a daily, weekly, and monthly basis. Projects that are completed early and under budget can be directly attributed to UC productivity enhancement throughout the project plan.
  - **KPIs**—KPIs for projects include project completion dates, early completion of tasks and projects, and tracking and monitoring the time required to complete a task or deliverable compared to the original project plan.
  - **Metrics**—It is possible to track the actual time and dollar amount for projects. When a project is completed early and under budget, this dollar amount contributes to the project's profitability and job costing calculations. Use these financial metrics to track and calculate billable consulting project profitability, based on number of hours under budget for fixed-fee contracts.

- **Improved resolution of customer inquiries and issues**
  - **UC driver**—UC tools enhance real-time communication between customer service and subject matter experts. Experts with UC tools are more easily accessible by customer service representatives.

- **Financial impact**—Enhanced customer service delivery starts with a customer service–focused strategy in which high-value customers are aligned with high-value services, such as first-call problem resolution and preferred agent responsiveness. Each high-value customer has a calculated customer lifetime value to the organization that is derived from repeat business and profits.

- **Tracking and monitoring**—Contact center performance reports can be used to track and monitor customer service effectiveness (ability to close out customer inquiry or problem) and efficiency (first-call problem resolution, shortened response times). By tracking responsiveness, customer purchases and repeat purchases can be tied back to customer service delivery and UC enablement.

- **KPIs**—Customer service KPIs include customer service effectiveness (number of customer service calls that can be handled), customer service efficiency (amount of time it takes to solve customer problems or issues), customer lifetime value, customer retention time, quantity and dollar value of customer repeat purchases, frequency of customer repeat purchases, and the average dollar amount and profit per customer purchase.

- **Metrics**—KPIs can be translated into a quantitative metric. KPIs can be translated into financial metrics if accurate sales information and CRM intelligence is available.

- **Customer experience and retention**

  - **UC driver**—UC tools enhance real-time communication between customer service and subject matter experts. Experts with UC tools are more easily accessible to customer service (expert anywhere).

  - **Financial impact**—Positive customer experiences generally lead to long-term customer relationships. Happy customers purchase more products and services, which contributes to customer retention and the customer's lifetime value. The longer the relationship, the greater the revenue and profit to the organization.

  - **Tracking and monitoring**—Customer retention and repeat customer purchases can be tracked and monitored over time. Customer purchasing history and buying behavior can be tracked with back-end CRM systems that aggregate customer information, including previous purchases. This information provides customer lifetime valuations, used to determine whether customers are high-value or low-value customers based on retention.

  - **KPIs**—Any customer who purchases products and services more than once is a KPI with associated financial metrics. Customer lifetime value, repeat purchases, revenue, and profitability are all measurable customer retention KPIs.

  - **Metrics**—Metrics for customer retention include customer lifetime value, average price for repeat purchase, and average gross profit margin per repeat purchase. A direct relationship between customer retention, UC enablement, and customer repeat purchases (revenue and profitability) can be extrapolated after UC enablement has been implemented as part of the customer retention strategy.

- **Employee retention**
  - **UC driver**—Use UC tools to provide employees with a flexible work environment (for example, home-based workers, mobile workers, or teleworkers) and roll out UC tools that permit employees to use their preferred methods of communication.
  - **Financial impact**—Employee retention means the employee does not want to leave the organization. With less employee turnover, organizations can minimize expenditures associated with hiring and retraining staff.
  - **Tracking and monitoring**—Employee retention can be measured by examining average employee tenure from hire date to termination or resignation date for each type of position. Employee retention for UC-enabled job positions and non-UC-enabled job positions can be compared.
  - **KPIs**—Measure employee retention correlated with UC enablement by identifying each employee's length of service and comparing the metric for UC-enabled and non-UC-enabled employees.
  - **Metrics**—Employee retention includes average or actual length of time for different types of employees.

UC enablement provides plentiful benefits and solutions, but these benefits cannot be validated without the ability to track and monitor KPIs and metrics tied to a financial ROI model. Many organizations use UC proof-of-concept pilot projects to test UC enablement and its ability to lower TCO, enhance productivity, and optimize business processes.

Forrester Consulting UC Business Value Tool v1.5

The Forrester Consulting UC Business Value Tool v1.5 is a financial ROI model currently used by Nortel and Microsoft to help customers justify UC enablement deployments. It is intended to be a forecasting and estimation tool used to determine whether UC enablement can be justified financially. It is not intended to be a definitive decision-making tool for UC enablement investments. This tool is an excellent example of an ROI financial analysis model used to assist UC enablement deployment decisions.

The UC Business Value Tool is best used as a forecast and UC proof-of-concept pilot project benchmark solution that provides milestones and financial goals and metrics to track and monitor a UC enablement project. It was designed to help vendors and customers understand the potential value of UC enablement prior to investing in UC solutions.

Forrester Consulting used the following approach to formulate this UC financial ROI tool:

- interviews with customers who use a Nortel voice infrastructure coupled with Microsoft applications, server, and desktop environment
- interviews with Nortel and Microsoft stakeholders who regularly calculate UC financial ROI
- extensive research in UC to develop the value proposition framework on which the tool is based

UC Business Value Tool v1.5 positioning

The UC Business Value Tool v1.5 is intended to be used by Nortel, Microsoft, or end users who want to build financial benchmarks and forecast financial calculations based on the proposed UC enablement project. The tool is positioned for VoIP, convergence, and UC-enabled environments consisting of the following:

- Nortel Communication Server 1000 IP communication system
- Nortel Multimedia Conferencing
- Microsoft Office Communications Server 2007 (OCS2007)

When a customer is already engaged and has a specific vision for UC enablement, the UC Business Value Tool v1.5 can provide compelling information about UC deployment benefits. This financial ROI tool is typically used during the sales cycle or UC business case analysis when the potential customer asks to learn more about the ROI that UC enablement can provide.

Total Economic Impact model

Forrester Consulting's financial investment cost-justification approach is based on its Total Economic Impact (TEI) model, a proprietary set of tools and techniques that offers the following benefits:

- aligns project goals with business goals and assigns accountability
- supports decisions with a business case
- takes risk and flexibility into account
- facilitates what-if scenarios
- supports future benefits realization and optimization through metrics and accountability
- supports IT governance efforts
- assists in a portfolio management approach to IT
- positions IT as a value-producing entity

The TEI approach and financial cost justification model is shown in Figure 8-4. The TEI model and approach examines a technical solution's TCO, benefits, and flexibility in adapting to future requirements and needs. This is compared to a risk analysis or uncertainty weighting. Assumptions and inputs, made by the customer or by the vendor, may affect the UC financial ROI results; the effects of these inputs are indicated here prior to the TEI calculation and results.

FIGURE 8-4: FORRESTER CONSULTING TEI FINANCIAL JUSTIFICATION APPROACH.

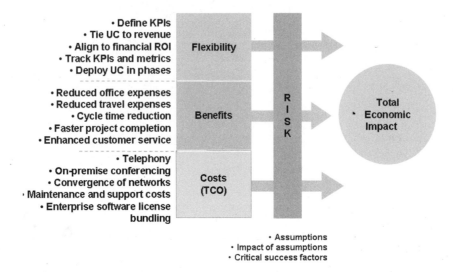

Inputting data into the UC Business Value Tool v1.5

The UC Business Value Tool v1.5 is based on customer-selectable data inputs. Interviews are conducted with customers in an effort to capture the true business drivers and requirements commonly found in UC enablement projects. The following requirements are incorporated into the tool's overall design:

- Customers describe the ways in which their businesses can be enhanced with UC enablement; they do not focus on specific products or capabilities.

- The tool's design is based on Forrester Consulting's understanding of how UC enablement's value is perceived.

- The tool is organized around business process change and quantifies how UC enablement can increase revenue and profitability while lowering operational costs.

- Calculations are based on customer selection of key business processes and benefits most commonly found in UC deployments.

The UC Business Value Tool v1.5 is organized into five sections:

- **Section 1: Describe your organization's profile**—Customers answer general questions about their organization to develop an accurate profile.

- **Section 2: Identify potential business benefits from UC**—Customers view a list of nine potential business benefits. The first area, which is automatically selected, is technology cost savings from UC. The customer may also select up to four other potential business benefits that are most relevant to their business.

- **Section 3: Calculate business benefits**—Customers answer detailed questions about each selected benefit.

- **Section 4: Calculate UC technology requirements**—Customers select the UC technology capabilities of interest.

- **Section 5: View results**—UC financial ROI results are displayed, based on the selections in the prior steps.

Figure 8-5 provides a front view of the UC Business Value Tool v1.5 developed by Forrester Consulting.

FIGURE 8-5: FORRESTER CONSULTING NORTEL AND MICROSOFT UC BUSINESS VALUE TOOL V1.5.

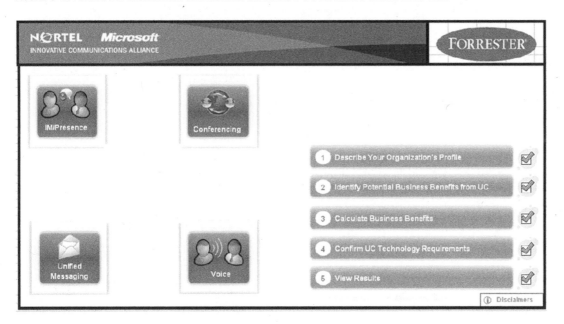

From this financial ROI model, customers and vendors can identify their unique potential UC enablement success by tracking KPIs and validating financial metrics as UC-enablement cost savings and productivity-enhanced revenue generation come to fruition. This success is based on accurate cost information entered in the financial model. Cost elements include, but are not limited to, the following:

- **Lifecycle costs**—This includes software, hardware, deployment and installation, maintenance and support, administration and training, and systems integration labor (outsourced or in-house).

- **Nortel costs**—This includes CS1000 VoIP system hardware and software cost elements (upgrades can be included in the UC enablement financial ROI model) and associated software licensing. All costs for convergence readiness should be incorporated into Nortel cost components, particularly if Nortel hardware and software is included in the overall solution.

- **Microsoft costs**—This includes Microsoft software licensing costs, including Office Communicator Server 2007 (OCS2007), Standard CAL, Enterprise CAL, Enterprise Server, Office Communicator Client software, and endpoint devices.

Additional detailed information about the financial ROI tool is contained on the CD in the back of the book.

Building the UC enablement business case

The Nortel and Microsoft UC Business Value Tool v1.5 developed by Forrester Consulting is uniquely positioned to map business drivers to UC requirements. This, in turn, provides you with KPIs that can be tracked, monitored, and aligned to financial metrics. This mapping to financial metrics brings true financial value to UC enablement solutions. Business drivers, KPIs, metrics, and a financial ROI model can strengthen your business case by linking UC requirements, benefits, and features to increased financial return and lower operating costs as a result of UC enablement.

UC Business Value Tool v1.5 financial outputs

Once necessary customer data has been entered, including the customer's organizational profile, cost elements, and UC features and benefits, the financial ROI analysis can begin. After successful input of the organization's cost elements, the UC Business Value Tool v1.5 displays a breakdown of an organization's cost elements, using a macro-enabled pie chart along with itemized cost elements in a spreadsheet, as shown in Figure 8-6.

FIGURE 8-6: FORRESTER CONSULTING UC BUSINESS VALUE TOOL COST ELEMENTS (USING ILLUSTRATIVE COSTS).

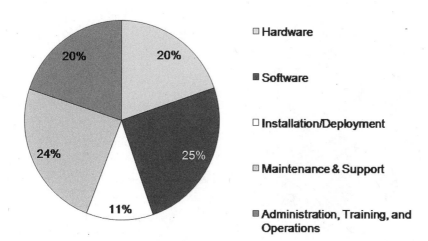

☐ Hardware

■ Software

☐ Installation/Deployment

☐ Maintenance & Support

■ Administration, Training, and Operations

	Original	
Hardware	$	297,900
Software	$	376,884
Installation/Deployment	$	169,817
Maintenance & Support	$	363,304
Administration, Training, and Operations	$	301,950
Total 3 Year Costs	$	1,509,855
Total 3 Year NPV	$	1,439,520

8 | Building a Measurable Financial ROI with KPIs

FIGURE 8-7: FORRESTER CONSULTING UC BUSINESS VALUE TOOL BENEFITS.

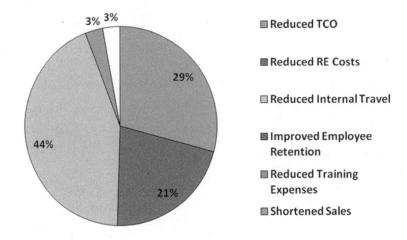

	Original		Risk-Adjusted	
Reduced TCO	$	1,356,750	$	1,288,913
Reduced RE Costs	$	988,500	$	939,075
Reduced Internal Travel	$	2,025,000	$	1,923,750
Improved Employee Retention		-		-
Reduced Training Expenses		-		-
Shortened Sales	$	137,700	$	130,815
Reduced Project Completion	$	135,000	$	128,250
Improved Project Resolution		-		-
Improved Customer Experience		-		-
Total 3-year Benefits	$	4,642,950	$	4,410,803
Total 3-year NPV	$	4,003,094	$	3,802,939

UC Business Value Tool v1.5 final ROI outputs include a risk-adjusted profit–loss analysis. An example of a risk-adjusted profit–loss chart is shown in Figure 8-8.

In the preceding figure, the break-even point crosses the line at approximately six months. Figure 8-9 shows how financial ROI analysis and metrics are presented, in a chart depicting ROI, payback in months, costs net present value (CNPV), benefits net present value (BNPV), and internal rate of return (IRR).

FIGURE 8-8: FORRESTER CONSULTING UC BUSINESS VALUE TOOL RISK-ADJUSTED PROFIT-LOSS ANALYSIS.

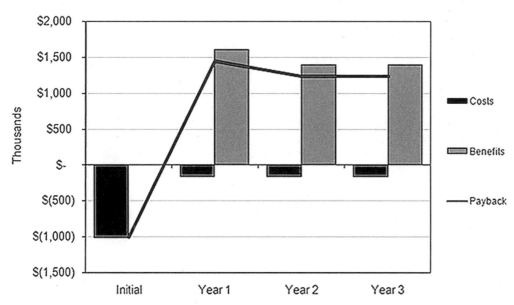

FIGURE 8-9: FORRESTER CONSULTING UC BUSINESS VALUE TOOL FINANCIAL ROI AND METRICS.

Three Year ROI and Payback Summary		
	Non-Risk Adjusted Estimate	Risk Adjusted Estimate
Return on Investment (ROI)	165%	152%
Payback period (months)	8	9
Total NPV of Costs	$1,439,520	$1,439,520
Total NPV of Benefits	$4,003,094	$3,802,939
Total NPV	$2,373,679	$2,188,351
Internal Rate of Return (IRR)	131%	122%

The Forrester Consulting Nortel and Microsoft UC Business Value Tool v1.5 is an excellent example of a tool used to forecast and estimate the financial ROI of UC enablement. Its accuracy depends on accurate and realistic data, including cost elements, anticipated UC features and benefits, and other pertinent organization profile data. This financial ROI tool is not intended to represent a formal business case to justify UC enablement, but it can illustrate potential costs and benefits over a three-year period to help organizations build their own customized business cases for UC.

Knowledge Check 8-1: Building a Measurable Financial ROI with KPIs

Answer the following questions. Answers to these Knowledge Check questions are located in *Appendix A: Answers to Knowledge Check Questions.*

1. Many organizations require financial justification to make a major technology investment. Forrester Consulting's financial justification approach for technology investment is called:

   a. Cost benefit analysis

   b. Total Economic Impact

   c. Financial ROI justification

   d. Forrester Consulting ROI Model

   e. None of the above

2. For every cost savings element, there might be an equivalent cost element for UC enablement.

   a. True

   b. False

3. Which of the following individuals does not usually participate in UC business decision making for an organization?

   a. CIO

   b. CFO

   c. Desktop systems analyst

   d. Director of networking and security

   e. Director of telecommunications and voice services

4. Examining the cost savings from replacing current technologies and cost elements with UC enablement is called examining the total cost of ownership.

   a. True

   b. False

5. Which of the following is not a UC benefit?

   a. Increased costs for software licensing requirements

   b. On-premise–based audio and video conferencing services

   c. Lower real estate costs through transformation of workforce

   d. Enhanced people-to-people communications, using presence, availability, and instant messaging

   e. Reduced travel expenses for conducting business meetings and internal training through UC

6. _____ expenditures are required to pay for monthly SG&A overhead expenses, such as office lease payments and utility bills.

   a. Office

   b. Capital

   c. Operational

   d. Software and hardware

   e. Travel and entertainment

7. When conducting a financial ROI calculation, you must capture all cost elements and all cost savings that can be derived from UC enablement.

   a. True

   b. False

8. If the ROI value is the ratio of money gained or lost on an investment relative to the amount of money invested, then an ROI value of less than 100 percent results in a favorable result.

   a. True

   b. False

9. Which of the following purchases typically requires a financial ROI model and justification if that purchase is to be made in the same fiscal year?

   a. OPEX

   b. CAPEX

   c. Lease

   d. Credit

   e. None of the above

10. Net present value calculations are needed because of the time value of money variable.

    a. True

    b. False

11. If an organization can obtain a financial ROI from UC enablement but it takes more than two fiscal years to break even, what should that organization do?

    a. Wait two years before deploying

    b. Cancel the UC enablement project

    c. Obtain funding approval from the board of directors

    d. Develop a phased migration plan that spreads out CAPEX and OPEX payments over three fiscal years so that negative returns are minimized

    e. None of the above

12. You should never invite the CFO to participate in a UC enablement business decision.

    a. True

    b. False

Chapter summary

In this chapter, you learned a financial cost justification approach for UC enablement investments that can be used by both vendors selling UC solutions and by end-user customers who want a financial benchmark to support a decision about funding a UC project. Without a financially justified approach, many organizations will struggle with whether to pursue UC enablement. For this reason, it is critical to build a financial ROI model with aligned KPIs and metrics. Many organizations propose UC proof-of-concept pilot projects coupled with a financial ROI model to track cost elements, UC-enablement benefits, financial returns or metrics from lower TCO cost elements, increased revenue and profitability, and long-term financial gains and returns from UC enablement. When a UC proof-of-concept pilot project is complete and proves to be financially successful, organizations will have the confidence and experience to conduct an enterprise roll-out of UC enablement.

9: Conducting a Unified Communications Proof-of-Concept Pilot Project

Unified Communications (UC) enablement can enhance productivity and support real-time person-to-person communication through Session Initiation Protocol (SIP)-enabled endpoint devices. In previous chapters, you saw several examples of business challenges that affect many organizations. Enterprise transformation, mapped to technology and UC enablement, can solve these challenges. Many organizations choose to test UC in their enterprise through a proof-of-concept pilot project. Before a pilot project can be started, executive management—especially the CFO and CIO—must support the project. Because the best way to approach technology investments is to determine whether its success can be linked to return on investment (ROI), executive approval is typically based on measurable key performance indicators (KPIs) and metrics that support a financial ROI model with positive results.

Because UC enablement requires a significant technology commitment, the UC proof-of-concept pilot project allows IT organizations to address software interoperability and systems integration issues before making an enterprise-wide investment decision. This is particularly true for organizations concerned about interoperability, functionality, and ongoing support within a heterogeneous voice infrastructure. SIP functionality, for example, brings many technical challenges, including multivendor Voice over Internet Protocol (VoIP) systems, UC application servers, and client device interactions. This chapter describes how to build a UC or proof-of-concept pilot project, including discussion of detailed project budgets. Designing a UC project will give you the information you need to sell the project internally and justify the cost of UC enablement.

Chapter 9 Topics

In this chapter, you will learn:

- how to identify the advantages of conducting a UC pilot project prior to full-scale deployment

- how to find risks and concerns related to a UC enablement project

- how to sell a proof-of-concept pilot project for UC enablement within your organization

- how to define the scope of the proof-of-concept pilot project for UC enablement

- how to set goals and objectives for a UC proof-of-concept pilot project

- how to align requirements to the goals and objectives of the UC proof-of-concept pilot project

- how to build a UC proof-of-concept pilot project budget

Chapter 9 Goals

Upon completion of this chapter, you will be able to:

- position a UC proof-of-concept pilot project as a preliminary step toward UC enablement

- define the goals, objectives, and requirements for a UC proof-of-concept pilot project

- identify the cost components for a UC proof-of-concept pilot project budget

Key Terms

Critical success factor	197	Shortened sales cycle	205
Line-of-business champion	198	UC Business Value Tool v1.5	203

Unified Communications pilot project planning considerations

There is some risk in any new technology deployment and investment, including investments in UC. UC touches many domains within an IT organization, including voice communications, IP networking, software applications, security, and desktop systems. Figure 9-1 shows how UC enablement affects many elements of an IT infrastructure. Because UC deployments are so complex, many organizations choose to run a UC pilot project prior to an enterprise-wide deployment. Pilot projects are a good way to evaluate and assess UC enablement, including risk exposure, KPIs, and metrics that can be aligned to a financial ROI. KPIs and metrics should be aligned to measurable outcomes that will act as the project's performance criteria. Throughout the UC pilot project's life, KPIs, critical success factors, and performance criteria can be tracked and analyzed. This analysis provides executive management with specific metrics that reflect the project's degree of success.

FIGURE 9-1: UC ENABLEMENT TOUCHES MANY DISCIPLINES WITHIN AN IT INFRASTRUCTURE.

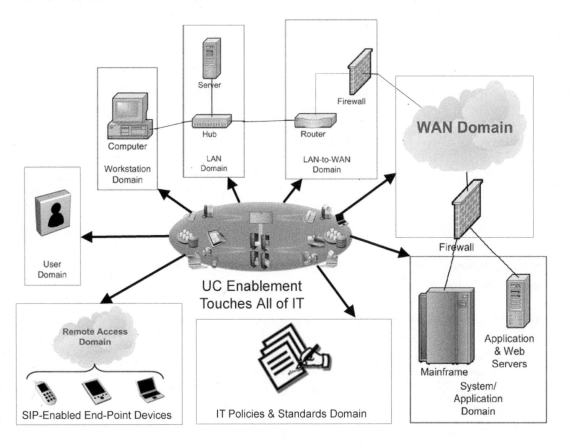

9 | Conducting a UC Proof-of-Concept Pilot Project

Purpose of UC enablement

In addition to tracking performance criteria, the purpose of UC enablement is to identify a business challenge that can be solved and mapped to a technology solution. Many organizations build a financial ROI model for UC enablement to justify the investment. Aligning KPIs and metrics to a financial ROI model is the only way to track the financial returns or competitive advantage that can be gained through UC enablement. The UC pilot project must be able to prove that the UC enablement solved the business challenge and enhanced productivity. UC enablement can be measured and analyzed from many perspectives, including the following:

• financial ROI results that track capital expenditures (CAPEX) and operational expenditures (OPEX) costs associated with changes in operating costs and expenses before and after UC enablement

• speed of, or increase in, revenue generation before and after UC enablement in comparison to previous fiscal periods

• measurement of cycle time to perform specific functions before and after UC enablement

• systems integration effort (labor hours) required to implement VoIP systems, UC application and communication servers, and quality of service (QoS)-enabled IP data networks, including the level of complexity, the required systems integration effort, and the cooperation of IT departments toward a common goal before and after UC enablement

• speed of end-user acceptance and adoption of UC enablement, once trained

Cost justifying a UC project

Organizations under financial duress or in changing economic conditions closely monitor CAPEX or OPEX. A UC proof-of-concept project allows organizations to analyze technical challenges and lets executive management review the results before making financially driven decisions about UC deployment, using KPIs, metrics, and financial ROI model results as validation. An organization typically conducts a UC pilot project prior to a full-scale deployment for the following reasons:

• minimized financial risk in the event of UC deployment failure or end-user nonacceptance

• minimized technical and systems integration failure because technical challenges and issues can be resolved in the pilot project prior to production deployment

• consolidated effort from the IT organization because UC enablement affects all disciplines within it

• collaboration between the UC pilot project's line-of-business champion and the IT organization toward a common goal

• thorough planning and assessment of a successful enterprise-wide UC deployment strategy to address systems integration issues

• a working model for executive approval, which in turn eases the internal sell for the full-scale project

> **Note**
>
> In some organizations, a pilot project is required before building a business case to validate both the financial investment in new technology and the ability to achieve desired goals and objectives. Depending on the scope, the UC project may require funding for additional expenses: VoIP system upgrades, purchase of servers, software licensing, data networking upgrades, security solutions, systems integration labor, and so on. All costs must be included in the financial ROI model. Any hidden costs that are discovered during the pilot project must be identified and added to the financial ROI model.

Define the scope of the project

There is a direct relationship between the scope of a UC deployment and the ROI obtained. The deeper the scope and breadth of a UC deployment, the greater the potential financial and productivity returns. However, as the scope widens, the project's success may be affected. For example, UC deployments affect many IT disciplines, including Private Branch Exchange (PBX) or IP-PBX systems, UC application servers, UC client and endpoint devices, networking, and security. As a UC pilot project scope becomes more complex, it may become increasingly difficult to meet scoped goals and objectives.

Project technical requirements and capabilities

It is critical to understand the technical disciplines involved in a successful UC implementation. It is also necessary to have hands-on systems integration experience. The following technical areas may be required within the scope of a UC proof-of-concept pilot project:

- telephony (IP-PBX) and computer telephony integration (CTI), including system configuration and administration of vendor IP-PBX and VoIP systems
- local area network (LAN) and wide area network (WAN) data-link and IP network layer protocols and networking: in particular, QoS and traffic prioritization
- Transmission Control Protocol/Internet Protocol (TCP/IP) family of protocols: IP protocols, VoIP, SIP, and voice signaling protocols
- VoIP and SIP security, particularly layered security designs
- UC application servers, including system configuration and administration of vendor UC application servers
- UC clients and endpoint devices, including selection and profiling of UC clients and endpoint devices

Because a UC project scope may include many of the areas just listed, a proof-of-concept pilot project is a good way to solve integration issues. Using a small-scale project to monitor issues with the breadth and complexity of required technologies will help to prepare the IT organization and staff for the upcoming network and communications transformation required in a full-scale UC enablement.

9 | Conducting a UC Proof-of-Concept Pilot Project

UC enablement projects have two major phases

UC enablement projects have two phases: requirements definition and implementation. The requirements definition phase is critical because it introduces the concept for the UC pilot project. This phase defines the business challenges to be resolved in the project. The implementation phase is critical because it provides proof and validation of the solution. The solution can be identified by defining KPIs, metrics, and the returns of a financial ROI model, and mapping those elements to the UC features, functions, and benefits that were enabled in the pilot project.

Figure 9-2 shows the three steps of the requirements definition phase:

- **Step 1: Identify the business challenges**—Identify clear and distinct challenges of business applications such as customer service (CS), customer relationship management (CRM), supply chain management (SCM), enterprise resource planning (ERP), or sales force automation (SFA). A line-of-business champion must also be identified to take on the identified business challenge and sponsor the UC proof-of-concept pilot project.

- **Step 2: Solve the business challenges**—Develop streamlined process flows and UC enablement options to solve these challenges. Enterprise transformation analysis and business process consulting are often required to build streamlined processes and create greater operational efficiency.

- **Step 3: Map the solutions to technologies**—Map each solution to a technology, using UC enablement features and functions. Identify cost elements and incorporate them into a financial ROI model that tracks all costs and budget components.

FIGURE 9-2: UC PILOT PROJECT REQUIREMENTS STEPS.

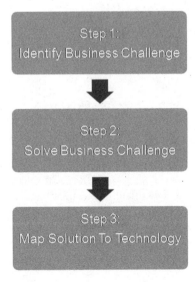

UC Pilot Project Requirements

Step 1: Identify Business Challenge

Step 2: Solve Business Challenge

Step 3: Map Solution To Technology

Once the requirements definition phase is complete, the line-of-business champion must decide whether to implement the UC pilot project. The project can focus on a single application or process within a particular business unit or department. The line-of-business champion typically takes ownership and financial responsibility for the project. The project must have full collaboration between that business unit and the IT organization supporting the UC pilot project implementation. It is much easier to sell the UC project internally if it is supported by an executive sponsor directly affected by the business challenge.

FIGURE 9-3: UC PILOT PROJECT IMPLEMENTATION REQUIREMENTS.

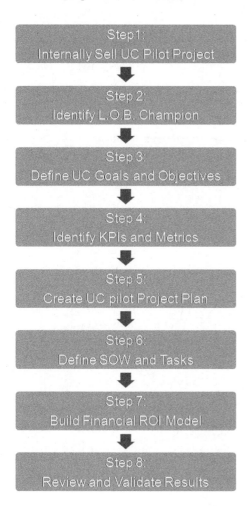

UC Pilot Project Implementation

Step 1:
Internally Sell UC Pilot Project

Step 2:
Identify L.O.B. Champion

Step 3:
Define UC Goals and Objectives

Step 4:
Identify KPIs and Metrics

Step 5:
Create UC pilot Project Plan

Step 6:
Define SOW and Tasks

Step 7:
Build Financial ROI Model

Step 8:
Review and Validate Results

9

Conducting a UC
Proof-of-Concept
Pilot Project

Figure 9-3 shows the eight steps typical of a UC proof-of-concept pilot project implementation. The following list describes these steps:

- **Step 1: Sell the UC pilot project internally**—Once the requirements definition phase is complete, the line-of-business champion must sell the project internally. The champion must also engage the CIO and CFO if the UC pilot project is driven by a financial ROI model.

- **Step 2: Identify line-of-business champion**—The line-of-business champion leads the UC enablement effort and pilot project. The champion is not from the IT organization, but controls the line of business targeted in the UC pilot project: for example, software development, professional services, customer service, supply chain, manufacturing, sales, or training.

- **Step 3: Define UC project goals and objectives**—The scope of the UC pilot project must be large enough to incorporate KPIs and metrics that can be aligned to a financial ROI model. At the same time, it must be limited to minimize pilot project complexity and potential for failure. The goals and objectives provide validation of the proof-of-concept pilot, if the project succeeds.

- **Step 4: Identify KPIs and metrics**—These tools measure and track the enabled UC features and functions. Examples include tracking cycle time reduction, cost savings, increases in revenue and profitability, repeat customer purchases, and lower operational costs through operational efficiencies.

- **Step 5: Create UC project plan**—The UC project plan has two phases: requirements definition and implementation. Tasks, deliverables, resource allocation, project milestones, and critical decision points are identified in the project plan. Specific reporting and review of KPIs, metrics, and financial returns is done throughout the life of the project.

- **Step 6: Define statement of work (SOW), tasks, and deliverables**—Specific tasks and deliverables are defined and documented in the SOW. The time required to perform tasks and provide deliverables is defined and allocated to the UC project implementation team's resources. It is important to track the time and work effort required to conduct a UC deployment and implementation to identify implementation challenges and streamline future enablement.

- **Step 7: Build financial ROI model**—The financial ROI model must contain startup data before the pilot project starts. The model's results serve as the financial KPI and metric for tracking lower operational costs. The model also tracks revenue and profitability throughout the life of the project.

- **Step 8: Review and validate results**—As data is collected through the life of the project, regular reviews, assessments, and validations are performed. Results are compared to the original goals and objectives to determine the ongoing success or failure of the UC pilot project.

UC project goals and objectives

Once the implementation process has been defined, identify achievable goals and objectives for the UC pilot project. In earlier chapters, you learned how to define functional requirements for workers who require real-time person-to-person communications, streamlined processes, and real-time access to information. These functional requirements are translated into technical requirements, which are mapped to technological solutions with UC enablement. From this mapping and translation, the goals and objectives are derived for the project. This is the most important part of a UC project because the goals and objectives are aligned to KPIs, metrics, and financial ROI.

Minimizing the risk associated with a UC project

The organization must decide whether or not to pursue the UC proof-of-concept pilot project, or future enterprise-wide UC deployment, based on a risk assessment conducted by the UC project team. The risk assessment team must answer the following questions before finalizing the goals and objectives:

• Are the goals and objectives functionally achievable?

• Are the goals and objectives technically achievable?

• Do the functional and technical goals and objectives map to feasible technology solutions?

• What are the critical success factors that must be achieved to ensure the success of a specific goal or objective?

• Are there any unknowns or risks pertaining to the desired goals and objectives?

• What is the financial budget required to conduct the UC project?

• What constitutes success or failure of the project?

Risk assessments help the organization anticipate challenges or technical issues as the UC project progresses. Additionally, such assessments help the project sponsor understand the risks, success factors, and financial implications if the project fails. The results of the risk assessment should be shared with the line-of-business champion to identify potential expectations and challenges. This helps to ensure the overall success of the UC project.

Scope of defining goals and objectives

Goals and objectives are generally defined for the end user and for the executive management review team responsible for assessing the overall performance of the project. Because goals and objectives are typically high level, they must incorporate KPIs and metrics that can be aligned to a financial ROI's cost elements and financial benefits. This alignment was shown in the UC Business Value Tool v1.5, introduced in Chapter 8, "Building a Measureable Financial ROI with KPIs."

> **SFA UC Pilot Project**
>
> **Sample Goals and Objectives**
>
> Depending on the UC pilot project scope and its functional and technical requirements, the goals and objectives may vary. Goals and objectives will be different for each type of worker participating in the UC project. For example, in an SFA UC proof-of-concept pilot project, the following workers will likely participate, each with different goals and objectives:
> - **Sales professionals**—The actual end users of UC endpoint devices
> - **Sales support specialists**—Sales engineers, sales overlays, and technical specialists
> - **Sales managers**—UC-enabled with sales professionals and executives for real-time presales support and sales reporting to executive management
> - **Sales executives**—UC-enabled with sales managers and other internal business executives with whom the sales organization must interface
> - **Customer service agents**—If the SFA UC project extends to enhanced customer service delivery, a UC-enabled contact center provides real-time access and collaboration with sales professionals and managers for high-value customers

Table 9-1 summarizes sample goals and objectives for the various participants in an SFA UC proof-of-concept project:

TABLE 9-1: SFA UC PILOT PROJECT GOALS AND OBJECTIVES.

	Primary Goal or Objective	Secondary Goal or Objective	Tertiary Goal or Objective
Sales Professionals	Real-time access to presales support specialists	Faster and simpler sales order entry	Shortened sales cycle
Sales Support Specialists	Real-time support for sales professionals	Real-time access to subject matter experts	Real-time audio/video conferencing and collaboration
Sales Managers	Driving revenue and profitability faster	Real-time access to sales professionals	Real-time access to sales figures
Sales Executives	Driving revenue and profitability faster	Real-time access to sales management and other executives	Real-time access to sales figures
Customer Service Agents	UC-enabled contact center linked to sales professionals	Driving customer retention	Increasing customer satisfaction

Many organizations cannot accurately track reductions in cycle time or shortened sales cycles. These organizations can still evaluate KPIs and metrics by comparing the end-of-project results to previous periods, and by asking each participant for a review of the project's goals and objectives. Some organizations track goals and objectives by comparing the end results to the financial ROI metrics determined during the pilot project requirements definition phase.

> **Note**
>
> In the SFA UC example just shown, each type of worker in the sales organization has specific goals and objectives to attain. Success is determined by measurable KPIs and metrics that can be aligned to cost elements and savings in a financial ROI.
>
> When the organization has decided how to track and monitor productivity enhancements, as well as cost savings and cost elements, the UC proof-of-concept pilot project can proceed. The review and validation of ongoing performance data should continue to establish the ongoing benefits of UC enablement.

Align requirements, goals, and objectives with key performance indicators and metrics

In Chapter 7, "Mapping the Solution to Technology," you learned to identify functional and technical requirements, which form the basis for the UC proof-of-concept pilot project's goals and objectives. Once goals, objectives, and requirements are determined, measurable KPIs and metrics are established to assess the project's success or failure. Goals and objectives must be mapped uniquely for different worker groups and UC project participants for everyone to benefit from UC enablement features and functions. The final step in this process is to map KPIs and metrics to measurable financial ROI cost elements: in particular, cost savings and increased revenue, profitability, and lower overhead for sales, general, and administrative (SG&A) functions.

> **SFA UC Pilot Project**
>
> **Sample KPIs, Metrics, and**
>
> **Alignment to Financial ROI**
>
> In an SFA project, a powerful sales force infrastructure can be created from a broad scope of person-to-person communication requirements, integrated business process, and real-time access to information. UC enablement can result in operational efficiency, which shortens the sales cycle and ultimately drives revenue and profitability.

Table 9-2 shows how goals and objectives are mapped to measurable KPIs, metrics, and financial ROI elements.

TABLE 9-2: Goals and objectives mapped to KPIs, metrics, and financial ROI elements.

	KPIs	Metrics	Financial ROI Element
Sales Professionals	Speed of access to presales support specialists	Average time to respond to customer	Did deal flow increase due to greater efficiency
Sales Support Specialists	Speed of access to sales professionals	Average time to respond to sales professionals	Did deal flow increase due to greater efficiency
Sales Managers	Driving revenue and profitability faster	Revenue and profitability figures compared to previous results	Increased revenue and profitability
Sales Executives	Growth in revenue and profitability compared to previous results	Revenue, profitability, SG&A overhead figures compared to previous results	Increased profitability and lower SG&A overhead
Customer Service Agents	Increased customer retention and customer lifetime value	Customer surveys, repeat purchases, first-call problem resolution metrics	Increased revenue profitability from customer repeat purchases

Forrester Consulting Business Value Tool v1.5 KPIs and metrics

The Forrester Consulting UC Business Value Tool v1.5 provides examples of additional KPIs and metrics that can be aligned to financial metrics. For example, KPIs and metrics can be tracked in the financial ROI model for a sales branch office participating in an SFA UC proof-of-concept pilot project, as well as for an organization that is not part of the project. Using the UC Business Value Tool, the organization can track the following areas:

- reduced real estate costs and SG&A overhead for sales branch office
- reduced travel expenses, compared to previous periods, for all sales professionals
- reduced training expenses and SG&A overhead for sales branch office
- shortened sales cycles and increasing revenue and profitability
- faster collection of revenues due to shortened project completion times through operational efficiencies
- total CAPEX or OPEX required to fund the UC proof-of-concept pilot project
- monthly, quarterly, and yearly sales forecasting figures, booked sales, revenue, profitability, and growth from previous time periods

Specific examples and figures of the cost elements and financial ROI benefits that can be tracked using the UC Business Value Tool v1.5 are provided in Chapter 8.

> **Note**
>
> Every CFO must ensure CAPEX and OPEX investments are wise financial decisions. Historically, it has been difficult to map IT investments to measurable KPIs and metrics and align these costs to a financial ROI model. Because UC enablement can enhance and streamline person-to-person communications, the opportunities for growth in revenue and profitability are promising for highly efficient, UC-enabled sales forces.
>
> Organizations that can identify CAPEX or OPEX funding for a UC proof-of-concept pilot project must engage their organization's CFO. Some CFOs prefer to examine two fiscal quarters of KPIs, metrics, and financial ROI results to assess growth figures from one UC-enabled financial quarter to the next.

Develop a financial budget for the project

The final, and most important, step in building a UC proof-of-concept pilot project is to build a financial budget for the project. It is critical to define an accurate project budget because UC projects typically include hardware, software, infrastructure, and systems integration labor costs. Note that the financial ROI model is based on CAPEX investment costs, on which the ROI is calculated.

UC project budget scope

The outline for a UC project financial budget should mirror the project scope definition. The following list contains some categories to consider for the UC project budget:

- enterprise transformation consulting services, including professional service fees that can be folded into the financial ROI model
- solutions to identified deployment prerequisites that may require funding for external systems or applications: for example, WAN upgrades, bandwidth increases, hardware, software, or systems integration costs
- technology purchases and upgrade or refreshment costs: for example, QoS network, hardware, software, applications, or VoIP and SIP security solutions
- installation and systems integration professional services
- maintenance and support
- ongoing systems administration and technical support, which may be done in-house or be outsourced throughout the term of the pilot project

In the UC Business Value Tool, project costs are collected and tracked on the view results screen, which displays the actual costs associated with the UC enablement project (see Figure 8-6 in Chapter 8). Financial cost and expense tracking spreadsheets can be built from these cost categories. The ability to track, report, and capture accurate cost elements and savings is key to project success.

Note

Funding a UC proof-of-concept pilot project requires a line-of-business champion or sponsor to commit CAPEX or OPEX funds for the pilot project. Once the champion or sponsor has been identified, the organization must examine the UC proof-of-concept scope. To do this, compare the advantages and disadvantages of a more complex project scope and the required financial or resource commitments based on the results of the preliminary financial ROI results.

The UC Business Value Tool v1.5 can serve as the UC project's roadmap once the project has commenced. The project will require ongoing program management by the line-of-business champion and project team members to track and report the identified KPIs, metrics, and financial results.

Knowledge Check 9-1: Conducting a Unified Communications Proof-of-Concept Pilot Project

Answer the following questions. Answers to these Knowledge Check questions are located in *Appendix A: Answers to Knowledge Check Questions.*

1. Which of the following is not a benefit of conducting a UC proof-of-concept pilot project?

   a. Mitigates any risk prior to production deployment

   b. Allows an organization to define best practices for future deployments

   c. Requires that funds be committed for the UC proof-of-concept pilot project

   d. Provides valuable cost, effort, savings, and complexity information for future deployments

   e. Supports a cooperative and collaborative implementation effort within all disciplines of an IT organization

2. The greater the need to identify financial ROI cost savings, the greater the scope and complexity of the UC enablement implementation.

   a. True

   b. False

3. Why should an organization include the UC pilot project requirements definition in a UC proof-of-concept pilot project?

   a. Minimizes risk

   b. Project budget is needed

   c. Line-of-business champion needs to build a financial ROI model and obtain acceptance from the CFO if needed

   d. Forces a detailed analysis and solution for a unique business challenge that can be solved with UC enablement

   e. None of the above

4. Which of the following steps is not included in UC pilot project implementation?

   a. Map the solution to technology

   b. Review and validate results of the financial ROI

   c. Define KPIs and metrics aligned to a financial ROI

   d. Build a financial ROI model with actual cost elements

   e. Define UC proof-of-concept project goals and objectives

5. A UC proof-of-concept pilot project does not need a line-of-business champion and can be driven by the IT organization.

    a. True

    b. False

6. _____ risk is an important task when an organization is deciding whether or not to pursue a UC proof-of-concept pilot project.

    a. Studying

    b. Defining

    c. Minimizing

    d. Maximizing

    e. Understanding

7. A KPI or metric must be quantifiable and measurable to have validity in a proof-of-concept pilot project.

    a. True

    b. False

8. Which of the following is not an example of a measurable KPI or metric?

    a. Time

    b. Sales cycle time

    c. SG&A overhead

    d. Revenue per month

    e. Productivity enhancement

9. How do you fold the cost of a UC proof-of-concept pilot project into the budget if you do not have CAPEX to spend?

    a. Wait until next fiscal year but budget for it this year

    b. See if other cost centers are willing to help contribute to the project budget

    c. Lease it and use OPEX to pay for the project based on a forecasted financial return

    d. Convince the CFO to commit to the investment using CAPEX based on the projected financial ROI model

    e. None of the above

10. UC proof-of-concept pilot projects are easier to sell as a first step for organizations considering UC enablement.

    a. True

    b. False

Chapter summary

In this chapter, you learned the benefits of conducting a UC proof-of-concept pilot project prior to a full deployment. You also learned how to build a UC pilot project and how to deploy it. There are two initial project phases: the requirement definitions phase, which defines functional and technical requirements for the UC enablement initiative, and the implementation phase, which minimizes risk and maximizes UC enablement success throughout the organization. The final step in the process is evaluation, where KPIs, metrics, and financial ROI results are reviewed and validated to determine the success or failure of the pilot project.

In Chapter 10, "Creating a Unified Communications Project Statement of Work," you will learn how to manage a project and build a project plan. UC proof-of-concept pilot projects and deployment projects are more likely to succeed when project team members understand how all parts of the project fit into the scope definition.

10: Creating a Unified Communications Project Statement of Work

When an organization is ready to consider a Unified Communications (UC) or proof-of-concept pilot project, it may be necessary to create financial and cost-benefit analysis models as a basis for the final decision. These models may include key performance indicators (KPIs) and metrics for financial return on investment (ROI). If the organization decides to implement the project, a statement of work (SOW) must be created. Building an SOW requires determining an acceptable financial ROI, minimizing the complexity of the project, building a project plan, and defining the project scope. It is necessary to perform these steps prior to scheduling purchases, defining system integration tasks, or creating project deliverables.

This chapter describes how to write an SOW, build a UC project plan, and map the project scope to a budget against which the ROI will be compared.

Chapter 10 Topics

In this chapter, you will learn:

- the major phases, tasks, and deliverables for a UC project

- how to develop the SOW for a UC project

- the major project milestones and checkpoints for a UC project

- how to build a UC project plan that includes key project decision points

- how to align the UC project scope to a budget that incorporates all cost elements into the financial ROI analysis

- how to identify UC project team resources and the skill sets required of each team member

Chapter 10 Goals

Upon completion of this chapter, you will be able to:

• develop an entire UC project SOW

• create a UC project plan with key milestones and decision points

• build a UC project team that ensures the success of the UC project

Key Terms

Acceptable use policy (AUP)   224

Functional requirements   227

Implementation plan   222

Project milestone or checkpoint   215

Project plan   215

Requirements definition   215

Statement of work (SOW)   217

10

Creating a UC Project
Statement of Work

UC project phases, tasks, and deliverables

A UC or proof-of-concept pilot project has two components: defining the project requirements, and implementing the project. Once the project scope, goals, and objectives have been determined, the project phases, tasks, and deliverables can be defined. These must then be incorporated into the SOW and aligned with a detailed project plan. In turn, the SOW supports the scope and budget of the UC project.

This section of the chapter contains a sample project element definition, constructed with the three-step method introduced in Chapter 9, "Conducting a Unified Communications Proof-of-Concept Pilot Project":

• **Step 1**—Identify the business challenge

• **Step 2**—Solve the business challenge

• **Step 3**—Map the solution to technology

These steps are also the project phases for the requirements definition. Each step has its own tasks, deliverables, and project milestones unique within the project scope. The following example shows sample tasks and deliverables typical of a multiphased UC requirements definition project.

UC Project Requirements

Step 1—Identify the Business Challenge

Certain tasks and deliverables are typical elements of identifying the central business challenge:

Task 1—Identify challenges in all aspects of the organization.

Task 2—Interview key executives to identify the source of existing challenges, problems, or inefficiencies.

Task 3—Assess the impact on productivity, financial performance, and employee satisfaction (ESAT) in an effort to prioritize the challenges.

Task 4—Determine if the challenge can be linked to a financial ROI and, if so, show how it can be quantified with KPIs and metrics.

Task 5—Prioritize challenges according to their impact on financial performance, productivity, and ESAT.

UC project requirements for step 1 deliverables typically include the following:
• evaluation matrix of identified challenges
• assessment of challenges based on prioritized criteria
• analysis of challenges and their impact on productivity, financial performance, and ESAT
• prioritization of challenges based on assessment criteria

Once the challenges are identified, assessed, and prioritized, the next step is to identify solutions. This process was introduced in Chapter 6, "Solving Business Challenges," where sample business challenges were solved with streamlined processes and real-time access to information.

Step 2—Solve the Business Challenge

These tasks and deliverables are typical elements of identifying solutions to the business challenge:

Task 1—Analyze what is needed to enhance each prioritized business challenge identified in step 1.

Task 2—Engage in enterprise transformation analysis to determine how best to solve the challenge.

Task 3—Identify process flow improvements where manual processes or human intervention in decision making can be eliminated.

Task 4—Make recommendations for a new application or streamlined process, based on what is achievable.

Task 5—Interview key business and operations managers responsible for the challenge and its solution.

UC project step 2 deliverables typically include the following:

- prioritized business challenges and processes mapped to identified solutions
- solutions mapping, which may include multiple alternatives with cost magnitude estimates for each solution
- assessment and recommendation for whether or not to move forward with the technology solution

---

Once the solution alternatives are identified for the challenges, they need to be mapped to UC enablement. This mapping was introduced in Chapter 7, "Mapping the Solution to Technology," which described how technology and vendor solutions are introduced into the UC enablement solution. Mapping the solution to technology must include a detailed cost matrix identifying all costs associated with the UC project. This information will be incorporated into the project's financial ROI model.

Step 3—Mapping the Solution to Technology

These tasks and deliverables are typical elements used when mapping the solution to technology:

Task 1—Map each viable solution alternative to technology.

Task 2—Break technology mapping down into telephony, Internet Protocol (IP) networking, server/ desktop application software, endpoint devices, Voice over Internet Protocol (VoIP), Session Initiation Protocol (SIP), security, and systems integration categories.

Task 3—Assess each solution and its technology mapping in the following areas: scope, complexity, cost, ability to achieve goals and objectives, critical success factors, and risk assessment.

Task 4—Map UC features and functions to each involved worker.

Task 5—Make recommendations for the best solution alternative to pursue.

UC project step 3 deliverables typically include the following:
- solutions to technology that map UC features to specific workers and end users, based on functional need
- technology cost budget identifying all associated costs to implement the UC project
- assessment and justification of each solution along with recommendation for the UC enablement technology solution to implement

---

Once the requirements definition part of a UC project is completed, implementation of the project can continue. The next section describes the tasks and deliverables associated with the implementation of the project.

Note
Some organizations require that a preliminary financial ROI be calculated before deciding whether to move forward with the UC project. In this case, the requirements definition and preliminary ROI analysis can be conducted prior to the implementation phase. The results of the preliminary ROI analysis must yield a positive or acceptable ROI estimate to make a sound decision regarding the UC project.

Defining the statement of work for a UC project

When shifting from the requirements definition component of a UC project to implementation, use the implementation process introduced in Chapter 9. The eight-step process includes the following steps, all of which can become part of the SOW:

- **Step 1**—Sell the UC project internally
- **Step 2**—Identify a line-of-business champion
- **Step 3**—Define UC goals and objectives
- **Step 4**—Identify KPIs and metrics

- **Step 5**—Create UC project plan
- **Step 6**—Define SOW and tasks
- **Step 7**—Build financial ROI model
- **Step 8**—Review and validate results

Depending on the UC project scope and the particular steps required by the organization, the following examples show the tasks and deliverables associated with each implementation step.

UC Project Implementation

Step 1—Sell the UC Project Internally

The following tasks and deliverables are typical elements of selling the UC project internally:

Task 1—Identify key business leaders in different organizational disciplines.

Task 2—Define the audience with which to share the UC enablement vision.

Task 3—Invite or collaborate with vendors and technology partners to develop content for the UC enablement value proposition.

Task 4—Invite the CFO, CIO, and other business leaders to a UC enablement briefing.

Task 5—Schedule and deliver the UC enablement briefing to the business leaders.

Task 6—Customize the UC enablement value proposition based on the confirmed audience.

Task 7—Review and evaluate further interest in pursuing UC enablement.

Step 1 deliverables typically include the following:
- executive summary of the UC enablement value proposition, describing the challenges that can be solved with UC enablement
- presentation of the customized UC enablement value proposition

---

One of the objectives in step 1 is to identify an internal line-of-business champion who is interested in learning more about how UC can solve business challenges and process inefficiencies. The more backing and support for UC enablement from business leaders, the greater the probability that UC enablement will be implemented.

Step 2—Identify Line-of-Business Champion

The following tasks and deliverables are typical elements of identifying a line-of-business champion:

Task 1—Identify key business leaders who showed interest in the value proposition.

Task 2—Drill down on that leader's challenges and demonstrate how UC enablement can solve them.

Task 3—Discuss the UC proof-of-concept pilot project approach and how it will be tied to a specific financial ROI model.

Task 4—Obtain the line-of-business champion's support and ask for sponsorship.

Task 5—Encourage the line-of-business champion to engage the CFO and obtain executive sponsorship to proceed with a UC project.

Step 2 deliverables typically include the following:
• preliminary financial ROI model aligned to the UC enablement solution in step 1

UC enablement is first driven by identifying a business challenge that can be fixed with UC enablement. The next step is to identify a business leader or line-of-business champion who will sponsor the project. Without a sponsor, the UC project will proceed without enthusiastic internal support for the initiative. The success of the UC project is in the hands of the line-of-business champion, who must drive it through implementation and validation.

> **Note**
>
> Steps 3 through 5 of the UC pilot project implementation process were introduced in Chapter 9: Step 3, define UC goals and objectives; Step 4, identify KPIs and metrics; Step 5, create UC pilot project plan.
>
> Step 6, defining the SOW and tasks, is the subject of this chapter.
>
> Step 7, building a financial ROI model, was introduced in Chapter 8.

Review and validation is the final step in UC project implementation.

> **Step 8—Review and Validation**
>
> These tasks and deliverables are typical elements in review and validation of a UC project's results:
>
> Task 1—Prepare a monthly UC project assessment report template.
>
> Task 2—Identify and assemble the measurable KPIs and metrics that were defined for the UC project.
>
> Task 3—Assemble, organize, and align the KPIs and metrics to the financial ROI model.
>
> Task 4—Prepare a monthly UC project assessment and financial ROI tracking report.
>
> Task 5—Summarize KPIs, metrics, and financial ROI benchmarks for management review and validation.
>
> Step 8 deliverables typically include the following:
>
> • UC project assessment report template
> • ongoing tracking, monitoring, and documenting of KPIs, metrics, and financial elements
> • monthly and quarterly review and validation of the UC project goals and objectives

Each part of a UC project has major milestones. These milestones act as checkpoints throughout the UC project to ensure that it is on track to achieve the defined goals and objectives. The major UC project milestones are presented in the next section of this chapter.

Major UC project milestones and checkpoints

In both components of a UC project, each step has its own milestones. A milestone can be described as a critical success factor, meaning that the milestone must be completed successfully to move forward with the project. The following list describes the major milestones for the requirements definition component:

- **Step 1—Identify the business challenge**
  - Milestone 1: Challenges are identified in one or more lines of business.
  - Milestone 2: Challenges are prioritized and agreed on by executive management.
  - Milestone 3: Executive management agrees to listen to UC enablement value proposition.
- **Step 2—Solve the business challenge**
  - Milestone 4: Challenges that can be solved with UC enablement are identified.
  - Milestone 5: The line-of-business champion or sponsor is identified and willing to fund the UC project.
  - Milestone 6: The line-of-business champion engages the organization's CFO to discuss the project's financial ROI model approach.
- **Step 3—Map the solution to technology**
  - Milestone 7: Alternative technology approaches for the solution are identified.

- Milestone 8: Costs associated with the UC project's solutions are identified.
- Milestone 9: Sponsorship and funding from the line-of-business champion and CFO are pursued to proceed with the recommended solution and UC project.

Note	At this point, some organizations may require that a preliminary financial ROI model be generated, based on identified assumptions, critical success factors, and expected outcomes. Positive model results will ensure that the line-of-business champion and CFO have greater confidence in the project, its achievable goals and objectives, and its favorable results.

The following list describes the major project milestones for the implementation component:

- **Step 1—Sell the UC project internally**
  - Milestone 1: Executive management agrees to listen to the UC value proposition.
  - Milestone 2: UC value proposition is presented to executive management.
  - Milestone 3: Executive management agrees to proceed with implementation of the UC project.
- **Step 2—Identify line-of-business champion**
  - Milestone 1: Line-of-business champion candidates are identified.
  - Milestone 2: UC value proposition is presented to a short list of line-of-business champions.
  - Milestone 3: Line-of-business champion agrees to sponsor implementation of the UC project.
- **Step 3—Define UC goals and objectives**
  - Milestone 1: Goals and objectives are identified.
  - Milestone 2: Line-of-business champion prioritizes and accepts the goals and objectives.
  - Milestone 3: Achievable goals and objectives are identified and incorporated into the UC project scope.
- **Step 4—Identify KPIs and metrics**
  - Milestone 1: Measurable KPIs and metrics are identified for the scope of the project.
  - Milestone 2: KPIs and metrics are aligned to the financial ROI model.
  - Milestone 3: Method of tracking KPIs, metrics, and financial ROI elements is defined.
- **Step 5—Create UC project plan**
  - Milestone 1: Line-of-business champion accepts and approves goals, objectives, KPIs, metrics, and financial ROI model.
  - Milestone 2: Project plan is crafted based on the scope of the UC project.

10 | Creating a UC Project Statement of Work

- Milestone 3: Detailed implementation plan is incorporated into the project plan template and calendar schedule.
- **Step 6—Define SOW and tasks**
  - Milestone 1: Finalized project plan template is reviewed and accepted.
  - Milestone 2: Tasks and deliverables are identified and assigned to the project plan.
  - Milestone 3: Resources, both internal and external, are identified to perform the tasks and deliverables.
- **Step 7—Build financial ROI model**
  - Milestone 1: CFO is engaged and supports the financial ROI approach to the UC project.
  - Milestone 2: All cost elements and savings are identified and incorporated into the financial ROI model.
  - Milestone 3: Preliminary financial ROI model is utilized to compare to actual data as it is collected.
- **Step 8—Review and validate results**
  - Milestone 1: UC project data points are incorporated into the reporting template.
  - Milestone 2: KPIs, metrics, and financial ROI elements are tabulated and compared to the preliminary financial ROI estimate.
  - Milestone 3: UC project benchmarked KPIs, metrics, and financial ROI are achieved.

> **Note** Financial ROI models for a UC proof-of-concept pilot project may require six to nine months of data to assess and analyze the financial impacts of the UC project. The line-of-business champion and CFO will typically determine the length of the UC project based on this analysis. They can then use this analysis to make decisions about deploying UC enablement throughout the entire organization.

Aligning a UC project scope to a project budget

As described in Chapter 9, the project scope dictates the amount of funding required to complete the UC project. It is critical to align the UC project scope to a budget as accurately as possible. Accurate budget alignment is necessary to develop a financial ROI model with expected outcomes. When finalizing the project scope and budget, consider these elements: mapping the scope to achievable goals and objectives, SOW tasks and deliverables, KPIs, metrics, and the financial ROI model. All identified UC project costs must be incorporated into the financial ROI model as part of the overall financial analysis. These costs may include upgrades to existing voice systems, IP data networks, servers, endpoint devices, and software application licenses. All of these elements must be identified to capture an accurate financial ROI picture.

The following list shows UC project scope elements that must be incorporated into the final project requirements definition:

- identified business challenges
- alternative solutions to challenges
- solutions that are mapped to technology and UC enablement
- achievable goals and objectives
- measurable KPIs, metrics, and financials
- financial ROI model
- identified cost elements and preliminary financial ROI model

These UC project scope elements must be mapped to a UC project plan and implementation budget. The line-of-business champion will be required to fund and sponsor this budget. In many cases, the UC project is driven by someone outside the IT organization, and is sponsored by the line-of-business organization itself. The following list summarizes the mapping of a UC project's requirements to an implementation budget:

- **Identified business challenges**—When done using outside business consultants, this will bear a cost.

- **Alternative solutions to business challenges**—This should include a cost analysis.

- **Solutions that are mapped to technology and UC enablement**—All hardware, software, upgrade, support, licensing, and systems integration costs should be included.

- **Achievable goals and objectives**—No cost element is involved.

- **Measurable KPIs, metrics, and financials**—No cost element is involved unless tools or systems are needed to capture data and report on results.

- **Financial ROI model**—No cost element is involved, except for resource time required to review, analyze, and validate results.

- **Identified cost elements and preliminary financial ROI model**—All cost elements should be identified before the total UC project budget is derived.

Note	Defining the total budget for a UC project is a critical success factor in moving forward with the investment. The total budget must be accompanied with identified cost-saving elements, particularly for those costs that are being replaced with UC enablement features and functions. All up-front capital expenditures (CAPEX) or operational expenditures (OPEX) must be identified and incorporated into the financial ROI model as up-front costs. These expenditures must also be funded by the line-of-business champion's business unit. The amount of available project funds may limit the scope of the UC project. Therefore, it is important to focus on achievable goals and objectives that have measurable KPIs and metrics that can be aligned to a financial ROI output.

Building a UC project team

A UC project affects many IT disciplines and other lines of business. When building the UC project team, all affected internal departments should be consulted about necessary applications, processes, finances, and technology. Because the UC project affects multiple departments, the project team must be built within the sponsor's line of business, but separate from IT support for the UC project. This group is called the UC business leadership team, and typically includes the following members:

- line-of-business champion

- directors and managers within that line of business who share a common challenge or problem

- end users within that line of business who currently use an inefficient application or process with human delay and latency issues

- CFO of that line of business or parent organization who can provide financial analysis support and input into solving the challenge

As explained in Chapter 9, UC enablement affects every IT discipline. Therefore, a UC project or proof-of-concept pilot project is not always easy to implement successfully. This is particularly the case if there is animosity among key players within the IT department or the organization as a whole. Working in a collaborative manner toward a common goal is critical for successful UC enablement deployment. The UC technology implementation team typically includes the following members:

- human resources and IT policy organization to define acceptable use policies (AUPs) for use of UC applications and tools

- IT workstation or desktop applications organization

- local area network (LAN) applications and systems administration organization

- wide area network (WAN) network engineering organization

- LAN-to-WAN or network engineering organization responsible for firewalls and ingress/egress points in the IT networking infrastructure

- remote access network engineering organization responsible for secure and authenticated remote communications for mobile workers

- systems and software applications development organizations

- IT security organization

- voice and telephony organization

- CIO of the business unit or entire organization taking a leadership role in assisting with the financial ROI model

The diversity of an organization's IT and non-IT disciplines must be utilized to implement the UC project successfully. At the end of the project, the organization's performance in working together toward a common goal must also be evaluated. The fewer complications in the implementation, the easier it may be to achieve acceptance across the organization for a full UC enablement deployment. If the UC project's goals and objectives are achieved, the KPIs and metrics will identify favorable financial ROI results. These results will determine whether or not the organization moves forward with its UC enablement deployments.

Knowledge Check 10-1: Creating a Unified Communications Project Statement of Work

Answer the following questions. Answers to these Knowledge Check questions are located in *Appendix A: Answers to Knowledge Check Questions.*

1. Why is it important to identify and solve a business challenge as the foundation of a UC proof-of-concept pilot project?

   a. Measurable KPIs and metrics can be identified.

   b. Measurable KPIs and metrics can be linked to a financial ROI.

   c. It is easier to get a line-of-business champion sponsor if you solve his or her specific business challenge or problem.

   d. Solving a business challenge or problem means the UC solution can positively impact financial performance, revenue, and profitability.

   e. All of the above.

2. The larger the UC proof-of-concept pilot project scope, the larger the SOW and funding required to obtain a positive financial ROI.

   a. True

   b. False

3. Why should an organization include part 1 of the UC pilot project requirements definition step in a UC proof-of-concept pilot project?

   a. It minimizes risk.

   b. Project budget is needed.

   c. A line-of-business champion needs to build a financial ROI model and obtain acceptance from the CFO if needed.

   d. It forces a detailed analysis and solution for a unique business challenge that can be solved with UC enablement.

   e. None of the above.

4. Which of the following steps is not included in part 2 of the UC pilot project implementation?

   a. Map the solution to technology

   b. Review and validate results of the financial ROI

   c. Define KPIs and metrics aligned to a financial ROI

   d. Build a financial ROI model with actual cost elements

   e. Define UC proof-of-concept project goals and objectives

5. A UC proof-of-concept pilot project does not need a line-of-business champion and can be driven by the IT organization.

   a. True

   b. False

6. _____ risk is an important task when an organization is deciding on whether or not to pursue a UC proof-of-concept pilot project.

   a. Studying

   b. Defining

   c. Maximizing

   d. Minimizing

   e. Understanding

7. A KPI or metric must be quantifiable and measurable to have validity in a proof-of-concept pilot project.

   a. True

   b. False

8. Which of the following is not an example of a measurable KPI or metric?

   a. Time

   b. Sales cycle time

   c. SG&A overhead

   d. Revenue per month

   e. Productivity enhancement

9. How do you fold the cost of a UC proof-of-concept pilot project into the budget if you do not have CAPEX to spend?

   a. Wait until next fiscal year but budget for it this year

   b. See if other cost centers are willing to help contribute to the project budget

   c. Lease it and use OPEX to pay for the project based on a forecasted financial return

   d. Convince the CFO to commit to the investment using CAPEX based on the projected financial ROI model

   e. None of the above

10. UC proof-of-concept pilot projects are easier to sell as a first step for organizations considering UC enablement.

    a. True

    b. False

Chapter summary

This chapter described the method used to plan a UC or proof-of-concept pilot project and subsequent UC enablement deployment. After an organization has decided to pursue a UC project or UC enablement deployment, a statement of work (SOW) must be built. The SOW must define tasks, deliverables, and project scope. It must also align the goals and objectives to KPIs, metrics, and a financial ROI model, and must include key milestones and a project budget. Showing how all project pieces fit into the project scope definition helps to ensure the UC project's success. Aligning project milestones with a project plan and budget keeps the UC project on track to achieve its goals and objectives.

Corporate UC and data security should be the priority of the deployment design. Considerations such as vulnerability, cost of mitigation, ease of use, and mitigation of risks to reward must be part of the overall deployment discussions. Security issues are covered in the final chapters of this book, including requirements for ensuring the confidentiality, integrity, and availability of VoIP and SIP communications. Sensitive security issues, such as how the organization's and customer's privacy data will be contained within a UC dialogue, must be included in the overall functional requirements and implementation plans of a UC project.

11: Conducting Unified Communications Systems Integration

A successful Unified Communications (UC) solution requires the cooperation and involvement of many individuals. It requires business leader support because a UC project can drastically affect how business activities are delivered when the project is complete. It requires in-depth application knowledge because specific applications must be made communications-aware. It also requires detailed knowledge of the communications methods that are included in the UC solution.

In this chapter, you will learn the elements of a successful UC systems integration, from preparing the network to modifying dialing plans and integrating the client at the user desktop. This chapter also describes the impact of UC systems on the rest of the information technology (IT) infrastructure.

Chapter 11 Topics

In this chapter, you will learn:

- steps required to integrate Microsoft Office Communications Server 2007 with a Private Branch Exchange (PBX), as explained in reference to the Nortel Communications Server 1000

- steps required to implement the Voice Services capabilities of Office Communications Server 2007

- services that can be configured with Office Communications Server 2007

- steps required to integrate Office Communications Server 2007 with the traditional voice infrastructure

- method used to prepare Active Directory directory services for the installation of Office Communications Server 2007

11

Chapter 11 Goals

Upon completion of this chapter, you will be able to:

- identify the key elements in delivering a successful UC integration project for Office Communications Server 2007 and Nortel Communications Server (CS) 1000

- clearly articulate the integration elements required for voice elements of the UC solution, based on details for the Nortel Communications Server 1000

- fully understand the capabilities configured with Office Communications Server 2007

- fully understand the integration elements required to facilitate interoperability between Office Communications Server 2007 and the traditional voice infrastructure

- fully understand the role of directory services in general and Active Directory specifically

Key Terms

Application Module Link (AML) 237

Associated Set Assignment (AST) 234

Call detail records (CDR) 236

Dual tone multifrequency (DTMF) 235

Fully qualified domain name (FQDN) 236

Multimedia Convergence Manager (MCM) 235

Network Routing Service (NRS) 236

Personal call assistant (PCA) 234

Remote call control (RCC) 234

SIP Proxy 235

Twinning 234

Value added server (VAS) 237

Putting it all together in an enterprise UC ecosystem

UC is a unique experience for every enterprise. Deployment involves a continuous process of assessment, strategy and review, planning and design, implementation, management, and ongoing support. It is a continuous process because there will be many new opportunities to apply UC technology to many facets of the business. As industry standards both evolve and become more widely adopted, new features and solutions will be developed to meet the ever-increasing demand for real-time communications and collaboration.

Before effective planning can begin, the existing environment must be thoroughly assessed. This analysis should include the following questions:

- Is there a line of business in which removing human latency will materially affect profitability?
- Can the existing network infrastructure support real-time communications?
- Is the existing voice infrastructure Session Initiation Protocol (SIP) ready?
- Can the IT infrastructure support the 24/7 high-availability demands of a real-time communications application?
- Are there existing information security policies and procedures that acknowledge the changing nature of the organizational information flow?

The answers to these questions are fundamental in creating a baseline for an effective strategy, implementation, and transition plan.

Existing voice and data infrastructure vendors may have conflicting UC strategies. Because every UC deployment is unique, it is important to establish a strategy tuned to business objectives rather than to technical capabilities.

When the assessment is complete and the shared strategy has been determined, the organization can begin to plan and design the UC environment. It is best to begin with a proof of concept or pilot project, which will provide training and familiarity with UC deployments before a full-scale implementation. This plan should define the pilot project, address every aspect of the infrastructure, and propose a long-term rollout strategy.

When these initial steps are completed, implementation can begin. In this chapter, you will learn about the technical implementation considerations involved in a UC enablement. However, business considerations represent the true value of a UC deployment, so the business must also commit to defining the process changes expected from the implementation.

When the UC project is complete, the company must create effective day-to-day operating and information security policies and procedures. It is critical to ensure that business performance is continuously monitored to ensure that problems do not affect profitability. Metrics must be defined and monitored so that generated reports are delivered to management. The transition to UC enablement requires clear communication of results.

Organizations must also design an effective support plan that defines procedures for both system maintenance and business process change management. The support system must acknowledge that transition to UC is a fluid activity.

Building the UC system may involve cooperation among resources that do not ordinarily interact. UC crosses organizational boundaries, vendor boundaries, and even individual boundaries. The transition must be managed to ensure that the system thrives throughout the UC enablement process.

TDM-PBX, IP-PBX, and IP Softphone system integration requirements

Every telecommunications vendor has a published strategy that explains why its customers should migrate to the Voice over Internet Protocol (VoIP). Even for systems not already IP-enabled, vendors offer gateways that allow VoIP integration with the traditional PBX. Figure 11-1 shows a logical view of the interconnection of a traditional phone system connected to the public telephone network through Integrated Services Digital Network (ISDN) primary rate trunks.

FIGURE 11-1: PBX NETWORK INTERFACE (NO IP).

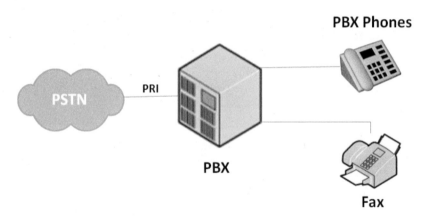

It can be expensive to IP-enable a traditional PBX. Before making that decision, the organization should consider whether a software-based IP-PBX could coexist with the traditional PBX and allow migration to VoIP. Coexistence does require support for two operational systems from separate vendors, although the organization can manage change across the internal organization more effectively. IP-enabling the traditional PBX essentially creates a coexistent environment; the only difference is that it is delivered by a single vendor. Figure 11-2 shows how the traditional PBX can act as a gateway for an IP-PBX. Notice that a gateway is used to translate between the IP-PBX and the traditional PBX.

If the organization decides to deploy a coexistent environment, an IP gateway solution must be implemented to allow interoperation with the PBX. Gateways emulate standard extensions from the PBX and provide call control, which translates SIP addresses to phone numbers and SIP requests to tone generation and translation echo cancellation, along with other operations. Gateways also use voice codecs to transform the media stream between IP packets and serial streams.

FIGURE 11-2: IP-PBX WITH PBX AND GATEWAY.

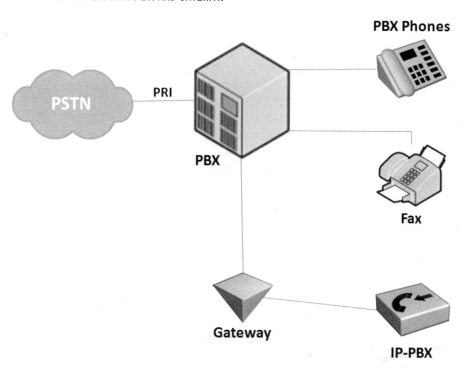

With rare exceptions, these gateways also exist in an IP-PBX environment. The difference between coexistence in the PBX environment and implementation of an IP-PBX is the physical location of the gateway within the network architecture. In a coexistence environment, one gateway lies between the PBX and the IP-PBX, with the PBX providing interconnection to the carrier services.

In the pure IP-PBX environment, the gateway lies between the IP-PBX and the carrier services. With the IP-PBX, this gateway requirement exists because the carrier does not deliver gateway services within the core network. Carriers who deliver IP Centrex services currently provide the gateway as part of their services, although a small gateway should be located at the customer premises as well to improve availability.

Integration requirements on the PBX are dependent on the defined configuration. The examples in this section describe integrating Office Communications Server 2007 as the IP-PBX with the IP-enabled Nortel CS 1000 (CS 1000). Although the specific integration steps are unique to CS 1000 and Office Communications Server 2007, other vendor products will require similar configurations.

One of the first requirements is to ensure that adequate licenses have been acquired for the CS 1000. Various licenses may be required, including the following:

• **SIP ports**—Enough SIP ports (trunks) must be licensed to support the number of concurrent users between Office Communications Server 2007 and CS 1000.

- **PCA**—Personal call assistant (PCA) trunks are required for each Office Communicator 2007 client that uses the Twinning feature. Twinning allows two phones to act as if they share the same extension number. Typically, this is used to link a user's desk phone with some form of wireless extension or Wi-Fi handset.

- **SIP CTI TR87**—TR87 is the international standard that defines interoperability standards between servers and communications equipment. These licenses are required for remote call control (RCC).

- **AST**—Associated Set Assignment (AST) is required to enable control of a secondary number, which rings to alert the called party that an incoming call is waiting.

After all appropriate licenses have been acquired, integration activities can begin. Figure 11-3 shows a flow chart of activities to be completed during the integration.

FIGURE 11-3: DEPLOYMENT FLOW CHART.

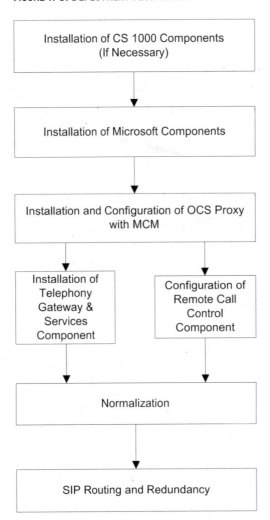

The remainder of this section covers activities associated with the CS 1000 hybrid PBX. The process explained here assumes that the PBX has the necessary hardware and software, and addresses only the incremental pieces required to enable UC. Office Communications Server 2007 and Active Directory must be configured prior to completing the tasks in this section.

Installation and configuration of Office Communications Server 2007 proxy with MCM

Within Office Communications Server 2007, the proxy has a defined server role. The SIP proxy is the core protocol platform upon which all other services are built. It provides the basic structure for networking and security and performs connection management, message header parsing, routing, authentication, and state management. When integrating with the CS 1000, Nortel's Multimedia Convergence Manager (MCM) must be installed on this server. MCM has two main components: MCM Service, which handles call processing, and MCM Management Console, which interfaces with the MCM Service for configuration, administration, and maintenance. The MCM call processing service handles SIP telephony traffic between CS 1000 and Office Communications Server 2007. To install MCM, use the installation wizard delivered on the distribution media.

Installation of Telephony Gateway and Services component

Office Communications Server 2007, Active Directory, and MCM must be configured properly before configuring the Telephony Gateway and Services component. PBX configuration involves two functions: signaling server configuration and call server configuration.

- **Configuring the codec**—The Office Communications Server 2007 mediation server supports the G.711 (20 milliseconds) codec. This codec must be enforced on the network by defining only the G.711 codec on the PBX.

- **Loss plan configuration**—For dual tone multifrequency (DTMF) digits to be transmitted at the correct volume, especially for communications from Office Communications Server 2007 to Public Switched Telephone Network (PSTN), the loss plan for the PBX must be correctly configured.

- **Dialing plan configuration**—For calls to be routed using PCA to Office Communications Server 2007, a dialing plan entry must be entered on the call server to send the call to the SIP trunk. The dialing plan entry is used only to route the call to the MCM and should not correspond to any number that can be dialed within the network.

- **Personal call assistant**—For incoming calls to be extended to the twinned Office Communicator 2007 client, a personal call assistant terminal number must be defined for that extension. A new class of service has been introduced to distinguish between PCAs associated with Office Communications Server 2007 clients and PCAs associated with other types of clients.

- **Caller ID table configuration**—The caller ID table is used to build the correct Caller ID (CLID) for private and public network calls from a number, an extension, or both. This table is used by all CS 1000 telephones and is required for Office Communicator 2007 calls to work properly.

- **Home Location (HLOC) and Home Number Plan Areas (NPA)**—For the CLID to be correctly displayed for Office Communications Server 2007 calls to the public network, both the HLOC and NPA require configuration.

- **DNS server configuration**—Domain Name System (DNS) configuration allows up to three DNS server IP addresses. The DNS server must be correctly configured with the fully qualified domain name (FQDN).

- **SIP trunk configuration**—For Office Communications Server 2007 to use the PBX as a SIP gateway, SIP trunks must be configured on the PBX. For a SIP trunk to communicate with Office Communications Server 2007, the SIP transport protocol must be configured as Transmission Control Protocol (TCP) and not as User Datagram Protocol (UDP).

- **Domain name**—In most configurations in which the PBX acts as a SIP gateway for Office Communications Server 2007, the SIP trunk domain name and the Office Communications Server 2007 domain name should be an exact match.

- **URI Mapping**—The SIP Uniform Resource Identifier (URI) map must be configured to register correctly with the Network Routing Service (NRS).

- **SIP gateway CLID parameters configuration**—The SIP gateway CLID parameters are used to adjust the format and appearance of telephone numbers for incoming calls. For Office Communicator 2007, these settings affect the format of numbers that appear on the incoming call pop-up for Telephony Gateway and Services.

- **SIP proxy server configuration**—The SIP proxy server is configured through MCM. Within this configuration, settings are created for primary and secondary IP addresses, three modes may be set, and the type of transport is defined.

- **NRS configuration**—The server running the MCM application must be configured on the NRS as a dynamic SIP endpoint or gateway and not as a collaboration server. An Office Communications Server 2007 service domain must be created for the signaling server and MCM. The signaling server and MCM register to the Office Communications Server 2007 service domain on the NRS.

- **Call detail records configuration**—Call detail records (CDR) is supported for outgoing calls from Office Communicator 2007. When a call is made, the CLID (extracted from Active Directory) is identified.

- **E.164 International Format (INFO) numbers from Office Communicator 2007 calls (SIP gateway)**—Calls to international format numbers are handled by the SIP gateway and arrive with a request URI in the SIP INVITE.

Remote call control

By default, users are configured for PC-to-PC communications within Office Communicator 2007. Configuring remote call control (RCC) and PBX integration is done from the User properties in Active Directory and on the Office Communications Server 2007 client. Specific licenses are required on the PBX to enable RCC functionality. Although the examples provided here are for Nortel CS 1000, configuration requirements are similar for other PBX products.

- **Configure the Application Module Link (AML)**—A new local area network (LAN) link, with a link number between 32 and 47 on a small CS 1000 system and from 32 to 127 on a large CS 1000 system, must be defined to indicate that communications will be across a TCP link.

- **Configure the value added server (VAS)**—The value added server configuration defines the connection of the link used to communicate with the RCC server and enables TR/87 front-end applications on the signaling server to acquire extension numbers. This number is associated with the AML number defined in the previous step.

- **Configure the license limit for the SIP CTI TR/87 users**—This limit allows the maximum number of RCC-enabled extensions to be specified. Computer telephony integration (CTI) provides coordination of activities between a telephone and computer.

- **Configure a station**—Any IP, digital, or analog extension can be configured as RCC-enabled. However, some features depend on handsfree capabilities, which might be available only with a specific telephone set. The use of certain RCC features will be reduced on sets with limited capabilities. When configuring an extension that is part of a Multiple Appearance Directory Number (MADN), the T87A class and the AST are configured only on the Multiple Appearance Redirection Prime (MARP). For RCC to work properly, the MARP must be defined on a PBX station and not on the PCA.

- **Configure the NRS**—NRS is an optional gatekeeper service that supports highly scalable implementation in a Nortel CS 1000 environment. If NRS exists, MCM and the signaling server identified as the TR/87 front end must be configured as gateway endpoints.

- **Configure the signaling server**—The TR/87 front-end application shares one instance of the SIP stack with the SIP gateway and correspondingly uses some existing SIP gateway configuration parameters. The IP address and domain name of any Office Communications Server 2007 proxy server responsible for forwarding TR/87 traffic to the signaling server must be added to the signaling server host table. Other SIP CTI-specific parameters must also be configured.

- **Configure the DNS server**—A LAN configuration setting within the PBX names up to three DNS servers that the PBX will query for servers running Office Communications Server 2007.

- **Configure the SIP CTI Services settings**—The calling device URI format must be properly configured to support Office Communications Server 2007 remote call control. The dial plan prefix section values under SIP CTI services must also be configured. Several configuration settings are required to enable RCC services.

- **Configure the SIP CTI CLID parameters**—These parameters adjust the format of phone numbers for display of incoming calls. For Office Communicator 2007, these settings affect the format of numbers that appear on the incoming call pop-up for RCC.

- **Configure the SIP URI map**—The SIP URI map configured for the SIP gateway application is used by the TR/87 front-end application to parse incoming URIs within SIP CTI service requests.

- **Configure the CDR records**—CDR records are produced for calls controlled with the RCC feature. These records are in the same format as those for calls dialed directly from a telephone's keypad.

- **Dialing E.164 International Format numbers from Office Communicator 2007 – Phone Calls with SIP CTI**—The TR/87 specification calls for these service requests to be passed through a SIP INFO message. The TR/87 Front End (FE) that resides on the signaling server contains a feature to insert the appropriate dial plan prefix, depending on the location of the call server and the destination of the call. This feature is either enabled or disabled.

Normalization

Office Communicator 2007 requires all phone numbers to be in standard TEL URI format (as defined in RFC 3966) for dialing and reverse number lookup. Office Communications Server 2007 uses phone numbers that are provisioned in directory servers and numbers that users have entered through the user interface. These sources do not enforce a standardized format, which is inconsistent with the TEL URI specification. Normalization means that all numbers will be transformed to a plus sign and a sequence of numbers prior to making successful connections.

SIP routing and redundancy configuration

Office Communicator 2007 is a soft phone application as well as a SIP user agent. The Office Communications Server 2007 front-end server is a SIP user agent (UA) and hosts Office Communicator. Office Communicator 2007 establishes a SIP dialog in one direction only: from the application to the TR/87 front end. The SIP proxy and the Nortel MCM are required to provide support for authorization because the Office Communicator 2007 clients cannot handle redirect messages.

- **RCC SIP routing using phone addressing configuration**—The TR/87 front end recognizes the TR/87 mime type within a SIP INVITE and intercepts the INVITE if the front end is co-resident with the gateway. This ensures that both TR/87 sessions and phone calls with the same request URI are handled properly, either by the front end or by the SIP gateway, which coexist on the same signaling server.

- **Redundancy configuration**—RCC redundancy is specific to the PBX environment. In a Nortel CS 1000 environment, RCC services are supported with single-node redundancy, campus redundancy, or geographic redundancy.

  - Single-node redundancy leverages the same master and follower mechanism used for Virtual Trunk and Terminal Proxy Server applications. After the master of one node fails, one of the followers takes over the node IP address and continues to deliver service. VoIP-mode session state is preserved when a new master is elected.

- Campus redundancy increases the distance between the two central processing unit (CPU) cores of a CS 1000E and operates similarly to single-node redundancy.

- Geographic redundancy can be supported with limitations that currently exist for gateway SIP traffic. During transition periods, situations may arise when IP phones are registered to a PBX that is different from the one that provides support for RCC. NRS is required to support redundancy in the CS 1000 environment.

It may seem as if an excessive number of steps are required to integrate the PBX with Office Communications Server 2007. However, this effort is miniscule compared to the work required to replace the PBX completely to derive similar benefits. Many enterprises believe that it is critical to have a transition path to new technology and that allowing IT vendors to integrate with legacy voice platforms is an effective approach to new product evolution.

UC enablement with the Office Communications Server 2007 application server

Office Communications Server 2007 offers a wide variety of functions to support UC enabling of all sizes. The following list includes a brief overview of some UC features supported by Office Communications Server 2007:

- **Instant messaging (IM) and presence for internal users**—Instant messaging is a communication format between two or more people based on typed text conveyed over a network. For internal use, the corporate network provides IM transport.

Presence is a status indicator that conveys the ability and willingness of a potential communications partner to communicate. IM clients provide presence state information through a network connection to a presence service. Office Communications Server 2007 maintains presence information as part of the user's personal availability record. The service distributes changes in presence status to convey users' availability for communication.

Because a user may have multiple clients (laptop, desktop, phone, PDA, mobile phone, and more), the service must receive input from all possible sources and maintain the correct status for the user at all times.

- **On-premise Web conferencing**—Office Communications Server 2007 enables enterprise users, both inside and outside the corporate firewall, to create and join real-time Web conferences hosted on the organization's internal servers. Conferences can be scheduled or unscheduled and can include IM, audio, video, application sharing, slide presentations, and other forms of data collaboration.

Enterprise users can invite external users without corporate IT accounts to participate in these conferences. Federated users can also join conferences and, if invited to do so, may act as presenters.

- **Audio and video conferencing**—Office Communications Server 2007 conferences provide rich multimedia capabilities that include data collaboration, group IM, audio and video, and multiparty conferencing. As many as four conferencing servers can be integrated into the Office Communications Server 2007 solution:

- **IM conferencing server**—Provides group IM capability

- **Web conferencing server**—Enables multiparty data collaboration

- **A/V conferencing server**—Enables network audio and video conferencing

- **Telephony conferencing server**—Enables audio conference integration with audio conferencing service providers

- **Address book**—The address book server provides global user information to Office Communicator 2007 clients. The address book retrieves contact information from Microsoft SQL Server and uses this data to generate a set of compressed full files and change files, which are stored in a standard folder. The user replicator updates the user database to synchronize with Active Directory.

Office Communicator 2007 uses Microsoft Internet Information Server (IIS) to download address book server files when the client is outside the corporate firewall, providing an advanced level of security for Active Directory. Office Communicator 2007 also relies on the address book for the phone number normalization required for reverse number lookup.

- **Archiving and CDR**—CDR records collect both IM and meeting data and generate reports on usage characteristics, which can assist in capacity planning and performance analysis. Administrators can specify the data to collect and should specify retention policies.

CDR records do not record the content of IM or conferences; they simply record information about the communication.

Administrators can archive IM conversations for all users, no users, or select individual users.

- **External user access**—Office Communications Server 2007 supports multimedia conferencing with external users. This capability requires the deployment of media-specific edge services, including:

  - Access Edge Server, which validates and forwards SIP signaling traffic between internal and external users.

  - Web Conferencing Edge Server, which enables data collaboration with external users.

  - Audio/Video (A/V) Edge Server, which enables audio and video conferencing and peer-to-peer communications with external users who also have the Office Communicator 2007 client. Only the control signaling, not the peer-to-peer communication, goes through the audio and video conferencing server.

- **Federation**—A trust relationship between two or more SIP domains (enterprises) permits users in separate organizations to communicate in real time across network boundaries as federated partners.

- **Public IM connectivity**—Many consumers have IM accounts with either their ISP or other consumer-oriented IM networks. Office Communications Server 2007 supports communication between the enterprise IM server and the public consumer-oriented IM networks run by the Microsoft MSN division and by rivals such as Yahoo! and America

Online. Many business partners who do not have federated status can participate in IM, using a subscription to a consumer-oriented network.

- **IM and presence through a browser-based client**—Office Communicator 2007 Web Access is a server that provides access through a browser-based client to Office Communications Server 2007. This client supports IM, presence, and the conferencing features of Office Communications Server 2007. There is no support for application sharing, whiteboard, audio/video conferencing, or file transfers in the Web client.

- **Enterprise voice**—The IP telephony component of Office Communications Server 2007 gives Microsoft a significant differentiation between their product and competitors' in the desktop productivity software market. The Office Communications Server 2007 IP telephony is a SIP-based implementation that does not rely on proprietary hardware investments. Gateways provide interoperation with the PSTN and enterprise PBXs. Calls can be placed from PC to PC, PC to PBX/PSTN phone, or PBX/PSTN phone to PC. Users working from home or any other remote location can call any other similarly connected client without incurring long-distance charges or even resorting to virtual private network (VPN) connection to the corporate network.

These capabilities will be enhanced by third-party, value-added offerings now in development. Office Communications Server 2007 is an industry standards–based platform with a well-defined application programming interface (API) for which there is already a huge development community.

System integration requirements for the Office Communications Server 2007 application server

The integration path of any particular Office Communications Server 2007 installation depends on planning and engineering work completed before project initiation. Figure 11-4 shows a flow chart that identifies the required steps. Initial integration steps focus entirely on the Office Communications Server 2007 platform, whereas integration with other voice platforms requires planning that extends beyond Office Communications Server 2007 integration.

The scenario presented here assumes that Office Communications Server 2007 is to be deployed as the telephony solution for an individual team, while the rest of the organization continues to use the PBX. This integration places the enterprise voice behind the PBX. All calls from the PSTN arrive at the PBX, which routes calls to enterprise voice users through a media gateway and calls PBX users in the usual way. This allows Office Communications Server 2007 users to keep existing phone numbers and minimize disruption for their potential communications partners. This approach also minimizes changes with carriers.

When the PBX receives a call destined for an extension associated with Office Communications Server 2007, the PBX forwards that call through a defined route on a mediation server to the Office Communications Server 2007 Standard edition server or to the front-end server in an Enterprise edition configuration. In a Nortel environment, MCM software is located between the mediation server and CS 1000. MCM configuration was discussed earlier in this chapter.

FIGURE 11-4: DEPLOYMENT FLOW CHART.

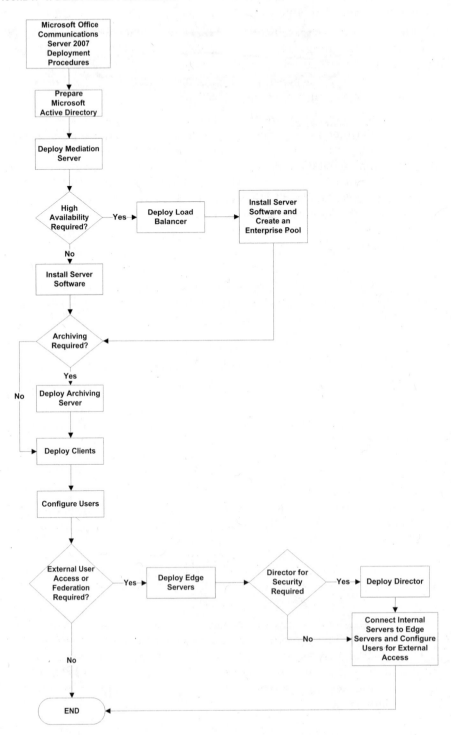

Mediation server configuration requires input of the FQDN and IP addresses, specification of edge servers and authentication services, default location profile, next-hop connections, and the media port range to be assigned. The mediation server has several functions:

- translating SIP over TCP on the gateway side to SIP over mutual transport layer security on the Office Communications Server 2007 side

- encrypting and decrypting Secure Real-Time Protocol (SRTP) on the Office Communications Server 2007 side

- translating media streams between Office Communications Server 2007 and the media gateway

- connecting clients outside the network to internal components when media traversal is enabled through firewalls

- acting as an intermediary for call flows that a gateway doesn't support, such as calls from remote workers on an Office Communications Server 2007 voice client

When introducing telephony support to an Office Communications Server 2007 system, the following Office Communications Server 2007 front-end entities must be configured:

Location profiles—A location profile defines all phone numbers that can be dialed from a named location. A location contains one or, typically, more normalization rules.

Normalization rules—These are regular expressions that define a phone number pattern.

Phone usage records—These specify a class of call (internal, local, long distance) that can be made by various users or groups of users.

Voice policy—This policy associates one or more phone usage records with one user or a group of users.

Route—The route configuration associates target phone numbers with particular IP-PSTN gateways and phone usage records. Source-based routing must be used for integration with Nortel CS 1000.

Define users—This configuration associates users with extensions and enables their voice and RCC capabilities.

Active Directory and enterprise systems integration requirements

User authentication is an important consideration when implementing UC services. Understanding who a user is, defining that user's access privileges, and having easy access to relevant attributes (such as phone number or SIP URI) are basic elements of directory services. The objective is for all applications in the enterprise to interact with a single repository used to gather access control information, thereby simplifying the password and account information that must be retained by a user. Active Directory provides authentication and user information repository services for Office Communications Server 2007 and many enterprise applications. Any application that integrates effectively with Office Communications Server 2007 must leverage this common infrastructure element.

Office Communications Server 2007 installation requires that the directory service domain services schema be extended and that Active Directory objects be created and configured. These schema extensions add new attributes and classes, such as telephone number and SIP URI, necessary for Office Communications Server 2007 to operate. Three steps are involved in Active Directory preparation:

- **Prepare the Active Directory schema**—Extend the schema so that new attributes and classes can be added. This preparatory step is run once per Active Directory forest. It is strongly recommended that SchemaPrep be run at a time of low network usage. This process must be run by someone with Schema Administrator credentials and administrator credentials on the schema master. After this step, let enough time pass to ensure that replication is complete before continuing.

- **Prepare the Active Directory forest**—Create the Office Communications Server 2007 objects and attributes in the root domain or under the configuration naming context. This preparatory step is run once per Active Directory forest. This process must be run by someone with Enterprise Administrator or Domain Administrator credentials for the forest root domain.

- **Prepare each Active Directory domain**—Add permissions on the objects in the domain for universal groups. This preparatory step must be run once in each domain in which Office Communications Server 2007 is being deployed. This process must be run by someone with Domain Administrator credentials in the domain in which Office Communications Server is being deployed.

After these three steps are complete, configure certificates on each server running Office Communications Server 2007. Use the provided Certificate Wizard to create and configure a Web certificate with an enhanced usage key for server authentication.

Next, create DNS A records and services (SRV) records to enable clients to locate and connect with Office Communications Server 2007.

Install additional components, such as Web conferencing or A/V conferencing servers, after the preceding steps are complete. IIS should be pre-installed on any servers that will act as Office Communications Server 2007 front-end servers.

Create user accounts only after this preparatory work is complete. User accounts must be configured to enable Office Communications Server 2007. After user accounts are created and configured properly, you can begin to deploy Office Communications Server clients.

If you plan to support external users for IM, A/V features, and conferencing, install and configure the edge servers at this point.

When this sequence of steps is complete, you may begin rollout of enterprise voice services.

Knowledge Check 11-1: Conducting Unified Communications Systems Integration

Answer the following questions. Answers to these Knowledge Check questions are located in *Appendix A: Answers to Knowledge Check Questions.*

1. What must be done before effective UC planning can occur?

   a. Purchase PBX licenses

   b. Survey the user community

   c. Purchase Microsoft licenses

   d. Complete an assessment of the existing environment

2. What can be integrated into the existing environment to allow non-IP-enabled PBXs to participate in UC?

   a. DSL modem

   b. Gateway server

   c. Network registration server

   d. Non-IP-enabled PBXs cannot participate in UC

3. Which role does the Office Communications Server 2007 Proxy server provide?

   a. Routing

   b. Authentication

   c. Header parsing

   d. State management

   e. Connection management

   f. All of the above

4. What must be configured to allow routing calls from the PBX to Office Communications Server 2007?

   a. Q-Sig

   b. Dialing plan

   c. SS7 signaling

   d. Emergency services

5. What is the purpose of personal call assistant on the PBX?

   a. Forward calls to voice mail

   b. Enable automated call distribution

   c. Forward fax messages to a multimedia mailbox

   d. Allow calls to be extended to the twinned Office Communicator 2007 client

6. What does a normalized phone number look like?

   a. 5613462348

   b. +15613472348

   c. (561) 3472348

   d. (561) 347-2348

7. Federation is a trust relationship between multiple SIP domains.

   a. True

   b. False

8. The Office Communications Server 2007 Web client can be used for enterprise voice services.

   a. True

   b. False

9. No configuration changes must be made to Active Directory to implement enterprise voice services with Office Communications Server 2007.

   a. True

   b. False

10. Which of the following is not a valid Office Communications Server 2007 server role?

    a. Telephony server

    b. Collaboration server

    c. IM conferencing server

    d. Web conferencing server

    e. A/V conferencing server

Chapter summary

Implementation of enterprise-wide IM and on-premise conferencing capabilities prepares organizations for the true return on investment (ROI) of converged voice and data networking. As users become more familiar with this integration, demand for communications-aware enterprise applications will grow. Corporations will see an immediate return in the number of interactions resolved on first contact and in reduced e-mail and voice mail retention. Between these benefits and the reduced expense of conferencing, enterprises will likely see a rapid return on their Office Communications Server 2007 investment.

Office Communications Server 2007 promises to be a robust IP voice services platform; however, in the early stages, corporations are likely to benefit most from coexistence of Office Communications Server 2007 with traditional voice telephony platforms. This enables select resources to exploit the new features of Office Communications Server 2007 without completely disrupting voice services for all staff. Many activities associated with the Office Communications Server 2007 deployment will be required only once, making rollout to other user communities faster and simpler.

12: Applications Integration with Endpoint Devices

This chapter describes the various endpoint devices that can be integrated into a Voice over Internet Protocol (VoIP) and Unified Communications (UC) deployment. Each endpoint device is described, and relevant integration, monitoring, and security issues are explained.

Chapter 12 Topics

In this chapter, you will learn:

- how to manage endpoint device application integration: cell phones, personal digital assistants (PDAs), and wireless tablets

- how to integrate endpoint devices with desktop and laptop applications and the general enterprise system

- how to configure access for mobile devices during application and system integration

- how to handle VoIP and Session Initiation Protocol (SIP) application system integration

- how to secure network access and configure authentication requirements

- how to track and monitor endpoint device access and security policies

Chapter Goals

Upon completion of this chapter, you will be able to:

- describe the various endpoints that can be connected in a UC-enabled network

- explain how applications support mobile endpoints

- explain how endpoint devices interoperate in the UC environment

- explain the requirements for integrating VoIP and SIP applications

- explain endpoint security and authentication implementations in the UC environment

- explain the registration process for endpoint devices

- identify the security policies necessary to protect UC endpoints adequately

Key Terms

Asset tag	262	Mobile endpoint device	251
Endpoint device	251	Radio frequency identification (RFID)	252
Global Positioning System (GPS)	262	Smartphones	252
Local endpoint device	251		

Endpoint device application integration

Enterprise networks are usually created from the interconnection of multiple local area networks (LANs) through connections provided by wide area networks (WANs). Endpoints usually connect to the LAN, which, in turn, can be subdivided into separate functional networks. For example, a LAN might be subdivided to create virtual workgroups or to satisfy differing priorities of VoIP and traditional data traffic.

Endpoint devices are interfaces that enable the user to gain access to network services such as VoIP or e-mail. Laptops and IP phones are not the only endpoint devices available to users; cell phones and PDAs can also be endpoint devices. Endpoint devices used in an enterprise VoIP or UC deployment can be divided into two categories:

- local endpoint devices
- mobile endpoint devices

Local endpoint devices

A local endpoint device uses the enterprise network from a single location. This device can be a computer, a phone, or even a copier or fax machine. It can also be a specialty sensor associated with System Control and Data Acquisition (SCADA) systems, badge readers in a security system, or security Web cameras. These devices are expected to stay in the same physical location for the full deployment unless the device's user must relocate. Because they are in a static location, security measures used to access, monitor, and track local endpoint devices are different from those used for mobile endpoint devices. These security policies and procedures, specific to local endpoint devices, can work within existing security measures deployed in the core network because local endpoint devices do not move.

Because local endpoint devices are used frequently, they tend to be standardized with approved versions of operating system code, applications, and hardware. Security policies and procedures can thus treat these devices as identical and predictable. Services the local endpoint device will access within a VoIP and UC network can also be supported with fewer modifications within the service or through specialized versions of the software.

Mobile endpoint devices

Unlike local endpoint devices, mobile endpoint devices require access from outside as well as inside the enterprise network. Traditional mobile devices include laptops and PDAs. Laptops accessed the enterprise network through modems from a remote location, whereas PDAs helped enterprise users by providing a corporate address book, notepad, and calendar that could be synchronized with a desktop calendar. Over the past decade, laptops and PDAs have evolved into more versatile and powerful devices.

Laptops are now powerful enough to replace traditional desktop computers, enabling end users to take work home or on the road without the need to synchronize computers or make paper copies. With smaller, faster, and low energy–drawing chips, PDAs have shrunk in size while gaining power. PDAs can now handle UC services as well as e-mail, wireless connectivity, and third-party video applications. UC technology has helped the PDA industry join the enterprise mobile endpoint device market.

Cell phones expand the range of communications between the enterprise and its clients. Cell phones have also become smaller and more powerful. Modern cell phones provide the same features as a standard PDA while enhancing basic cell phone service with digital services and short message service. The newest cell phones, with a more robust operating system and application suite, are called smartphones.

Mobile devices include more than just cell phones and PDAs:

- tablet PCs
- laptop computers
- PDAs
- cell phones
- smartphones
- radio frequency identification (RFID) readers
- portable IP phones

Each of these devices has specific uses in a VoIP and UC environment. Each device supports a specific subset of UC applications that are designed for that specific device type and how it is typically used. VoIP and UC security policies and procedures must be based on whether the device is a local or mobile endpoint and whether that device will reside outside the enterprise network infrastructure.

Desktop and laptop application and system integration

All users on an enterprise network must have a reliable endpoint device for daily use. These endpoint devices normally reside on a desk or in an office. For several decades, the desktop computer served as the single point of application access, information access, and data storage. As users have become more mobile, the laptop has become commonplace. Laptops allow users to work outside the office without losing functionality.

Desktop and laptop devices are designed to be interchangeable. These local endpoint devices run the same operating systems, applications, and tools. Using a single platform and application base can reduce the amount of time an IT group requires to test and deploy new applications and hardware.

Unified user interface

The same standard deployment of hardware and software can be applied to the VoIP and UC environment. With the use of a single operating system, VoIP and UC applications can be consolidated into a single release, deployed on each desktop and laptop as they are assigned to end users. Users do not need to relearn commands or applications when all computers in the organization use the same application suite and operating system. The reduced learning curve increases productivity and ease of use, which is a primary requirement for VoIP and UC deployments.

Although the back end of the VoIP and UC network can be complicated, this complexity should not be apparent to the user. If an enterprise requires local and mobile endpoint devices to support VoIP and UC applications and services, that complexity must stay hidden. The best way to reduce complexity is to reduce the learning curve for any service that might span multiple endpoint devices. As with desktop and laptop applications, all endpoint devices should use the same graphical user interface (GUI) whenever possible. VoIP and UC vendors in the current market support this trend.

Each endpoint device that supports a particular UC service, such as messaging, uses a different physical application binary. This is due to the different platforms on which the service must run. Although the machine-readable code is different from device to device, what the user sees is always the same whether the device is a laptop, tablet, PDA, or smartphone. UC vendors such as Microsoft require each version of their UC applications to look and act the same on every supported endpoint device. However, application support for every endpoint device is not assured because some device operating systems or hardware might not support a particular application, whereas other endpoint devices might not be supported due to how the devices are used.

Application and service support

Endpoint devices might enable the enterprise user to access the VoIP and UC environment, but without applications and services, that access is useless. In a normal enterprise environment, the end user accesses VoIP and UC applications and services through a local endpoint device. Normally, these devices handle UC applications such as messaging and presence as well as video and VoIP. These can be used seamlessly within the same device because the device was designed to handle multiple simultaneous robust applications. Additionally, these devices use a high-speed network interface to access the enterprise data and VoIP network. With high-speed access, endpoint devices can run applications with real-time video feeds, as well as interactive Web conferencing, without latency or loss of content quality. Note that not all local endpoint devices can support these features.

A wired IP phone is a basic local endpoint device with a specific set of functions. Because it has limited functions, the IP phone does not have to support each application used on the desktop or laptop. Newer IP phones have more power and faster network interfaces that could be used to support a large suite of VoIP and UC applications and services, whereas other IP phones handle only the applications needed to service VoIP calls, presence, and possibly messaging. Still, others support a full complement of Web browsing and video capabilities. This same model is used for other endpoint devices such as thin clients and mobile devices.

Although some hardware can support video conferencing or e-mail integration, it might not make sense to create a specialized version of the application for each supported device. The same hardware might require specialized code to enable a user interface that matches the desktop version. In many cases, the endpoint hardware will not support the same user interface, which might determine whether the application is ported to the mobile endpoint device.

Mobility and computing application and system integration

Desktops and IP phones are the core of VoIP and UC deployments. However, as the workforce becomes more mobile, VoIP and UC applications must adapt to work on devices as mobile as their user, ranging from mobile laptops to cell phones. Each of these devices can participate in a UC environment through limited application and feature support. Mobile devices with UC support enable an enterprise user to access communications mechanisms anywhere in the world. Enterprise data, collaborative sessions, and communications tools all follow the user. The enterprise user thus becomes a mobile corporate information and communications center.

Tablets

The idea behind the tablet computer is to give users the power and functionality of a laptop with a PDA-like interface. Tablets are now produced in a size and weight comparable to a paper legal pad without reducing the device's versatility. Most tablets support wireless and Bluetooth interfaces. Each tablet can support a modern enterprise operating system, usually the same operating system deployed on the enterprise's desktop and laptop computers. This versatility has brought the tablet into environments usually reserved for either specialized devices or pen and paper.

Using multiple wireless network interfaces, a tablet can access an enterprise LAN anywhere in the company's offices. Car dealerships, warehouses, and factories deploy tablets to track inventory, handle billing, or order parts. Hospitals and doctors' offices deploy tablets for each doctor on staff, who use them to access patient records and transmit prescriptions. With location-enabled capabilities, the hospital system can even verify the room in which the doctor is located, to ensure that the information is appropriate to the patient for whom the data is being entered. This mobile information platform can help save lives and raise employee productivity while still being lightweight and easy to use. With the addition of VoIP and UC, tablets can become a major asset in an enterprise environment.

Tablets and UC

Although a tablet is normally thought of as an information center, it can be used for a more robust set of jobs. By including several features within a UC deployment, the tablet can do more than just return information; it can act as a communications center for the mobile user. Because most tablets support an enterprise operating system such as Microsoft Windows, the tablet usually supports the same UC applications. Messaging, presence, and VoIP through a soft phone are all UC features and applications suitable for a tablet computer.

PDAs

The PDA was one of the first mobile devices to bridge the gap between a basic organizer and an enterprise support device. The first PDAs provided an address book, calculator, clock, and notepad and were quite large compared to modern devices. Over time, PDA functionality grew to include offline e-mail, spreadsheets, and even games, due to development of the operating systems. Today, most PDAs support some form of robust operating system, for example, Microsoft Windows, Palm OS, Blackberry, or Symbian. Operating system development and evolving hardware have permitted the PDA to adapt and grow. Today, a PDA can support wireless networking and use enterprise applications such as a robust word processor or Web browser.

A fully functional Web browser allows the PDA to be used as a mini–tablet computer. It can gather information, access references through the Web, and update data on Web-based applications. This robustness gives it a new role as a communications center. Because PDA operating systems now emulate the more robust enterprise operating systems, UC vendors have adapted VoIP and UC applications for wireless communications–enabled PDA devices. A PDA with these applications installed is a tablet computer small enough to fit in the user's pocket. Although PDAs are functional and useful devices for VoIP and UC deployments, they are quickly being replaced by a versatile and sometimes smaller competitor, the smartphone.

Smartphones

Like PDAs, cell phones have been evolving since their introduction. As technology improved, cell phones got smaller and gained new features, replicating features and interfaces normally seen on PDAs. The cell phone has become the briefcase of an enterprise employee. Due to faster and more powerful hardware, the cell phone acts as both phone and PDA. The operating systems used on modern cell phones are as complex as those used on PDAs, leading to the term "smartphone." A smartphone is any cell phone that can act as a PDA and allows the user to add third-party applications and software to leverage the growing data network now supported by most smartphones.

Smartphones are relatively new to the enterprise environment. They have only recently been integrated into an enterprise's basic set of services such as e-mail and corporate address repositories. These versatile phones can even support VoIP and UC features. Presence and messaging can both be used on a smartphone, linking the user to anyone in the company while he or she is anywhere in the world. VoIP services can also be used with some smartphones through a wireless 802.11 interface. All these features make the smartphone the new PDA of the enterprise world.

Dual-mode devices

The latest advance in technology for wireless devices, whether mobile phones, PDAs, or smartphones, is dual-mode operation. Inside the corporate environment, these devices connect to the corporate network through Wi-Fi without incurring commercial charges for minutes of use. When outside the range of corporate access points, the devices connect through public wireless networks. Higher-quality devices can shift between networks without disrupting active sessions.

Mobile applications

When an enterprise initially designs a VoIP and UC solution, it must understand the different devices used throughout the company. Each device must be reviewed, based on what the device can support and how the device will be used. Mobile devices generally support basic VoIP and UC applications, depending on the device type; applications that work on a tablet might not be supported on a smartphone. The software version for supported applications can also be different from mobile device to mobile device. Several applications can be used with reasonable consistency on mobile devices:

- SIP-based VoIP

- presence

- messaging

- Web-based conferencing

- video conferencing

Enterprises should also identify the location of mobile devices and how they are used. A PDA or smartphone that travels with a user as he or she moves outside enterprise offices, or even outside the country, must be handled differently than endpoint devices that reside in offices. An application on a highly mobile device might have easy access to confidential information. If the device is lost or stolen, the thief could access these trusted parts of the network. Additionally, not every employee or department needs all the mobile VoIP and UC features. Reducing the number of features could save licensing costs. Each of these issues must be evaluated and understood before a mobile device can be integrated into a VoIP or UC solution. Table 12-1 shows a matrix of UC functions mapped against mobile client capabilities. (Clients with a check and a dash mean the function is supported in a limited fashion.)

TABLE 12-1: CLIENT/UC FUNCTION CAPABILITIES MATRIX

Function\Client	Personal Computer	Converged Desktop	Notebook Computer	Tablet PC	PDA	Smart-phone	Mobile Phone	PBX Phone	IP Phone
Update Presence	✓–	✓	✓–	✓–	✓–	✓	✓		✓
View Presence	✓	✓	✓	✓	✓	✓	✓		✓–
Instant Messaging	✓	✓	✓	✓	✓	✓	✓		
Text Messaging	✓	✓	✓	✓	✓	✓	✓		
Location					✓	✓	✓		
Audio Conferencing	✓	✓	✓		✓	✓	✓	✓	✓
Web Conferencing	✓	✓	✓–	✓–	✓	✓	✓		✓–
Video Conferencing	✓	✓	✓		✓				

Secure network access and authentication requirements

Network security is often taken to mean the core of the network and how to permit or prevent access from the rest of the world. Sound core network security design is a key component to any enterprise network. However, securing the network edge is just as important, if not more so, as securing the core itself. The edge of the network is any place where a user, malicious or otherwise, can gain access to the network and the data that resides within it. The network's edge is more than just the points where the enterprise's LAN connects to the Internet or telephony networks; it also includes each access point where enterprise users can access the network and its data. This includes the desktops and IP phones that reside on user desks as well as the mobile devices that access the enterprise network around the world.

Local vs. mobile UC devices

When a user is assigned a desktop computer and an IP phone, it is expected that those two devices will stay in a single location. These devices rarely move, doing so only when the user moves to a new office or the devices move to a new user. These VoIP and UC devices are static and thus can be secured with basic policies and procedures. These devices use security solutions to defend against network attacks or enterprise user attacks. These policies are designed with the assumption that network core and edge security mechanisms are in place. If either assumption is untrue, these devices are partially open to attack and data theft or fraud. Although this can lead to a higher security threat, the configuration must give the enterprise user the least restrictive access possible to these devices. Because these devices are used daily, any restriction on the devices that constrains productivity must be evaluated before it is applied.

Mobile devices must be treated in a different light. Although mobile devices enable enterprise users to work remotely while in the car, at the airport, or in line for lunch, they add a huge risk to an already threat-laden enterprise VoIP and UC network. Mobile devices can access everything from the corporate intranet site to presence, messaging, and e-mail services. Each of these services resides on a device about the size of a hand. Enterprise security teams should secure mobile device access to the enterprise network, using policies and procedures that require the mobile device to use authentication and encryption to access the network. This is similar to the process used to secure a local endpoint device. Unlike a local endpoint, however, a mobile device can be easily stolen, lost, or broken. In these cases, the mobile device might land in unauthorized hands. If the mobile device is not properly secured, these unauthorized users could have trusted access to the enterprise's network without alarm.

Encrypting the call on mobile devices

In any networked environment, encryption is one of the best ways to secure a communication stream. VoIP or UC applications can use encryption to secure signaling and media data so that a malicious user cannot access or control the VoIP and UC call. This same logic should be applied to mobile devices. Most mobile devices will use one of two methods to access the enterprise network and VoIP or UC services. The first method is through the cell phone service provider's data network. Although this might seem secure, intercepting a digital cell phone call is a relatively trivial task for a malicious user, even when it is a data call. Unencrypted voice, video, or data can then be collected by these users and used at will. Voice and data calls and application flows should be encrypted by the enterprise. The cell phone service provider or service itself should not be trusted, even if the cell phone service provider supports a network-based encryption solution on each cell phone call that terminates at the cell phone or mobile device.

The second way to access the enterprise network is through a wireless connection using the 802.11i protocol. This is the same protocol used for wireless access from a laptop device. This technology is not considered secure by any means. However, the 802.11i wireless protocol supports several encryption solutions inherent to the protocol, including those listed here:

• Wired Equivalent Privacy (WEP)

• Wi-Fi Protected Access (WPA)

• Wi-Fi Protected Access version 2 (WPA2)

Each of these protocols supports some form of encryption algorithm to protect the data stream it carries. WEP was the first encryption method deployed for 802.11i and is the most commonly supported encryption solution on mobile devices. Although WEP was a good starting point, it has a serious and well-known security flaw. It is easy to find an application that can breach an 802.11i data stream secured using WEP. WEP is considered about as secure as having no security on the wireless stream.

WPA and WPA2 are newer encryption solutions, created by the Wi-Fi Alliance, that support a hardened set of algorithms to secure data. Because these solutions are relatively new, they are not yet fully supported by every mobile device. They are a better solution than WEP but are not totally secure; a dedicated hacker can breach a WPA- or WPA2-secured 802.11i stream within a short time. Like WEP, WPA should not be considered the sole solution for mobile wireless connections. If WPA or WPA2 are available, they should be deployed as a complementary security measure on top of any other measure used. The problem, however, is that a mobile user is, by definition, mobile, and 802.11i networks can be accessed from more networks than just the enterprise network. Do not assume that all wireless networks support WPA and WPA2.

Every mobile device that uses a wireless connection should employ point-to-point encryption between the endpoint mobile device and the enterprise's network. This can be done through an IP security virtual private network (IPsec VPN) connection. An IPsec VPN connection starts at the mobile device and terminates in the enterprise network, creating a virtual network connection that encrypts everything traveling across it. An IPsec VPN resides above the IP transport layer and can work in conjunction with WPA, WPA2, or a cell phone service provider's encrypted cell phone calls.

Encrypting the data on mobile devices

Data streams and VoIP calls are not the only data at risk on a mobile device. Most mobile devices store confidential information about the enterprise or its clients. This can be in the form of e-mails, contact information, or proprietary documents and applications. All must be secured in case the mobile device is lost, stolen, or thrown away. At a minimum, access to the mobile device should be password-protected, but the data stored within the device should also be encrypted. The mobile device should allow access to the data only if the correct authentication mechanism is used to access the data. This can be a password, a thumbprint, or even a one-time password from a secure token. A secondary measure can also be configured to lock the mobile device if the user fails authentication too many times in a row. This stops a malicious user from attempting to figure out the password through trial and error but could also cause a legitimate user to be locked out if the password is forgotten or the access code input incorrectly. A comprehensive authentication method must complement the encryption solution.

Encryption on a local endpoint device

Signal handling on a local endpoint device is less complicated than on a mobile device. Local endpoint devices consist of an IP phone or a desktop computer. These devices conform to the enterprise standard operating system and feature set. This permits a unified encryption solution for any VoIP signaling traffic. SIP, the most commonly used signaling protocol in VoIP, can be encrypted when paired with Secure Socket Layer (SSL) encryption or Transport Layer Security (TLS). Although support for both of these encryption protocols is small at the moment, new and more dangerous VoIP security threats have pushed IP phone and softphone vendors toward this solution. These encryption protocols can also be used on the data stream for VoIP and UC sessions. These protocols are discussed in more detail in Chapter 14, "Best Practices for VoIP Security."

Authentication on an endpoint device

Secure access to the enterprise network should not rely solely on encryption. Although encryption can protect the data, it cannot dictate what the mobile or local endpoint device can access. Access control requires authentication and authorization. Authentication can be performed through several means:

- certificate authentication
- single sign on (Active Directory) authentication
- one-time password token authentication
- strong password authentication
- existing VoIP authentication

Each of these authentication methods can be used when connecting to the enterprise network from a mobile device. Base your solution choice on the mobile devices that need to be secured as well as on what they will access.

Smartphone authentication—Smartphone authentication methods are limited to what the operating system can support. The most common methods use strong passwords, VoIP proxy authentication, or certificate key authentication.

PDA authentication—PDAs come in various sizes and operating systems. Like smartphones, PDAs can support strong passwords, VoIP proxy authentication, and certificate key authentication. Additionally, some PDAs support the Active Directory authentication mechanism.

Tablet and desktop authentication—Tablets are computers that can be used like PDAs. Both tablets and desktop computers support any of the authentication methods listed earlier, if the operating system also supports it. Some tablets can also support a biometric authentication mechanism, such as a thumbprint identifier, to access the tablet itself.

IP phone authentication—IP phone authentication is limited due to vendor support and the operating system. Most IP phones support strong passwords linked to a UC ID such as a user's Active Directory user name. MD5 hashing is supported with password authentication in some IP phones. Certificate authentication can also be supported, but this is a much newer feature.

Registering an endpoint device

Another aspect of authentication occurs when an endpoint device attempts to use VoIP and UC services. In a secure VoIP and UC network, each device that will use any of the UC services must register with a VoIP proxy server or VoIP Private Branch Exchange (PBX). When an endpoint device turns on, it initiates an authentication session with the VoIP proxy or PBX. This authentication uses either a certificate key authentication scheme or an MD5 hashed user name and password scheme. If a device fails to authenticate to a VoIP proxy or PBX, VoIP and UC services will not be enabled on that endpoint device. An alert will also be sent to the security team to alert them of an unauthorized attempt to use the service.

Endpoint device registering should be used for all VoIP and UC deployments in conjunction with a primary authentication scheme used to access the endpoint device itself. It should also be understood that VoIP registering can be bypassed in certain situations, especially when using the SIP protocol for signaling.

Endpoint authorization

After a mobile or local endpoint device has been authenticated, access can still be restricted through an authorization access list. The ability to restrict access to specific areas of the network is based on the third-party authentication and authorization software used. With each of these security measures incorporated in a comprehensive mobile and local endpoint device deployment, an enterprise user can securely access data and communication channels in any part of the office, campus, or world. Chapters 13–17 contain more detail about security best practices for VoIP and UC deployments.

Tracking and monitoring endpoint device access and security policies

With a mobile workforce, security does not end at the device. A secure device is secure for only a limited time. Given enough time, a dedicated hacker will eventually break any security solution outside of encryption. Even strong encryption has a chance of being breached. In the long run, securing the endpoint device though encryption and authentication is only a delay tactic. A security team must be able to track and monitor the user and the endpoint device that user uses. After an endpoint device is stolen or lost, the clock starts ticking. If rapidly alerted to a breach attempt in progress, the security team can attempt to recover the device.

A security team should be tracking several aspects of an endpoint device—who is using the device, how it is being used, and where it is being used from.

Monitoring end-device access

Access monitoring should be one of the first items deployed by the security team for each endpoint device. Every endpoint device should support a way to monitor which user is logged on to the device and for how long. An authentication scheme that supports a separate user logon and password is called per-user authentication. Per-user authentication is easily monitored and tracked. Each user who accesses the endpoint device is logged with a time and date stamp. Some per-user authentication solutions support a way to log where the user initiated access if access is requested from somewhere outside of the endpoint device.

Each access is stored in a log that is local to the endpoint or that is sent remotely to a log correlator. The best practice is to send a copy of the logs to a remote server that analyzes device usage and alerts the security team if a breach is in progress. This logging should be as discreet as possible, so that a malicious user does not notice the log update being sent. Although this solution will work in most endpoint cases, some devices do not support a per-user authentication scheme.

Most smartphones and PDAs support only a password authentication scheme for device access. Although this is not an ideal solution, a secure password can dissuade all but the most determined hackers from accessing the device. A secure password is any password that is at least 16 characters in length. These characters should include at least one letter, one number, and one special character such as !@#$%^&*. The password should also not repeat any two characters in a row and should avoid any known words. Another issue with PDAs and smartphones is their inability to send logs to a remote location.

Monitoring end-device usage

Security protocols are designed to protect the integrity of confidential data while still allowing appropriate users and devices to access that data. Security policies and procedures are revised each day to keep the data secure. This does not mean that an unauthorized user cannot access the data. As explained previously, a determined user, whether authorized or unauthorized, can eventually gain access to restricted data. Monitoring activity on an endpoint device is the next step to control and mitigate a breach before it happens.

After a user logs on to an endpoint device, he or she will want to use the device for some service or job. Access must be authorized before the user can do anything past accessing the GUI. Some operating systems found on endpoint devices support the ability to restrict access to part of the operating system and the data that resides on that endpoint device. These systems can also restrict how the endpoint device then accesses the enterprise network. Each time the user authenticates onto an endpoint device, the authentication device assigns authorization credentials to the endpoint device and the network. As the user runs applications or accesses data, the authentication server is notified. If the user tries to access restricted data, the authentication server notifies the security team. In this way, the user's access is controlled and tracked from logon to logoff. This solution can work on a per-user authenticated system only.

On smartphones and PDAs, it can be impossible to track what the user does if the operating system does not support it. Most smartphones and PDAs on the market cannot track or log each command or application that the user starts, nor can they alert a remote security team of unauthorized access to an application. Even with this limited authorization ability, smartphones and PDAs can restrict access to specific parts of the device or data and can limit or remove access to enterprise or telephony networks.

Tracking an endpoint's location

An endpoint device is one of the first targets for a malicious user. Desktop computers, IP phones, laptops, and smartphones can all be easily removed from the enterprise office or stolen from the user. Limiting access to the endpoint device after it is removed, as well as controlling what can be accessed if a user's device is compromised, will slow down the malicious user or thief but will not always stop him or her. The best solution is to know when an endpoint device is being removed and where the device has been moved. This can be done in several ways. The best solution might be to use multiple location tracking solutions.

Asset tagging—The easiest way to help recover an endpoint device is to place an enterprise-specific asset tag on the device. This tag marks the device as owned by the enterprise, enabling the police to verify ownership. These tags can be on the outside chassis of the device or hidden so that thieves cannot find them. Although an asset tag is a good start, it can be removed from the endpoint device if found. The asset tag cannot know the location of the device and will not be able to inform the security team of its new location. Asset tags should always be used in conjunction with another tracking solution.

RFID—RFID tags are increasingly popular. They are used for inventory tracking and security at warehouses, toll booths, and retail stores. RFID tags hold a select amount of information that identifies the device and provides limited information such as ownership. Although the most commonly deployed RFID is a passive chip that responds to cues from an RFID antenna, RFID does support an active version that broadcasts the information stored in the chip. RFIDs have a restricted range but can be used to tag and track endpoint devices as they enter and leave the premises. If RFID antennae are placed throughout the physical office location, endpoint devices can even be tracked throughout the building. Due to range limitation, however, after an endpoint device moves out of the last RFID antenna's range, it cannot be tracked.

Global Positioning System (GPS)—After the endpoint device has left the range of an RFID antenna, a GPS receiver can take over. A GPS receiver uses an array of satellites to track its location at all times. The GPS receiver can hear the satellite signals with a clear line of sight to the sky. If the receiver is blocked by a building or other obstruction, it might not be able to hear the satellites, and the endpoint device cannot then be tracked. GPS requires at least four satellites to triangulate the receiver's location.

Each of these tracking devices can be used to monitor and track the endpoint device's location. Each tracking solution can be countered through different means. If all the tracking solutions are used together, one tracking device will pick up where the next left off. The only way to counter all these tracking mechanisms is to house the endpoint device inside a building or container. Although these are not foolproof solutions, they help the enterprise security team track and recover the endpoint device if it is ever lost.

Knowledge Check 12-1: Applications Integration with Endpoint Devices

Answer the following questions. Answers to the Knowledge Check questions are located in *Appendix A: Answers to Knowledge Check Questions*.

1. Which of the following are considered local endpoint devices?

   a. Tablet

   b. Laptop

   c. IP phone

   d. Desktop computer

   e. All of the above

2. Which of the following can be considered mobile endpoint devices?

   a. Tablet

   b. Laptop

   c. IP phone

   d. Smartphone

   e. Answers A and B

   f. Answers A, B, and D

3. Which is one goal for a unified endpoint device application?

   a. Use the same code base

   b. Restrict access to a single user

   c. Have a consistent user interface

   d. Work on only a select amount of devices

   e. None of the above

4. A PDA can support encrypted wireless VoIP sessions.

   a. True

   b. False

5. Which tracking system can be used to monitor a mobile device's location in a building?

   a. GPS

   b. RFID

   c. Asset tag

   d. Magnetic sensor

Chapter summary

The emergence of high-powered, mobile devices has added many new endpoints to modern computer networks. The applications they support provide a way for mobile workers to have constant access to information upon which they can base decisions, regardless of the time of day or their current location.

Historically, a user was associated with a physically static device and was then limited to what that device could do. The shift to mobile work means that the user has defined privileges, and devices have defined capabilities. Applications must be able to incorporate the right functionality, given the user privileges and the device capabilities, without inadvertently restricting what that user can do.

Mobile devices require a different approach to security than traditional endpoint devices. Mobile devices can use a variety of security methods, although the individual device's operating system might not permit use of all possible security schemes. In addition to access and authorization control, mobile devices can be tracked with a variety of physical tags. Although all security schemes should evolve regularly to stay ahead of malicious users, a combined strategy should protect most mobile devices and proprietary data when used within a UC-enabled deployment.

13: VoIP Threats and Vulnerabilities

This chapter describes the risks, vulnerabilities, and threats within a Voice over IP (VoIP) network and Unified Communications (UC) deployment.

Chapter 13 Topics

In this chapter, you will learn:

- the security definition of a vulnerability

- the security definition of a threat

- how to determine the actual security risk involved in deploying a network component

- how threats, vulnerabilities, and risks apply to VoIP and UC

- common VoIP vulnerabilities that may affect a VoIP or UC deployment in an enterprise environment

Chapter 13 Goals

Upon completion of this chapter, you will be able to:

- describe the common security challenges in deploying a VoIP and UC environment

- list the common threats, vulnerabilities, and risks to VoIP and UC

- understand the security challenges that exist for each VoIP protocol

Key Terms

Black hat	269	Risk	268
Denial of service (DoS)	270	Script kiddie	269
Gray hat	269	Session Initiation Protocol (SIP)	267
H.323	267	Threat	268
Media Gateway Control Protocol (MGCP)	267	Vulnerability	268
Phishing	274	White hat	269

13

VoIP Threats and Vulnerabilities

Introduction

As VoIP becomes a mainstream technology, the enterprise sector has started to employ it within corporate networks. VoIP, also known as IP telephony in an enterprise environment, creates a scalable solution to the growing costs of traditional telephony. When paired with a UC solution, VoIP becomes a truly compelling solution. Voice and video over IP, matched with messaging, presence, and multimedia, enhance employee productivity. Although these tools are useful, they bring new risks to the enterprise network and IT groups. These risks may outweigh the reward, and might not be as obvious as the benefits.

It can be complicated to deploy a VoIP network over the top of an existing Internet Protocol (IP) network. Many variables must be considered. The IP network must be able to support multiple protocols that may be used by the VoIP deployment; for example, new access through existing firewalls, VoIP dedicated network virtual local area networks (VLANs), and new application servers that handle VoIP switching. New hardware specifications must be supported, such as Power over Ethernet (IEEE 802.3af standard). This may require additional power to existing network gear, or new modules for the same gear. IP phones will be required at each end user's desk to support the feature set of the enterprise's new VoIP deployment.

Vendor compatibility must also be considered. An enterprise may have the correct hardware and software within the network to support a particular vendor's VoIP equipment, but the hardware may not be fully compatible with a different vendor chosen for the VoIP hardware or software. Stable compatibility may require a change in vendor for either the network gear or the VoIP hardware and software, which could reduce cost savings realized from the VoIP infrastructure deployment.

Vendor compatibility and interoperability also add a new layer of complexity at the security level. Interoperability may seem like an easy way to have the components from two vendors working together, as it will streamline deployment and possibly reduce costs. However, if interoperability requires deviation from known standards or requires some form of interpretive gateway to allow the vendors' products to interoperate, new and unknown security vulnerabilities can appear where they normally would not exist. A simple deployment of VoIP hardware can open an enterprise network to risks it has never known or anticipated. If a layer of UC applications is added to the VoIP deployment, this risk becomes even greater.

UC adds additional features to a basic VoIP network. A voice and video over IP infrastructure enhanced with added UC features can support new enterprise tools, such as integrated instant messaging (IM), personal conference bridging, call redirection, Web conferencing, presence, and Voice to Exchange gateways. Most of these applications must be integrated with an enterprise user's operating system, such as Microsoft Windows Vista. Operating system integration requires an enterprise's security group to reevaluate how security is handled on the desktop, from the firewall to virus and malware detection applications, so that security elements do not hinder UC features but still keep the desktop as secure as possible. Each time the existing enterprise deployment becomes more complex, more risk is added.

This additional complexity can be separated into several elements. With a new VoIP deployment, new protocols are required throughout the network, including new session signaling protocols such as the Session Initiation Protocol (SIP), H.323, or Media Gateway Control Protocol (MGCP). Signaling requires protocols that govern the transfer of data, such as Real-Time Protocol (RTP), Real-Time Streaming Protocol (RTSP), Real-Time Control Protocol (RTCP), H.261, H.263, and H.264. Each new protocol brings new threats and vulnerabilities. Note that several of these protocols, such as SIP, are not always compatible from vendor to vendor, even if there is an open protocol standard. This is an additional burden for an enterprise IT group, as it adds another layer of complexity to an already complex VoIP deployment.

Voice and video over IP, as well as messaging and multimedia, are applications that ride on an existing enterprise data network. Specific protocols are used to signal, control, and pass data traffic for these applications, but they still rely on the underlying IP network to get from point to point. These protocols inherit the existing vulnerabilities and security issues within the deployed enterprise IP network. These issues must be compared with the VoIP-related vulnerabilities and threats to guarantee that all issues are covered with the fewest security modifications.

What is a vulnerability?

What does it mean when a vendor describes a device, application, or operating system as secure? Is it truly safe from known and unknown attacks? Will it stand up to black hat hackers who pride themselves on proving how insecure a product is? It is quite common for a vendor to make a relatively broad statement that a product is secure, only to see the product breached within hours or days. Security patches are regularly released within days of a product or device release to address newly discovered vulnerabilities. Why would an enterprise allow such insecure devices onto or inside their network? Because security is relative.

Security policies and procedures of enterprise organizations often contain similar rules and regulations, but there are considerable differences in the way these policies are implemented. One enterprise may see a particular security risk as less of a priority than another. Each security risk, vulnerability, and threat has an associated cost, which represents the real money it takes to mitigate the issue. It also represents the loss of potential person hours for each user as a result of new policies, as well as the likelihood that the vulnerability will ever be exploited. All of these factors make up the risks, vulnerabilities, and threats that an enterprise must review to decide whether it is possible to mitigate the threat, or if it costs less to ignore it. When a new vulnerability is found on a device or application within an enterprise network, the enterprise must revisit these issues to identify the proper mitigation procedure. First, however, the enterprise must understand the vulnerability; this is not always easy.

When a vulnerability is found, a select group of IT professionals usually receives a description of the vulnerability and how to re-create it. The group evaluates the vulnerability's severity and announces it to the vendor or clients. These groups may not share the IT group's opinion about the vulnerability or how it could be used. One group might see it as a severe threat that could open up an enterprise's network to theft or damage, whereas another group might see the vulnerability as too obscure to threaten a real-world network.

If everything has vulnerabilities, does this mean that nothing is secure? With the right deployment of policies and procedures derived from an understanding of the risks, vulnerabilities, and threats, any network can be made adequately secure. However, it is not an easy task, especially when securing a less than mature VoIP and UC infrastructure. Because so many products have been introduced over the past five years, the number of vulnerabilities has risen exponentially.

As the Internet has become more widespread, many obscure and small product lines have become popular. Because the pool of implemented hardware and software is now much larger, malicious users can attack a wider range of devices and services to find and exploit vulnerabilities. Users who search for vulnerabilities can be divided into several types. Although these users are popularly called hackers, this term does not classify them correctly. The following list describes the major types of users who search for vulnerabilities:

- **Black hat**—A black hat is a malicious user who intends to use vulnerabilities to harm, steal, blackmail, or create chaos. Black hats are not always driven by money. They work in private and talk only with others within their niche. They never expose or announce exploits they find outside of their niche.

- **White hat**—A white hat is a hacker whose sole purpose is to find an exploit or vulnerability before the black hats, to notify vendors and customers who use the device or application. White hats are the "good guys" and can be found in many organizations, from Security Focus to CERT.

- **Gray hat**—Gray hat hackers will eventually announce the vulnerability or exploit, but want to profit from the find before releasing it.

- **Script kiddie**—These are not real hackers. They break things because they can, and use scripts or applications created and leaked by the black hats because they do not have the skills to crack networks or programs on their own. These users are truly out to cause harm, and usually do not have any idea what they have breached. The breach itself is their goal.

The growing popularity of UC provides a new range of products and services that a black hat can attack. The rewards have become much more lucrative as well, as UC and VoIP vulnerabilities may allow access to financial or personnel information, proprietary documents, and even free access to phone services. This creates even more incentive to find and abuse vulnerabilities in every UC and VoIP product.

Hardware

A VoIP deployment utilizes more than software applications. Software must run on some form of hardware. The IP phones used in a VoIP deployment may require an application-specific integrated chip (ASIC) to support encryption or voice compression. A VoIP media gateway may also require a specific Digital Signal Processor (DSP) that can handle multiple VoIP calls concurrently. A switch may require a specific module that supports 802.3af. Although adding specialized components to a device reduces the number of vulnerabilities because job functions are reduced for each component, any specialized component with a vulnerability may actually cause more harm. Chip-specific vulnerabilities can remain unfixed for a long time due to the difficulty in repairing or replacing the chip with a new piece of silicon or copper.

13

VoIP Threats and Vulnerabilities

Common chips in VoIP calls

A basic VoIP call requires three different chips to transform sound from the phone or microphone into a format that can be transmitted across the Internet to the destination end without a significant amount of loss to the original signal.

- **Analog to Digital Conversion (ADC) chip**—This chip converts the voice signal from the original analog to a digital format. The process uses an algorithm that can handle lossless conversion from one format to the other.

- **Digital to Analog Conversion (DAC) chip**—This chip is the opposite of the ADC. It converts a digital signal back to analog so that it can be played on a user's telephone or speakers.

- **Digital Signal Processor (DSP)**—The DSP chip applies a codec to the digital signal it receives from the ADC. It also removes the codec and hands it back to the DAC. The DSP can also apply a codec that compresses the digital signal into a lossy codec, which compresses a sound or set of sounds using a method that does not keep all of the original sound. This means that the new version of the sound is of lower quality than the original sound. Newer DSP chips can handle more than a single data stream (concurrent calls) at a time.

These chips handle the majority of signals within a VoIP call and can become a target for denial of service (DoS) attacks. This is especially true of the DSP. A malicious user can use code that ties up the channels within a DSP so that new voice calls will not have a DSP channel available for the call.

Beyond the audio aspect of a VoIP call, the VoIP device still needs to utilize a processor for signal handling and process management. These processors, although specialized, can have vulnerabilities that cause the device to reset or that allow a remote user to create a buffer overflow. Vulnerabilities in a processor or ASIC can be devastating for enterprise infrastructures that deploy them if the processors or ASICs cannot be updated with some form of patch.

EEPROM updating

Newer technology gives hardware vendors the ability to update ASICs, as well as processors, with a new or modified instruction set. This is usually done through an electronic erasable programmable read-only memory (EEPROM) chip within the device or ASIC. This can give a device new features that did not exist at the initial product release. This feature can update a chip or processor if a security vulnerability is found. Because the EEPROM update must be done manually, the process may require an outage and could cause other conflicts if the updated instructions are not designed to work in the enterprise's specific environment.

Software

Although vulnerabilities can be found within the hardware of a device, most are found within the software that interacts with the different parts of the hardware. Each device that is part of a VoIP deployment in an enterprise network requires some form of software. This may include an operating system, application software, or firmware that allows the device to use the services and applications required to support VoIP. On soft switches or media gateways,

·this may require a combination of software applications, with an operating system and application software residing on the same device. IP phones tend to have some form of firmware that handles the user interface and communications for the appropriate VoIP signaling and media protocols. Soft phones that reside on an end-user desktop can add complexity to software vulnerabilities management because their underlying operating system must be added to the mix of possible security vulnerabilities. An enterprise technician might have to manage several different sets of software images and firmware releases, based on the deployment size and design. This could include everything from multiple operating systems to the firmware on each IP phone and the images used on a router or switching device.

Code vulnerabilities

New vulnerabilities are often discovered in favorite applications or operating systems. Whether a security hole in Windows Vista or a kernel vulnerability in Linux, there is no application that is completely secure. Some attribute this to poor vendor testing or obvious neglect, but this is not usually the case. Every year, more applications are brought to market, each more complex then the last one. This complexity is partially due to the new features and options the product may offer, but is also due to the complexity of the hardware on which it will be used and the compatibility it may require. This leads to complex situations not easily duplicated in a testing environment. Some vulnerabilities can be so tiny that a specific situation must be in place for the vulnerability to work.

The alerts from security groups show that the most widely used and well-known software products top the list of active vulnerabilities, whereas lesser known or seldom-used products are at the bottom, if they appear at all. The more pervasive an application, the more breaches will be attempted. The less the software is used, the less important it is to black hats. This may give a false sense of security to enterprises that use less popular software, following the security theory of "security through obscurity." This theory proposes that the less public your company or product, the less interesting it is to black hats, and thus it is less likely to have a security vulnerability exploited. This does not mean that the piece of software is secure, only that it is not advantageous for others to find a weakness within it. If the software is a widely used operating system or an application used by governments or banks, the incentive becomes much greater.

An enterprise security group must still manage and test these applications, but should understand each application's possible threats and vulnerabilities. Public-facing applications should take precedence, but software deployed in private should be tested with the knowledge that security holes will exist that have not yet been identified by the vendor or the industry as a whole.

VoIP phone code

The software used on IP phones has grown dramatically over the last decade. Modern IP phones often use Java as the back-end operating system to drive the graphical user interface (GUI). Using an open standard like Java makes IP phone software more versatile, offering new features and options as each phone gets a more powerful processor. However, this also means that the phone is susceptible to the known vulnerabilities of the underlying operating system, whether Java, Linux, or some other system.

Although the underlying system may be a problem, IP phones also require interpreters that support the various VoIP signaling and media protocols. These interpreters must be as vendor-neutral as possible, because an enterprise might not use the same vendor for IP phones as for the network gear or VoIP switching. These issues create a complex set of code that can be exploited.

Because the majority of IP phones have such small processors, an attack on a single protocol, through a vulnerability or a simple protocol or packet flood, can cause a DoS that could allow a remote attacker access to information on that phone. This could also open the phone up to worms that can breach the VoIP protocols and vulnerabilities within the operating system, and then access the IP phone's address book to spread throughout the enterprise VoIP network.

Luckily, IP phones can be updated with firmware patches to resolve most of these security holes. These patches can usually be sent from a central point to all network IP phones when they reset.

XML

As IP phones become more sophisticated, customization becomes a major differentiator. IP phone vendors have focused on customizations such as interface modifications, feature additions, and the ability to update phones with event notices and news. Vendors are now using the Extensible Markup Language (XML) open standard language to create profiles and manage the phone interface. XML is used in Internet applications and Web sites around the world. This means that XML is very much in the public eye and is a target for black hats. Vulnerabilities within the XML standards must be considered when deploying IP phones that support XML. Be aware that a vendor may deviate from the XML standard in how it parses and interprets the XML code. These new parsers may have vulnerabilities of their own that are unique to the vendor.

UC on the desktop

When UC is integrated within the enterprise, it adds new tools such as integrated voice and e-mail, IM, Web conferencing, presence, and soft phones. These tools are designed to enhance productivity within the enterprise, but bring some security risks. As UC applications are deployed onto the desktop, enterprise IT departments must consider the security ramifications. Additional ports must now be supported on the desktop, such as User Datagram Protocol (UDP) 5060 and 5061 for SIP, and UDP ports 1719, 1720, and 1731 for H.323. Dynamic ports must also be available for all video and voice media streams set up beyond port 1024.

Application control is another important aspect of UC on the desktop. Because end users control the UC applications, they also control how each phase of the VoIP or UC session setup is handled. If end users install a modified version of the UC application—for example, a modified soft phone—they will have the ability to do more than just make a voice call. The enterprise group must continue to provide security for UC applications, while verifying that the ability to use that application has not been diminished and ensuring that new holes are not opened within the operating system through new or modified UC applications.

Protocol vulnerabilities

Each protocol used in a VoIP deployment can be considered a standard. Although some of these standards are closed or proprietary, such as Nortel's UNISTIM signaling protocol, vendors can still use recommendations from the standards to handle and interpret a specific protocol to use or interoperate with that protocol. You might assume that, if each vendor has the same template to use in building their software, each vendor's software should interoperate predictably with products from all other vendors that use the same protocol. Sadly, this is not normally the case. Most vendors utilize the standards as the base for their protocol interpretation, rather than the complete framework.

Vendors always want to outpace their competition, often with new features or enhancements to existing standards. A vendor may add new variables or options to SIP, and another group may change the arrangement of an H.323 or SIP message streamline packet processing. Such changes can cause vendor incompatibility, but can also create vulnerabilities within a protocol that are not inherent to the protocol itself. This is not to say that the VoIP protocols are free of vulnerabilities without tampering; VoIP protocols have some inherent vulnerabilities, but as vendors add more functionality, the existing vulnerabilities may become more dangerous and new vulnerabilities will start to find their way into the VoIP network.

Some common vulnerabilities span several VoIP protocols; they are described in the following list. The majority of these vulnerabilities can be exploited to access calls or create new calls without authorization, thus allowing fraud within a VoIP infrastructure.

- **Message header rewriting**—Several VoIP protocols, such as RTP and SIP, allow a user to manipulate the message header to inject new information and replace existing information in the message. A malicious user can then redirect a call or media stream to a local device instead of its intended destination, and can allow the user to disrupt calls.

- **Data piggybacking**—Through the widespread use of soft phones, an application on the user desktop can handle VoIP signaling and media streaming. Users can also use modified soft phones to implant new data into the media stream. This method can carry actual data traffic to a remote server through the media stream, similar to a file transfer, and thus permit a potential security breach of proprietary information.

- **Denial of service**—The protocol parser's ability to handle incoming packets is based on how the vendor built the parser. Although recommendations within the standard describe the most common way to handle packets and loads, a vendor may try to enhance the parser to make it faster or feature-rich. This can cause errors in how the parser interprets the packet, resulting in problems that range from buffer overflows to resets. If the device is flooded with these badly formed packets, the end user may create a DoS for that device. If the device happens to be a SIP proxy or H.323 gateway, the DoS can be enterprise-wide.

- **Spam over Internet telephony (SPIT)**—The spread of VoIP has led to a new form of spam. SPIT is a new way for spammers to send ads and offers to an end user. SPIT is far more devious than simple short message service (SMS) text messages. By exploiting known vulnerabilities within the VoIP protocols, spammers can send voice mail directly to your e-mail if you are using a UC voice-to-mail solution. If access to the media streaming protocol is gained through packet sniffers or other means, the spammer can inject a voice advertisement within an active voice call. This is especially true with open source SIP, as malicious users can easily build tools to abuse SIP's signaling vulnerabilities.

Specific VoIP protocol vulnerabilities are described later in this chapter. Remember that VoIP protocols must run on an IP network, and IP is not in and of itself a secure protocol. When IP was designed, security was not at the top of the feature list to be supported. This means that applications using IP require security through the use of another protocol. IP has a wide range of vulnerabilities that can be used to disrupt a VoIP network, or to assist in fraudulent calls or identity theft.

Social engineering

The human factor is the hardest thing to control when dealing with security. Software can be patched and hardware can be updated or locked down, but a person cannot be forced to follow standards. Remember that each person is different; although a security method may work with one group of people, another group may neither understand nor care. This is due to the perceived impact of new security measures.

Social vulnerabilities come in many forms. How often have you seen a desk with a set of passwords written on a note and stuck to the monitor? You probably know someone who uses their birthday or anniversary as their password. Do you use the same password for everything? Does it have at least eight characters with at least one number, one letter, and one special character, and is not a dictionary word? When you walk into a secure building, do you hold the door open for the people behind you, even if they haven't gone through the security process, because you know them? All of these are security failures based on the human factor.

People tend to choose the easiest method to complete a task, instead of a complicated or work-intensive solution. It is much easier to look at a password taped to your screen than it is to memorize it. People are also more likely to trust the new or unknown, whereas a security group will always treat new information as suspect. Enterprise security groups must take human nature into account to keep the enterprise infrastructure as safe as possible.

Phishing

Phishing is a major issue that threatens security and privacy. Phishing is a tactic used by malicious users to gain restricted or private information from an end user. It relies on human nature, gambling that an end user is too trusting and lazy to verify information before divulging whatever the phishing attempt is trying to gather. Phishing occurs in several ways:

- **Fraudulent call**—A malicious user can utilize a breached VoIP network to call that network's end users. The user then impersonates a member of the enterprise staff to gain information from the end user. If a call comes from the corporate VoIP network and the originating caller says he or she is from human resources, especially in a large enterprise, an end user will trust that the malicious user is truly who he or she claims to be and will answer honestly. This can lead to additional breaches of security, fraud, or theft.

- **Worms**—E-mail is an important weapon for the phisher. A phishing user may send an e-mail that appears legitimate to a select group of users at an enterprise network. The e-mail, which may refer to a corporate event or client, contains a worm or virus. If successful, the phisher has placed a worm that could utilize the VoIP network to make calls, steal from the address book, or even shut down the VoIP network. A virus may allow the phisher the ability to automatically obtain a copy of every media stream created by the end users' computers. These actions can be truly damaging to an enterprise.

To reduce the possibility of such intrusions, the enterprise security group must make sure that end users are as informed as possible. If the enterprise's intrusion detection applications catch a phishing scam, or it is determined that some users have weak passwords, the end users must be quickly notified and trained to stop or limit the damage within the network. Policies must be put into place to audit user security practices, so that users who do not follow standard security policies can be found and corrected.

What is a threat?

As you learned earlier in this chapter, new vulnerabilities are found every day in VoIP and UC products, as well as in the underlying infrastructure used by VoIP and UC. Once you understand how each vulnerability works and how it affects a product deployed in the enterprise network, the next step is to determine the threat these vulnerabilities pose to the enterprise. The enterprise security group must understand what a threat is, and how to determine if the threat is real.

The United States Army's definition of a threat is appropriate for environments that handle information every day, such as an enterprise environment. The Army's Information Assurance Security Officer Training Guidelines define threats as "capabilities, intentions, and attack methods of adversaries to exploit, damage, or alter or any circumstance or event with the potential to cause harm to information or an information system." Threats are comprised of who a person is, what that person is supposed to do within the enterprise, and what the person actually does. These threats must be secured and monitored continuously.

Known threats

An enterprise security group should always have an understanding of the possible threats to the enterprise network. If the enterprise network is connected to the Internet in any way, nothing should be considered safe by default. Even the most remote servers and devices on a small enterprise network can be used in a DoS attack. The enterprise security group's advantage is in its knowledge of devices and applications deployed within the enterprise network. This knowledge will help the security group defend against potential threats by understanding existing vulnerabilities to the network and mitigating them.

The industry and services that the enterprise offers will also help the security group determine what must be protected and what can be left more vulnerable. The enterprise can use tracking and trending to understand traffic and service patterns so that when an anomaly, such as a DoS attack, occurs on the enterprise network, it can be noticed and understood immediately.

Malicious users

One of the most obvious threats to an enterprise network is the malicious user or hacker. A malicious user is someone who has decided to access the enterprise network through means that are illegal and nonintuitive. These users also attempt to find vulnerabilities within common and uncommon applications and protocols. Their intent varies, but can include the following reasons: money, terrorism, espionage, chaos, sabotage, respect, glory, and proving the attack can succeed.

It should never be assumed that a security measure can be put into place that will always stop such a user. The only true way to be secure from a malicious user is to turn a device off.

Known vulnerabilities

Vulnerabilities can cause havoc on an enterprise network. They can be used by malicious users to enter the network. They can also be triggered accidentally, which may open a new security hole or cause damage or downtime within the enterprise network. The security group should evaluate several aspects of the vulnerability to determine how it might threaten the enterprise network:

- **Ability to reproduce the vulnerability**—Some vulnerabilities are easy to reproduce, whereas others may require a special set of events to be triggered. Some are so hard to reproduce that they can only be seen in a lab. A security group should note the difficulty of using a vulnerability when determining the threat level.

- **Relevance to the enterprise**—A vulnerability may be easy to reproduce, but how often does it actually happen within a specific enterprise infrastructure? A vulnerability may never be seen by an enterprise if the affected feature is never or rarely used. An enterprise security group should evaluate the relevance of the vulnerability and if it can even be accessed within the network.

- **Risk to the enterprise**—An enterprise network is often split into multiple zones, each with different security requirements, such as a trust zone, a demilitarized zone (DMZ), and an untrust zone. A vulnerability may reside in a zone that has a very low security requirement because it represents a noncritical part of the company. These zones or sections of the network may not have access to more critical zones, so a security breach may only affect that area, if at all. The threat of theft or malicious damage may be small enough that an enterprise would spend more money to secure the vulnerability than it would to handle an actual breach in the zone.

Although a vulnerability may be marked at a low threat level, this does not mean that these vulnerabilities should be taken lightly. All vulnerabilities should be considered as possible threats to the enterprise network and should be continuously reviewed and audited to determine the current level of threat the vulnerability might present to the enterprise.

Social threat

Because the human factor is hard to secure and control, all users should be treated as possible threats to the enterprise network. End user access to the network should be tracked and monitored, and any opportunity for unauthorized access should be removed. This should not be the only security consideration for end users. Their job responsibilities, productivity, and privacy must also be taken into consideration.

Industry threat

Specific industries tend to draw more security attacks than others. In recent years, malicious users have migrated from wanting the prestige of breaching a big firm to wanting monetary reward for doing it. The desire for financial reward has led to the rise of phishing schemes or fraud run through unauthorized use of a VoIP network. As VoIP and UC are deployed in more critical environments, such as financial institutions, these services have become a way for black hats to steal money from end users and the financial institutions themselves.

This is not unique to financial institutions, though. Security firms that must protect their image have become targets for malicious users intent on defacing the firms' credibility and showing how insecure they really are. Because there is no such thing as a completely secure infrastructure, these users will eventually succeed.

Governments and universities have also become large targets, due to the growing trend of identity theft. These institutions store private data of employees, students, and taxpayers that includes Social Security numbers, birth dates and places, and other personal information that can be used by identity thieves.

Unknown threats

No matter how vigilant a security group, some threats will be missed. These threats are not always obvious and are rarely easy to predict. As an enterprise network grows, it adds new products, services, and personnel that might not have been included in the last security audit. The company might have also become more visible in the industry, thus becoming more of a target for black hats. Either way, the enterprise security group must be diligent in resolving new threats as quickly as they are found.

Unknown vulnerabilities

When an enterprise purchases a new device or application, the IT staff usually researches known vulnerabilities of the device or application. Thorough security groups will perform additional security tests on the new products to ensure vulnerabilities related to their specific deployments are identified and understood. Even with extra testing, new vulnerabilities may be found by the vendor, security group, black hats, or the enterprise itself. While these vulnerabilities are identified and resolved, the gear in the field is vulnerable to attacks. It is difficult to be proactive toward this type of threat without continuous testing that could end up being very expensive.

Unauthorized hardware or software

Although desktops may be locked down to a specific point and switches secured, an end user may install new hardware or software to get around these security measures. Some end users may add a noncertified piece of hardware to the network to get a product up and running. Other users might want to use the same VoIP provider at work as they have at home and install proprietary VoIP software on their desktops. Still others may add wireless access points, without security, to the network so that they can work away from their desks.

These choices may seem trivial to the end user deploying them, but to the security group they are security holes waiting to be breached. This type of activity must be controlled as much as possible with diligent audits and monitoring to stop a malicious user from exploiting a vulnerability within a device that is not even known to the security group.

The human factor

No one can predict how employees will react when they are under stress. This includes events such as being fired, being demeaned, or losing a promotion. Although an enterprise security group should attempt to head off threats from disgruntled users, they will not catch everything. Determined end users will find a way to disrupt or steal what they want, even if it means breaking or breaching security. This is not just the realm of the disgruntled employee. Some employees earn extra money by selling secrets, or steal voice minutes to call overseas. These problems can be handled with a simple solution: Make sure that everything is properly monitored and recorded. This is a good idea for security as a whole, but also gives an enterprise the ability to show and track what the user has done so that the proper authorities can be notified.

What is risk?

Once the threats and vulnerabilities of a specific enterprise network are identified, a level of risk can be associated with each aspect of the network. In a basic IP network, these risks are well known as they have been evaluated, researched, and analyzed for over a decade. The IP protocol has specific security risks that must be taken into consideration when deploying a network, such as the ability to monitor and capture traffic, network-based attacks and DoS attacks, and the fact that it is easy to learn how an IP network works. Malicious users don't need to be geniuses to breach an IP network, because widely available scripts and programs will do it for them.

To assist in reducing the damage caused by a breach, enterprise networks often place critical data behind a firewall while allowing Internet-facing devices to exist in their own zone. This reduces the risk that a malicious user can gain access to the Internet-facing box and then use it as a jumping-off point to compromise critical data. Most enterprise networks place their corporate VoIP and user base within the same zone as the critical data. This is because the enterprise security group allows a limited amount of trust to the end users.

With the deployment of VoIP and UC, this trust should be reevaluated. VoIP requires that an end user be able to access the network, and possibly the Internet, with a suite of protocols that are normally not handled by firewalls. Because most VoIP media streams require dynamically assigned ports, a firewall will not know ahead of time which ports to allow through. This requires the enterprise security group either to open up a range of ports above 1025, or enable application layer gateways (ALGs) that can create dynamic pinhole filters in the firewall on a per-stream basis. The ALG does not necessarily verify that the VoIP signaling protocol requesting the pinhole is valid, so a malicious user could force a hole in the firewall by abusing the ALG.

Both of these solutions add risks to the network because part of the critical infrastructure may now be accessed from a different zone, or the Internet, through the use of holes in the firewall. End users can also use UC applications, such as soft phones, to make valid calls to remote locations and transfer information through the firewall and around a content evaluation device. This also permits viruses and worms to access the critical part of the network by utilizing UC and VoIP protocols and the trust of the end user. The enterprise must understand and evaluate these additional risks.

Product solution

When designing VoIP and UC infrastructure, the solution should take the risks associated with such a deployment into account. Several factors must be understood before the infrastructure can be green-lighted.

- **User access**—Will the user base require access to the VoIP network? Does each user need each application within the UC deployment? If they do, what additional risks will be added?

- **Department**—Should a critical department or infrastructure use VoIP if 99.999 percent uptime cannot be guaranteed? If these departments lose access to the voice network, how will productivity be affected?

- **Content using VoIP/UC**—What will be said over the VoIP calls or through instant messages? Because privacy is an important legal concern, patient health or employment information may be at risk if the VoIP network is breached and a malicious user gains access to that voice stream or instant message.

Industry

The enterprise's industry can also affect the potential risk of VoIP and UC. Emergency services, such as police or fire departments, might not be able to allow a less secure, less reliable telephony option within their networks. Health care or financial firms must implement additional security measures to ensure that private or confidential information cannot be stolen through vulnerabilities in the VoIP or UC deployments.

The enterprise's industry may also affect the required amount of monitoring and auditing. Companies that support IP telephony may be required to support wiretapping ability for law enforcement. The enterprise may also be required to record and store the media streams of one or more voice calls for auditing and security reasons. All of this adds new risks and responsibilities to an existing and complex security environment.

Accessibility

Adding new security measures can create a problem for end users. If a security measure is considered a hindrance, tedious, or useless, end users may find a way to get around the security measures. These methods then create a new security vulnerability that may not be apparent to security groups within the enterprise network. When ease of use is compromised by security measures, policy adjustments must be made.

Security measures should be as thorough as possible, but must take ease of use into consideration, and should determine how often each measure must be used by an end user. An enterprise may consider taking on risk by reducing some security measures to provide a more accessible way to use the measure. This can avoid the more dangerous risk from end users by substituting a small managed risk.

13

VoIP Threats and Vulnerabilities

VoIP protocol vulnerabilities

VoIP utilizes several different protocol suites and deployment methods. Each of these suites fills a specific role and resolves a specific VoIP problem. These protocols sit above IP, an insecure transport protocol. IP's vulnerabilities are widely known, and methods to breach them are easily found on the Internet. Although a security group must understand IP vulnerabilities, those specific issues are not covered in this book.

Because VoIP rides on an insecure transport protocol, the protocols governing VoIP require some measure of security. The applications in which VoIP will be used can allow a malicious user access to confidential and private information, or possible access to secure data. This gives black hats a good reason to breach a protocol or protocol suite used in a VoIP deployment. VoIP deployments might counter these issues with proxy or registration servers. This allows a limited amount of security by validating who can use the VoIP network, but is not a completely secure solution.

Encrypting signaling and media traffic can add some security. Signaling can utilize strong encryption to avoid permitting a black hat to see the content or call information of the VoIP protocol. Encrypting the media stream can help remove the ability of malicious users to gather the media packets and attempt to reassemble them, which then allows someone to listen to the entire conversation. Encryption does reduce the amount of risk within a VoIP deployment, but has yet to be widely deployed. Equipment cost and lack of vendor support have hampered the deployment of encrypted VoIP solutions.

Even these solutions will not remove all vulnerabilities and risks associated with VoIP. The main reason is the vulnerabilities within the VoIP protocols themselves. These vulnerabilities can thwart competent security measures added to the VoIP deployment to reduce risk.

H.323

In the mid-1990s, a signaling protocol had to be placed between media gateways to support the new application called VoIP. Because there was no existing standard, the International Telecommunications Union (ITU-I) decided to utilize the current open video conferencing standard, H.323. This became official in 1995 when the first Internet phone used H.323 as its signaling protocol. Although this particular protocol is usually called H.323, H.323 is actually an umbrella protocol with several protocols contained within it.

H.225.0 protocol

When an H.323 call is initiated, the first protocol used is H.225, which has two purposes. During the setup and teardown aspect of an H.323 call, H.225 handles the communication between the two ends and determines how the call will be set up or the process required to end the call, once completed. H.225 requires another protocol for this action, Q.931. Figure 13–1 shows an H.225 setup and teardown call flow between two soft phones.

FIGURE 13-1: H.225 CALL FLOW.

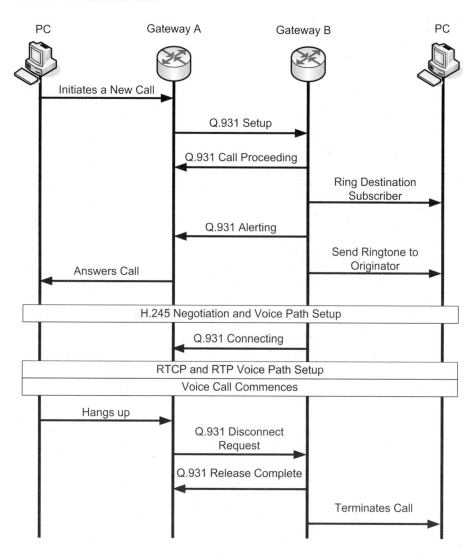

H.225 can also handle the registration process if an H.323 gatekeeper is present. This process is commonly known as Registration, Admission, and Status (RAS). This changes the call flow by adding a step, before the Q.931 setup, in which both of the H.323 gateways must send an RAS request message to the H.323 gatekeeper, which in turn sends an RAS request to the remote gateway. Once this process is complete, the H.225 call flow continues unchanged. When a call is terminated, the gateways inform the gatekeepers that the call has been released.

13

VoIP Threats and
Vulnerabilities

H.245 protocol

During the call setup process, H.245 negotiates the channels that will be used for the media stream once the call has been connected. It must do this in conjunction with both the H.225 and Q.931 protocols. After the H.225 protocol receives the Q.931 Altering message, it hands off the setup process to the H.245 protocol. The call flow for an H.245 setup process is shown in Figure 13–2.

FIGURE 13-2: H.245 CALL FLOW.

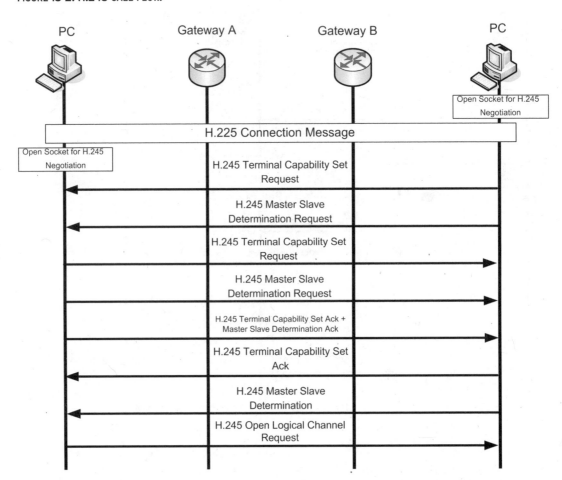

H.450 protocol

H.450 is a protocol that handles additional services not originally included in the H.323 standard. These features mirror the ITU-I QSIG feature set used on Integrated Services Digital Network (ISDN) connections between multiple Private Branch Exchange (PBX) devices:

- **H.450.1**—Supplemental Services Framework
- **H.450.2**—Call Transfer
- **H.450.3**—Call Diversion
- **H.450.4**—Call Hold
- **H.450.5**—Call Park
- **H.450.6**—Call Waiting
- **H.450.7**—Message Waiting
- **H.450.8**—Name Identification
- **H.450.9**—Call Completion
- **H.450.10**—Call Offer
- **H.450.11**—Call Intrusion
- **H.450.12**—Common Information Additional Network Feature

H.235 protocol

The H.235 protocol was created to manage the security aspect of the H.323 protocol. H.235 handles the specifications for encryption, featuring several encryption algorithms, as well as the ability to encrypt the voice stream by defining profiles. The H.235 protocol defines nine different profiles that suggest how H.323 should be deployed securely:

- **H.235.1**—Baseline Security Profile
- **H.235.2**—Signature Security Profile
- **H.235.3**—Hybrid Security Profile
- **H.235.4**—Direct and selectively routed call security
- **H.235.5**—Framework for secure authentication in RAS using weak shared secrets
- **H.235.6**—Voice encryption profile with native H.235/H.245 key management
- **H.235.7**—Usage of the MIKEY Key Management Protocol for the Secure Real-Time Transport Protocol (SRTP) within H.235
- **H.235.8**—Key exchange for SRTP using secure signaling channels
- **H.235.9**—Security gateway support for H.323

The H.235 protocol can also work hand in hand with an H.323 gatekeeper to assure that both ends of the call are legitimate and authorized users.

H.239 protocol

When H.323 is used for video conferencing, the H.239 protocol comes into play. H.239 governs how H.323 will use a dual stream for video conferencing. One stream is dedicated to the live video from the presenter, and the other feed handles any presentation media that may go with the live video feed, such as slides.

H.460 protocol

The H.460 protocol defines optional extensions that may be assigned by an endpoint, such as a gateway or IP phone. Additionally, the extensions for Network Address Translation (NAT) and firewall transversal are governed by this protocol.

Q.931 protocol

The Q.931 protocol is used extensively with ISDN networks. It is the signaling protocol used to set up and tear down ISDN channels on a primary rate interface (PRI) or basic rate interface (BRI). H.323 also utilizes it as a signaling protocol to set up and tear down channels when talking with an IP-PBX over a non-LAN-based connection. All VoIP-related configuration and setup information is injected into the Q.931 protocol by embedding within it the H.245 protocol.

RTP with H.323

Once a call is set up, H.323 uses RTP to carry the media streams. This protocol is an Internet Engineering Task Force (IETF) standard used in conjunction with the ITU-I standard H.323. RTP is explained in more detail in the next section of this chapter.

RTCP

RTCP returns the status of the media stream handled by RTP. RTCP works closely with RTP to understand the quality of the media stream and report back to the H.323 server the state of the media stream, including bytes sent, packets sent, lost packets, jitter, feedback, and round-trip delay. Reports are then created for the sending and receiving ends of the call.

T.120

To allow more than voice and video interaction, H.323 utilizes the T.120 protocol for all other multimedia data. This can include file transfers, application sharing, live chat, and interactive multimedia. Because this protocol handles applications that are sensitive to packet loss, T.120 uses Transmission Control Protocol (TCP) channels instead of UDP.

G.7xx codecs

The G.7xx codec set (G.711, G.723, G.723.1, G.726, G.728, G.729, and G.729a) is used to encode the analog signal to a digital signal for transmission. G.711 is used for uncompressed voice encapsulation, and the rest are different compression algorithms that take into consideration quality over bandwidth use. When G.711 is not used, G.729 is the most common compression algorithm. These codecs are also used with the SIP protocol.

H.26x codecs

Like the G.7xx codecs, the H.26x codecs convert an analog signal to a digital signal. These codecs are specifically used for video signals that are part of multimedia applications and video conferences.

H.323 gatekeeper

When deploying H.323 in a VoIP infrastructure, an H.323 appliance can act as several different parts of the deployment. Whereas a single end-to-end VoIP deployment only needs to communicate between the two ends, an H.323 gateway is commonly deployed in an enterprise VoIP infrastructure to handle all incoming and outgoing calls, while adding a layer of security to the transaction. This requires both ends of the H.323 VoIP call to register with the H.323 gatekeeper so the call can be set up.

H.323 gateway

When a VoIP call must be created between two different protocols, such as H.323 and SIP, an H.323 gateway is used. The H.323 gateway can be used in conjunction with an H.323 gatekeeper to support call registry, while still supporting the ability to talk with other protocols.

H.323 vulnerabilities

H.323 is a versatile protocol with a complex structure. A technician can use H.323 in many different applications, but must continuously review each subset protocol for new vulnerabilities that may affect the VoIP deployment. This can become time consuming, and permits a possible breach in security before the technician is notified of a new vulnerability. Patching the subset protocols can become an issue if they can no longer interact fully with the rest of the H.323 suite of protocols.

In addition to maintaining each subset protocol, an enterprise technician must be able to utilize H.323 in a secure environment. In an enterprise infrastructure, the H.323 gateway and gatekeeper usually reside behind a firewall and may even utilize a NAT device to access the Internet. This can be problematic because the protocols within H.323 are not clear text. When the H.323 protocol and its subset protocols were designed, the ITU-I required that they use the ANS.1 standard. This standard requires protocols to use a binary format and the ANS.1 low-level interpreter. Because the protocol is in a binary format, the firewall or NAT device must interpret the protocol through special readers that also follow the ANS.1 standards. This can increase the time it takes for a packet to get to the endpoint, but it also allows the interpreter to misunderstand the contents of the packet and thus create a vulnerability that can crash the device or allow access to internal data.

There are some common vulnerabilities within the H.323 protocol that should be understood before deployment:

- **Registry hijacking**—If a malicious user can acquire the initial setup and register H.225 packet sent from the end user or phone to the H.323 gatekeeper, the user can modify the header messages and switch the IP address source from the original sender to the malicious user. All further setup messages will then move between the malicious user and the H.323 gatekeeper.

- **Corrupted H.225 packet**—Due to the design specifications of the H.225 protocol, an H.323 end device, gateway, or gatekeeper does not perform sufficient error checking on the user-supplied part of Setup-PDU messages. If a malicious user provides specific corrupt data as part of user-supplied content in the H.225 message, the remote phone, gateway, or gatekeeper can experience a buffer overflow within the H.225 stack and cause the device to stop answering H.225 requests, or even reboot. Continuous use of this vulnerability can cause a DoS attack. This attack is sometimes called fuzzing.

- **Gatekeeper flooding**—It is possible for a user to send large amounts of gatekeeper requests to an enterprise gatekeeper to the point at which the gatekeeper cannot keep up. This may cause the H.323 gatekeeper to drop active IP phones that have already registered with active calls.

Session Initiation Protocol (SIP)

SIP is the IETF's answer to a standard VoIP signaling protocol. SIP uses a protocol layout similar to that used by Hypertext Markup Language (HTML), and is an open source peer-to-peer signaling protocol that utilizes a clear text protocol format that can be read without additional interpreters. SIP was initially designed as the IETF's replacement for H.323, because H.323 was not designed for VoIP signaling over IP. Although SIP was originally a VoIP protocol, it is now used in many applications, including video over IP, instant messaging, Web conferencing, events notification, and presence applications. SIP is defined in RFC 3261, and can utilize UDP or TCP port 5060. It commonly uses the UDP protocol because SIP has a TCP-like acknowledgment system that can get around UDP's stateless design.

SIP utilizes a separate protocol to handle the media stream. Like H.323, SIP uses RTP to transport the media between each end. Unlike H.323, SIP uses a separate protocol, Session Description Protocol (SDP), which piggybacks SIP to carry the media content information. SDP handles the IP address, available codecs, and the ports that will be used for the media stream. The same vulnerabilities found in H.323's implementation of RTP can also be found in SIP's implementation. A sample SIP call flow is shown in Figure 13–3.

FIGURE 13-3: BASIC SIP CALL FLOW.

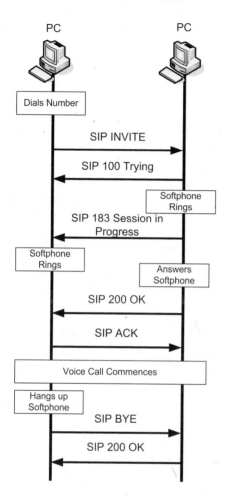

The SIP protocol has more than 20,000 currently known vulnerabilities. These vulnerabilities range from minor to severe, with many of them giving an attacker the ability to disrupt service or even seed worms or viruses into a network that would normally block them through a firewall or antivirus mechanism. The following list describes some of the more common SIP protocol vulnerabilities:

• **Media stream redirection**—A SIP packet can be modified to create a modified header that may have a new To:, From:, or CC: field. SIP message modification can also be used to inject a new IP address for the source or destination endpoint of the media stream. This can allow a malicious user to hijack an existing call or gain a valid copy of the media stream with a minor modification.

- **Message tampering**—SIP messages can also be modified to get around a registering proxy. If a malicious user can acquire a valid SIP INVITE message, the message can be modified and reused to make fraudulent calls through the SIP proxy without being denied.

- **DoS**—Although SIP is an industry standard with a set text format for each legitimate field, SIP message interpreters will have issues with content that may be within a SIP message field. In a process called fuzzing, a malicious user can modify a once-valid SIP message with an abnormally long set of characters within single or multiple fields of a SIP message and transmit it to a SIP speaking device or proxy. If the right set of characters is used, the receiving device will fail to understand the packet and crash. If this is done repeatedly or to a large amount of SIP-speaking devices within a network, the malicious user can create a DoS attack that will seriously disrupt an existing VoIP network.

- **Worms**—With the ability to modify the SIP message and change To:, From:, or CC: fields, a malicious user can redirect an end user to an unwanted site. In particular, end users who use SIP for Web conferencing or events notifications can unknowingly be redirected to a Web site that will install a virus, worm, or Trojan on the user's desktop. Additionally, worms can be seeded inside an instant message signaled by SIP. This is similar to the worms currently used on common public IM platforms.

- **Eavesdropping**—SIP is a text-based protocol that can be easily read on the wire, especially in an archived packet capture. If an IM product uses SIP to pass all messages, a malicious user can intercept these packets and eavesdrop on the conversation without either party knowing. This can also allow a malicious user to learn the possible whereabouts of an end user based on the information gathered from SIP messages used in a presence application.

SIP registrar and proxy

SIP supports two additional services: registrar and proxy. A SIP device can act like a registrar. The registrar authenticates each SIP session through a configured authentication scheme, such as Lightweight Directory Access Protocol (LDAP) or RADIUS. A SIP media gateway or a firewall can be configured to force all SIP INVITE messages to the proxy, reducing the chance that an unauthorized SIP session will be created. This does permit a registrar bypass vulnerability, as a SIP INVITE can have the CC: field modified by a malicious user to redirect all further SIP messages for that session to the user's IP address. This causes the registrar to think that the session has been authenticated while an unauthorized SIP session is in progress.

The SIP proxy is used when a NAT transversal or firewall bypass is required. A SIP proxy can also parse SIP messages for invalid content and drop the message before it can harm the end devices. The SIP proxy is the intermediary through which the SIP messages for both ends of the SIP session pass. Once the session has been set up, the proxy gets out of the way and does not participate in the session until the session is terminating. Although a SIP proxy can help control SIP sessions and weed out bad messages, it can also be used to breach security by injecting itself into a SIP message flow.

Because a SIP device can sometimes act as a SIP proxy, an end device can redirect a SIP session to an insecure endpoint by acting like a proxy and modifying the SIP message headers.

SIP over Transport Layer Security (TLS)

SIP can also utilize TLS to encrypt all messages between each endpoint. SIP over TLS utilizes a different port than regular SIP. Port 5061 is used for SIP over TLS signaling. When TLS is used to encrypt signaling messages, malicious users lose the ability to intercept a SIP message and modify the SIP headers. It also stops eavesdropping based on SIP's text-based design. Although this is a more secure way to handle SIP signaling, it is not yet widely used, due in part to lack of vendor compliance and in large part to the false sense of security that many enterprises have with SIP and their network security as a whole.

UNISTIM

UNISTIM is a proprietary signaling protocol developed by Nortel Networks. UNISTIM is considered a closed protocol, as the complete specifications for the protocol, packet headers, and content format are not available to the public. UNISTIM is a UDP-based signaling protocol used between Nortel IP telephony devices to handle the setup and teardown of all VoIP calls. Vulnerabilities found for this protocol are announced by the vendor, with a patch to follow.

RTSP

RTSP was created in the late 1990s (RFC 2326) and has been mainly used by media streaming applications to push video and audio. The protocol is an open standard, used by companies such as Microsoft and Apple for media streams and conferencing. Video conference calling applications have also utilized this protocol. The largest set of RTSP-related vulnerabilities comes from malformed RTSP packets. These packets tend to cause a buffer overflow on the receiving application server, giving the malicious user who sent the packet the ability to run arbitrary code on the application server. RTSP can also use RTP as its media streaming protocol, and inherits all vulnerabilities known for RTP.

RTP and RTCP

Used by SIP and H.323, RTP carries the media stream of a VoIP or video session between two or more endpoints. RTP is a UDP-based protocol that utilizes any port from 1025 to 65535. RTP sees all ports below 1024 as restricted. If an administrator notices that RTP is using these lower ports, an unauthorized backdoor may have been installed. RTP is an IETF standard media protocol (RFC 1889) for real-time applications, although it is mainly used for VoIP and media streaming.

During a VoIP call setup, the VoIP protocol negotiates with the remote end to determine what port each end will use to terminate the RTP stream, as well as what compression algorithm will be used for the stream itself. Although UDP is the most common form of RTP used for VoIP media streams, RTP can utilize TCP and encryption to help secure the media stream during transmission.

In addition, RTP, SIP, and H.323 can utilize RTCP to monitor the status and quality of an end-to-end voice call. RTCP is designed to gather information on bytes sent, packets sent, lost packets, jitter, feedback, and round-trip delay for each end of the voice call, as well as any intermediate section of the network for which it can retrieve feedback.

13

VoIP Threats and Vulnerabilities

RTP vulnerabilities

By itself, RTP contains several vulnerabilities that can be used to disrupt a VoIP installation or end user. When using RTP through a VoIP signaling protocol, the media stream can be moved around or intercepted. The most common vulnerabilities using RTP are described in the following list:

- **Media stream redirection**—Malicious users can inject different IP addresses as the source or destination of a media stream during the negotiations between endpoints to determine the specifications that will be used for the RTP stream. The stream can thus be redirected to the malicious user's IP phone, soft phone, or other device. This is usually done by modifying a SIP or H.323 signal packet during RTP negotiations.

- **Voice injection**—A malicious user can gain information about the RTP stream through the use of an arbitrary RTP packet flood to a VoIP call recipient during an active call. If enough information is gathered, the user can inject sound into the existing RTP stream, disrupting the call and allowing possible unsolicited advertisements through a voice recording.

- **Message tampering**—An RTP packet can be modified to create an invalid header or payload. If this packet is sent to an end device, such as an IP phone or media gateway, the end device may fail to parse the packet and force a reset of that device. If this is used as a DoS attack, it can bring down multiple end-user IP phones or all DS0 channels on a media gateway by continuously resetting them.

- **Theft**—VoIP soft phones provide a new way to steal data. RTP can be used to send more than just sound between two endpoints, because it can carry normal data. If the soft phones on both ends of the call are modified, a SIP call can become a file transfer. This file transfer can get past firewall and content filters because these filters do not interrogate the RTP payload.

- **RTP quality of service (QoS) degradation**—If a malicious user can capture an RTCP packet, the information gathered from that packet can be used to build a new RTCP packet that gives false QoS reports back to the endpoints or IP-PBX. This can cause the endpoint or IP-PBX to reserve additional bandwidth when none is needed, or move packet queuing around to adapt to the false report. This causes quality to drop on other calls.

MGCP

Some enterprise networks utilize PRI or intermachine trunk (IMT) circuits to pass voice calls to a local telephone provider, such as a regional Bell Operating Company (RBOC) or a competitive local exchange carrier (CLEC). These circuits terminate on an appliance called a VoIP media gateway. This gateway formats an outgoing VoIP call so that it can be passed over a digital service channel to the telephony provider. MGCP is used between an IP soft switch or IP-PBX and an IP media gateway to signal and control how these digital service channels are assigned, and what calls will utilize them. MGCP is an IETF standard (RFC 2705) that utilizes UDP ports 2427 (MGCP Gateway) and 2724 (MGCP Call Agent). This protocol is very restrictive in how it is deployed, and is less likely to be the target of security attacks than a more versatile protocol like SIP. However, this does not mean that MGCP lacks vulnerabilities.

MGCP vulnerabilities

There are several known vulnerabilities for MGCP, but a majority of them are not directly protocol-related. The major vulnerability of the MGCP protocol is that it is a trusting protocol. The MGCP protocol is designed to answer all requests sent to it with a valid answer. This means that if a malicious user sends a packet to an MGCP gateway (usually an IP soft switch), the user can request a list of all known DS0 channels in service or managed by that soft switch. The list of channels can then be used for several purposes:

- **Disrupt calls in progress**—Because the channel list identifies DS0 channels with active calls, the malicious user can send an MGCP packet with a Delete Connection (DLCX) command to disconnect the channel from service, thus disconnecting the call in progress.

- **Eavesdropping**—A malicious user can gain access to the voice data stream between the media gateway and the remote caller through a series of requests to the soft switch. This can only be done if the call is a conference call, as the user must request to be added to the bridge silently. This cannot be done with an end-to-end call.

- **Fraud**—Knowing which channels are controlled by the MGCP protocol means that a malicious user can use the soft switch to dial outbound calls. This could allow the user to place long distance calls or to call emergency numbers, potentially requiring the enterprise to pay large fines for fraudulent calls. It can also enable the user to lock all channels so that the enterprise cannot use any outgoing lines to the local telephony provider, effectively removing access to emergency numbers and all local, and possibly long distance, calling.

- **Man in the middle attacks**—A malicious user can use the channel list to take over a VoIP call while it is being set up. This ability is also known as call hijacking. If the user can intercept the initial signaling before the call is complete, the signaling setup can be redirected to steal the call from the original caller. The malicious user then becomes the original caller and the call goes through to the remote user.

These are severe threats, but they can easily be resolved by restricting permission to talk with the MGCP soft switch and media gateway, or by creating a trust design through certificates or other means.

The rest of the MGCP-related vulnerabilities are rooted in how a soft switch or IP-PBX handles an MGCP packet. The interpretation of these packets seems to lend itself to vulnerabilities that can lead to several different outcomes:

- **Buffer overflow**—A malformed MGCP Audit Endpoint response message (AUEP) packet can create a remote buffer overflow within an IP-PBX. This buffer overflow allows the remote user to run arbitrary code within the IP-PBX. With knowledge of the IP-PBX, a malicious user can cause havoc within the server by adding or removing data, gaining access to make calls that are not logged, and other disruptions.

- **Failure to handle exceptional conditions**—An MGCP packet using TLS can be used to create an exception within the MGCP stack. If this exception is interpreted incorrectly by the IP-PBX, soft switch, or media gateway, an unintentional DoS attack may result. A malicious user who can create the same type of MGCP packet can actively cause a DoS attack on an enterprise network, disabling the ability to utilize local telephony networks and possibly emergency services.

Knowledge Check 13-1: VoIP Threats and Vulnerabilities

Answer the following questions. Answers to these Knowledge Check questions are located in *Appendix A: Answers to Knowledge Check Questions.*

1. What is a black hat?

   a. A telco engineer

   b. A normal end user

   c. A malicious hacker

   d. A spy versus spy reference

2. What three things should be understood to make good security decisions?

   a. Network traffic flow

   b. The user-level experience

   c. Vulnerabilities, risks, and threats

   d. Authorization, authentication, and availability

3. Everything can be completely secured.

   a. True

   b. False

4. What can contain vulnerabilities in a VoIP deployment?

   a. End user

   b. Application

   c. Signaling protocol

   d. Hardware platform

   e. All of the above

5. What kind of vulnerability allows an attacker the ability to listen to calls?

   a. Phishing

   b. Link start

   c. Proxy DoS

   d. Man in the middle

Chapter summary

With the multiple risks associated with a VoIP deployment, why would an enterprise deploy VoIP into an existing network? Although there are some risks, the benefits outweigh the potential costs and liabilities associated with VoIP. The key to a secure VoIP deployment within an enterprise is to match security with productivity. For many years, security groups have joked that "if you can get your work done, we have failed in our jobs." Although this might seem harsh, there is some truth to it. Good security tends to hamper productivity, as it forces end users to think before they do anything within the enterprise network.

A good security group can mitigate the majority of risk associated with VoIP and UC while allowing end users access to the new features. Methods for secure VoIP installation, and industry best practices, are introduced in the next chapter.

13

VoIP Threats and Vulnerabilities

Chapter 14: Best Practices for VoIP Security

This chapter explains the need for security in a Voice over Internet Protocol (VoIP) network deployed in an enterprise environment. It describes various security policies, suggests when certain security policies should be used, and defines best practices for deploying security in a VoIP network.

Chapter 14 Topics

In this chapter, you will learn:

- the need for VoIP security

- confidentiality goals and objectives for VoIP

- integrity goals and objectives for VoIP

- availability goals and objectives for VoIP

- compliance and VoIP security

- best practices for enterprise VoIP security

- vendor solutions for VoIP security

Chapter 14 Goals

Upon completion of this chapter, you will be able to:

- describe the confidentiality goals and objectives needed for a VoIP deployment

- describe the integrity goals and objectives needed for a VoIP deployment

- describe the availability goals and objectives needed for a VoIP deployment

- list the major compliance laws and regulations that must be considered in an enterprise VoIP and Unified Communications (UC) deployment

- understand the best security practices for an enterprise VoIP and UC deployment

- describe how using different vendors through the deployment can help or hinder a security solution

Key Terms

Access control	298	Confidentiality	297
Application layer gateway (ALG)	308	Information system	297
Availability	297	Integrity	297
CIA	297		

14

Best Practices for
VoIP Security

The need for VoIP security

An enterprise environment is controlled by the data and services that use the network and infrastructure. An enterprise's data should be considered its lifeblood. Each user will access various data elements throughout the day, week, and month and, as the user's job, customers, or field changes, the data also changes. Access to data is a critical aspect of the enterprise infrastructure, and data security is paramount. If information is lost, stolen, corrupted, or copied, an enterprise's entire business could be jeopardized. If the data contained personally identifying material, whether of an employee or a customer, regulations and legal investigations might be required, causing a publicity nightmare. Controlling data is a critical part of enterprise security.

To ensure this control, all data transport services must be scrutinized before access to requested data is allowed. In an enterprise, various services are used to move data: e-mail, file transfers, interactive services such as a Web site or database access, and others. These services are designed to maintain a steady productivity rate. Each service must be stable and secure to reassure users that the data will not be lost, stolen, or corrupted. Comprehensive security policies help to control the movement and access of data on the enterprise network without hindering productivity through overly complex practices.

VoIP deployment and data security

When deployed in an enterprise network, VoIP and UC replace several traditional and trusted applications. VoIP implementation replaces existing phone systems, exchanging older handsets for Internet Protocol (IP) phones and soft phones. Voice mail can be accessed through the IP phone, through an application on the desktop, or even through an e-mail application such as Microsoft Outlook. UC deployment gives each user access to a private conference bridge, and the ability to control the bridge. Employees can use an enterprise standard instant messenger client to manage multiple simultaneous conversations. These tools facilitate productivity, but how do they affect the security of data in the enterprise network?

When IP and soft phones are deployed within a network, data normally secured through the traditional phone system, including voice and fax data, now must cross over an IP network. If the enterprise did not consider security requirements based on the protocols in use before installing the VoIP network, data that was once secure is now vulnerable to theft, manipulation, and deletion. VoIP must also match its predecessor's stability. The IP network must also maintain availability to services it was never designed to handle. When these requirements are added to new UC services such as Web conferencing and instant messaging (IM), the security structure of an IP network can easily become overburdened. Security must be redesigned to handle the new risks associated with VoIP and UC deployment.

Confidentiality, integrity, availability, and VoIP

It is standard practice for security teams to evaluate information systems. In an enterprise infrastructure, the deployment of an IP network with VoIP and UC is considered an information system. The evaluation benchmarks for information systems are confidentiality, integrity, and accessibility (CIA); these benchmarks pertain to the data within the information system. Each aspect of CIA describes a way in which data can be handled:

- **Confidentiality**—Confidentiality describes who can access specific data, how they can access it, and what they can access.
- **Integrity**—Integrity suggests how to handle data content and state, including copying, removing, editing, or replacing the data. This also includes who has access to make these changes. Integrity and confidentiality methods must work together to operate effectively.
- **Availability**—Data availability evaluates security linked to how data is accessed. This is generally more of a concern at the enterprise level.

When planning or evaluating a VoIP and UC deployment, the CIA methods should be used. Data to be secured is not restricted to the media session of a voice or video call, but may include data stored on a desktop, information transferred through a fax, or contact information stored in a directory. Access to this information can be restricted in many ways, based on the services used and the user requirements. Even while still bound to the underlying IP network, service availability can be secured to remove as much risk as possible to both the services and the IP network without hampering productivity.

Defining confidentiality goals and objectives for VoIP

Discussions of confidentiality often focus on a single issue: privacy. Personal information is closely controlled so that, when an authorized person requests the information, it can be provided in a clean and untainted form. Controlling the data in our lives also includes how it is delivered, to prevent unauthorized people from looking through the wrapper and seeing what is inside. For example, a delivery service must obtain a signature at the destination address before it can deliver the package. If this same approach is applied to an enterprise, information and data access control expands to cover much more than just the personal information of its employees.

An enterprise must control data related to the organization as well as information related to its employees. This includes the enterprise's financial data, proprietary information, software, and customer dealings, as well as all conversations internal and external to the enterprise. Traditionally, enterprises use the International Organization for Standardization (ISO)'s definition of confidentiality:

> " . . . *ensuring that information is accessible only to those authorized to have access*"

This definition has been used for decades as the basis for many enterprise policies and procedures. These policies and procedures have been adapted from the standard corporate environment to the enterprise network environment, to help handle data within the insecure world of IP. Adding a VoIP and UC deployment layer onto an existing IP infrastructure will create more challenges in controlling access to data.

Confidentiality and VoIP

In a traditional telephony world, it is not easy to access a live voice call or tap into an ongoing data stream without special equipment or a legal document such as a wiretap, or by seriously disrupting the actual flow of the voice call or data during a breach. Security in the traditional telephony network has been tweaked and refined for decades, with most security holes related to data stream access control closed off. This includes the use of Private Branch Exchange (PBX) telephony in enterprise networks. Although toll fraud and eavesdropping do still happen today in traditional telephony, it is rare. This is not the case with VoIP and UC.

VoIP and UC are new to the telephony field, having been around for only about a decade. However, VoIP and UC have become common within both enterprise and home user environments, and users depend on the service for the same reliability and security expected from traditional telephony. VoIP and UC services and applications have not had the time to mature enough to be considered highly secure. Many VoIP and UC protocols contain vulnerabilities in their defined standards, as well as in the way vendors deploy these standards, which can allow unauthorized access to a voice or data stream. These vulnerabilities include eavesdropping on active voice and data sessions, unauthorized access to voice mail or stored contact information, and hijacking of applications that can lead to direct access of any piece of data on the desktop of an end user. Additionally, new laws and regulations have been applied to VoIP and UC infrastructures, which must be considered when implementing an enterprise security design focused on confidentiality.

New policies and procedures, such as encryption and authentication, must be put into place. All policies and procedures must be evaluated so that they add security to the overall VoIP and UC deployment, but do not hamper efficiency to the point of the user trying to circumvent onerous security procedures.

VoIP and UC confidentiality goals and objectives

The enterprise IT team that designs and deploys the VoIP and UC infrastructure must create several confidentiality objectives specific to their enterprise's needs. These goals should focus on productivity, ease of use, and cost, as well as on VoIP and UC security.

VoIP and UC service access control

A VoIP and UC deployment requires access to the different services of each enterprise business unit and group. Some services might not be required by all business units, such as Web and video conferencing. Other businesses or units will restrict certain services, such as long distance. When evaluating confidentiality-related security for a VoIP and UC deployment, all services must be listed and each business unit matched to the specific services it requires for productivity. If a business unit does not require access to a specific service, users within that unit should not be allowed to use that service. Thus, a definitive service access list can be created and used to apply policies and procedures throughout the VoIP and UC deployment.

Different types of users require access to different services, with some unique to a particular business unit. Policy-based access control should allow these user types without creating additional security risks and vulnerabilities:

- **Office user**—An office user works from a desk and uses services there. This may require an IP phone or a soft phone, and will require access to UC. The devices used by this user will already be on the office's enterprise network and will follow the VoIP security deployed there.

- **Sales and marketing user**—A sales and marketing user needs additional services, such as Web conferencing, to use beyond the enterprise network. Policies designed to secure VoIP and UC data must include remote access from networks not controlled by the enterprise.

- **Traveling user**—A traveling user employs a software application, such as a soft phone, to access VoIP or UC. The traveling user may also be on an insecure network. This is a security risk if there is no secure, controlled, and encrypted way to access the services. Security solutions must include a way to allow secure access to the enterprise network through VoIP and UC services, and must be flexible enough to support varying network designs and network access methods.

- **Home office user**—The home office user is similar to the traveling user, but the network can be more stable. The same precautions should be applied to the home office user as to the traveling user.

- **Support or operations user**—A support or operations group might require additional access to troubleshoot VoIP or UC issues, and might also require a vendor to have privileged network access. Security measures must track what the vendor does, accesses, and removes while troubleshooting, so that an audit can determine whether confidentiality has been breached.

- **Third-party access**—One of VoIP's benefits is the ability to build virtual telephony trunks between multiple institutions, such as a telephony company, Internet service provider, and another enterprise, using the IP network. This requires a procedure to limit access between the enterprise and the other institutions, so that only authorized VoIP and UC services can be used between the different institutions. Additional safeguards must also be created to ensure that services shared between the institutions and the enterprise's users do not allow the other institutions access to confidential or private data.

VoIP and UC service access authentication

Limiting access to a service reduces the number of potential threats to a VoIP or UC deployment, but it can also give the enterprise security team a false sense of security. Vulnerabilities in some IP and VoIP protocols allow a malicious user to impersonate a legitimate user and gain access to services or data. An enterprise must use a second layer of defense to help mitigate these vulnerabilities. This can be done through authentication.

When deploying authentication within the VoIP and UC network, the enterprise must compare a single authentication solution to a service-specific authentication solution. The objective is to create a method that is not overly complex to deploy or use, but that cannot easily be breached. It must also reduce the chance that a breach will allow access to all VoIP or enterprise devices or data.

Signaling control

Access control and authentication are still not enough to create a truly secure environment for VoIP and UC data. More must be done to ensure confidentiality, especially when Session Initiation Protocol (SIP)–based instant messaging is deployed, and because voice and video data streams can still be redirected or copied even after access and authentication have been approved. Protocols that signal a call or Web conference, pass messages for IM, and carry media data require an additional form of control, which can be set up through encryption.

Many protocols, such as SIP, support Secure Sockets Layer (SSL) or Transport Layer Security (TLS) encryption-based communication protocols. Traditional encryption methods that use IPsec can also be considered when native SSL or TLS support does not exist. An enterprise should evaluate whether these protocols can be deployed within the network and how they can be applied to each service, and should aim to encrypt as many of the signaling and transport protocols as possible. Consider the following elements when pursuing this goal:

- **Protocol compatibility**—Not all VoIP and UC protocols can be used with native encryption. Each protocol should be evaluated for support. A unified encryption solution might not be available, and the enterprise must consider the risk to each service for which the signaling or transport protocol cannot be secured.

- **Equipment compatibility**—The IP phones, soft phones, signaling gateways, and IP-PBX devices deployed on the network might not support encryption. When deploying a VoIP and UC infrastructure for the first time, the enterprise should purchase devices and software that either currently support SSL and TLS or will soon offer upgrades to do so.

- **Performance**—Adding encryption to a device that does not natively support it can reduce the number of calls per second, amount of data throughput, or even stability. This situation can be mitigated if encryption is performed through a hardware chip within the device.

- **Cost**—Hardware encryption can add to the high cost of IP phone and signaling devices. Additional costs may be involved when purchasing certificates from authorized sources such as VeriSign and Comodo.

Network deployment of VoIP and UC devices

Physical VoIP and UC devices require specific access control that allows only authorized users to manage, use, or even see them on the network. Locking down control of these devices also removes one way for a malicious user to gain access to the data. This requires the following set of controls:

- **Device management**—Only a select group of users should be granted secure and authenticated access to the devices. All other attempts should be blocked and recorded.

- **Device access**—Device services should be accessible only through an authenticated, secure means, as described earlier in this chapter.

- **Device visibility**—Although the device should be visible to authorized users on appropriate service ports or applications, it should be hidden in all other ways and visible only to authorized monitoring and troubleshooting tools and users.

- **Monitoring and reports**—All access to, and use of, these devices must be monitored and tracked. This surveillance must be available for every device and should include detailed information about the services used, how the device was accessed, and what was done on the device when it was managed. This may include call detail records (CDR), which track call source, destination numbers, and the length of each call.

Regulations and laws

The location, market, and services in which the enterprise does business might require that specific practices and regulations be followed. If any private or confidential data is stored, transported, or accessed through the VoIP, UC, or IP networks, the implemented security solution must review and comply with these regulations, practices, and laws. Compliance with legal requirements is discussed later in this chapter.

Defining integrity goals and objectives for VoIP

It is important to maintain an environment in which access to data in an enterprise network is restricted to authorized users. Access control can only secure access to the data, not safeguard the integrity of that data. The state of data content, and whether it has been corrupted or tampered with, is one aspect of integrity. However, there are other aspects that must be understood before full data integrity can be secured.

When securing data integrity, enterprises must identify different states of the data and how they should be achieved. Data can be recorded, stored, copied, modified, or removed, but in a secure environment, these actions should be performed only by authorized users and applications. A serious breach of privacy and security can occur when it is possible to erase or copy data without authorization. For example, America's Watergate scandal centered on unauthorized recording of conversations, followed by unauthorized copying and removal of those records. Although the first part of the Watergate scandal was a breach of confidentiality, the second part could have been avoided with proper security policies.

In addition to the data's state, security policies must require the data to be verifiable in some way, to prevent unauthorized data insertion or replacement. Data integrity also promotes tracking the state of the data. Data integrity in an IP or VoIP infrastructure is different than the traditional implementation of data integrity. If data has been tampered with, or the configuration permits data tampering, it becomes pointless to control who can use the VoIP and UC services.

VoIP data integrity

A VoIP call has several components, from signaling to the media stream, but the most important part is the content within the media stream. If end users cannot trust that the content they send is the original content, whether as a voice call, an instant message, or a Web conference slide, they will choose not to use such an untrustworthy service. Insertion, replication, modification, and deletion of the content can be controlled through three aspects of a VoIP or UC deployment:

• application software

• media content

• identity of the user

Application software

Every VoIP phone requires some type of firmware to run the services supported by that phone. Soft phones on the desktop might be required for more mobile installations. Video conferencing and interactive Web conferencing both require applications and software to manage the different UC services. These critical applications must run in a trusted environment. It is detrimental to the enterprise when these applications can be tampered with, permitting access to malicious users. For example, a malicious user may either modify existing applications software or replace the application with a compromised version to gain access to VoIP services or data on the user's desktop or to commit other malicious actions. The enterprise user assumes these applications are safe because they were deployed by the enterprise's IT personnel, so the user might not think it strange to see the applications perform additional actions beyond the services they were intended to provide.

Media content

The most vital information in a VoIP and UC deployment is the media content: voice, video, Web conference data, voice mail, and instant messages created to communicate efficiently throughout the enterprise and with customers. When VoIP protocols are not secured, a malicious user can access the media stream and inject a different version of the call, or can disrupt the call altogether. The same protocols can allow a malicious user to send false instant messages to an end user, without the recipient knowing that the message came from someone other than the parties currently in the conversation. At a minimum, these interceptions and disruptions can cause confusion between the calling parties, but there is a real possibility of greater damage.

Identity of the user

The final aspect of VoIP and UC integrity is controlling the identity of the user. When an enterprise employee calls another employee, the call's recipient assumes that the caller is the person identified by the IP or soft phone. It is also critical for the enterprise to control use of its VoIP connections call outside the enterprise. Through known vulnerabilities, such as registration hacking and soft phone modifications, a malicious user can originate calls from within the enterprise and then make fraudulent calls to disrupt business or gather private or confidential information.

This can also be a problem if the enterprise loses user control for outbound calls. With the ability to falsely represent the enterprise, a malicious user could call customers and get confidential information, such as financials, call news media and spread false rumors, or call financial institutions to make false financial accusations. When an enterprise's VoIP phone system and UC are used without the knowledge of the end users or the enterprise itself, there is fundamental risk to the enterprise's business and reputation.

VoIP integrity security goals and objectives

It can be daunting to validate the integrity of data within a VoIP and UC deployment. VoIP applications support multiple protocols that can carry media content from one user to another, or to many other users. Web conferencing adds interaction to the data, allowing some or all users to have access to some state of the data. IM enables users to send data in real time to one or more other users. All these components of the VoIP and UC environment must be controlled and secured.

Compliance with privacy and corporate regulations

Earlier in this chapter, you learned that an enterprise may be bound to specific privacy practices, regulations, and laws. This is particularly true for data integrity. Certain data types, such as voice mail messages, voice call recordings, or even video conferences, may carry regulated data. If the enterprise must handle data that identifies the medical, financial, or legal state of a person, that data must be secured and its integrity guaranteed. This can also include the financial or legal state of the enterprise.

Policies and procedures must be created that control data integrity based on several aspects of integrity security.

Application integrity

One of the easiest ways to access data without authorization is through applications used for VoIP and UC. A malicious user can modify or replace applications to bypass network security policies. These same applications can be attacked through known vulnerabilities, such as buffer overflows, that enable a malicious user to run applications on a user's desktop without anyone knowing. Policies must be created to authenticate the integrity of the applications installed on any device used within the VoIP or UC infrastructure. This might incorporate a range of tools, from malicious software (malware) detection software to antivirus software. The solution must be adaptable to fit the various devices and operating systems used in the enterprise network.

User authentication

Control over access to data and the devices on which the data resides is instrumental to safeguarding a VoIP and UC deployment. This is especially true with data integrity. If the media stream of a voice or data session is secured, if voice mail or video recordings can be accessed only by authenticated means, and if instant messages can be sent only between two authenticated users, less data can be lost or compromised. The authentication method must incorporate the requirements for confidentiality as well as for data integrity. This might require a multilevel authorization scheme, or some other means to restrict specific data states from a set of users.

Encryption

Although access control and user authorization can mitigate much of the risk associated with VoIP and UC data integrity, these measures cannot help if the media stream is hijacked or replicated. However, some form of encryption can minimize that risk. An enterprise must evaluate the shortcomings of encryption, as described earlier in this chapter, against the amount of security needed on the data. The more robust the encryption, the longer it will take a malicious user to break it and gain access, if at all. Ideally, the solution will be compatible with existing technology deployed within the enterprise network, and will require only a small expense to upgrade equipment if necessary.

Change control

Sometimes authentication and authorization can be circumvented, or users with access can abuse the privilege. In either case, an enterprise requires the means to track what has happened to the data. Policies must be in place to track all changes to the state of critical data, as well as link each change to the user who changed the state. This monitoring also needs security for its data so that it is equally protected from tampering.

Defining availability goals and objectives for VoIP

Confidentiality and data integrity are very important parts of the CIA security model; some consider them to be the most critical of the three parts. However, when most enterprise organizations think about securing VoIP and UC, their first concern is availability. Availability of services within a network is the most visible aspect of that network. If the mail or Domain Name System (DNS) server fails, it will be noticed long before fraudulent calls or missing data. If a hacker can create a program that does not disrupt the visible aspect of the network—its availability—unauthorized access to data is available for a much longer period of time.

This problem is not unique to VoIP and UC; it also exists in the underlying IP infrastructure. It is well known that IP is an insecure protocol, and VoIP and UC rely on different aspects of IP. Known vulnerabilities within IP leave the unsecured enterprise network open to attacks on the enterprise's domain name servers, IP address spoofing on a specific network or switch, or exploitation of known buffer overflow vulnerabilities in an application's IP implementation. A malicious user can bypass the VoIP and UC security policies for availability and cause disruptions to the VoIP and UC infrastructure. These issues must be considered in addition to the specific availability issues of VoIP and UC. If availability fails through a vulnerability, within either IP or VoIP, productivity within the enterprise may be reduced, if not halted.

Availability encompasses both whether the service is up and whether the data can be accessed. If a user cannot gain access to crucial data, disruption and production loss may occur, which affects the enterprise environment's financial state. Attacks on the authentication and authorization system can lock users out of their IP and soft phones, and attacks on the VoIP signaling gateways can cause an active VoIP call to drop. This could be critical if that call was an emergency call reporting that lives are at risk. Availability means access to the services and infrastructure, but it also means stable access to the data within those services.

VoIP availability security goals and objectives

Authentication availability

Access to the data within a VoIP and UC network can mean access to voice mail, to old video and voice recordings, or to live streams for an active voice call. All data types should require the user to be authenticated before accessing the data. Authorization can also be required. If the services that handle authentication and authorization ever fail, such as Active Directory directory services or a SIP proxy, access to these data types will be closed. The enterprise, therefore, must deploy a resilient authentication and authorization service that enables some form of active failover if a device is compromised or taken offline.

Core device availability

If the signaling gateways, media centers, or PBX are offline or under attack, access to these services will be disrupted even if authentication systems are operational and functioning properly. Like the authentication and authorization systems, the signaling and routing systems used for VoIP and UC should be deployed in a high availability (HA) design. This may require the HA design to support stateful failover so that calls in progress will not be disrupted if a signaling or routing device fails.

Network availability

By nature, a normal IP network has bursts of data, or is "bursty." This behavior is not friendly to a VoIP or UC environment, which requires a steady amount of bandwidth moving at a sustained rate of speed until the VoIP or UC session is complete. If the IP network suffers a denial of service (DoS) attack, the bursty behavior can cause congestion in which the VoIP and UC packets compete to use bandwidth on the attacked link. If a form of quality of service (QoS) is deployed on the enterprise network, VoIP and UC traffic can be prioritized over less critical and bursty traffic. Deploying QoS can also help during DoS attacks because it allows critical VoIP calls to get through even under high traffic loads.

If a QoS solution is deployed, remember that a malicious user might try to augment DoS packets to look like they belong in a higher QoS priority than they should be. A QoS solution must support a method that assigns QoS priorities to packets, and that ignores unauthorized QoS assignments.

Emergency services availability

An enterprise can deploy a VoIP infrastructure that supports local, long distance, and international calls without ever passing a call to the local telephony carrier near each office. This might help the enterprise to save money on toll calls, but may create a potentially serious risk to employee safety. Because VoIP relies on the underlying IP infrastructure, the ability to make calls through VoIP might not exist if that infrastructure fails. This could mean that calls to emergency personnel such as the police, medical facilities, or fire department would not be possible. An enterprise must allow these calls at all times, so it must deploy some form of connectivity to the local telephony carriers that do not rely on the IP infrastructure.

Compliance and VoIP security

An enterprise works in a world of rules and regulations. Some of these rules dictate how the enterprise can hire or fire personnel, and others dictate how it must handle medical, legal, and financial information for each employee. Laws and regulations may require the financial and legal operations of the enterprise to be audited every year, or to be made public. All these requirements bind the enterprise in how it handles information. These requirements are not limited to information on paper, but also apply to the enterprise's network and VoIP infrastructures. Most of these regulations and laws center on data integrity.

CALEA

For many decades, law enforcement has been granted the ability to eavesdrop and record conversations on one or more voice lines. This is called wiretapping. Not all telephony equipment supports this activity. Wiretapping has become more difficult as phone lines and circuits have moved from twisted-pair cable to fiber optics wire. A law passed in 1994, the Communications Assistance for Law Enforcement Act (CALEA), required telephony providers to support wiretapping on all equipment by 2007. This included digital telephony switches that had not always offered the ability. The requirement was expanded to companies that provide IP telephony services, including enterprise, higher education, and public facilities such as libraries. Compliance is not always about securing the data for the enterprise; sometimes that data is secured for another reason.

HIPAA

Health care facilities require strict control over access to patient records, regulated through the Health Insurance Portability and Accountability Act (HIPAA). HIPAA is not restricted only to health care facilities; any enterprise or corporation that offers some form of health care or insurance must follow HIPAA regulations. This includes discussions of medical and insurance information over a VoIP session. If a voice mail is routed to an incorrect user or a media stream somehow leaks to an unsuspecting user, critical and private health information can be leaked to an unauthorized user. Worse, if the VoIP network is breached, that information can be sent to the media or stockholders, or even used for blackmail. These requirements must be considered when developing security for a VoIP and UC infrastructure.

Sarbanes-Oxley

The Sarbanes-Oxley (SOX) Act is the corporate and financial equivalent of the HIPAA regulations. Like HIPAA, SOX regulates data integrity and confidentiality. SOX compliance is required for all corporate and financial institutions.

ISO 17799/2005

ISO 17799 is a standard of practice created in collaboration between the ISO and the International Electrotechnical Commission. This standards document contains 12 sections related to information security, from risk assessment and security policy to business continuity management. These standards form the basis for many corporate and enterprise information security policies and procedures. They are mirrored in the equivalent standards of other major countries in documents such as the BS ISO/IEC 27002:2005 (United Kingdom) and JIS Q 27002 (Japan). If an enterprise will have offices outside of the United States, these standards must be read and understood before any form of information or VoIP security policy is solidified.

Breach laws

In the United States, some states, such as Virginia, have enacted breach laws. Breach laws dictate that a company or enterprise must inform all its employees if a security breach has compromised any privacy data. This includes any medical, financial, legal, or personal data that the company might hold. A breach in the VoIP network would allow someone to obtain data about any of these subjects, triggering the breach law and possibly causing an enterprise-wide panic and a marketing mess. There are financial repercussions if a breach of this kind is not brought to the employees' attention within a specific period of time.

E911 services

Federal law requires that all phone systems have the ability to contact emergency services. According to the Federal Communications Commission, a phone system must have access to E911 servers at all times, even if all other phone services are disabled. If E911 access is lost or disabled, the provider will be in serious breach of the regulations. These regulations cover enterprises that deploy internal voice networks, such as a VoIP network. All IP and soft phones must be able to access E911, and security measures must be in place to ensure that a breach or attack cannot stop this ability.

Best practices for enterprise VoIP security

A network designed to handle VoIP and UC, or any IP network, should be built with a layered security policy. A network that uses layered security places multiple security checkpoints throughout the network, so that one device does not handle all the security measures. With a VoIP and UC installation, security measures will rely partially on existing IP security measures, such as firewalls, while also deploying new measures specific to VoIP and UC, such as a SIP proxy or signal protocol encryption.

Firewalls and VoIP

In an IP security design, firewalls separate a trusted zone in which critical data might reside from the untrusted rest of the world. The network within the trusted zone is exclusively controlled and secured by the enterprise. Some implementations also require a demilitarized zone (DMZ) that straddles the trusted and untrusted zones. A DMZ usually contains Web or application servers that must talk with both the Internet and systems housed in the trusted zone. The path between a DMZ and the other two zones is highly filtered so that only applicable services and protocols can gain access to the DMZ from either zone, and vice versa.

Adding VoIP to the IP network requires that the firewall be updated to address how the new protocol must be handled over the firewall. VoIP protocols require two or more users to communicate through each other's dynamically assigned media ports. Although the signaling protocol uses a known port number, the media protocols use a range of ports that are negotiated during the call setup. This can cause problems through a firewall because the security team cannot open a specific port for all media traffic, nor would it be wise to open a range of ports for Real-Time Protocol (RTP) traffic. Another way to resolve this issue is with an application layer gateway (ALG).

ALG

ALGs are used in conjunction with firewalls to open ports dynamically, based on the negotiated media port numbers assigned during the setup process. This is done by reviewing the VoIP signaling protocol for the agreed-on port numbers and adding them into the firewall rules. This is also known as pinholing. When the call ends, the ALG removes the firewall rule from the firewall to stop any chance that the hole will be exploited.

Media port assignments are not the only use for the ALG. In many enterprise deployments, the trusted zone uses RFC 1918 space. This space, known as nonroutable space, can be used freely by anyone within a network, as long as it stays within that network. This includes the 10.0.0.0/8, 172.16.0.0/12, and 192.168.0.0/16 IP address spaces. When an enterprise assigns these to the IP network in the trusted zone, end user desktops will have nonroutable IP addresses. When accessing the Internet, and therefore sending packets outside the enterprise, the firewall usually handles Network Address Translation (NAT) from the RFC 1918 space to a public IP address. Although this will work for many IP applications, it will break most VoIP services because VoIP and UC rely on the end user's IP address to set up and send the media stream. If the address is unreachable, media can't be sent.

An ALG mediates this situation by rereading the VoIP signaling messages, rewriting the IPs that designate the user in RFC 1918 space, and entering the NAT IP address. The ALG does this for both the VoIP signaling setup messages and the RTP messages, so that dynamic ports are mapped to the RFC 1918 address from the NAT IP. ALGs exist for the majority of the VoIP protocols and should be mandatory for any firewall policy that must support a VoIP deployment.

User registration and proxies

Many VoIP services allow both caller and recipient to register with an authoritative device before a call or UC application can be set up and used. These can be H.323 Gatekeeper (H.323 proxy) or SIP proxy devices, but both should verify the user's claimed identity before a VoIP or UC application allows possible critical data to flow to that user. User registration can rely on existing authentication and authorization mechanisms to unify and streamline the process. Note that the proxy will handle only the initial setup of the call. After the call is set up, the proxy will allow all media messages to pass between the actual endpoints. Only when the session is complete will the proxy return to the VoIP signaling path to close out the session and remove access for both endpoints.

A VoIP proxy should be deployed within an enterprise network, especially if VoIP sessions must connect outside of the enterprise network. This will help to ensure that the correct parties are using the session.

Session border controllers

Some enterprise networks deploy a VoIP proxy within the DMZ that handles both signaling and media control for all VoIP and UC sessions that leave the enterprise network. These devices are called session border controllers (SBCs). An SBC handles all VoIP signaling by acting as an endpoint for each half of the VoIP or UC session. The SBC negotiates the supported media types and connects the calls through the SBC. Therefore, an SBC can act as a VoIP protocol middleman, allowing different VoIP protocols to accept and set up calls between each other. An example of this is the H.323 to SIP setup described earlier. Another SBC feature is the ability to inspect signaling and media packets for malicious use. This can help reduce the chances that a protocol vulnerability is abused or that a malicious application is sent over the media stream.

This also means that VoIP and UC services not known or supported by the SBC cannot be used through the SBC. Newer features and options will take longer to deploy because the SBC must now support that feature or option. This is the side effect of a more secure VoIP and UC session. SBCs can also be expensive because they act as a signaling gateway as much as they act as a proxy. Deployment may seem cost-prohibitive, but if VoIP and UC sessions are critical and must be as secure as possible, an SBC should be deployed to validate all media streams and signaling in and out of the enterprise.

Intrusion detection systems

When VoIP and UC services are deployed, the enterprise's intrusion detection systems must be updated to integrate the new protocols and services. Otherwise, too many false alarms will mask the real problems.

Encryption for VoIP

As you have learned in this chapter, encryption is a requirement for a VoIP deployment. All IP and soft phones should support both a signaling and a media encryption solution based on SSL or TLS. An enterprise should use this encryption policy for all applications that will use a VoIP signaling protocol.

Application authenticity

The last part of a layered security policy is a method to validate that the applications used on an end user's desktop or IP phone are still the expected software. Applications that detect VoIP viruses and malware should be installed as part of the default installation in all enterprise desktop environments. These applications must be updated frequently because new VoIP and UC exploitations are found daily. This will not stop what is known as zero-day exploits: exploits that are newly discovered, but against which no established protections are yet applied.

Applications must also be verified regularly because they may already be corrupted, or their exploitations database may have become stale. The 802.1x authentication protocol on network switching devices as an authentication service can safeguard against these situations. 802.1x, used as an authentication solution, allows only devices that have the proper security applications and up-to-date databases. 802.1x interrogates the device for the appropriate data. If the device fails to answer correctly or at all, the 802.1x protocol prevents access to the network, or places the request in a holding zone for further investigation.

VoIP usage policies best practices

Even with these security layers in place, a user who has been given excess permissions can circumvent these restrictions and cause disruptions within the VoIP network. A policy and procedure must govern who can have access, how that access is given, and how it is removed. These policies must themselves have safeguards so that they cannot be abused, circumvented, or breached through social engineering.

Who gets access

Each business unit should list the services to which it would like to have access within the VoIP and UC toolset. The security team must define the services that apply to each business unit in the following manner:

- **Required services**—VoIP services required for the business unit to do its job.
- **Productivity enhancers**—Services that might not be required by the business unit, but that enhance productivity and may save money in the long run.
- **Luxury services**—Services that are tools to some business units and toys to another. These services could also open security holes, depending on the nature of the business unit. Although the business unit might require a VoIP or UC service, it should not be allowed to dictate how that service is deployed. Any exceptions to the enterprise's standard security rule set should be evaluated and approved by the security team.

How business units use access

A user within a business unit can be granted access to a specific service, but might not be allowed to use that service everywhere or on every device that supports the service. Some users may have access to the VoIP network through an IP phone, but are restricted from using a soft phone on the desktop. There are many reasons why a user might be granted access through a single means. For example, the user might have a desktop that is considered a high security risk because it uses an application that is too risky for an operations technician to use outside of the enterprise network.

A policy should list all the requirements to access and use a VoIP or UC service. These requirements must be verified on the requester's environment before access to the service is allowed as requested.

A policy must also be employed to audit the requester's environment over time, to validate that the environment has not changed and fallen out of the required specifications.

How business units remove access

One common security issue within an enterprise infrastructure is the slow rate at which users' permissions are removed from VoIP and UC services. An enterprise IT group should have a policy designed to remove individual access to the entire IT environment quickly if a user is fired, quits, or loses access for any other reason. These policies do not always cover VoIP and UC because those services are normally handled by the enterprise's telephony group. A unified policy must be implemented that covers both IT and VoIP/UC requirements so that no doors are left open through which a disgruntled user can keep or regain access to the enterprise network and breach data integrity.

Validation of security policies best practices

Security policies and procedures are usually designed and initially implemented within an enterprise network. However, upkeep and maintenance—and even enforcement—of these policies often become lax. Over time, an enterprise environment changes, new services are deployed, and new equipment or vendors are used. These changes must be reflected in existing service policies within the enterprise network for VoIP, UC, or even IP services.

Enterprise environmental change review policies

Each change to the enterprise environment must be reviewed to determine the impact it will have on the security of the network. This review must be performed before the change is implemented, as well as after the change has had time to be deployed and used. The security team should perform these reviews in conjunction with the team that will be making or requesting the change. New hardware may need to be put through a certification process to verify that it meets the appropriate security standards. In addition to these reviews, a monthly review should be performed to examine each change and how it has affected the overall enterprise security policy deployment. This meeting can also be used to review upcoming changes so the security team can be proactive in validating the change.

Enterprise enforcement policy audits

Although security policies can be defined and required for all enterprise users, they might not be fully enforced, perhaps because the policy is too restrictive, complicated, or time consuming. Lack of compliance could also be due to a lack of user awareness about which policies they should use. In addition, users who want to use unauthorized services might have found a way around the policies. Whatever the reason that enforcement has failed, any potential security risk can be reduced by auditing the use of existing policies.

An enterprise security team can use a wide variety of tools to validate existing policies and procedures. These tools should include applications that probe for security vulnerabilities, as well as network management systems that review device configurations. The IT team can use tools that review an enterprise desktop image for unauthorized installations to validate that all applications are within the security policies and that a user has not gained additional access without specific approval. This should be done on a regular basis, with no more than a week between verifications of the security policies.

Audit of software and images best practices

One of the most common ways to breach a network is through security vulnerabilities within the software a device uses. These vulnerabilities can be very dangerous; they can cascade into a serious problem if multiple vulnerabilities are found across multiple platforms that use the same code base. One way to mitigate this is to create a procedure in which each of the enterprise's vendors sends an alert to the security team when a vulnerability has been found in its hardware or software. This alert should include any patches or image updates. The security team must request access to any mailing lists the vendor uses to disseminate these updates. The majority of these lists are archived, and the security team needs searchable access. These lists should be watched diligently for new updates that can affect the enterprise IP or VoIP infrastructure, and updates should be immediately acted on when a vulnerability is found.

The security team and operations team need a policy that governs how they handle a vulnerability to a network device. This policy should contain the following elements:

- **Evaluate the risk**—The first step is to evaluate the risk to the enterprise. The risk should be based on the vulnerability's accessibility and ease of use as well as what it exposes to the malicious user.

- **Evaluate affected devices**—Once the risk is understood, the affected devices must be determined. These devices should be grouped by how vital they are to the network and how much access that device will give the malicious user if the vulnerability is exploited. This ranking identifies the devices that must be fixed first. It also helps determine which devices must stay active if a fix has not been found and devices must be disabled to remove the risk to the enterprise.

- **Certify the fix**—Although a vendor may say that the fix or patch or new code will not cause any additional issues, the enterprise must validate the fix within its own environment. Based on how strong a threat the vulnerability is to the enterprise, a regression test might be the only test allowed within the time available. If there is time, a complete certification should be done on the fix before deployment.

- **Deploy fix**—A procedure should exist that enables a security and operations team to deploy a patch or new software image onto devices quickly.

- **Validate security**—The security team should use the same procedure that validates security enforcement to verify that a breach has not happened and that data integrity is still intact.

- **Notification process**—A process must be created to notify users or customers of a service disruption due to the vulnerability or its remediation. This notification should contain only the minimum information required for the user or customer to understand the issue. This will help prevent panic or false rumors from spreading but still allows the user or customer to learn about the situation.

Vendor solutions for VoIP security

During a vulnerability situation, an enterprise's decisions about selecting and deploying different vendors can become an issue. If the operations and security teams did a thorough job during the evaluation and set up the appropriate channels of communication with each vendor, vendors will have access to the notification, fix, and deployment procedure quickly. If the enterprise deploys a vendor-diverse environment, a vulnerability might not hurt the enterprise as much as it might if the enterprise was using only one vendor's products.

Multiple-vendor solutions

One way to mitigate a large vulnerability can be to use multiple vendors within a single deployment. Because each vendor uses its own brand of software or application, the product diversity might reduce the spread of a vulnerability if it can be limited to only one vendor's devices or applications. The exception to this is when a standards-based vulnerability is found. Vendor diversifications cannot help reduce that type of vulnerability and might actually hurt the situation. With unique code for each vendor, the process for fixing a standards-based vulnerability can quickly become very complex.

The same issue may arise when dealing with compatibility between devices that must work with each other in a VoIP deployment. Because vendors use standards as a starting point, tweaks within standards might not be compatible between vendors, or at least may not be fully stable. This can create problems for the telephony department as well as hinder troubleshooting of a problem. Although a vendor might promise that its equipment is compatible with another vendor's VoIP gear, enterprise technicians should investigate; these claims are not always accurate.

Testing before deploying

An enterprise should have procedures that outline the requirements of each VoIP and UC device. These requirements should state what deviations from the standard are acceptable and what will cause the device to become noncompliant. This outline should include interoperability with any existing VoIP devices. Every device must be put through this certification procedure before it can be deployed on the network.

A certification procedure will almost never end with a perfect grade. Every device will have some form of incompatibility or deviation from the standard. Additionally, any bugs that are found during the certification process should be brought to the vendor to be fixed.

Knowledge Check 14-1: Best Practices for VoIP Security

Answer the following questions. Answers to these Knowledge Check questions are located in *Appendix A: Answers to Knowledge Check Questions.*

1. Privacy and confidentiality regulations do not apply to Voice over Internet Protocol (VoIP) and Unified Communications (UC) deployments.

   a. True

   b. False

2. When referencing the security standard called CIA, the A stands for:

   a. Auditing

   b. Availability

   c. Accessibility

   d. Authorization

   e. Authentication

3. A VoIP proxy should be used when:

   a. Access to voice mail is down

   b. An IP phone needs to be replaced

   c. VoIP protocols need to be translated

   d. User authentication through registration is deployed

   e. None of the above

4. What is the easiest way to reduce the chances that a VoIP signaling message cannot be intercepted and read?

   a. Reroute the message path through at least 15 hops

   b. Accelerate the packet speed to make it harder to capture

   c. Use encryption protocols such as Transport Layer Security (TLS)

   d. Obfuscate the message content so that a reader cannot understand the critical information being delivered

   e. None of the above

5. When a vulnerability is found that might affect deployed VoIP or UC applications for devices, the first step in the remediation process is to:

   a. Notify end users and customers of the issue.

   b. Evaluate the risk the vulnerability might cause the enterprise.

   c. Gather a list of devices that might be affected by the vulnerability.

   d. Start deploying a new patch of code onto the affected devices or applications.

Chapter summary

Deploying a VoIP and UC network requires a great deal of preparation. A security team should understand how the new network will be used, who will use it, and where it will need to be accessed. A detailed review of the protocols and equipment should be completed before any device or application is deployed. Any policies and procedures should be formed, reviewed, and deployed before the network is up and running. If all these factors are addressed prior to the VoIP and UC deployment in conjunction with a layered security model, the enterprise user base can feel confident in the trust level of the information crossing the new network. The security team should not treat network security as complete after the network is built. A VoIP and UC network is always being attacked. New services must be added. New parts of the company might need to be integrated. Keeping the network secure through each change is a never-ending task. With a good foundation, the security team will manage a more controlled and predictable network.

14

Best Practices for VoIP Security

15: SIP Threats and Vulnerabilities

In this chapter, you will learn about the Session Initiation Protocol (SIP) and the role it serves in an enterprise VoIP implementation. SIP has some known vulnerabilities, but an awareness of common attacks against the protocol can help when designing a strong set of security policies and procedures.

Chapter 15 Topics

In this chapter, you will learn:

- how SIP works

- what is at risk with a SIP deployment in an enterprise network

- common SIP threats

- common SIP vulnerabilities

- known SIP protocol vulnerabilities

- how a SIP attack can occur on the enterprise network

- how SIP is extended into other federations

Chapter 15 Goals

Upon completion of this chapter, you will be able to:

- describe how SIP works between two devices

- define common SIP vulnerabilities threats, and risks

- list common SIP protocol vulnerabilities that might affect an enterprise deployment

- discuss how SIP attacks occur within an enterprise environment

- describe how SIP is used outside of the enterprise environment

Key Terms

Black hat	338	Session Initiation Protocol (SIP)	321
Denial of service (DoS)	327	Threat	326
Risk	326	Vulnerability	321

15

SIP Threats and
Vulnerabilities

SIP in the enterprise IP network

In previous chapters, you learned about the various Voice over Internet Protocol (VoIP) protocols used in an enterprise VoIP and Unified Communications (UC) deployment. Most of these protocols have limited use, particularly with telephony-based applications, with the exception of H.323 and SIP.H.323 was initially created to handle video over IP and media streaming, and was later adapted to support VoIP. Because H.323 is a mature protocol, it has fewer security vulnerabilities than newer protocols. However, its lack of support for applications outside of VoIP and video conferencing has kept it from wider use. Although H.323 can be used in a UC deployment, the protocol itself is cumbersome and is not easily adapted to newer applications, such as messaging. It also does not support some features expected from a UC deployment, such as presence and messaging. In response to H.323's weaknesses, the Internet Engineering Task Force created SIP.

SIP

Initially created in 1996, SIP has become the preferred VoIP and UC protocol because it is much simpler than H.323 or any other VoIP protocol deployed today. SIP is an application-layer protocol that can use either the Transmission Control Protocol (TCP) or User Datagram Protocol (UDP) transport-layer protocols. This enables a flexible deployment that is customized to the requirements of each application that will use SIP. If the statefulness of TCP is required, SIP can use port 5060 over TCP; otherwise, UDP will be deployed. In a typical SIP deployment, SIP uses UDP through port 5060.

SIP messages use an easy-to-understand text-based format that is similar to Hypertext Markup Language (HTML). This makes it easy for a device or service to read and interpret a SIP message quickly, without a proprietary parser or the extra cycles required to convert a message from a binary format to a more manageable format. The following example shows a SIP proxy message in which the SIP proxy has sent a SIP INVITE from Josh Smith's IP phone to Sandra Livingston's IP phone:

sip:1234@companyabc.com:5060 SIP/2.0

Via: SIP/2.0/UDP 192.168.65.132:5060;branch=z9hG4bK100BE5B15

Remote-Party-ID: <sip:1161@192.168.65.132>;party=calling;screen=no;privacy=off

From: "Josh Smith" <sip:1161@192.168.65.132>;tag=FD0AB738-1C18

To: "Sandra Livingston" <sip:291@192.168.65.70>

Date: Wed, 25 Apr 2007 15:00:51 GMT

Call-ID: 97FBFACD-F27411DB-904BEC43-DBD99238@192.168.65.132

Supported: 100rel,timer,resource-priority

Min-SE: 1800

Nortel-Guid: 2549833381-4067693019-2420698179-3688469048

User-Agent: Nortel-SIPGateway/IOS-12.x

Allow: INVITE, OPTIONS, BYE, CANCEL, ACK, PRACK, UPDATE, REFER, SUBSCRIBE, NOTIFY, INFO, REGISTER

15

SIP Threats and Vulnerabilities

CSeq: 101 INVITE

Max-Forwards: 70

Timestamp: 1177513251

Contact: <sip:1161@192.168.65.132:5060>

Expires: 180

Allow-Events: telephone-event

As the example shows, the SIP message format is simple and relatively easy to understand. The SIP Uniform Resource Identifier (URI) is an important field in the message; in the example, the SIP URIs are 1234@companyabc.com and 291@192.168.65.70. These URIs identify the initiating and target callers, and they can use IP addresses or fully qualified domain names (FQDNs). If FQDNs are used, they will be translated to the IP address they represent in the rest of the message.

SIP request message codes

SIP signal flows use a standard set of message codes. In the preceding example, the CSeq field contains the message code used with that SIP proxy message. In this case, it is an INVITE message code. This message type is considered a request message and uses SIP request codes, which are standardized. There are 14 SIP request message codes shown in the following list. Each message code represents a different aspect of a SIP call.

- **INVITE**—Message that invites a destination client to participate in the application session (call)

- **ACK**—Message that acknowledges that the client has received the final message for a signal flow, such as a call setup (INVITE) or termination (BYE)

- **BYE**—Message request to terminate an existing SIP session, usually sent by the party that closes the application or hangs up the phone on a VoIP call

- **OPTIONS**—Message that sends the capabilities of the application or VoIP server applicable to the SIP session being initiated

- **REGISTER**—Message that registers the SIP URI listed in the To: header field with a SIP REGISTER or PROXY server

- **SUBSCRIBE**—Message that subscribes a SIP application for an Event of Notification

- **PRACK**—Provisional acknowledgment

- **NOTIFY**—Message that notifies a SIP client of a new event

- **CANCEL**—Message that terminates any existing queued searches but does not terminate the existing SIP session

- **MESSAGE**—Message that transports the content of an instant message (used in messaging applications that use SIP)

- **UPDATE**—Method that modifies the state of an existing session

15

SIP Threats and Vulnerabilities

SIP response message codes

When a client receives a SIP request code within a SIP message, it responds with a SIP message containing a SIP response code. These codes provide informative status responses to the request message, and notify the requesting client of changes that may need to be made to the SIP session (such as redirection) to continue the session. There are more than 63 standard SIP response messages, and vendors use additional proprietary messages. Response message codes can be categorized into six types of responses:

- **(1xx) informative responses**—These responses announce the application's progress in servicing the SIP request message. The most common codes in this category are 100 Trying, 180 Ringing, and 183 Session In Progress.

- **(2xx) successful responses**—These responses confirm that the application has successfully completed a SIP request initiated by the other end of the SIP session. The most common response from this category is 200 OK.

- **(3xx) redirection responses**—These responses announce when a SIP session's destination URI has moved to a different URI. This is generally used when a SIP proxy is involved or when a UC service, such as presence, is used. Redirection responses inform the requesting SIP application where to find the URI it initially requested. The most common responses from this category are 301 Moved Permanently, 302 Moved Temporarily, and 305 Use Proxy.

- **(4xx) client failure responses**—These responses announce that the client receiving the SIP request message fails to understand, authenticate, or complete the requested service. The most common responses from this category are 401 Unauthorized, 403 Forbidden, and 404 URI Not Found.

- **(5xx) server failure responses**—These responses announce that a server, such as a registry or Private Branch Exchange (PBX), is not responding to SIP request messages. The most common responses from this category are 500 Server Internal Error, 503 Service Unavailable, and 504 Server Time-out.

- **(6xx) global failure responses**—These responses confirm a final response when a request spans multiple applications, servers, or clients. This includes searches for presence. The most common responses from this category are 600 Busy Everywhere, 603 Decline, and 606 Not Acceptable.

FIGURE 15-1: BASIC SIP CALL FLOW.

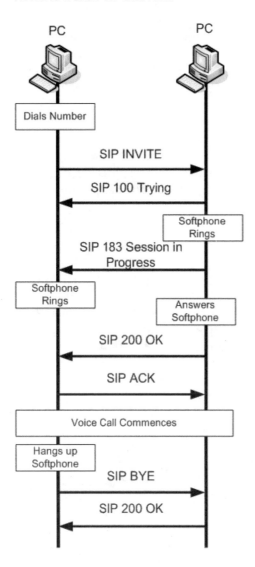

SIP requires specific message fields within the SIP message, but the fields do not need to be in any particular order. The SIP message can also contain fields that are proprietary to a specific vendor or application. For example, these fields may be seen when the SIP protocol message contains information about how the media session for the application is set up. This is usually done through a second protocol, the Session Description Protocol (SDP). The SDP message is embedded at the end of the SIP message. The following example shows the same SIP INVITE message shown earlier, with SDP media information embedded:

sip:1234@companyabc.com:5060 SIP/2.0

Via: SIP/2.0/UDP 192.168.65.132:5060;branch=z9hG4bK100BE5B15

Remote-Party-ID: <sip:1161@192.168.65.132>;party=calling;screen=no;privacy=off

From: "Josh Smith" <sip:1161@192.168.65.132>;tag=FD0AB738-1C18

To: "Sandra Livingston" <sip:291@192.168.65.70>

Date: Wed, 25 Apr 2007 15:00:51 GMT

Call-ID: 97FBFACD-F27411DB-904BEC43-DBD99238@192.168.65.132

Supported: 100rel,timer,resource-priority

Min-SE: 1800

Nortel-Guid: 2549833381-4067693019-2420698179-3688469048

User-Agent: Nortel-SIPGateway/IOS-12.x

Allow: INVITE, OPTIONS, BYE, CANCEL, ACK, PRACK, UPDATE, REFER, SUBSCRIBE, NOTIFY, INFO, REGISTER

CSeq: 101 INVITE

Max-Forwards: 70

Timestamp: 1177513251

Contact: <sip:1161@192.168.65.132:5060>

Expires: 180

Allow-Events: telephone-event

Content-Type: application/sdp

Content-Disposition: session;handling=required

Content-Length: 193

    v=0

    o=NortelSystemsSIP-GW-UserAgent 5421 883 IN IP4 10.164.65.132

    s=SIP Call

    c=IN IP4 192.168.65.132

    t=0 0

    m=audio 18768 RTP/AVP 0

    c=IN IP4 192.168.65.132

    a=rtpmap:0 PCMU/8000

    a=ptime:20

SIP can embed other protocols within itself, if required by a particular application. Although this feature is supported, nonstandard protocols could cause a SIP parsing application to fail on the unknown protocol. Even with this protocol hazard, SIP has become a widely accepted and diverse signaling protocol for applications over an IP network.

What is at risk?

Many applications have begun to implement SIP as their signaling protocol over IP networks. This permits increased UC and applications design, but also means that issues with SIP security or handling can be riskier than if each service or application used a separate signaling protocol. As the cost of deploying an enterprise IP network has become more affordable, IP-based services have become commonplace. With an IP infrastructure, applications that were once independent have become unified. E-mail applications can now talk with a voice mail server and receive voice mail messages. Phone services can now use multiple databases to help a caller trying to contact a user by determining the user's presence and the services on which the user is available. These features can help create a more productive enterprise environment, but they also link applications and information into an accessible network that did not exist before.

Confidentiality

In the past, confidential documents and data were held in a closed environment that either could not be accessed from a public network or had limited access to the network. This limited possible security breaches mostly to internal attacks. As enterprises shift to unified services and applications around an IP-based, SIP-signaled environment that can be used across the Internet, documents and data that were once secure are now vulnerable to theft, modification, or destruction.

Financial considerations

A network breach that allows confidential information to be stolen, modified, or removed can cause more than just a public relations nightmare. It can cost an enterprise money. Although many breaches are never reported to the public, publicized breaches can cause an enterprise to lose its reputation as a responsible company. This could cause clients to leave or sue, based on the severity of the security breach. Additional money can be lost if the breach triggers state or federal regulations that impose fines. As VoIP and UC become more common, risk increases because confidential information is easier to access and harder to audit and control.

VoIP across the Internet

Many organizations are eager to permit their users to use UC and VoIP anywhere in the world. In this situation, VoIP calls, voice mail, instant messaging (IM), and other services are now open to attack by anyone on the Internet. These sessions may contain confidential information or be used to gain confidential information. Security measures that work within a closed or restricted enterprise network must be adapted to address the higher risk that can come from the Internet.

With all these risks, why would an enterprise allow Internet access to the VoIP and UC infrastructure instead of restricting VoIP and UC services to the enterprise network? Although that is one solution, it does not account for one of the largest threats to a UC and VoIP deployment. Internal users are the largest risk for any enterprise network, with or without VoIP and UC. Because internal users have easy access to the devices and have some level of trust, enterprises often find that the source of a security breach is an internal user who leaked confidential or proprietary information.

SIP-based UC and VoIP deployments carry significant risks. Threats must be taken seriously, and must take external and internal access into account. SIP threats are well known, and a security group should review and understand common threats and vulnerabilities before they ever deploy a VoIP or a UC network.

Common SIP threats

In Chapter 13, "VoIP Threats and Vulnerabilities," you learned about the VoIP threats common to most VoIP and UC signaling protocols. SIP also contains potential threats. Because its protocol design is much more open and it uses a text-based message format, SIP can be easy to exploit. Common SIP threats must be considered when deploying a SIP-based VoIP and UC network.

Internet accessibility

One benefit of SIP is ease of deployment over common Internet protocols. This could give the enterprise confidence to implement an Internet-wide solution for its UC deployment. However, this makes it easier for attackers to gain direct access to SIP applications. Most SIP deployments contain a SIP proxy that handles all intranet and Internet SIP signaling, but that SIP proxy can become the target entrance point for attacks. Using known SIP and VoIP vulnerabilities, attackers can gather employee information from the proxy, redirect calls, steal media streams from existing call sessions, or even attack the proxy to disable it, creating a denial of service (DoS).

Although these issues are common to all VoIP signaling protocols, SIP has the distinct problem of being open and trusting; the SIP standard does not require encryption or authentication. If an enterprise deploys a SIP solution in a standard configuration and does not include these security features, the network is vulnerable. SIP messages are also easy to read and modify on the fly through man-in-the-middle attacks or through viruses, Trojans, or modified applications on the user's desktop or IP phone.

Application tampering

Centralizing UC and applications on a single communications protocol enhances deployment and interoperability. Using SIP as the communications protocol makes it easier to allow each application to talk to any other application. However, if proper security policies are not implemented, this interoperability may not be a good idea. A network unified around SIP means that a single breach in an application can be used to attack a wide variety of other applications that may yield confidential information or cause harm. Breaching an application becomes easier when applications are linked, and a known security vulnerability in one application can enable an attacker to compromise another application.

For example, the unification of e-mail and VoIP can lead to security problems. E-mail is a common source of security breaches because users regularly open attachments or click URLs within messages. These URLs or attachments then add an application onto the operating system, or modify an existing application. Many worms use this method to infect computers, but the same method can modify VoIP soft phones or instant message clients. An attachment, URL, or even an ActiveX vulnerability can replace, modify, or redirect calls from a soft phone to an attacker who can then use that information and access in many ways.

The more integrated SIP becomes within an application and application suite, the more dangerous a single SIP vulnerability becomes for an enterprise network.

Social engineering

Even when ideal security measures are deployed within a network, a single user can cause a breach by sharing the wrong information. A user might give out his or her SIP URI to an unauthorized user, or might decide to use an IM service to talk with a friend outside of the enterprise network and share confidential information, passwords, or other critical information across the unsecured SIP session. Such users compromise security inadvertently, but an enterprise may also have users who intend to steal information. With modified applications and the limited trust that applies to every user on the network, a malicious user can use a soft phone to make an unauthorized transfer of data over a VoIP session. Note also that SIP and SDP are open-format protocols, which makes it easy to develop protocol-compliant programs. A plethora of open-source SIP and SDP applications is available to be used for these attacks or thefts.

VoIP is a significant threat to any enterprise that implements it without understanding the common risks and threats of VoIP-related protocols. SIP's known vulnerabilities give attackers the opportunity to breach the network. Common vulnerabilities must be understood before a full assessment of their potential threat can be made.

Common SIP vulnerabilities

Like any protocol, SIP has vulnerabilities that can be used to breach security or create a DoS attack. SIP-based VoIP deployments should be designed to stop common attacks. This will help secure the enterprise's data and network devices.

Message tampering

SIP permits fields to be modified without validation. This is how registration hijacking is possible, and is the basis for several different vulnerabilities within SIP. This vulnerability can be exploited successfully to produce four common results: DoS, theft, misdirection, and spam over Internet telephony (SPIT).

Registration hijacking

An attacker can exploit SIP's text-based and nonvalidated nature to create a new registration packet that uses the attacker's information instead of the real user's information, as shown in Figure 15-2.

FIGURE 15-2: FSIP REGISTRATION HIJACKING.

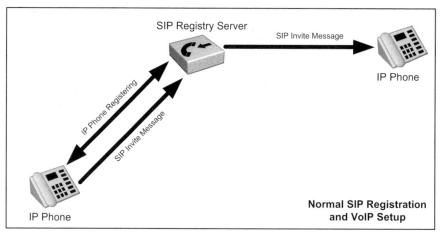

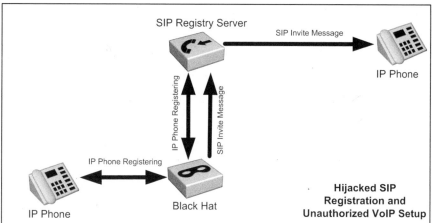

An attack can also register a SIP device by hijacking an existing SIP registration message with a computer that is placed between the initiating user and the user's SIP proxy. First, the attacker intercepts the initial SIP registration message and modifies the SIP message to point a single field URI to the attacker's computer. Then, the attacker sends the SIP registration message to the SIP proxy for delivery. A call that would have been set up to the original user is now set up to the attacker, without the proxy or end user knowing anything has happened.

Registration hijacking tools are available on multiple platforms. These tools can intercept a call registration message and modify it on the fly. Some of these programs can also crack HTTP Digest authentication. All are open source and freely available on the Internet.

Fuzzy denial of service

Although SIP message fields are standardized and the format is easy to interpret, vendors often modify how these fields are interpreted to gain a competitive advantage. The fields within a SIP message have no set size limit, but the maximum character length of some fields can be predicted. A vendor can thus reduce the time it takes to parse a SIP message, as well as reduce their interpreter's application footprint. However, these changes can cause problems. Because there is no set field length and because anything can be added to a field, an attacker can create a SIP message that contains more characters than the vendor expected, resulting in an out-of-bounds error within the interpreter, as shown in the following example:

sip:1234@companyabc.com:5060 SIP/2.0

Via: aaaaaaaaaaaaaaaaaaaaaaaaaaaaaaaaaaaaaaaaaaaaaaaaaaaaaaaaaaaaaaaaa

aaaaaaaaaaaaaaaaaaaaaaaaaaaaaaaaaaaaaaaaaaaaaaaaaaaaaaaaaaaaaaaaaaaaaaaaaaaaaaaaaaaaaaaaaa
aaaaaaaaaaaaaaaaaaaaaaaaaaaaaaaaaaaaaaaaaaaaaaaaaaaaaaaaaaa

Remote-Party-ID: <sip:1161@192.168.65.132>;party=calling;screen=no;privacy=off

From: "Josh Smith" <sip:1161@192.168.65.132>;tag=FD0AB738-1C18

To: "Sandra Livingston" <sip:291@192.168.65.70>

Date: Wed, 25 Apr 2007 15:00:51 GMT

Call-ID: 97FBFACD-F27411DB-904BEC43-DBD99238@192.168.65.132

Supported: 100rel,timer,resource-priority

Min-SE: 1800

Nortel-Guid: 2549833381-4067693019-2420698179-3688469048

User-Agent: Nortel-SIPGateway/IOS-12.x

Allow: INVITE, OPTIONS, BYE, CANCEL, ACK, PRACK, UPDATE, REFER, SUBSCRIBE, NOTIFY, INFO, REGISTER

CSeq: 101 INVITE

Max-Forwards: 70

Timestamp: 1177513251

Contact: <sip:1161@192.168.65.132:5060>

Expires: 180

Allow-Events: telephone-event

The vendor's interpreter will probably have problems with the Via: field shown in the example. The Via: field normally has an associated SIP URI and tag, but the example shows a string of characters. This field will cause an out-of-bounds error on the interpreter, and the interpreter should drop the message and ignore it. That is not normally the case. Instead, interpreters tend to crash if unexpected behavior occurs once or several times in a row, stopping the service.

Although this behavior might be expected on a soft phone or a SIP proxy, it has actually been confirmed on IP phones from every vendor. It is easy to fix the issue when the SIP message is seen by modifying the interpreter to account for the new entry type in the Via: field, but after this issue is repaired, a new tool will be released that uses either special characters (such as $, %, *, or #) or another field to create the same results. This is one of the biggest concerns for any enterprise deploying SIP, because freely available programs for Microsoft Windows and UNIX can create and send these fuzzy messages.

Termination denial of service

Another way to disrupt an existing SIP deployment is to send BYE messages (see Figure 15-3) to each existing SIP session, unexpectedly terminating the session.

To implement this DoS attack, the attacker must intercept at least one SIP message on an active session by either capturing one on the wire or making a registration query to a proxy for all active calls. In either case, the attacker needs the Call-ID for this attack. After acquiring the Call-ID, the attacker can create a SIP BYE message. This message needs only the correct Call-ID; the other fields will not be checked. The application or SIP proxy will accept the BYE and terminate the session.

This works because the majority of SIP devices never authenticate a BYE. They assume that the BYE is trusted, and look only at the Call-ID for verification. To initiate a DoS attack, an attacker simply needs to set up an automated script that pulls Call-IDs from the wire and terminates each call. This would quickly affect the usability and reliability of an enterprise VoIP and UC network.

This authentication issue also includes SIP proxy devices (see Figure 15-4). Using this same method on a SIP proxy, an attacker can convince the proxy that a call has been completed even if it has not, and then take the proxy's place within the SIP message flow. Because the proxy thinks the call is over, a security alert will not be generated; clients will think the attacker is now the proxy and continue with their sessions.

FIGURE 15-3: SIP BYE DENIAL OF SERVICE.

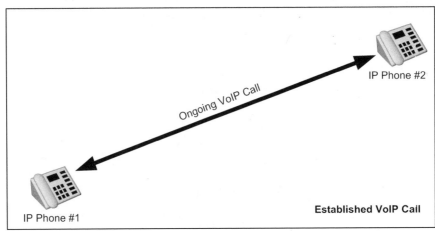

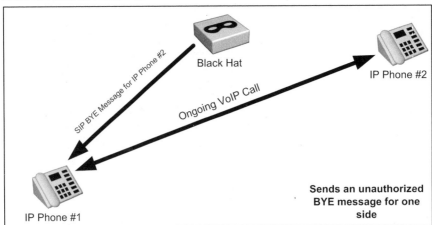

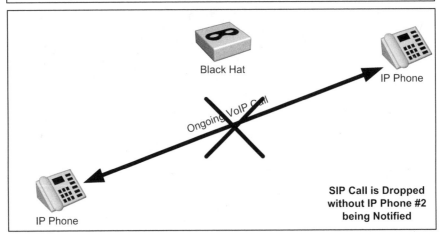

FIGURE 15-4: SIP BYE PROXY ATTACK.

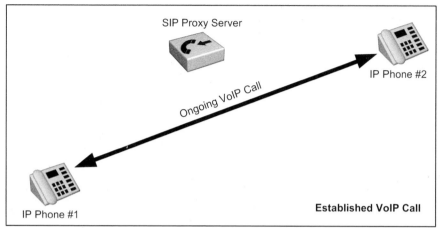

IP Phone #1   **Established VoIP Call**

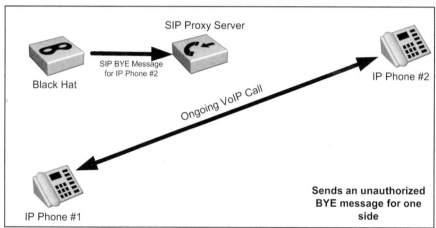

IP Phone #1   **Sends an unauthorized BYE message for one side**

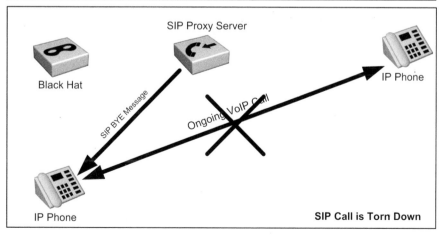

IP Phone   **SIP Call is Torn Down**

Flooding DoS

Of all the possible DoS attacks, the easiest is a flooding DoS attack. Flooding DoS attacks require that an attack create so many SIP messages that the device, whether an IP phone or a SIP proxy, cannot keep up and crashes. This is similar to a traditional IP SYN or Internet Control Message Protocol (ICMP) attack, but can cause problems other than bandwidth usage.

A flooding DoS uses a large amount of bandwidth, but it will also fill the device's maximum call-per-second allotment. If a device is spending its time trying to answer requests from the attacker, it will never answer requests from valid users. Because the attacker can mask the originating IP address and rewrite SIP messages to hide identity, it is very hard to trace a flooding attack over UDP.

Eavesdropping

Eavesdropping is the ability to capture the media stream of an active session and record it for later playback. This can occur on active calls or on a Web or voice conference. SIP supports the ability to create conference calls with few speakers and many listeners, and can be used in the same way for Web conferences. An attacker can spoof a registered user to gain access to the conference and obtain a copy of the media stream (see Figure 15-5).

FIGURE 15-5: SIP CONFERENCE EAVESDROPPING ATTACK.

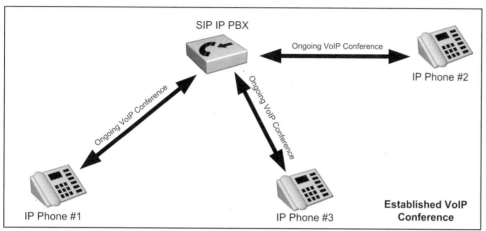

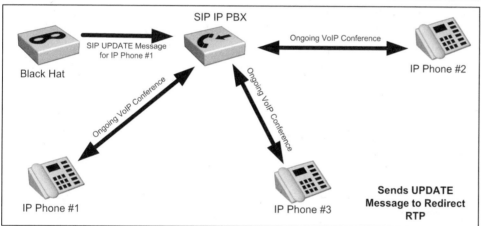

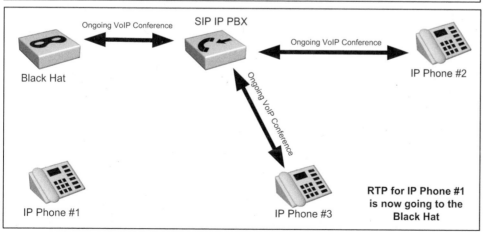

The attacker must gather information about the conference, perhaps by capturing a SIP INVITE message to the conference or through a breached application on a user's desktop. After the Call-ID has been obtained, the attacker can then send a new message to the SIP proxy, using a SIP UPDATE message to request that the media stream be redirected to a new location. Because the Call-ID has been sent correctly and the message contains other expected information, the proxy will accept it. The only element that changes is the SDP field that designates the IP to which the media stream will be sent. Now the attacker can access the conference media data. This can also be done on normal calls in the same way. This technique is shown next, using the example shown previously. Only the SDP c= field is changed.

sip:1234@companyabc.com:5060 SIP/2.0

Via: SIP/2.0/UDP 192.168.65.132:5060;branch=z9hG4bK100BE5B15

Remote-Party-ID: <sip:1161@192.168.65.132>;party=calling;screen=no;privacy=off

From: "Josh Smith" <sip:1161@192.168.65.132>;tag=FD0AB738-1C18

To: "Sandra Livingston" <sip:291@192.168.65.70>

Date: Wed, 25 Apr 2007 15:00:51 GMT

Call-ID: 97FBFACD-F27411DB-904BEC43-DBD99238@192.168.65.132

Supported: 100rel,timer,resource-priority

Min-SE: 1800

Nortel-Guid: 2549833381-4067693019-2420698179-3688469048

User-Agent: Nortel-SIPGateway/IOS-12.x

Allow: INVITE, OPTIONS, BYE, CANCEL, ACK, PRACK, UPDATE, REFER, SUBSCRIBE, NOTIFY, INFO, REGISTER

CSeq: 200 UPDATE

Max-Forwards: 70

Timestamp: 1177513251

Contact: <sip:1161@192.168.65.132:5060>

Expires: 180

Allow-Events: telephone-event

Content-Type: application/sdp

Content-Disposition: session;handling=required

Content-Length: 193

    v=0

    o=NortelSystemsSIP-GW-UserAgent 5421 883 IN IP4 10.164.65.132

    s=SIP Call

    c=IN IP4 10.168.57.3

    t=0 0

    m=audio 18768 RTP/AVP 0

a=rtpmap:0 PCMU/8000

a=ptime:20

SIP protocol vulnerabilities

It is easier to exploit these vulnerabilities through SIP than it is with H.323 or other VoIP protocols. This is due to inherent design decisions within the protocol itself. For example, SIP was designed to be as user-friendly and usable as HTML. This means that some of HTML's known design issues are also found within SIP. These issues must be understood and assessed before SIP should be considered to be an enterprise's communications protocol of choice.

Message format

Message format and layout were early design decisions for SIP. As described earlier, SIP sessions send text-based messages between applications, which is similar to the HTML format. These messages can easily be manipulated on the fly. An attacker can intercept a SIP message and change any field without using a compiler or proprietary application. Additionally, SIP does not require the message content to be validated or passed through a checksum, so a user will not know if anything has changed within a message. A change as simple as the URI in the From: field will not be seen by either party.

UDP versus TCP

Although SIP can be used on TCP, it is more commonly deployed using UDP. The SIP standard recommends that it be deployed over UDP using port 5060. The recommended standard for SIP deployment does not refer to TCP, although TCP is a far safer transport protocol. TCP is a stateful protocol that uses a validation system to acknowledge that a packet has reached its destination and to determine whether that packet has been changed during the trip. UDP does not have these features. UDP is stateless and never validates that a packet reached its destination before sending the next packet. Using UDP means that even the transport protocol itself can be modified by an attacker. It also means that the security team cannot rely on the underlying transport protocol for packet validation.

The disadvantage of TCP is that it can cause a great deal of latency in a session and can generate inconsistent response times. This is due to the validation feature, as well as to congestion management built into TCP. These two issues are why TCP is not part of the official recommendation for SIP transport protocols.

Authentication

The SIP standard does discuss an authentication standard that can be used for SIP messages: the HTTP Digest mechanism. This method embeds an MD5 password challenge and response in the SIP message to validate a message's authenticity. The server must compute the MD5 checksum each time a message is received, which can slow the server. Additionally, a flood of SIP messages that require MD5 verification can create a DoS attack on the server or device. Although this is a potential danger, the added security of MD5 authentication outweighs the risk of using an unauthenticated solution. However, SIP does not require the use of HTTP Digest and can run successfully without authentication.

Encryption

As described earlier, SIP's text-based messages are sent unencrypted between multiple SIP-speaking devices. The standard deployment for SIP does not require encryption to accept or send messages. The SIP request for comments (RFC) does suggest that deployments use some form of Secure Sockets Layer (SSL) encryption for all messages, but this is not mandatory and is rarely deployed.

SIP attacks

Because SIP has many vulnerabilities, one might expect that SIP deployments are frequently attacked, but this is not yet the case. SIP VoIP and UC deployments have not gathered enough mainstream success to warrant the large-scale attacks that occur on other applications and services, such as Windows servers, UNIX servers, and traditional telephony systems. Of course, this does not mean that no attacks occur. It actually means that attacks against SIP deployments are often not random, but have a defined goal.

SIP attacks require some knowledge of the network. This is not trivial information to gather, because even small enterprise networks have some form of IP security. The attacker must find a way to gain access to the messages or SIP applications without anyone knowing. With the growing demand for UC and SIP, this has become easier. However, traditional methods to access a user's desktop cannot be used for SIP and UC/VoIP access, so new methods must be developed.

For example, someone who uses an enterprise instant messenger for public and work messaging might be vulnerable to a messaging worm. This worm can be used to gather VoIP and UC-related information from the user, either by redirecting the user to a URL or by hijacking the messaging session itself. After several valid SIP messages are obtained, the attacker will have enough information to begin probing the enterprise network for specific SIP applications.

A message sent in e-mail as an ActiveX call, an attachment, or even an image, can install an application that sends this reconnaissance information to the attacker for further exploitation. This is a common technique for other security vulnerabilities, and UC with SIP allows the attacker to take advantage of the same holes. An attacker must put effort into gathering information, and often does so to steal specific confidential data from the enterprise.

SIP attacks in the future

In this chapter, each description of SIP's vulnerabilities mentioned that the applications used to abuse these vulnerabilities are open source. The applications are freely available for anyone to download, configure, and use as desired. At this point, these applications are not trivial to use, but that will change. As SIP is more widely deployed, more attackers will want to exploit its vulnerabilities to access a network. This will push black hat programmers to build more intuitive programs to access these holes.

15

SIP Threats and Vulnerabilities

Automated scripts for SIP will also become a standard part of future rootkit suites. Rootkit suites are sets of programs, applications, and scripts used to attack a network and find a vulnerable device that the suite's tools can compromise to give an attacker entry to a network. When the attacker has device access, the suite can be run again to compromise more devices and gain access and control of more of the network. This is particularly dangerous because telephony is a critical part of an enterprise, especially for emergency services. If an attacker has full control over the communications network, lives could be in danger.

SIP extension into other federations

The enterprise environment is not the only place where SIP is used as a communications protocol. SIP is also used throughout the traditional telephony network of signaling communications. As the SIP protocol extends into other telephony federations, its vulnerabilities and capabilities will follow.

Traditional telephony

Many telephony providers have begun to migrate to SIP and VoIP for their communications and for media transport of voice calls. This is especially true for countries outside of the United States. South Korea and Japan use SIP and VoIP for a great deal of their cellular communications, as well as for all noncopper telephone services. In the United States, telephony and cable providers are migrating to SIP-based VoIP phones that are packaged with Internet services for residential clients.

Intertelephony use

SIP is also used between telephony carriers to pass voice traffic over the Internet. You might wonder why traditional carriers or competitive local exchange carriers (CLECs) would use Internet connections to pass voice traffic between each other, especially because IP is a less stable environment than dedicated circuits. These companies have found that running voice traffic next to normal IP data traffic uses existing Internet bandwidth more efficiently, and enables cheaper communications with other carriers. Instead of using their dedicated circuits, carriers can sell them to Internet service providers (ISPs) or other carriers. SIP also enables the carriers to communicate more easily with carriers across the ocean. A large amount of long-distance traffic is now carried using VoIP and signaled through SIP trunks between carriers.

SIP trunks

In a traditional telephony world, an enterprise would obtain a private line, such as a primary rate interface (PRI), and use it to pass all voice traffic, including incoming and long-distance calls. SIP methods have begun to replace dedicated circuits. An enterprise can now get a SIP trunk to a carrier and use it for all local and long-distance signaling. Voice traffic then passes over Internet circuits between the carrier and the enterprise. This new feature can also be used to create SIP trunks between remote offices and a central hub office, saving money on voice calls.

Knowledge Check 15-1: SIP Threats and Vulnerabilities

Answer the following questions. Answers to the Knowledge Check questions are located in *Appendix A: Answers to Knowledge Check Questions.*

1. Which transport protocols does SIP use? (Choose two.)

   a. TCP

   b. UDP

   c. ICMP

   d. SNMP

2. Which SIP request code is used when sending a call request?

   a. INVITE

   b. CANCEL

   c. CALLING

   d. REGISTER

   e. SUBSCRIBE

3. SIP is encrypted by default.

   a. True

   b. False

4. Which applications use SIP?

   a. Presence

   b. Video over IP

   c. Instant messaging

   d. Voice over Internet Protocol (VoIP)

   e. All of the above

5. Which is the most widely exploited vulnerability in SIP?

   a. Packet breakdown

   b. Social engineering

   c. Message manipulation

   d. Flooding denial of service

Chapter summary

SIP is an immature, and therefore insecure, protocol. More than 2,000 SIP vulnerabilities are already documented, most of which are variations on message manipulation. As SIP deployment expands, new vulnerabilities and exploits will be discovered. SIP will not be considered secure for some time, but its simple nature and design will make it an appealing solution despite the risk. This simple design is part of SIP's security problem. However, when SIP is teamed with a solid authentication and encryption solution, it becomes a powerful tool for UC that cannot yet be matched.

16: Best Practices for SIP Security

This chapter describes the best practices, goals, and objectives to consider when deploying a Voice over Internet Protocol (VoIP) and Unified Communications (UC) environment by using the Session Initiation Protocol (SIP). It also covers best practices relevant to SIP.

Chapter 16 Topics

In this chapter, you will learn:

- why SIP security is necessary and how it might differ from generic VoIP security

- confidentiality goals and objectives for SIP applications

- integrity goals and objectives for SIP applications

- availability goals and objectives for SIP applications

- how compliance laws and regulations affect SIP security

- best practices for enterprise and federation SIP security

- challenges of adding multiple vendor solutions into a SIP security deployment

Chapter 16 Goals

Upon completion of this chapter, you will be able to:

- describe confidentiality goals and objectives for SIP applications

- describe integrity goals and objectives for SIP applications

- describe availability goals and objectives for SIP applications

- list applications that might be affected by compliance laws and regulations

- define security best practices for deploying SIP in an enterprise VoIP and UC deployment

- describe how using different SIP vendors during the deployment can help or hinder a security solution

Key Terms

Access control	351	Integrity	345
Application layer gateway (ALG)	363	Secure Sockets Layer (SSL)	348
Availability	345	Transport Layer Security (TLS)	348
Confidentiality	345	Virtual local area network (VLAN)	365

The need for SIP security

In previous chapters, you learned that VoIP or UC deployments must take security into consideration. In the enterprise environment, confidential information commonly passes over a deployed VoIP service, including data through fax services. VoIP protocols used on critical or confidential services are not inherently secure. Without proper security measures, VoIP conversations can be interrupted, copied, or eavesdropped upon, allowing unauthorized access to confidential information. These security measures make it easier to identify illegal access to VoIP conversations.

When UC is deployed within the enterprise, the communications system is leveraged by emerging technologies that enable the end user to access UC services from a variety of devices and services. Because this is a new concept, an enterprise communications group might overlook it when designing security for the VoIP platform. Services such as instant messaging and e-mail are not normally part of communications security audits because they are usually part of an IP network security audit. Historically, these applications have not needed to access VoIP-related features and services.

The IP network security audit also does not address new VoIP and UC application layer services that rely on the network and on existing IP-based services and applications. Until recently, a VoIP and video-over-IP network was contained within an enterprise and did not need to access the IP data network. Each network required different security parameters, and, therefore, different security practices were deployed. UC combines these two network types and adds the Internet to the mix. IP security teams must reconfigure IP network security to accommodate these new services and applications, incorporating known security measures that affect several signaling and transport protocols. Because both VoIP and UC applications use SIP, it is easier to manage the network's communications aspect but more difficult to control security.

The Internet Engineering Task Force (IETF) developed SIP to replace H.323 for communications and applications signaling. The SIP request for comments (RFC) offers several suggestions on security, but they are not required. SIP has quickly become a standard signaling protocol for most VoIP and UC applications and services, although H.323 is still used. SIP is also an open standard that can be reviewed and used by anyone. Applications and tools are written daily to access and test SIP-based products, and many applications have added SIP support when designing interoperability with other applications. Security audit teams must consider SIP and communications threats, risks, and vulnerabilities when testing new applications such as e-mail, instant messaging, and Web conferencing applications.

SIP quickly penetrates an organization. IP phones use SIP to handle voice calls, desktops use SIP for UC applications such as voice mail through e-mail and instant messaging, and media servers that house and service corporate-wide conferences use SIP. Even cell phones and personal digital assistants (PDAs) can deploy it. However, SIP is an easy path for illegal access to a network. For example, consider a financial institution in which confidential information crosses multiple media types. The SIP deployment must conform to existing corporate regulations such as the Sarbanes-Oxley (SOX) Act. Sarbanes-Oxley requires financial reports and audits that take Internet access into account. The act requires that financial businesses apply confidentiality, integrity, and availability (CIA) to their intranet and Internet facilities.

SIP, as you learned, is not a particularly secure protocol, and does not require security mechanisms to work. SIP also uses insecure transport protocols (Transmission Control Protocol [TCP] or User Datagram Protocol [UDP]) that can exacerbate the problem. Security measures must be applied to a SIP deployment, but the organization must first determine the various ways in which SIP will be used. This requires an audit that defines the confidential information that can be accessed through SIP applications. This audit should also validate policies that prevent a deployed SIP system from being used to modify or remove confidential information without activation. SIP can be used in mission-critical applications, but the availability of each SIP-deployed application, as well as SIP use itself, must be gauged and understood.

Defining confidentiality goals and objectives for SIP applications

VoIP and UC deployment in an existing network requires access to the network and its contents to be reevaluated. In most cases, a separate internal network handles VoIP traffic and signaling, and the main network handles normal IP data. This design gives a security group strict control over access to either network at the edge between the networks. Figure 16-1 shows this configuration, including the single point at which management applications or one-off VoIP applications can cross the border to the data network and vice versa.

FIGURE 16-1: TRADITIONAL VoIP AND DATA NETWORK.

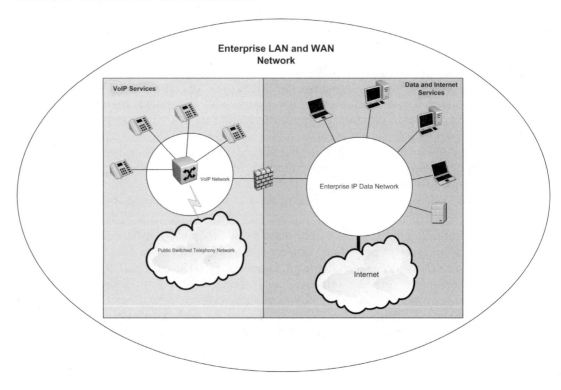

In traditional networks, there has been little worry that a device breach on one side of the network could access user data or services on the other. The firewall between the two networks controlled access. When SIP and UC are deployed, practices must change. UC application deployment means that specific services, previously existing only in the VoIP network, may be required within the IP data network. Some applications might also need to access the VoIP network from the Internet. Such a versatile design is possible with SIP, but the data network and the Internet will have direct access to the data on the VoIP network (see Figure 16-2).

FIGURE 16-2: UC-ENABLED VoIP AND DATA NETWORK.

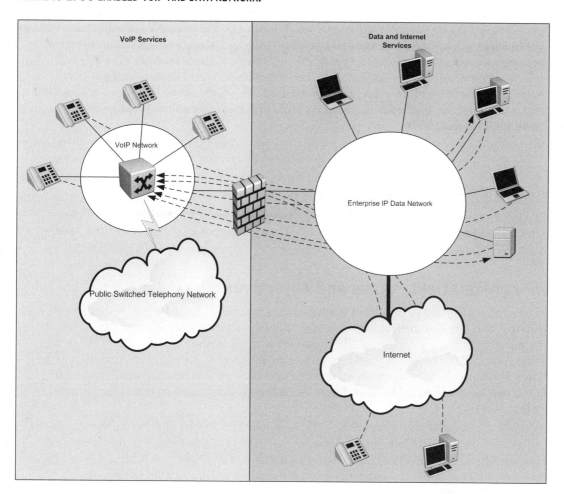

This also means that the VoIP network can access the data network and all data stored on, or crossing, that network. Improperly secured information could easily leak or be stolen.

Confidentiality and SIP

As more applications are unified under SIP, the vulnerabilities within SIP become more susceptible to security breach. When SIP is used within a VoIP network, specific aspects of a call can become open, allowing a hacker to eavesdrop on an existing call, capture a copy of an existing call, or modify the media within that call by injecting new sound or data. This is also the case with other applications such as instant messaging (IM) and Web conferencing. Confidentiality is not only about stored or live information; it is also about convincing someone to provide access to that information.

• It is necessary to develop policies that govern how and where SIP can be deployed within the VoIP and IP data networks. These policies must consider existing policies that already place restrictions on the IP or VoIP network. For example, IP networks should already have policies that govern data confidentiality and use of encryption through Internet Protocol Security (IPsec), Secure Sockets Layer (SSL), or Transport Layer Security (TLS). These policies must be updated to include SIP-based applications and devices that support encryption. As SIP matures, the protocol must add this form of security into the signaling and media process. When SIP is deployed with TLS, it is often called Secure Session Initiation Protocol (SIPS).

• SIP is not a secure protocol, and other protocols, such as H.323, could be used to handle VoIP calls. Although H.323 is a more secure protocol than SIP, it is also more complicated to deploy and maintain because it uses a binary format instead of an easily parsed text format. Complexity can also make it more difficult to audit H.323 installations.

• It is necessary to develop procedures for a manageable audit trail of SIP usage. These procedures might include the source and destination of each user that requests a session through SIP.

SIP confidentiality goals and objectives

When a security group defines confidentiality goals and objectives for SIP, it should address issues beyond simple vulnerabilities, threats, and risks. Because SIP is widely used for communications, new policies can affect devices and applications outside the VoIP or UC realm. Also, SIP is a new and relatively immature protocol. Commercial devices that help control or secure SIP communications can be expensive. A VoIP security team using SIP should use the goals and objectives described in this chapter as the starting point for an initial deployment audit.

The audit itself can be time-consuming. The time required will be affected by the number of devices and applications linked together with SIP. If the enterprise uses multiple networks, such as multiple remote offices linked to a single office or multiple hub offices, the audit could grow into a large endeavor. A security team must adapt goals and objectives to the organizational capabilities and budget.

SIP and application deployment

A traditional phone service deployment requires a single Private Branch Exchange (PBX) server, a voice mail server, copper trunks connecting the PBX to the phones, and phones. VoIP deployments are simpler, but the phones are replaced with IP phones, and the trunks are replaced with an IP network. Adding SIP and UC to the deployment adds other devices not traditionally used in a voice network, such as proxies, messaging servers, and soft phones. SIP-enabled devices should be considered applications when evaluating security. These devices include software to handle SIP signaling and Real-Time Protocol (RTP). They should be included in the VoIP and UC security evaluation audit.

Each application might have a different use or interpretation of SIP or its media signaling protocol, Session Description Protocol (SDP). Policies and procedures created for one application might not work for another. Policies should be used to control various aspects of an application to mitigate information leakage during a VoIP or UC application session. The following list recommends some policy and procedure elements as the starting point for all application security measures:

- **Application use**—In a deployed VoIP or UC application, each application is used for a different service or feature. The specific use must be documented and understood by all users and technicians. The documentation must include which users will require this feature and the types of information that can be provided. If an application will support several information types or several levels of confidential data, this must also be noted as well. Some applications allow different users to access different features. Each feature must have a specified list of users, and users who can use multiple features of the application should be identified. If an application has features that will not be used, these elements must be documented. A definitive list can then be generated that contains all the services the applications support, which users can use all or some of, and what information will be allowed through these services by which users.

- **Application communications**—After a definitive application list has been created, the security group must determine how each application communicates or implements its feature within the VoIP and UC deployment. Each device that transports or passes an application's signaling and media protocols must be defined, including routers, switches, firewalls, and other such devices. The security group must also compile a list of other protocols and services that will use these network paths and devices, including all possible vulnerabilities that could affect how information sent through VoIP and UC applications is accessed or handled. Policies must be implemented to reduce the chances of any vulnerability allowing a malicious user to access transported information.

- **Application support for SIPS**—Although SIP does not require any security elements for it to operate properly, it can support security measures around the protocol. As you learned in Chapter 15, "SIP Threats and Vulnerabilities," SIP can be used with either SSL or TLS encryption. When encryption is active, SIP uses a different port (port 5061 instead of 5060) by default; the protocol is then called SIPS. SIPS allows signaling packets to be sent securely between two applications on the VoIP and UC network (or the Internet), reducing the chances of the session being redirected or eavesdropped upon. Although SIP itself can support encryption, not all SIP-based applications support it. Those that do might not support TLS. The comprehensive application list developed earlier in the audit must include the application's supported encryption system. Performance should also be measured after encryption is enabled, to discover any latency that might be created by using SSL or TLS. This is necessary because not all applications or devices can decrypt signaling through hardware. When decryption is performed through software, performance can be reduced to the point at which the application or device is too slow to be useful.

SIP signaling and media control

SIP signaling between devices and applications is the most vulnerable aspect of SIP-based VoIP and UC sessions. As a first step in creating a secure VoIP and UC deployment, these signaling messages must be protected through encryption. The media stream for a given session can also support encryption with the encryption protocols supported by SIPS. Although these are necessary solutions to secure content within a session on a VoIP UC network, they do not come without some challenges.

- **SIPS compatibility**—Although SIPS has become more mainstream and is supported by the VoIP and UC communities, it is not technically a standard. The SIP standard still recommends Hypertext Transfer Protocol (HTTP) Digest mode for authentication and Secure Multipurpose Internet Mail Extensions (S/MIME) for encryption (RFC 3853). Many vendors used in a VoIP or UC deployment might not support SIPS or SIP beyond S/MIME. Even S/MIME support is not widely deployed in VoIP and UC vendor devices. A new VoIP or UC deployment should evaluate each vendor's applications and devices for SIPS support and create a sound encryption strategy based on available authentication protocols.

- **SIP protocol compatibility**—Unlike SIPS, SIP is a standard and should be supported equally by all vendors, but this is not always the case. Vendors often use slightly different methods to interpret the contents of a SIP message to gain a market advantage. Other vendors add new fields within the message's SIP or SDP sections, which might not be understood by other vendor products. These tweaks can be used to gain unauthorized access to SIP signaling. Each vendor's devices and applications must be tested to validate support for SIP RFC 3261. Each device should also be audited and assessed to determine how the devices work together or if any changes have occurred during a software upgrade or other device change.

- **SIP performance**—When encryption is deployed, there is additional overhead for each application or device that must encrypt and decrypt each packet. VoIP is very unforgiving of latency. When the round-trip time of a VoIP signaling packet or RTP media packet exceeds 250 milliseconds (msec), the two ends of the session will notice delay or gaps in sound while they wait for a reply. If a VoIP or UC network is already stressed and encryption is added, the additional latency could cause quality issues across sessions. The organization must evaluate the VoIP and UC services that have this problem, based on the underlying IP network or how the service will be used (for example, remotely or internationally). At some times, service degradation might be so bad that the risk of information leakage does not outweigh the need for quality on that service.

- **SIPS encryption cost**—The cost of enabling SIPS encryption has two components. The first component is how the application or device will support the encryption algorithm. Many devices use software for encryption and decryption, which is slow and takes up many CPU cycles. Devices that manage encryption through hardware are more expensive but can boost speed and reduce the chance of failure or breach due to a software bug. However, hardware encryption might not be the right solution for a new enterprise VoIP network. The organization must consider the number of sessions per second that applications and devices will have to handle while encryption is enabled. This number, paired with performance data for the device or application, will help the enterprise team understand scalability for software encryption and which devices, if any, require hardware encryption.

The second component of encryption cost is whether the application or device requires a non-self-signed SSL or TLS certificate. These certificates must be purchased from a secure vendor. This cost is multiplied by each device or application that needs certificate-based encryption, which could be a large number.

SIP access authentication

Confidentiality-centered security for VoIP and UC is focused on controlling how a device, application, or user can access the SIP signaling and media streams with encryption. However, encryption does not resolve all information access control issues. Encryption hinders a hacker's ability to look at the content in a VoIP or UC session, but it cannot stop users from creating or using an unauthorized session to transfer information to an unsecured or unauthorized location. SIP can enable hackers to redirect an existing session or start an unauthorized new session as long as they have some basic information about the VoIP and UC network and its users, which can happen even with encryption enabled. To control this potential breach, SIP supports authentication through either a built-in mechanism or a proxy and authentication protocols.

In the original SIP RFC, the suggested authentication mechanism for a client and a SIP proxy is the same method suggested for the HTTP Authentication service on Web servers. HTTP Digest is an MD5-based authentication system that has been around for some time. HTTP Digest requires the user to send a user name and password to the SIP proxy, where the password is MD5 encrypted. This is normally done through a register message:

REGISTER sip: 192.168.3.41 SIP/2.0

Via: SIP/2.0/UDP 192.168.65.132:5060;branch=z9hG4bK100BE5B15

From: "Josh Smith" <sip:1161@192.168.65.132>;tag=FD0AB738–1C18

To: <sip: sip:1161@192.168.65.132>

Call-ID: 97FBFACD-F27411DB-904BEC43-DBD99238@192.168.65.132

CSeq: 1 REGISTER

Contact: <sip:1161@192.168.65.132>

Proxy-Authenticate: Digest realm="Corp," nonce="9eb714a7," algorithm=md5

Proxy-Authorization: Digest username="jsmith," realm="Corp,"

nonce="9eb714a7," uri="sip:192.168.3.41,"

response="549eb04688dcea6195e24fb1de1d41d0," algorithm=md5

max-forwards: 50

expires: 3600

Content-Length: 0

The SIP proxy responds with a SIP acknowledgment message or a SIP 401 message, based on whether the MD5 password is correct. With HTTP Digest enabled, an unauthorized user should not be able to get authorization to create new sessions or join existing ones. However, MD5 authentication has already been compromised. MD5 passwords can be decrypted, making this solution less secure than it should be.

Another form of authentication can replace MD5. Newer password encryption ciphers, such as Advanced Encryption Standard (AES), can be used through S/MIME instead of through MD5. Another solution is to use a public–private certificate key system in which each proxy stores a copy of a user's public key, and all authentication is done through key exchanges, using TLS:

REGISTER sip: 192.168.3.41 SIP/2.0

Via: SIP/2.0/UDP 192.168.65.132:5060;branch=z9hG4bK100BE5B15

From: "Josh Smith" <sip:1161@192.168.65.132>;tag=FD0AB738–1C18

To: <sip: sip:1161@192.168.65.132>

Call-ID: 97FBFACD-F27411DB-904BEC43-DBD99238@192.168.65.132

CSeq: 1 REGISTER

Contact: <sip:1161@192.168.65.132>

Identity: qEOQMvgss+F0pQHJCyarb8IMbDh1d1gi1r33af6G1bO+ug5ZQzo31xn

GRBAYe0tzNVoyOfmGUY2dIEWJ2iZlWER1RT4F5hGN9f0y39iCRqGEAE

N6JY3SocU4RzgXfK3Durle/66rkyCaLPJQ/pzgA+qW/nQytSuzewhrD

MErCBQ=

Content-Length: 6

These solutions are more secure than the MD5 solution but are more complex and might not be supported by every vendor. An enterprise security team must evaluate the authentication support mechanisms of each application and device to validate which protocol can be used. A SIP proxy can support multiple types of authentication schemes, and each should be used on a per-device basis.

Regulations and laws

As with any other VoIP and UC deployment, a SIP-based deployment must comply with existing local, federal, state, and international laws and regulations that govern access to, and use of, confidential data. When SIP is deployed beyond the traditional VoIP environment, the audit scope should include all aspects of the technology, network, and user base with which the SIP protocol will be used.

Defining integrity goals and objectives for SIP applications

Numerous SIP applications are available, ranging from software that supports soft phones or IM to SIP proxy and PBX servers that handle routing and switching for SIP sessions. Each application is designed to handle a specific part of the SIP session call or data flow. These applications are thus potential access points to existing or live session content, due to SIP's basic design.

SIP was not designed with data integrity in mind. For example, a standard SIP deployment uses the UDP transport protocol rather than TCP. UDP is a stateless protocol that does minimal error checking, relying solely on the application for sanity checks. Although SIP does support minimal features to acknowledge that a SIP message was received or to attempt another connection if a message is not answered, SIP does not check whether the receiving message is valid. After a session has started and the media stream has been initiated, the RTP protocol used to carry the media does not check that the content sent in the RTP packet is the same content that is received. This offers an easy way for hackers to replace or modify content within a SIP session without either party or any intermediate device knowing about the attack until it is too late. This is not entirely due to SIP, however, because access to SIP and RTP messages can be gained from the application itself.

Each application that resides on a device or desktop is another potential point of attack because it provides a clear view of the VoIP network and allows an intruder to send SIP messages while appearing to be a legitimate user. This allows access to any content that a user can potentially remove, modify, or copy elsewhere. A single solution to these issues is neither possible nor practical.

A layered approach must be used to secure data within a SIP-based VoIP and UC network. Each piece of the puzzle should be handled by a single solution, and the total design should avoid overlapping security measures. Layered security creates multiple obstacles for attackers before they can gain access to any form of data. As each obstacle is breached, the network will notice and react with enough time to resolve the issue before the attacker reaches the goal. A layered solution requires an understanding of each layer of defense and the goals these defenses support.

SIP application integrity goals and objectives

Integrity-centered security revolves around the ability to validate or authenticate information exchanged between all parties within a session. This includes standing information such as address books or documents. It is not easy to validate information between two or more VoIP or UC participants when SIP is deployed. Additional secure protocols are required to validate who is using SIP services and what is in the media stream. An organization must be aware of all types of data, not just what would normally be sent across a VoIP or UC session. With modified SIP applications, a user could send any kind of information through a media stream to a remote application or device.

Application integrity

It does not matter how well secured a network is against SIP attacks, or even IP attacks, if the basic applications are compromised. Because SIP supports a wide range of applications, including open source and third-party applications, it is imperative to create policies and procedures that audit the state of these applications. Trojans, worms, and viruses can come across applications that work in tandem with a SIP application, and these same applications can be used to compromise legitimate SIP applications. Hackers could use compromised SIP applications to get a copy of every SIP media session created or accessed from that machine. It could also enable malicious users to inject new media content into existing streams or taint what is already there with advertisements, spam, or even random sounds.

These policies should cover more than SIP applications. Enterprise IT groups know that users eventually add unauthorized software to their machines, whether as simple as a screen saver or as dangerous as a VoIP soft-phone product for a commercial carrier. These noncertified applications could be compromised and used to modify, copy, or remove information on the user's desktop. To make matters worse, the user could intentionally install compromised applications on a machine to affect information. These issues make it critical to track and restrict all application installations on any device that also houses a SIP application.

Message and content integrity

In other chapters, you learned that policies and devices can be used to restrict what users can do in the VoIP and UC environment and how they can access the network. Such policies and devices eliminate many integrity threats introduced by the SIP and RTP protocols. However, these solutions still have flaws that must be accounted for. One way to mitigate these flaws is to evaluate each SIP signaling message and RTP packet for corruption, compromise, or change, using a session border controller (SBC). An SBC acts as an intermediary between the initiating SIP application and the destination SIP application. Each SIP message from a SIP application is sent to the SIP SBC, where the SBC evaluates and validates the message or RTP packet before sending it to the final destination. The SBC is configured to look for the more than 20,000 known vulnerabilities for SIP and all vulnerabilities for RTP and then to remove any matching packets or messages, as shown in Figure 16-3.

This approach can significantly reduce the number of attacks on the VoIP and UC environment, but it has a cost. An SBC is a very expensive appliance because each SBC must have the power to handle large numbers of packets per second and concurrent calls per second. Another issue is that an SBC can handle only a select number of VoIP and UC protocols and, within those, only a select number of features. Beyond the hardware, latency caused by the SBC can carry an even larger cost. Because it must arbitrate all SIP session messages and RTP media packets, delay can quickly become an issue, especially if the SBC becomes overloaded with calls.

An organization considering deployment of an SBC should discuss these issues. Perhaps a SIP proxy will solve some problems, while others could be handled through encryption. If an SBC is the right device for the network, it should be deployed only at the edge of the network and used for all SIP sessions that must cross outside of the enterprise network.

FIGURE 16-3: SIP SBC CALL.

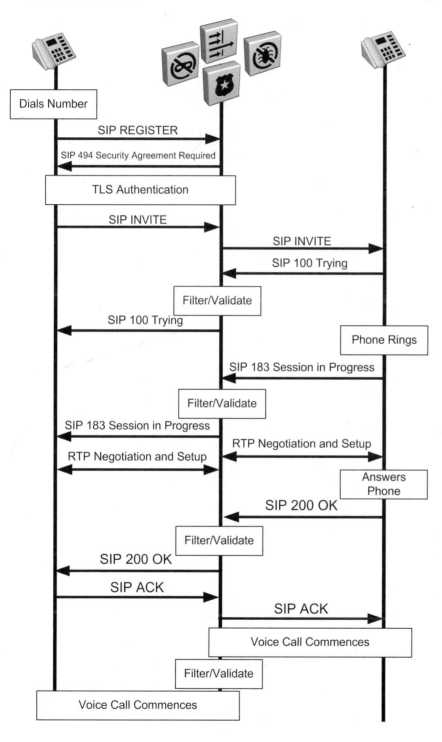

User authentication

Another way to control SIP application integrity is to track users as they create new SIP sessions, and validate that only a specific set of users can use a VoIP or UC service. As the number of mobile VoIP and UC users increases, more VoIP and UC deployments support access from outside of the enterprise network. Breaches in the software itself, through malware applications such as Trojans and viruses that can create SIP sessions, are also becoming more frequent. These attacks can be controlled through a SIP proxy device, as shown in Figure 16-4.

FIGURE 16-4: SIP PROXY CALL SETUP.

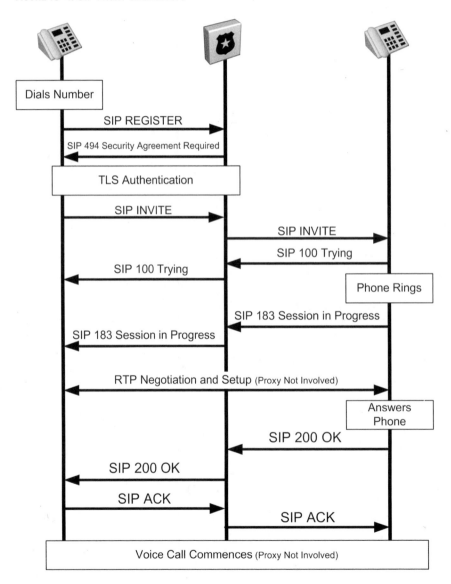

In this configuration, a SIP proxy is placed at the edge of the enterprise network, and all VoIP and UC sessions must use it for all signaling. This means that a SIP client on a user's desktop or IP phone must first send the entire normal SIP session setup message to the proxy, and the message is forwarded to the destination only after the proxy has verified that the initiating client is allowed to create the new session. Incoming SIP session requests also pass to the proxy first and then are forwarded to the local SIP-based application. Unlike an SBC, a SIP proxy handles only the signaling component of a SIP session. After the session has been set up, the SIP proxy gets out of the way, and all RTP traffic goes directly between the two SIP-speaking applications.

SIP proxies must support all SIP features used on the VoIP and UC network. These proxies can be quite expensive. The enterprise security team should evaluate whether VoIP or UC calls will ever leave the network. If so, the team must seriously consider the cost and ability to deploy a SIP proxy for security. This evaluation must also include support for an authentication and encryption solution because the SIP proxy should support the best possible authentication and encryption solution used by the SIP applications and devices.

The security group must create policies that designate which SIP applications must use the SIP proxy and which need direct client-to-client access.

Encryption

The best way to stop information tampering is to make sure the malicious user cannot see that information. For many years, encryption algorithms have been used to hide information; this method is equally useful with modern services such as SIP. Although SIP does not support encryption directly within its RFC, other protocols can be used in conjunction with SIP to encrypt both the signaling and media streams. This is shown in Figure 16-5.

A SIP-based device can implement SIPS for all signaling messages between the device and another remote device. This would also work through a SIP proxy. The SIP device that initiates the session uses port 5061 to negotiate the encryption requirements and challenge messages. After the encryption negotiations and validations are finished, the SIP application sends normal SIP messages wrapped in a TLS-encrypted envelope. Anyone looking at the messages sees only an encrypted packet without any markings to indicate the packet's intent or use as a SIP message.

FIGURE 16-5: ENCRYPTED SIP CALL.

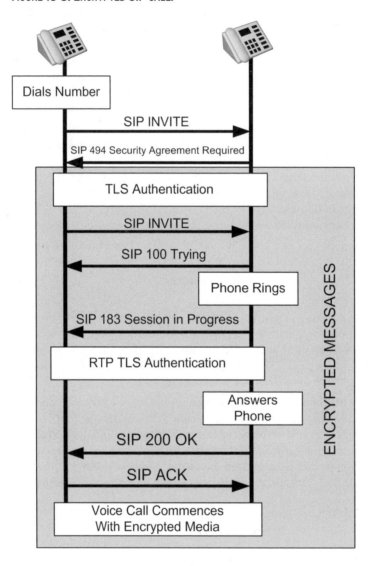

Hidden messages can keep intruders from gathering enough information to impersonate a SIP user on the enterprise network. However, malicious users can still see RTP media packets after the call is set up, because SIPS encrypts only SIP messages and not RTP media packets. To encrypt RTP packets, use the Real-Time Streaming Protocol (RTSP). RTP is negotiated during the SIP session setup. This negotiation is usually started within the SIP 183 Session in Progress message through the embedded SDP messages:

sip:1161@securityevolutions.com:5060 SIP/2.0

Via: SIP/2.0/UDP 192.168.65.132:5060;branch=z9hG4bK100BE5B15

Remote-Party-ID: <sip:1161@192.168.65.132>;party=calling;screen=no;privacy=off

From: "Josh Smith" <sip:1161@192.168.65.132>;tag=FD0AB738–1C18

To: "Sandra Livingston" <sip:291@192.168.65.70>

Date: Wed, 25 Apr 2007 15:00:51 GMT

Call-ID: 97FBFACD-F27411DB-904BEC43-DBD99238@192.168.65.132

Supported: 100rel,timer,resource-priority

Min-SE: 1800

Cisco-Guid: 2549833381–4067693019–2420698179–3688469048

User-Agent: Cisco-SIPGateway/IOS-12.x

Allow: INVITE, OPTIONS, BYE, CANCEL, ACK, PRACK, UPDATE, REFER, SUBSCRIBE, NOTIFY, INFO, REGISTER

CSeq: 183 SESSION IN PROGRESS

Max-Forwards: 70

Timestamp: 1177513251

Contact: <sip:1161@192.168.65.132:5060>

Expires: 180

Allow-Events: telephone-event

Content-Type: application/sdp

Content-Disposition: session;handling=required

Content-Length: 193

    v=0

    o=CiscoSystemsSIP-GW-UserAgent 5421 883 IN IP4 10.164.65.132

    s=SIP Call

    c=IN IP4 192.168.65.132

    t=0 0

    m=audio 18768 RTP/AVP 0

    c=IN IP4 192.168.65.132

    a=rtpmap:0 PCMU/8000

    a=ptime:20

During this stage, SDP negotiations can use the same TLS setup and validation mechanisms used for SIP messages. This sets up a TLS session that envelops all RTP packets. The SIP session is now almost completely encrypted from start to finish, but this high level of encryption can cause several issues.

The cost of heavy encryption can be staggering in the early stages of deployment. Without hardware acceleration, a large part of the cost, applications rely on software encryption solutions. This adds latency to the SIP session and could delay it to a point of uselessness. In addition, not all SIP applications support encryption, which might require support for multiple encryption algorithms in the VoIP and UC environment.

The enterprise security team must decide when and where to deploy encryption most effectively. The team must determine the uses of each SIP application, including where it will be used and on what platforms. The cost of encryption for each SIP-based application must include the criticality of the information to be secured. If the information or device is within a less critical service, or if it exists in a separate part of the network, encryption might cost more than a potential breach. All these elements must be evaluated before an encryption solution can be designed or deployed.

Defining availability goals and objectives for SIP applications

Availability goals were described in Chapter 14, "Best Practices for VoIP Security," as part of a general security plan, but SIP applications require unique availability goals due to the protocol's nature and the critical applications that require it. Phone systems, e-mail systems, and communications services all rely on the stability of SIP applications. As many call centers move to SIP-based applications, entire businesses rely on SIP. SIP, though, cannot be relied upon in its basic deployment state.

Network availability

SIP is commonly deployed with the UDP transport protocol on an IP network. UDP is not reliable because it is a purely stateless protocol that is not designed to resend a packet found to be corrupt or missing. UDP also lacks the congestion algorithms needed when a circuit within the path between two SIP session clients is overrun. This means that SIP must be relied on for state tracking; although SIP can handle some state tracking functions, it is not as well designed for these tasks as TCP. TCP is a stateful protocol that handles network congestion through an algorithm called TCP Congestion Control (RFC 2581). This algorithm allows TCP to manage the flow of packets over a link, based on how quickly they are acknowledged from the remote end. However, this method can backfire because latency is added to VoIP session calls as packets are delayed to handle congestion.

TCP can also handle the state of the session, resending packets that are corrupted or missing. This can reduce the number of jumps in a SIP session caused by missing media packets and reduce the chances of a session dropping due to unreceived packets that were never re-sent. Like the congestion algorithm, this feature can cause additional delay. These side effects might be a hindrance but should not prevent the use of TCP over UDP for one primary reason: to implement TLS encryption, SIP must run over TCP.

Authentication availability

Moving SIP to a more secure platform requires authentication. The authentication scheme might use a simple password or a public–private certificate solution. Either solution must be properly managed so that increased security is not negated by a leak of the security keys. The goal is to control availability of the authentication systems themselves as well as availability of the keys used by each user.

Each authentication device must be evaluated for high-availability support. Additionally, each authentication system should be audited to determine how it stores the passwords or keys used during authentication. Keys or passwords should be kept in a highly encrypted data file or files and should not be easily decrypted, if decrypted at all.

Another aspect of authentication is that users will have the key with them most of the time. They might have written their passwords somewhere or sent them in e-mail. If certificates are used, the private key might be stored on one or more machines or in e-mail where it can be obtained easily. User-side keys are critical and are dangerous if leaked. The security team must create policies that dictate how and where these keys can be stored and define procedures that ensure that each user follows current policies dictating how a password or key can be stored.

Core device availability

SIP has numerous vulnerabilities rooted in a SIP device or application's ability to parse and interpret each entry in the SIP message. This parsing can take some time, and many vendors take the liberty of assuming what should be in each field, how long each field can be, and other characteristics. These assumptions may cause a device to crash if unexpected data appears in the field. This applies to both client SIP applications and to SIP servers such as the PBX, communications server, proxy, SIP-aware firewall, or SBC. If any of these devices is attacked with modified SIP messages, it could fail, causing the service or the user to lose access to SIP applications and features.

Although there is no way to avoid these vulnerabilities completely, an enterprise should create proactive policies that predict problems well in advance. A security team must create procedures that test each device for known SIP message–parsing vulnerabilities. The goal should be an auditing solution that provides a clear idea of all known message vulnerabilities in a vendor's SIP application or device and predicts how likely it is to fail after an attack.

Each critical device must have policies that dictate how to control known vulnerabilities so an attack can be mitigated, or at least noticed, well before the attack affects the system.

Compliance and SIP security

Enterprises are affected by many laws, whether federal, state, or local. These laws also govern how confidential information, confidentiality, and employee safety must be handled. The following list shows some examples:

- Communications Assistance for Law Enforcement Act (CALEA)
- Health Insurance Portability and Accountability Act (HIPAA)
- Sarbanes-Oxley Act
- ISO 17799/2005
- breach laws
- E911

These laws affect how a VoIP and UC network may be deployed and specify the auditing, monitoring, and reporting requirements for all information transported through the VoIP and UC environment. Using SIP does not eliminate any of these regulations or requirements. In fact, SIP opens the VoIP and UC network to possible breaches that can cause an enterprise to violate these laws.

Because SIP is such a vulnerable protocol, each security measure must be validated over a set period of time to confirm that it is still functioning and that data has not been modified, copied, or removed. Additionally, procedures must dictate how to monitor and manage the audit trail so that a third party can validate all reporting mechanisms created by the enterprise. Taken together, these policies and procedures bring a SIP installation into compliance with local and federal laws. These laws and regulations, discussed earlier in this book, can encompass an entire IP network. The exception is the E911 regulation. E911 service must be carefully reviewed if SIP-based VoIP is deployed as the standard telephony solution.

E911 services

IP phones and soft phones use a network-based connection to a PBX or SIP gateway that handles all calls. This gateway can even use local Public Switched Telephone Network (PSTN) circuits to send calls to a local exchange carrier. These enable a user to call an emergency service, but the call cannot be placed if the network as a whole fails. In a traditional enterprise design, the PBX and its phones are separate from the data network. If one fails, the other is not affected. This is not the case with a fully deployed SIP voice solution because the IP phone has no access to physical circuits. Therefore, a solution must be designed to handle a network failure and the resulting phone system failure. Procedures might require the use of cell phones or public phones until service is restored or deployment of actual copper phones in each office, to be used in case of emergencies.

Problems with E911 extend beyond issues of network failure. In a mobile workforce, enterprise users begin to depend on SIP for regular phone service while on the road, through the use of soft phones or cell phones that support SIP-based VoIP services. This means that if a user calls 911 on a soft phone or mobile IP phone, the SIP voice network must provide the correct emergency service. If the user is visiting Texas and uses SIP voice service from an office in Maine, the Maine police and emergency services will not be able to respond to a local emergency. Mobile SIP solutions must direct emergency services to the appropriate local E911 call center. If this cannot be done, it is wise to disable this ability until a solution is found.

Best practices for enterprise and federation SIP security

In previous chapters, you learned overall best practices for deploying a VoIP and UC solution. These best practices do not change when SIP is deployed as the signaling protocol. Before designing a SIP-based VoIP and UC deployment, all best practices should be reviewed and, where necessary, configured differently to work with SIP.

Network security best practices

Most enterprise networks have a solid security solution that handles common IP traffic and that might handle rudimentary VoIP traffic. When SIP is added, security devices such as firewalls and Network Address Translation (NAT) devices must be adapted to work with SIP.

Firewalls and SIP

Although basic firewalls can handle common IP traffic, they are not designed to protect SIP-based applications and services. Because SIP uses a static port for signaling and a dynamic port for media traffic, traditional firewalls might not be able to open proper firewall holes for media traffic. This means that the firewall can have openings between the trusted and untrusted zones of a firewall that remain open even when SIP-based sessions do not exist outside of the enterprise network. A simple scan can find these holes.

Additionally, SIP-based applications must be modified to support a static set of ports that RTP can use instead of dynamically assigned ports from 1025–65536. This modification might not be possible for all SIP-based applications. Incoming session invitations from remote applications also might be unaware of this feature or might not support it. To mitigate this issue, a traditional firewall must be replaced with a SIP-aware firewall. These firewalls can assign dynamic ports to RTP through application layer gateways (ALGs).

Application layer gateways

ALGs allow a firewall to assign an RTP port dynamically on a per-SIP-session basis by monitoring SIP messages for an embedded SDP message:

Content-Type: application/sdp

Content-Disposition: session;handling=required

Content-Length: 193

    v=0

    o=CiscoSystemsSIP-GW-UserAgent 5421 883 IN IP4 10.164.65.132

    s=SIP Call

    c=IN IP4 192.168.65.132

    t=0 0

    m=audio 18768 RTP/AVP 0

    c=IN IP4 192.168.65.132

    a=rtpmap:0 PCMU/8000

    a=ptime:20

The ALG parses SDP messages from both endpoint SIP applications and captures the IP address, used for both the source and destination application, that will terminate the RTP media and the port information (seen in the m= field):

    o=CiscoSystemsSIP-GW-UserAgent 5421 883 IN IP4 10.164.65.132

    c=IN IP4 192.168.65.132

    m=audio 18768 RTP/AVP 0

With this information, the ALG creates a hole in the firewall policy that allows each RTP source and destination to access each other over the appropriate ports. This hole stays open until the ALG receives a SIP BYE message with the same Call-ID as the one contained in the initial SIP call setup messages for the RTP hole. The ALG then immediately removes the hole from the firewall rules. If an additional call is made, the ALG opens a new hole for that specific call. However, when ALGs are combined with NAT-based networks, things become more complicated.

NAT

Unlike a traditional network in which an ALG uses a source IP address from within the corporate network, newer enterprise networks use RFC 1918 space to conserve public IP space and create an additional layer of security. This poses a problem for SIP-based VoIP and UC deployments as well as for ALGs designed to protect these deployments. The culprit is the RFC 1918 network IP space.

RFC 1918 space is designated as nonroutable space. That is, if a SIP message reaches a remote SIP application with a source IP address taken from RFC 1918 space, the remote SIP application will not know how to answer the initiating client and thus will ignore the SIP message. This is also true for RTP because it uses a source or destination IP address in the SDP message to understand where to send the media packets. Dynamic RTP port assignments can be handled by the same ALGs used by the firewalls. These ALG features can be used in situations beyond firewalls because SBCs and SIP proxies require them when deployed in front of an RFC 1918 network.

SIP-aware ALGs already parse SIP messages for the SDP fields required to open the correct ports. After the ports are open, the ALG removes any reference to the RFC 1918 IP address within the message and replaces it with a public IP address assigned to the firewall. The SIP messages are then sent to the destination application. The firewall logs which Call-IDs go to which RFC 1918 IP addresses and monitors all incoming responses for these Call-IDs (see Figure 16-6).

FIGURE 16-6: ALG NAT.

When a return SIP message is received with the correct Call-ID, the ALG replaces the public IP address that it initially placed in the message with the actual RFC 1918 IP address and forwards it to the enterprise network. This same procedure happens for RTP packets. The ALG modifies embedded SDP messages with the appropriate public IP space for all outgoing messages and replaces it when replies are received. This allows the enterprise to keep its existing IP assignments without having to open the network to public access, while still allowing creation of SIP sessions to remote sources outside of the network.

User registration and proxies

Registering users for a VoIP network is relatively simple. The requirements and information stored within the VoIP registry also apply to VoIP calls. When SIP is added to the network, more work is required because devices other than IP phones will require SIP registration.

E-mail services, presence services, IM, and Web conferencing all have different authorization and accounting requirements. The easiest solution is a unified authentication mechanism that can be used beyond SIP applications. Most SIP proxies and SBCs support the ability to authenticate through Active Directory directory services.

Because Active Directory archives user information and group authorization rules, the SIP proxy or SBC can leverage this information when authorizing a user who wants to access UC applications or VoIP services through SIP. This also gives the security team a single location to manage all user information, passwords, and rights. When a user leaves the company, a single change in Active Directory disables all the user's rights on both the enterprise data network and the VoIP and UC network. This reduces the chances that a user will take advantage of the VoIP network to place calls, steal information, or cause disruption of any kind.

Virtual local area network support considerations

Many enterprise VoIP deployments place a VoIP network within a specific virtual local area network (VLAN) that does not overlap any part of the normal enterprise network. This is intended to prevent a VoIP service breach from carrying over to the data network and compromising additional confidential information. When SIP and SIP-based UC applications are deployed, some applications that formerly existed only on the VoIP VLAN now exist on users' desktops. This can pose a problem because the VLANs cannot communicate, and blindly opening the floodgates could be very dangerous. SIP and RTP messages must be able to cross dynamically between the two VLAN environments without opening either environment to malicious users or programs. This requires one of two solutions. The first, and least secure, is to place the SIP proxy, gateway, or PBX on the edge of both VLANs. This gives the device a connection into each network to receive incoming and send outgoing SIP and RTP packets to the SIP applications. This method works but does open a point for hackers who can gain access to both networks through the SIP server that now acts as a bridge.

The second solution is to deploy a SIP-aware firewall between the two VLAN environments. With this method, the non-VoIP environment is treated like an external network. This reduces the chance that a rogue application or packet can gain access to the VoIP VLAN. This method could cause some application issues and is more expensive but is a far more secure solution and should be implemented if critical information must pass between the two VLAN environments.

SIP encryption

Encryption is a new feature for VoIP and SIP. Although SIP has supported the ability to handle several protocols in conjunction with encryption, this is not a standard practice. However, as SIP continues to widen its deployment footprint, encryption must become an integral function. As the cost of SIP-based devices and applications drops, enterprises have more incentive to upgrade. The more enterprises support and use SIP, the more hackers will want to use it to breach networks.

It is imperative that new VoIP and UC deployments implement encryption at the beginning. This might delay the deployment slightly, due to additional cost and design considerations, but a new VoIP and SIP-based environment that is deployed without encryption will lead to many security threats and greater costs later, when the threat becomes unavoidable.

Knowledge Check 16-1: Best Practices for SIP Security

Answer the following questions. Answers to these Knowledge Check questions are located in *Appendix A: Answers to Knowledge Check Questions.*

1. Which password encryption protocol is recommended for use with a SIP deployment?

   a. MD5

   b. SSL

   c. TLS

   d. 3DES

2. Which applications can be supported in a SIP deployment?

   a. Voice

   b. Video

   c. E-mail

   d. Messaging

   e. All of the above

3. Which protocol is used to signal SIP media sessions?

   a. H.264

   b. RTP

   c. SDP

   d. TCP

4. Which transport protocol is considered to have higher availability?

   a. SIP

   b. TCP

   c. UDP

   d. HTTP

   e. ICMP

5. Using SIP instead of H.323 as the signaling protocol allows an enterprise to ignore VoIP-based compliance laws and regulations.

   a. True

   b. False

Chapter summary

We have said several times before that SIP is a standard, yet vendors still seem to have issues properly implementing this standard. This issue must be considered for all SIP-based applications and for all vendors. This should include more than just IP phones. SIP-aware firewalls and ALGs, as well as e-mail servers and even routers and switches, need to be reviewed for SIP support. These devices should also be tested to make sure they properly comply with the different SIP RFCs. This requires a battery of tests, using multiple open source and commercial tools. The more thorough the testing, the less likely a bug will be found in the future that will cripple the SIP service or open up a network to malicious users.

17: Implementing a Multilayered VoIP and SIP Security Solution

This chapter reviews the Session Initiation Protocol (SIP), and describes its common exploits and vulnerabilities. The following topics are included:

- review of SIP in the enterprise
- SIP review
- what is at risk with a SIP deployment
- common SIP threats
- common SIP vulnerabilities
- SIP protocol vulnerabilities
- SIP attacks
- SIP extension into other federations

Chapter 17 Topics

In this chapter, you will learn:

- how to design a layered defense strategy for enterprise Voice over Internet Protocol (VoIP) and SIP infrastructures

- about enterprise VoIP and SIP security policy creation

- how to implement secure federations between companies

- about VoIP and SIP security: ensuring confidentiality, integrity, and availability

- about Time-Division Multiplexing Private Branch Exchange (TDM-PBX) system hardening: securing the core voice infrastructure

- about IP-PBX and VoIP system and server hardening: securing systems and servers

- SIP application (Unified Communications [UC]) server hardening: securing UC application servers

Chapter 17 Goals

Upon completion of this chapter, you will be able to:

- understand how an enterprise should create new VoIP and SIP security policies and procedures

- describe the use of a layered defense in a security design

- explain how and why SIP federations need to be secure, internally and externally, for an enterprise

- describe how SIP security can ensure confidentiality, integrity, and availability at the different points within an enterprise:

  - endpoint devices

  - edge of the network

  - access or transit links

  - core backbone network

- understand how to harden a TDM-PBX

- understand how to harden an IP-PBX server or appliance, and how these security measures are different from hardening a TDM-PBX

Key Terms

Access control   386

Availability   377

CIA   377

Layered security   371

Virtual local area network (VLAN)   373

Introduction

Previous chapters described the risks that occur when an enterprise IT group deploys a VoIP and UC solution. These vulnerabilities, threats, and risks can be mitigated through policies and procedures that take into account the known and unknown. As each new threat is resolved, a virtual wall is built to stop that particular vulnerability. Without a unified solution, an enterprise could have security "walls" set up all over the network, each handling only one specific issue. Such a configuration can create a false sense of security; if a different type of attack is attempted, it will most likely get through because no wall has been built to counter it. This configuration is also difficult to manage because each vulnerability has its own wall that must be monitored and maintained. If one of these walls develops a "crack" or vulnerability, an attack against that wall might succeed and damage the infrastructure, unless there is a redundant wall behind the vulnerable one.

Designing a layered defense strategy for enterprise VoIP and SIP infrastructures

In good security infrastructure, a single solution is never adequate. Single solutions tend to be placed near the devices or data that require special security. This design can permit an attack to travel through a network, using bandwidth and CPU resources on every device that the attack crosses. Some solutions used for different kinds of risks are actually similar; if deployed separately, however, multiple versions of a similar policy or procedure may be created. This can be quite confusing. If a layered approach is used, most of these issues can be resolved and security can be increased.

A layered security model consists of multiple walls that must be penetrated to get to the protected device, information, or application. These walls are placed from the edge of the enterprise network inward. The closer to the edge of the wall, the broader the security measure. Deeper into the enterprise network, the walls become more specific to a particular product, service, or application.

- **Broad-based security layer**—This is the first layer of security that should be deployed in an enterprise network. This layer includes the access lists that filter Internet Protocol (IP) traffic at the edge of the network, as well as IP firewalls separating the local area network (LAN) from the wide area network (WAN). In this layer, threats like denial of service (DoS) attacks and basic spoofing attempts can be stopped before they enter the network. This is also the last defense for all outgoing traffic from the enterprise network.

- **Transport-protocol security layer**—Once traffic has been broadly inspected at the edge of the network, it enters the second layer of defenses. This layer handles the separation of an enterprise network into the different compartments that might be needed for a business unit, product, or application. This could mean separation of the VoIP IP space from the data IP space, or separation of the untrusted environment from the trusted. Additionally, Network Address Translation (NAT) and port address translation can be placed in the security layer. Although not technically security measures, these translation methods can be used to create a more obscure network image, as some of the enterprise network will be hidden behind a single address or port.

- **Service-based security layer**—At this point, the traffic entering the network should be traffic for known services only, and not for services used for DoS attacks. Additionally, traffic should have been directed to the appropriate compartment within the network. At each of these compartments, the traffic meets security measures specific to that compartment. This may include Web or VoIP proxies, e-mail sanitizers, session border controllers (SBCs), and remote access servers. This layer also includes authentication systems, such as a proxy, and authorization systems. These devices act as sentries for this layer of the network security design. Unlike the first two layers, the service-based layer is focused on protecting a specific area. However, the measures here are still broad enough to handle filtering and evaluating all traffic within the layer.

- **Application-based security layer**—Even though a layered defensive security design features security measures that can deal with multiple threats or vulnerabilities in one stroke, the application-based layer requires that the design deviate from that ideal. Once the security design reaches individual applications and devices, the measures become unique to those elements. General policies, such as requiring data encryption or device and application authorization, can still be applied to multiple devices or applications. This layer handles specific policies and procedures that dictate encryption on data and communication paths and validation of software images and binaries on the desktop or application devices, as well as watchdog systems that monitor the devices, applications, or systems for malicious applications, viruses, or Trojans.

- **End-user policy-based security layer**—The last layer of security contains security measures that deal directly with end users and how they use the network and its services. These security measures are usually policies and procedures that dictate how end users can access the applications or services, and what they can do with them. This layer also handles how to lock down the system when a user is fired or leaves, procedures used if there is a security breach, how new devices and applications are certified before deployment, and all other common security best practices.

These layers must work both ways. Most enterprise networks focus the majority of their efforts on securing how users, devices, and applications can access the enterprise network from the outside, and tend to put far too little effort into protecting what can leave the network. Because internal breaches are the most common form of information theft, this aspect cannot be ignored. This means that each wall must act as a sentry for traffic initiating from either direction. Each layer must compensate for this and be constructed accordingly.

VoIP and SIP and security layers

VoIP and SIP are considered application layer protocols. SIP uses IP for transport across a network and the Internet. As previous chapters have described, SIP is used within devices as well as in software applications such as soft phones and instant messaging applications on the desktop. In general, SIP and VoIP cannot be secured through a single wall. Because the different VoIP protocols affect many parts of an enterprise network deployment, each security layer must address VoIP-based threats, vulnerabilities, and risks.

- **Broad-based security layer**—At the edge, incorporate strategies to block IP spoofing and verify that SIP messages and Real-Time Protocol (RTP) messages entering and leaving the enterprise network actually originate from the expected real IP addresses. This means that any NAT or Port Address Translation (PAT) application must be done and any request for comments (RFC) 1918 IP address space must be removed. Blocking the ports specific to all unused VoIP protocols should also be done in this layer, especially if the enterprise decides to utilize nonstandard ports for SIP or RTP.

- **Transport-protocol security layer**—The entire network must be considered in the security design, but the network does not have to be flat or one large pool. Deploying virtual local area networks (VLANs) and NAT/PAT can help separate important traffic into network compartments that can then be secured much more easily. This could mean that all corporate data exists in RFC 1918 IP space, whereas the VoIP data within that space exists in its own VLAN domain. Network separation helps reduce the chances that a breach in one area can grant an attacker access to information that should be located in another area. These measures are all deployed in this security layer.

- **Service-based security layer**—All SIP proxies and SBCs should be deployed within this layer. Because this is just inside the edge of each compartment in the network, VoIP security measures placed here reduce the chances that an attacker can get a good view of the VoIP network and design. Placing SIP authentication and authorization devices in this layer will also stop rogue SIP applications from breaching the network and listening to or hijacking a VoIP session.

- **Application-based security layer**—By the time traffic reaches this layer, all common external attacks should have been effectively mitigated, but this will not stop the more complex attacks or attacks from inside; that is where this layer becomes important. Because VoIP-based applications are mainly software-driven, they can be tampered with or replaced. Security measures like MD5 checksum hash auditing from a reliable source can help reduce the number of tampered applications. If an organization has deployed 802.1x, the policies for the supplicant fall under this layer.

- **End-user policy security layer**—Best practice security policies and procedures also apply to SIP and VoIP deployments. Because these policies and procedures handle how, when, where, and why a user can access a device, application, or information, adding VoIP should not change existing policies beyond integrating the VoIP services into the documents.

In an enterprise VoIP deployment, most of these layers consist of some form of device or application. These devices and applications will each have a default way to secure a network, but they should never be installed right out of the box. The security team should create procedures for deploying these devices and what data, service, and information will be touched by these devices. These procedures must also involve the different business units within the enterprise itself. Otherwise, security might become so cumbersome that it is ignored in favor of efficiency.

Enterprise VoIP and SIP security policy creation

Policies and procedures are the navigation systems that every organization uses to give direction and purpose to end users, operations, and even clients. When an enterprise designs a layered security solution, the same practices should be followed; each security policy or procedure describes how applications, devices, or information are accessed, deleted, modified, or copied. These rules cannot be created by a small group of people. Because each of these rules affects the entire company, in areas ranging from productivity and confidentiality to the corporate image, the creation of rules must include input from the different parts of the enterprise.

A fluid process should be used to initiate and create a new policy or procedure that will handle a specific security rule or restriction. The process will require several steps, some of which will require time and patience to get through, but all of which should be followed if the new procedures are to be respected by all end users and staff.

Step 1: Defining the need

The first step in policy creation is to define the need for the policy. This might sound obvious, but each new policy must be created for a valid reason. If an enterprise deploys too many superfluous policies and procedures, the more important policies may be systematically ignored or enforced only when time allows.

Policies should only be created for issues that cannot be resolved by a one-off solution, such as a patch or upgrade. A policy should change the behavior of an organization's staff in a way that makes the whole network more secure without too much complication. If this can be accomplished, then the new policy will be worth taking the time to create and implement.

Step 2: Defining the policies' goals

Once need has been verified, the goals for the new policy should be defined. These goals should be discussed throughout the IT and security groups to verify that the problem this policy is trying to solve is not covered by an existing policy. In other cases, the new policy might aim to combine multiple policies and procedures into a unified single policy. Either way, the goals must be well defined to eliminate overlap with existing policies.

Step 3: Defining what will be affected

Each new policy will affect the enterprise in a different way. It might require modifications to how different groups do business on a daily basis; it might require a reconfiguration of the network; it might require additional funds. No matter what is required, how the enterprise will be affected and what will be affected must be understood before the procedure can be written. This will give the policy writers a good idea of whom to contact for more information or who can review draft or final versions of the policy.

Step 4: Defining the policy

With the need for the policy and its goals defined, the security team should draft the policy. This draft should be as detailed as possible and should include all information needed to understand the policy's goals, what the policy will affect, and how it should be implemented. At this point, the team should meet with each group affected by this policy, including those whose productivity may be affected, whose applications or equipment will need to be used or reconfigured to support this new policy, and those who might need to pay for these changes. Once the draft has been written with the help of the various other departments or business units, the draft must be reviewed.

Step 5: Review for comments

Each affected group should review the draft for any discrepancies. The reviewers should also take notes on the feasibility of deploying the new policy and make comments on how they think it could be streamlined. Once all of the comments have been received, the draft should be updated to a final version.

Step 6: Approval

The last step before deployment should be to ask affected stakeholders for their approval of the new policy or procedure. This will ensure that any political issues are handled before the deployment. It will also ensure that everyone is aware of the impending change.

Step 7: Deployment

After the final version of the policy has been approved, it must be deployed. This does not mean that a notice is simply sent out to the whole organization. A solid deployment of a new procedure includes the following:

• A copy of the new policy or procedure.

• A list of affected groups, business units, devices, and so on.

• A help line (e-mail or support numbers) that staff can use to ask questions or bring up support issues.

• If the policy is complicated or changes some part of how the enterprise does business, training classes should be part of the deployment process. These classes should help transition the staff into the new way of handling the policy.

If these steps are followed, new or modified procedures will be easier to create and deploy. With the proper deployments, these policies and procedures will be used and enforced without too much pushback, because the appropriate groups provided input during planning. Remember, though, that there will always be some complaints about any change in the enterprise environment, no matter how much approval or time is spent creating a sound policy.

Implementing secure federations between companies

As SIP has become a more commonly deployed protocol for VoIP, virtual voice trunks have become an increasingly common VoIP service deployed between two companies. These trunks are used to pass VoIP calls and to make SIP-based applications faster and more effective. A SIP trunk is used as a virtual VoIP signaling path between the companies and allows them to set up calls over a network without handing off the call to traditional local exchange carriers. This can reduce the cost of telephoning between the two companies, especially if one of the companies is a hub that can pass the call to a plethora of other SIP-enabled companies or service providers. SIP trunking can also allow a company to customize its telephony design to fit each company with which it will communicate, something that is not easy to do through traditional means.

Connecting two companies through a SIP trunk should not be considered a secure application of the SIP or VoIP service. If the VoIP security design was built to handle only internal office-to-office sessions with the occasional Internet session, opening up the enterprise's PBX to another company might not be covered. It should also be understood that each enterprise can only control its own side of the SIP trunk, and usually cannot dictate how the other company handles security. This means that a security wall must be put into place between the enterprise and all other companies to which the enterprise will connect through SIP trunks. As a standard practice, there are three security measures that should be put into place before any SIP trunking is enabled.

Session border controllers

SBCs can be used in four different ways. An SBC can act as a VoIP protocol translator. Although this is not a security feature, it does allow a company that uses H.323 to create VoIP sessions with another company that utilizes SIP, by having an SBC as a middle man.

SBCs can act as a SIP proxy for all incoming or outgoing calls. Like a normal SIP proxy, they can authorize a session through an authentication scheme (such as MD5-hashed passwords) or certificates. They can also authorize access through IP addresses or domains. This feature should be enabled if the enterprise will not be using the filtering and sanitizing features of the SBC.

An SBC can also be used to encrypt all signaling and media streams within a Transport Layer Security (TLS) envelope. This requires that both end devices support encryption. An exception is if both parties utilize encryption on their adjacent SBCs or SIP proxies. If this is the case, then encryption should be used for all signaling and media communications between the enterprise networks, even if the streams are unencrypted once they enter the enterprise networks.

Finally, an SBC can be used to review a VoIP signal or media stream by acting as a middleman or termination point for each end of the call. This is the most important set of features that can be enabled on the SBC, and the most controversial. When one end of a SIP session sends a setup signal, the SBC will intercept the signal, sanitize it, validate that it is an authorized source for a session, and then send it to the destination device or application. This is controversial because the SBC does not transparently send the signal to the destination.

Instead, it sends a new setup signal to the destination with the SBC as the originating device. When the SBC receives the SIP response signals from the destination, it replies to the originating device as if it were the destination. In this way, the SBC can review every signaling packet for malicious data or for unauthorized access attempts midstream. The SBC does not just handle the signaling packets, it actually injects itself into the Session Description Protocol's (SDP) media source and destination fields so that the SBC can monitor what is sent within the media stream in an attempt to control attacks such as spam over Internet telephony (SPIT) or eavesdropping.

Although controversial, these features should be enabled before any SIP session can be accepted across a SIP trunk. This might require that the enterprise disclose its use of an SBC to the other parties.

Session registration

Although there may be a contract between the parties involved, complete access to the VoIP networks between each company might not be authorized. Additionally, an enterprise neither understands nor controls the security practices of the other enterprises to which it connects through the SIP trunks. A malicious user might therefore try to use this other company to gain access to your enterprise network. To help mitigate this risk, each enterprise should support SIP session registration and authorization. This will reduce the chances that an attacker can create or hijack an existing SIP session without at least being logged. As with any security measure, this is not completely secure and should be used with other security measures to help reinforce the SIP layered security design.

Service restrictions

Although the intent may be to allow the setup of SIP sessions for multiple applications between two companies, opening up the network can create additional risks through other applications not related to VoIP. Because this is a service-specific application with known transport-layer protocols and application-layer protocols, access lists can be placed between the two companies to restrict access to SIP-based sessions only. This should be simple when securing SIP or SIP over TLS. Unlike traditional SIP, SIP over TLS uses a certificate-based encryption solution to encrypt the SIP messages over Transmission Control Protocol (TCP). Both SIP and SIP over TLS use standard static ports (5060 and 5061, respectively). With static ports, both SIP implementations can be placed into a static exception in a firewall or access list. This might not be as easy when securing RTP, due to RTP's use of dynamically assigned port numbers above 1024. RTP is the media transport protocol for SIP and over VoIP solutions. RTP is dynamic and a simple access list cannot be used without opening up the same ports to all User Datagram Protocol (UDP) or TCP traffic.

This can be mitigated through the use of application layer gateways (ALGs). ALGs can be used by an SBC, proxy, or firewall between the two companies to dynamically add and remove RTP ports as a session is set up and torn down. This is done through a review of the SIP signaling packets for the SDP attributes embedded within SIP. ALGs are very effective but can be temperamental.

ALGs rely on an understanding of the layout, attributes, and data within a SIP signal. Specifically, ALGs expect these to fit the SIP RFC standard. As mentioned earlier, SIP vendors try to gain an edge in signal parsing speed through modifications within the SIP signal. Some of these modifications can cause an enabled ALG to miss the appropriate SDP attributes, or even to fail. The SIP format that caused the failure, if known by an attack, can be used to crash the security device with an ALG enabled, creating a DoS attack. This should not dissuade organizations from using ALGs, as the benefits outweigh the problems, but each ALG implementation should be thoroughly tested before field deployment.

VoIP and SIP security: Ensuring confidentiality, integrity, and availability

With any security design, the main goals are to control confidentiality, integrity, and availability (CIA) of all network information and services. CIA can be achieved through a flat single-layered security design, but such a design is not thorough. Flat designs must make assumptions for the whole network so that the security measures deployed can somewhat fit all of the applications, services, and information being secured. These assumptions will require a more generic set of policies and procedures, which will in turn open up possible attacks to device-, protocol-, or application-specific vulnerabilities and threats that are not covered by the generic security measures.

A layered security approach is a far better fit when protecting an enterprise for CIA. This allows the same generic policies and procedures to be implemented, but also includes layers of additional application-, protocol-, and device-specific policies to be placed closer to the information or endpoints. There are several aspects of the enterprise network that must be considered when a layered security design is put into place.

Endpoint device: Cell, PDAs, wireless, and more

When initially designing a layered security system that must consider CIA, the end users' realm is one of the first places that must be controlled. As VoIP and SIP have grown in use, devices that traditionally were kept on a separate network are now being integrated into the IP and UC environment. The desktop environment has always been a confidentiality and integrity risk, but now that risk has expanded to the VoIP and UC realm.

There are many endpoint devices that can support SIP and UC applications and features, and all of them should be able to support several basic security functions that will help integrate the devices into several different layers of the network's security design.

Transport-protocol security layer

SIP has traditionally been deployed using UDP transport, which is a very quick and efficient transport protocol, but is not secure. A secure SIP and VoIP deployment should utilize a more secure transport protocol. TCP should be used instead of UDP for all SIP and VoIP sessions, including the media stream, if possible. This will allow the basic TCP handshake, traffic mitigation, and security features to apply to the SIP stream. Using TCP also allows the endpoint to implement TLS encryption. All endpoint devices that can support TCP as the transport method should have it enabled by default; UDP should be disabled and not used.

Service-based security layer

An endpoint should not be allowed to use the SIP or VoIP network without first being validated locally. Although this adds to the authenticity of the endpoint, the endpoint could still be spoofed or breached. A second authentication and authorization scheme should help remove the remaining risk. This can be done by forcing the endpoint to use a SIP proxy. Each endpoint should use a SIP over TLS communications scheme to talk with the proxy and authenticate through a certification private/public key.

Application-based security layer

For each end device, there are three aspects of the application-based security layer that can be applied:

• **MD5 hash validation**—Each endpoint device utilizes applications specific to SIP and VoIP. This includes IP phones, SIP-enabled cell phones, PDAs, and desktops or laptops. These applications are the easiest attack point for any attacker or malicious user because the end user cannot easily see or monitor the state of integrity of the application. To assist the end user, a security procedure needs to be put into place that will validate the state of the application through the use of MD5 checksum validation. This requires that an MD5 hash be created for each binary on the endpoint device. This hash is compared to one created by the vendor in a secure environment. If these hashes match, the applications have not been tampered with. Otherwise, the application and device should have all of the software reinstalled to remove any malicious code.

- **Encryption**—The device may have a secure platform and code base, but this does not mean that it is communicating securely with all SIP applications and devices. Endpoint devices or applications, such as a wireless laptop or SIP-enabled cell phone, can further complicate things as they utilize a layer 2 transport network that is not considered secure. If a wireless network is used as the layer 2 transport method for these devices, an encryption method should be enabled: specifically, Wi-Fi Protected Access version 2 (WPA2). WPA2 uses a new encryption model to encrypt each packet that will transmit over the wireless link. WPA2 has been cracked, but it has the longest time needed to breach a device of all of the supported encryption methods used on wireless devices today.

In addition to transport layer encryption, each device should use TLS over IP. This adds a second layer of encryption on the wireless connection, or even on the IP connections when using a traditional layer 2 network, and gives the data in the device a higher level of integrity and confidentiality. When TLS over IP is paired with WPA2, the probability of data theft within the IP stream is greatly reduced.

- **Authentication**—With encryption and a secure application, the endpoint devices are more secure then when they were initially installed. This, however, does not stop an internal or external user from utilizing the endpoints without authorization. Even with all of the security, gaining access through basic use can make the encryption and binary validation moot. Adding an authentication mechanism to each endpoint can help mitigate this issue. The best solution for authentication is the use of a two-factor authentication scheme. This scheme is designed to have the end user enter two passwords into the device or application before the device allows access to its services. Each two-factor authentication scheme uses the traditional user name and password authentication method. One of two elements can be added to this to create a second means of authentication:

- **Certificates**—A certificate public/private key solution can be used as a second authentication mechanism. Each end user or end-user device will hold a private key, and every device or application the end user or endpoint needs to access will have that private key's public key. In this way, each time the endpoint is used with another application or device, the destination device can challenge the endpoint to validate that it truly is an authorized device.

- **One-time passwords**—Another way to handle the second factor in a two-factor authentication scheme is to use a token that can deliver a one-time password. This one-time password, which can be time or sequence based, is used as a second password when authenticating. Because end users must carry the token with them and the password changes each time the token is used and is never repeated, this solution is considered a very safe authentication scheme.

End-user policy security layer

Although it can be difficult to control what end users do with the devices they use, procedures should instruct them how to operate the endpoint and what can be safely used on the endpoint. This means that end users must never install applications nor make modifications on the endpoint devices. Instead, the IT group should be the only people authorized for application installation.

To comply with laws on fraud and illegal use of long-distance voice mechanisms to bypass toll charges, the organization must ensure that end users know they cannot use the endpoint for non-work-related SIP sessions. Additional policies should dictate how the end user authenticates to the endpoints and how often that authentication mechanism must be refreshed.

Access to the enterprise network from a PDA or cell phone

Another current trend for organizations is to link users' PDAs or cell phones to the organization's intranet so that users have access to instant messaging, e-mail, and the corporate address book. All of these features, although convenient, can be risky. If an organization requires that these features be deployed, the underlying transport between the cell phone or PDA and the intranet must be secure. This might mean that the cell phone carrier must be audited to make sure its security is at least as sound as the security used by the organization. Additional service level agreements (SLAs) should be written to hold the carrier responsible for any breach if one ever happens, as the enterprise will have no control over the remote network.

Edge network: Branch office or remote locations

An enterprise can comprise just a single location, but this is rarely the case. Most enterprise networks support remote offices, or even home offices for employees. These offices must be included within the layered security design of the enterprise. Because these are not directly within the enterprise network's main infrastructure, they must be treated as smaller versions of the enterprise network. This means that firewalls, proxies, and other security procedures might be needed at these remote sites to maintain security integrity.

Firewalls

Each remote or home office will likely reside behind an Internet connection and not behind a dedicated circuit between the main enterprise network and the remote site. When this is the case, firewalls that are deployed between the main enterprise network and the Internet never see the traffic from the remote offices, and thus cannot secure it. Each remote or home office should have a separate, and possibly smaller, firewall that mimics the same policies and features deployed within the enterprise's main network. This will ensure that the same policies are enforced everywhere and that integrity is never lost.

These firewalls should be centrally managed by an operations or IT group and must never be managed by a remote office. This reduces the chance that unauthorized configuration changes will be made. This also allows for a centralized monitoring station that can be alerted if any firewall sends an alarm.

Network Address Translation

Placing filters and access lists at the edge of the remote office network will reduce the number of attacks and risks to the enterprise network, and a network that cannot be fully seen is made more secure. NAT can and should be deployed at remote offices for several reasons.

- Using NAT reduces the amount of public IP space that an enterprise will need to deploy. This was the original purpose of NAT and should not be disregarded when deployed as a security mechanism. Instead of using public IP space, the enterprise instead will utilize RFC 1918 IP space behind the firewall. RFC 1918 IP space is not routable outside of a network.

- Using RFC 1918 space, NAT separates the untrusted and trusted networks by placing each in a separate IP block that cannot reach the other. This means that the whole of the Internet will only see a small select set of public IP addresses that represent the whole remote offices network.

NAT requires the firewall to support and enable ALGs. This requirement is less necessary for security, and is required more because all SIP sessions will either terminate or originate in nonroutable RFC 1918 space. The ALGs must act as the interpreter so that a session can be set up across the firewall to the Internet.

Using the enterprise proxy

Even though the SIP sessions originate or terminate at a remote or home office, they should still be required to go through an enterprise SIP proxy for all signaling. This allows the enterprise to enforce the same authentication and authorization policies for all SIP sessions and keeps the proxy footprint to a manageable level. Another aspect of a SIP proxy is the ability to register all endpoint devices.

By registering all endpoint devices, including those from an external network, the enterprise can make sure that a remote office does not use unauthorized SIP applications or devices. It will also allow the enterprise the ability to track how and what is being used at the remote sites without the need for additional monitoring tools deployed at every remote office or home office.

Access network or Internet: WAN or public Internet

The Internet is not a safe place. Each hop that a packet crosses outside of the enterprise network can be to a compromised device. Communicating across the Internet to other corporate offices or to other Internet locations must be treated as if the endpoints are compromised. This means that each SIP session will need to be authorized and authenticated before it can be allowed to completely set up. In this security step, the WAN locks down the communications path among all of the offices.

Interoffice communications

As stated earlier, the majority of remote or home offices will use an Internet circuit to transport them from the remote office to the main office. Because the Internet is inherently insecure, all communications should be handled as crossing over a high-risk environment, so all communications should use strong encryption. This can become a problem, as not every application or device can support strong encryption. As we have seen, some devices or applications cannot support encryption at all.

This can be resolved by using an Internet Protocol Security (IPsec) virtual private network (VPN) between the main enterprise network and each remote office. These IPsec VPN tunnels will still travel over the Internet, but because they will be using strong encryption, an eavesdropper will not be able to hijack or steal the data within. There are some drawbacks to IPsec tunnels, however. Because each IP packet must be placed in an IPsec-encrypted envelope, additional bandwidth is used over the Internet connection.

Encryption also takes time. The strong encryption can cause additional latency to a SIP or VoIP session that might not have been calculated initially. If the IPsec tunnel is created through the use of software instead of hardware encryption devices, this latency could grow unmanageably high. Care should also be taken in how the IPsec tunnel is transported across the Internet. IPsec tunnels cannot handle fragmentation or too many lost packets.

Session Border Controllers

SIP sessions have historically been between multiple offices within an enterprise. With the expansion of SIP as the signaling protocol of choice, more and more communications applications and devices are being created to communicate with entities outside of the enterprise. As much inherent Internet risk as possible should be removed before SIP sessions can safely leave the enterprise network for a remote destination outside the enterprise.

The SBC can handle this task. Because the SBC is part proxy, part firewall, and part registry, it can act as the middleman to authenticate, authorize, and clean all signaling and media streams that pass into and out of the enterprise network. If the remote enterprises support encryption, the SBC can handle that function as well. The deployment of an SBC between the enterprise and all external destinations should be a mandatory part of any layered security solution.

Restricting SIP sources

Because we are at the edge of the enterprise network, filters should dictate which networks can talk to the enterprise via SIP. Because SIP is a standard protocol, if restrictions are not placed at the edge of the network initially, an attacker who sends DoS attacks can send that traffic into the enterprise network before it is mitigated. This wastes resources, time, and effort. Instead, it should be mitigated at the edge through the use of access lists. Each WAN circuit that connects to the Internet should have an access list applied that will allow only known SIP-speaking IP addresses into the network over the SIP, SIP over TLS, or RTP protocols. All other SIP packets should be dropped at the edge and not carried to the SBC or proxy.

Core backbone network: Enterprise IP backbone network

In this chapter, we have described methods to secure the endpoints, WAN, and remote offices, but we have not yet addressed the core enterprise network. There are several steps that can be taken within the core network to reduce the chances that a security vulnerability is accessible to an attacker. All of these recommendations should be implemented together to ensure that all paths to these vulnerabilities are locked down.

Partitioning the network

One of the first steps in preparing an enterprise network is separating the VoIP and SIP network from the data network (see Figure 17-1). This requires separate VLANs for each of the services (VoIP and data). This will restrict communications between the two environments and require them to first pass through a router or firewall for inspection and authorization. This should not be restricted to just the separation of VoIP and data. A core network should be separated into many different compartments for security reasons. Device and application updates and management should have their own VLAN compartment, as should each department within the network. It might even be necessary to create a VLAN specifically for the security team.

FIGURE 17-1: LAYERED SECURITY REALMS.

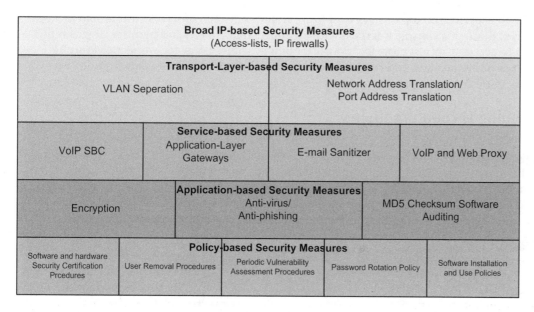

Each of these VLANs can have a routable interface on a router or firewall that allows them to communicate. If this access is not controlled, the separation of the network into partitions adds complexity, not security. Access lists need to be placed at each routable point on a VLAN that restricts which other VLANs and Internet IP addresses can access the VLAN itself. These access lists can be based on IP address, VLAN tags, services, or even protocols.

17

Implementing a Multilayered VoIP and SIP Security Solution

Logging the network

These restrictions should also be logged. Restricting access will help mitigate current issues, but if each unauthorized access attempt is logged, a security team can watch for trends that could lead to an attack. These logs might also help track down an attacker during or after an incident. All of these should be sent to a centralized logging monitor that can review, analyze, and alert to possible threats while storing the additional logging noise.

Logging can work against a security design. Because most devices use the main processor instead of customized application-specific integrated chips (ASICs), an attack that generates a large amount of logs can cause an inadvertent DoS. This is caused by all the cycles needed to create and send the logs to the monitoring device. Before logs are deployed, an evaluation of what the logs will be capturing and the possible growth rate of these logs during high traffic should be performed.

TDM-PBX system hardening: Securing the core voice infrastructure

In the last few decades, an enterprise that required a full-featured phone system would purchase a TDM-PBX. The TDM-PBX acted as a telephony gateway that contained the voice mail system, phone system, and interoffice communications. Everything ran on copper connections to the desktop or over telephony circuits between offices. A traditional PBX was managed through a console interface with an attached keyboard and monitor. It was much harder to access from a remote location, although possible. Consoles are secured through password authentication and can only be accessed through a modem apart from logging directly into it.

Managing through modems

TDM-PBXs do support a remote management solution through the use of a traditional modem connection, which gives the user access to the console. This can be a problem if the PBX has a weak password or none at all, or if the console is left open from the last user and the account does not time out after a set limit of idle minutes. This could give an attacker access to the PBX and thus access to the telephony system to create fraudulent calls or other chaos. One way around this is to secure the modem that is used on the PBX's remote connection.

Many vendors support password-authenticated modems. These modems utilize a set of user names and passwords that restrict and authorize access to the modem itself. Some of these modems even require a second password to access the serial connection between the modem and the PBX. In any installation that utilizes traditional TDM-PBX, a secure modem should be used to stop attackers from easily accessing the PBX console from a remote location.

Management through IP

As the Internet became a more common part of an enterprise network, more enterprise telephony managers started to request integration with the IP network. PBX vendors responded by adding the ability for a telephony technician to access the PBX through an IP connection. With this feature, the technician could conveniently work on the PBX from his or her desk. This change brought new security issues that must be mitigated.

A TDM-PBX with IP management must have the interface to which the PBX is connected locked down so that only authorized IP addresses can access the interface. In addition to the access list on the interface, all other traffic should be dropped, instead of being responded to. This means that Internet Control Message Protocol (ICMP) must be restricted to respond only to ICMP echo requests from known and trusted sources. This makes the PBX look like it does not exist and reduces the chances of a roaming attacker finding and trying to breach the PBX.

Securing telephony access

A PBX handles calls to and from the phones sitting on an end user's desk. These phones use lines that are directly connected to the PBX. Each line can be secured to a point at which that line can only call specific numbers, whether those numbers are internal, external, or international. Although this type of filtering works, it can become unmanageable. Another way to create access lists within a TDM-PBX is to create access groups. Blocks of phone lines can be assigned to the larger group access lists that restrict how the lines can be used.

Even this can be problematic. A third solution can be used to create an access code for specific services. If an end user would like to make a long-distance call, he or she must enter an authorized access code. These codes are often used to track costs and assign them to specific business units, but they can also be used for security purposes.

Call detail records

Security is never truly sound. There are always ways around security measures, policies, and procedures. If an enterprise does not monitor all of the devices within a security infrastructure, an attacker could slip through undetected. This is true even for TDM-based PBX systems. Toll fraud is a serious issue and the best way to track it, when security fails, is through call detail records (CDRs). The CDRs are a logging mechanism used by the PBX that tracks what phone number accessed the phone line, what phone number was called, and for how long. They can also show the circuit from which a call originated. A regular audit of these records can help track a malicious user using the PBX for unauthorized calls.

IP-PBX and VoIP system and server hardening: Securing systems and servers

As technology advances and IP support for voice becomes more common, enterprises have started to migrate to IP-based PBX systems. These systems can support VoIP and TDM phones as well as VoIP and TDM telephony circuits. With the move to a more IP-centric PBX comes a greater need to secure the PBX from IP-based attacks. With the IP network secured using best practices, the next step is to secure the actual IP-PBX devices.

Although these devices are considered appliances, certain issues must be secured before they should be allowed onto the network. The IP-PBX can accept authentication, authorization, and access restrictions. The devices that use its service should be segmented into a specific network pocket, with all external access sent to a VoIP firewall such as an SBC.

Access authentication and authorization

Access to the PBX has become a graphical user interface (GUI) that can be accessed through an integrated Web-based solution, or through a customized application. Both of these access methods should require some form of authentication and authorization. An IP-PBX should initially be set up to support a per-user authentication scheme if possible. This is different from a simple access password and another password to configure the box. A per-use authentication configuration requires a unique user name and password for each user. This will still include a universal configuration password, but allows for some authorization control that can be specific to the user. The user should use, if possible, a token-generated one-time password, as that is the strongest password security method currently available.

The use of specific commands, both configuration and nonconfiguration, should be organized into authorization groups based on the users who will be accessing the PBX, such as operations, management, and monitoring groups. Each command should be added to a group's list of authorized commands based on that group's need. All other commands should be restricted. This allows some control over how much access attackers can have if they successfully breached an account.

Restricting port access to the PBX

One of the quickest ways to start hardening an IP-PBX is to restrict the protocols and ports that can be used to access the IP-PBX. This can be done on the interfaces that connect to the IP-PBX, usually Ethernet or Fast Ethernet. These access lists can restrict access to the Ethernet connection so that only ports relevant to the VoIP services enabled by the IP-PBX are allowed through. All other packets should be dropped at the router and logged to a central monitoring system.

Create authorized device list

One of the benefits of an IP-PBX is that you can utilize an authorization list made up of media access control (MAC) addresses and IP addresses. This gives the enterprise a flexible way to control which devices will be allowed to make calls through the PBX, without relying on user identity. Each VoIP device must be added to the list as it is deployed on the network. This should work in conjunction with any user authentication and authorization deployed for access to the VoIP network through VoIP devices and applications.

Securing the TDM side of the IP-PBX

The IP-PBX handles VoIP services, and it can also handle TDM services. These calls must also terminate to a local exchange carrier at some point, and it can be cheaper for the organization to deliver the local calls to a local telephony carrier through a TDM circuit. All of this requires some form of security on the circuits. As described in the previous section on securing TDM-PBX systems, the carrier circuits can be restricted to specific calling areas. Incoming calls can also be restricted, if necessary.

Even though the IP-PBX might utilize VoIP trunks more than TDM circuits for terminating calls, the same auditing of the CDRs should be done for an IP-PBX. Toll fraud can be found in both situations, and even though the VoIP side might seem secure, the only way to verify is to check the records weekly.

Firewalling a PBX

The last security layer for a hardened IP-PBX is the firewall rules setup. Although this might not be part of the server itself, access to the server over specific ports, as well as access from the rest of the Internet, must be analyzed before it can be allowed to access the IP-PBX. Because traditional firewalls cannot handle this function, a VoIP firewall is needed. This can be a firewall with VoIP ALGs, or an SBC. Place these firewalls between the parts of the enterprise network that separate the Internet-accessible network from the internal network. In high-risk enterprise environments, a VoIP firewall may be required between the VoIP VLANs and the internal network to make sure that any internal attacks or malicious users are hindered in their attempts to breach the VoIP network.

SIP application UC server hardening: Securing UC application servers

Like the PBX that will be deployed in the VoIP infrastructure, the UC application server is more than just a customized appliance. The majority of the deployed application servers actually use common server hardware. They also utilize a common operating system, such as Windows or Linux, which introduces additional security vulnerabilities beyond those related specifically to the services and features the application server uses.

Each of these application servers consists of three layers that must be secured separately: the operating system, the application binaries themselves, and the transport mechanism the application uses to talk with the VoIP and SIP infrastructure.

Operating system security

Operating system security is the moving target of any application server deployment. When the application server is installed, the operating system should be installed with only the necessary modules, files, or services. This will require additional libraries or binaries that will never be directly used by the application, but that are required as a dependency by the services needed for the application server.

Understanding application dependencies

As more applications are added directly to the operating system, new vulnerabilities can be introduced. Because these modules might not be directly used or even known, each additional application must be scrutinized to figure out what additional software has been enabled. The additional modules and applications must be monitored for vulnerabilities, with each bug fixed as soon as possible. This is in addition to existing procedures that govern the operating system patch and bug management.

Once all applications have been installed on the application server, the security team should do a thorough check on all services that are enabled, disabling any unnecessary applications that could be used to breach security on the device.

Validation of operating system integrity

Another reason to use a custom solution rather than a standard operating system is that attackers already have access to software used to break into standard operating systems and modify them. The same viruses, Trojan applications, and hacking methods used to breach a desktop host can also be used to access servers. Be sure that all applications that reside on the server are truly needed. Once this has been verified, do not permit additional applications and software to be loaded onto the server. The IT security team must install additional safeguards that continuously validate the integrity of all installed applications, ensuring that no breach in security has happened through modification of existing application software.

These same validation methods should be used on the operating system itself. A standard operating system is widely distributed within the private and public communities. This gives potential black-hat hackers the ability to test proven and new attacks on any operating system. When standard operating systems are used in large enterprise deployments, attackers have a large pool of targets to attack, using known techniques. A custom operating system is generally not as inviting a target, because access to the operating system code and the code's deployment base may be too difficult to make it worth the effort.

Knowledge Check 17-1: Implementing a Multilayered VoIP and SIP Security Solution

Answer the following questions. Answers to the Knowledge Check questions are located in *Appendix A: Answers to Knowledge Check Questions.*

1. A layered security design can be compared with a set of objects aligned back to back. What are these objects?

   a. Water

   b. Walls

   c. Buckets

   d. Shields

2. Which of the following is gained through using a layered security design over a flat design?

   a. Less deployed equipment

   b. Less cost for the initial deployment

   c. Less specific security measures for specific applications and devices, supporting generic measures to the whole network

   d. More specific security measures for specific devices and applications, and still applying generic measures to the whole network

   e. None of the above

3. End-user policies are not considered part of a layered security model.

   a. True

   b. False

4. Interoffice VoIP communications should be secured using what encryption scheme?

   a. SSL VPN

   b. TLS VPN

   c. IPsec VPN

   d. DES encryption

   e. Packet over Sonet

5. Hardening an application server should include which of the following?

    a. Reduced operating system footprint

    b. MD5 checksum validation for all binaries

    c. Authentication, authorization, and accounting schemes

    d. All of the above

17

Implementing a
Multilayered VoIP and
SIP Security Solution

Chapter summary

When dealing with any security solution, a layered design always supports a greater number of devices within the security matrix compared to a flat design. With a layered security design, the security team can focus on the IP network vulnerabilities and threats and still have the flexibility to create specific mitigation solutions for VoIP devices and applications. This layered solution needs to encompass the whole network, starting from the edge and moving inward. The closer to the device or application, the more specific the security measure is. This reduces the amount of generic attack noise that can be found at the edge of an enterprise network and controls the truly important traffic at the destination. Think of it as if the security system is chipping away at the attacks, piece by piece, as they travel through the network. If there is anything left when an attack gets to the target device, the security solutions deployed at the devices can remove the small bits that remain.

The following list summarizes the suggested recommendations that should be reviewed before a SIP-based VoIP and UC deployment design is complete:

- The enterprise network should be partitioned into a separate VoIP and data network through the use of VLANs.

- SIP over UDP should be disabled and not used.

- SIP over TLS should be used as much as possible.

- When SIP over TLS is not supported, SIP over TCP should be used.

- All endpoint devices should be required to register with a proxy or SBC before the device can access any VoIP or UC service.

- Registration should use an MD5 hash for password encryption.

- Only authorized remote VoIP and UC devices should be allowed VoIP and UC sessions.

- All VoIP and UC services must pass through a VoIP-aware firewall or SBC.

- If wireless is used, WPA2 should be enabled for data encryption.

- If wireless is used, additional encryption at layer 4 should be enabled.

- VoIP and UC network and application devices should use strong authentication through the use of certificates and two-factor authentication.

- Policies should be put into place that dictate how and why an end user can access the VoIP and UC network and the data that resides within that network.

- SLAs should be written to hold the carrier responsible for any breach if one ever happens, as the enterprise will have no control over the remote network.

- All network devices and applications, as well as VoIP and UC service appliances, must log all events and access to a centralized location.

Appendix A: Answers

Use this appendix to check your answers to the Knowledge Check questions.

Table of Contents

Knowledge Check 1-1: Introduction to Unified Communications 394

Knowledge Check 2-1: Elements of Unified Communications 395

Knowledge Check 3-1: The Impact of Convergence, VoIP, and SIP 397

Knowledge Check 4-1: Current Unified Communications Landscape 399

Knowledge Check 5-1: Critical Business Applications and Processes 400

Knowledge Check 6-1: Solving Business Challenges 403

Knowledge Check 7-1: Mapping the Solution to Technology 406

Knowledge Check 8-1: Building a Measurable Financial ROI with KPIs 408

Knowledge Check 9-1: Conducting a Unified Communications
Proof-of-Concept Pilot Project 411

Knowledge Check 10-1: Creating a Unified Communications
Project Statement of Work 413

Knowledge Check 11-1: Conducting Unified Communications
Systems Integration 415

Knowledge Check 12-1: Applications Integration with Endpoint Devices 417

Knowledge Check 13-1: VoIP Threats and Vulnerabilities 418

Knowledge Check 14-1: Best Practices for VoIP Security 419

Knowledge Check 15-1: SIP Threats and Vulnerabilities 420

Knowledge Check 16-1: Best Practices for SIP Security 421

Knowledge Check 17-1: Implementing a Multilayered VoIP
and SIP Security Solution 422

A | Answers to Knowledge Check Questions

Knowledge Check 1-1: Introduction to Unified Communications

1. Which of the following is NOT a key capability of UC?

   a. **Paging services**

   b. Instant messaging

   c. Presence notification

   d. Multimedia conferencing

2. Which are the two companies that formed the ICA?

   a. Nortel and SAP

   b. SAP and Microsoft

   c. Oracle and Microsoft

   d. **Nortel and Microsoft**

3. What activity will drive business success for UC?

   a. Lower IT operating expense

   b. New, inexpensive IP phones

   c. Convergence of data and voice networks

   d. **Streamlining of business processes involving human interaction**

4. Which of the following is a key element of UC?

   a. Networks

   b. Business applications

   c. Communications channels

   d. **All of the above**

5. Which market influencers will be critical to the adoption of UC?

   a. System integrators

   b. Enterprise voice vendors

   c. Enterprise IT organization

   d. Enterprise application vendors

   e. **All of the above**

6. UC is focused on real-time communications.

   a. True

   b. False

7. UC will eliminate the need for e-mail and voice mail.

   a. True

   b. False

8. UC allows users more control of their communications channels.

   a. True

   b. False

Knowledge Check 2-1: Elements of Unified Communications

1. Which of the following is a standard presence status?

   a. Active

   b. Connected

   c. On the phone

   d. All of the above

2. When a user is logged on to a multimedia PC client or multimedia Web client, and no keyboard or mouse activity is detected for a predetermined amount of time, which presence state transition occurs?

   a. From Available to Unavailable

   b. From Connected to Unavailable

   c. From Unavailable to Connected

   d. From Active to Connected-Inactive

A
Answers to Knowledge
Check Questions

3. Which type of IM message is NOT included in the Internet Engineering Task Force (IETF) specification?

   a. Chat

   b. Trailer

   c. Normal

   d. Headline

   e. Groupchat

4. Which of the following is NOT a basic conferencing system requirement?

   a. Sidebar

   b. Discovery

   c. Video transmission

   d. Conference creations

   e. Conference termination

   f. Participant manipulation

5. Which of the following is expected to be supported for view sharing with remote control?

   a. Whiteboard

   b. View sharing

   c. Remote device control

   d. All of the above

6. Which collaboration type enables near real-time viewing of the same Web pages?

   a. Desktop sharing

   b. Co-Web browsing

   c. Application sharing

   d. Remote device control

7. UC increases user control of the user's voice environment.

   a. True

   b. False

8. A single-mode wireless device is supported with fixed mobile convergence.

   a. True

   b. False

9. No PBX configuration changes are required to support remote desktop operations with traditional digital phones.

   a. True

   b. **False**

10. Which of the following is NOT a personality of presence?

    a. Poller

    b. **Stalker**

    c. Fetcher

    d. Watcher

    e. Presentity

    f. Subscriber

Knowledge Check 3-1: The Impact of Convergence, VoIP, and SIP

1. Convergence as it applies to UC includes which of the following?

   a. Protocol convergence

   b. Application convergence

   c. Infrastructure convergence

   d. **All of the above**

2. In what year was the original specification of VoIP published?

   a. 1998

   b. 1988

   c. **1978**

   d. 1968

3. In what year was TCP/IP officially named the transport protocol for major U.S. government agencies such as the DOD?

   a. 2005

   b. 1995

   c. **1985**

   d. 1975

A

Answers to Knowledge Check Questions

A

Answers to Knowledge
Check Questions

4. What was the first specification published for voice over packet protocol?

   a. SIP

   b. NVP

   c. H.323

5. What is the primary function of LDAP?

   a. Access control

   b. Load balancing

   c. Performance reporting

   d. Packet assembly/disassembly

6. SIP is a relatively new, experimental protocol.

   a. True

   b. False

7. SIP is an ASCII-based protocol.

   a. True

   b. False

8. H.323 is a more mature protocol than SIP.

   a. True

   b. False

9. PBX systems must be completely replaced to effectively deploy UC solutions.

   a. True

   b. False

10. Personal mobility allows a user to do which of the following?

    a. Send calls from any location

    b. Receive calls from any location

    c. Send or receive calls on a wide variety of devices

    d. Present only one contact phone number regardless of the number of devices with which that user might communicate

    e. All of the above

Knowledge Check 4-1: Current Unified Communications Landscape

1. Which two products dominate the enterprise productivity tools market?

   a. Lotus Notes and Yahoo! Mail

   b. Yahoo! Mail and Microsoft Office

   c. Lotus Notes and Microsoft Office

   d. Microsoft Office and Adobe Acrobat Reader

2. Which feature(s) are required to enable PBXs to work cooperatively in a UC ecosystem?

   a. Twinning

   b. Call forwarding

   c. Remote call control

   d. All of the above

3. Which of the following products is designed specifically for the SMB market?

   a. Lotus Sametime

   b. Nortel Software Communication System

   c. Microsoft Office Communications Server 2007

4. Which of the following vendors has appeared most frequently in the Leaders quadrant of the Gartner Magic Quadrant for UC?

   a. IBM

   b. Nortel

   c. Oracle

   d. Microsoft

5. Which of the following is a limited capability of Microsoft Office Communications Server 2007?

   a. Conferencing

   b. Emergency services

   c. Presence management

   d. None of the above

6. Microsoft Office Communications Server 2007 can be used to build federations between enterprises.

   a. **True**

   b. False

7. The greatest value of UC is the reduction of human latency in business processes.

   a. **True**

   b. False

8. UC solutions can dynamically provide phone presence status without integrating with enterprise PBXs.

   a. True

   b. **False**

9. Carriers can effectively deploy UCAAS without having a presence at the customer presence.

   a. True

   b. **False**

10. Which of the following is not a UC requirement?

   a. Voice mail

   b. Presence management

   c. Telephony remote control

   d. **Audio/video conferencing**

Knowledge Check 5-1: Critical Business Applications and Processes

1. Enterprise transformation is similar to business process reengineering.

   a. **True**

   b. False

2. Enterprise transformation integrates which of the following? (Choose two.)

   a. People-to-people communications

   b. Enhanced customer service delivery

   c. Streamlined business processes and work flows

3. Which of the following challenges can be solved by SOA implementations?

   a. Flexibility to change operations based on changing dynamics

   b. Inability to share and access customer data in different repositories

   c. Communications with disparate IT systems, applications, and databases

   d. Inability to reuse software applications in a simple and cost-effective manner

   e. All of the above

4. SOA solutions are typically delivered as middleware software applications.

   a. True

   b. False

5. Organizations that implement a customer service–focused strategy can create a competitive differentiator.

   a. True

   b. False

6. Which of the following is NOT a common customer service challenge that organizations must overcome?

   a. Increasing contact center effectiveness

   b. Increasing contact center operating costs

   c. Mapping customer satisfaction to an overall customer service delivery strategy

   d. Enhancing customer service delivery through multiple modes of communication

   e. All of the above

7. CRM solves which of the following business challenges?

   a. Sales process inefficiencies

   b. Access to real-time financials

   c. Manual sales order entry processing

   d. Analysis of customer purchasing history and buying patterns

   e. None of the above

Answers to Knowledge
Check Questions

A

8. Enhanced customer service delivery requires a back-end CRM application and system, providing customer service agents with real-time access to customer information.

   a. **True**

   b. False

9. SCM challenges are related to which of the following?

   a. Cycle time reduction

   b. Lowering operational costs

   c. Implementing JIT inventory

   d. Implementing JIT manufacturing

   e. **All of the above**

10. CFOs track operational costs in the supply chain for which of the following reasons?

    a. To track cost of goods sold

    b. To determine when price increases may be needed

    c. Because they lack confidence in financial reporting information provided

    d. **Both A and B**

    e. None of the above

11. ERP systems are best suited for small- to medium-sized businesses.

    a. True

    b. **False**

12. Which challenge is the most important when trying to incorporate ERP systems into critical decision making?

    a. **Access to real-time financials**

    b. Inability to generate and obtain accurate financial reporting

    c. Inability to make sound business decisions based on financial priorities

    d. Inability to obtain financial cost elements and financial performance throughout the enterprise

    e. None of the above

13. Sales force automation is most concerned with shrinking which of the following?

    a. Cost of goods sold

    b. Size of the sales force

    c. Sales order data entry time

    d. Sales cycle time from start to close

    e. None of the above

14. Sales professionals typically have which of the following challenges to overcome?

    a. Time

    b. Inability to access sales order entry system remotely

    c. Real-time access to sales management for approvals on discounts

    d. Real-time access to subject matter experts and technical specialists during presales

    e. All of the above

Knowledge Check 6-1: Solving Business Challenges

1. Which of the following is not a potential benefit of UC enablement?

    a. Reduced real estate costs

    b. Reduced training expenses

    c. Cycle time reduction in decision making

    d. Real-time collaboration with team members

    e. Increased complexity of IT and decreased productivity

2. How can UC enablement enhance customer loyalty?

    a. By providing real-time access to sales professionals

    b. By offering lower cost customer service delivery solutions

    c. By providing presence and availability and IM chat functionality on a Web site

    d. All of the above

    e. None of the above

3. SOA is a new way to develop and deliver software applications and solutions based on software modules that are reusable.

    a. True

    b. False

4. SOA combines people-to-people communications, processes, and which of the following?

   a. Information

   b. Software modules

   c. Cost of goods sold

   d. Application programming interfaces (APIs)

   e. None of the above

5. An organization can implement an enhanced customer service delivery strategy by doing which of the following?

   a. Implementing a back-end CRM application and system

   b. Distinguishing between high-value versus low-value customers

   c. Diverting high-value customers to preferred or VIP customer service agents

   d. Diverting low-value customers to self-service Web sites and automated attendants

   e. All of the above

6. Investments in customer service solutions and technologies can be cost justified with a financial return on investment analysis.

   a. True

   b. False

7. CRM applications data warehouse which of the following?

   a. Real-time financials

   b. Current product inventory levels

   c. Manufacturing production schedules

   d. Customer purchasing history information

   e. None of the above

8. If an organization does not have a back-end CRM application or system, it cannot build an enhanced customer service strategy.

   a. True

   b. False

9. In SCM, which of the following KPIs or metrics is focused on elimination of human delay or latency in business decision making?

a. Cost of supplies

b. **Cycle time reduction**

c. Lower cost of goods sold

d. Cost of distribution and shipping

e. None of the above

10. When communicating using VoIP and UC with your business partners, suppliers, and distributors, you must do which of the following?

a. Define a security policy to allow VoIP and SIP protocols through both organization's IP firewalls

b. Identify who and what endpoint devices will be allowed to communicate using UC solutions

c. Extend the federation beyond your organization to allow VoIP and SIP protocols to permeate firewalls

d. Enable UC applications such as presence and availability, IM chat, audio and video conferencing, and collaboration

e. **All of the above**

11. ERP systems provide real-time access to accurate financial information for business managers to do what?

a. Plan for fiscal year budgeting

b. Analyze annual profits and losses

c. Analyze annual growth in relation to overhead

d. Determine revenue growth from previous fiscal year

e. **Make critical business decisions based on financial priorities and impact**

12. ERP systems do not provide granular financial cost elements or information about a business function or process.

a. True

b. **False**

13. Shrinking the sales cycle can generate revenue and profit faster for an organization.

a. **True**

b. False

A

Answers to Knowledge Check Questions

14. Which of the following provides a UC productivity enhancement for sales professionals?

   a. CRM applications integrated with customer service

   b. Manual data entry into the sales order entry system back at the branch office

   c. Manual, case-by-case approvals from sales managers for customer discounts

   d. Real-time access to presales support specialists, subject matter experts, and technical specialists via presence, availability, IM chat, and collaboration

   e. None of the above

Knowledge Check 7-1: Mapping the Solution to Technology

1. UC enablement encompasses all these functions except which of the following?

   a. Collaboration

   b. Unified messaging

   c. Presence and availability

   d. IM chat, voice, text messaging

   e. Audio and video conferencing

2. Cycle time reduction is a benefit provided by UC enablement in many business applications and processes.

   a. True

   b. False

3. What is the proper sequence of events for solving business challenges with convergence and UC enablement solutions?

   a. Functional requirements, identify business challenge, technical requirements

   b. Technical requirements, functional requirements, technology solutions mapping

   c. Functional requirements, technical requirements, technology solutions mapping

   d. Identify product and services solutions, functional requirements, technical requirements

   e. None of the above

4. SOA applications integrate people-to-people communications with new streamlined processes but cannot access data in real time.

   a. True

   b. False

5. Enhanced customer service delivery strategies typically include which of the following?

   a. Offshore contact center service agents

   b. Multimodal UC-enabled contact center

   c. Preferred VIP agents servicing high-value VIP customers

   d. Differentiated services for high-value versus low-value customers

   e. All of the above

6. Which of the following UC enablement functions can best shrink project time when multiple project team members are involved?

   a. SMS text messaging

   b. IM chat conversations

   c. Real-time collaboration

   d. Real-time presence and availability

   e. Audio conferencing and video conferencing

7. In SCM, which of the following can affect the cost of goods sold using technology and UC enablement?

   a. Providing an enhanced customer service delivery strategy

   b. Streamlining sales order entry, inventory, and purchasing processes

   c. Implementing quality assurance procedures that require human inspection and sign-off approval

   d. Negotiating more favorable costs in real time with suppliers to fulfill an emergency rush order for a high-value customer

   e. None of the above

8. CRM applications can provide sales professionals with valuable customer purchasing history information and discounts offered previously. This is of no value to the sales professional, and slows down the sales cycle.

   a. True

   b. False

9. ERP financial systems provide business unit and corporate financial managers with the information they need to make sound decisions based on financial priorities.

   a. True

   b. False

10. In SFA, UC enablement can be implemented internally for presales support personnel and externally for customers. Which of the following should not be implemented when using SFA externally with customers?

   a. Real-time collaboration to answer customer inquiries

   b. Real-time access to technical or subject matter experts

   c. Opening and extending UC federations between companies

   d. Presence and availability between sales representatives direct to the customer

   e. **Presence and availability to all presales support team members direct to the customer**

11. Why is SOA application integration, coupled with UC enablement, more effective?

   a. SOA incorporates people-to-people communications in the application itself.

   b. SOA, integrated with UC enablement, embeds UC functionality within the process itself.

   c. SOA integrates streamlined processes with real-time information access, and UC functionality can deliver it.

   d. SOA Web Services delivery is simple and easy through a browser, and real-time UC communications can be embedded in the Web site.

   e. **All of the above.**

12. Financial KPIs and metrics can be extracted from ERP systems in the form of a real-time financial dashboard for business managers and financial executives.

   a. **True**

   b. False

Knowledge Check 8-1: Building a Measurable Financial ROI with KPIs

1. Many organizations require financial justification to make a major technology investment. Forrester Consulting's financial justification approach for technology investment is called:

   a. Cost benefit analysis

   b. **Total Economic Impact**

   c. Financial ROI justification

   d. Forrester Consulting ROI Model

   e. None of the above

2. For every cost savings element, there might be an equivalent cost element for UC enablement.

   a. **True**

   b. False

3. Which of the following individuals does not usually participate in UC business decision making for an organization?

   a. CIO

   b. CFO

   c. **Desktop systems analyst**

   d. Director of networking and security

   e. Director of telecommunications and voice services

4. Examining the cost savings from replacing current technologies and cost elements with UC enablement is called examining the total cost of ownership.

   a. **True**

   b. False

5. Which of the following is not a UC benefit?

   a. **Increased costs for software licensing requirements**

   b. On-premise–based audio and video conferencing services

   c. Lower real estate costs through transformation of workforce

   d. Enhanced people-to-people communications, using presence, availability, and instant messaging

   e. Reduced travel expenses for conducting business meetings and internal training through UC

6. _____ expenditures are required to pay for monthly SG&A overhead expenses, such as office lease payments and utility bills.

   a. Office

   b. Capital

   c. **Operational**

   d. Software and hardware

   e. Travel and entertainment

7. When conducting a financial ROI calculation, you must capture all cost elements and all cost savings that can be derived from UC enablement.

   a. True

   b. False

8. If the ROI value is the ratio of money gained or lost on an investment relative to the amount of money invested, then an ROI value of less than 100 percent results in a favorable result.

   a. True

   b. False

9. Which of the following purchases typically requires a financial ROI model and justification if that purchase is to be made in the same fiscal year?

   a. OPEX

   b. CAPEX

   c. Lease

   d. Credit

   e. None of the above

10. Net present value calculations are needed because of the time value of money variable.

   a. True

   b. False

11. If an organization can obtain a financial ROI from UC enablement but it takes more than two fiscal years to break even, what should that organization do?

   a. Wait two years before deploying

   b. Cancel the UC enablement project

   c. Obtain funding approval from the board of directors

   d. Develop a phased migration plan that spreads out CAPEX and OPEX payments over three fiscal years so that negative returns are minimized

   e. None of the above

12. You should never invite the CFO to participate in a UC enablement business decision.

   a. True

   b. False

Knowledge Check 9-1: Conducting a Unified Communications Proof-of-Concept Pilot Project

1. Which of the following is not a benefit of conducting a UC proof-of-concept pilot project?

   a. Mitigates any risk prior to production deployment

   b. Allows an organization to define best practices for future deployments

   c. **Requires that funds be committed for the UC proof-of-concept pilot project**

   d. Provides valuable cost, effort, savings, and complexity information for future deployments

   e. Supports a cooperative and collaborative implementation effort within all disciplines of an IT organization

2. The greater the need to identify financial ROI cost savings, the greater the scope and complexity of the UC enablement implementation.

   a. **True**

   b. False

3. Why should an organization include the UC pilot project requirements definition in a UC proof-of-concept pilot project?

   a. Minimizes risk

   b. Project budget is needed

   c. Line-of-business champion needs to build a financial ROI model and obtain acceptance from the CFO if needed

   d. **Forces a detailed analysis and solution for a unique business challenge that can be solved with UC enablement**

   e. None of the above

4. Which of the following steps is not included in UC pilot project implementation?

   a. **Map the solution to technology**

   b. Review and validate results of the financial ROI

   c. Define KPIs and metrics aligned to a financial ROI

   d. Build a financial ROI model with actual cost elements

   e. Define UC proof-of-concept project goals and objectives

5. A UC proof-of-concept pilot project does not need a line-of-business champion and can be driven by the IT organization.

   a. True

   b. **False**

6. _____ risk is an important task when an organization is deciding whether or not to pursue a UC proof-of-concept pilot project.

   a. Studying

   b. Defining

   c. **Minimizing**

   d. Maximizing

   e. Understanding

7. A KPI or metric must be quantifiable and measurable to have validity in a proof-of-concept pilot project.

   a. **True**

   b. False

8. Which of the following is not an example of a measurable KPI or metric?

   a. Time

   b. Sales cycle time

   c. SG&A overhead

   d. Revenue per month

   e. **Productivity enhancement**

9. How do you fold the cost of a UC proof-of-concept pilot project into the budget if you do not have CAPEX to spend?

   a. Wait until next fiscal year but budget for it this year

   b. See if other cost centers are willing to help contribute to the project budget

   c. **Lease it and use OPEX to pay for the project based on a forecasted financial return**

   d. Convince the CFO to commit to the investment using CAPEX based on the projected financial ROI model

   e. None of the above

10. UC proof-of-concept pilot projects are easier to sell as a first step for organizations considering UC enablement.

    a. **True**

    b. False

Knowledge Check 10-1: Creating a Unified Communications Project Statement of Work

1. Why is it important to identify and solve a business challenge as the foundation of a UC proof-of-concept pilot project?

    a. Measurable KPIs and metrics can be identified.

    b. Measurable KPIs and metrics can be linked to a financial ROI.

    c. It is easier to get a line-of-business champion sponsor if you solve his or her specific business challenge or problem.

    d. Solving a business challenge or problem means the UC solution can positively impact financial performance, revenue, and profitability.

    e. **All of the above.**

2. The larger the UC proof-of-concept pilot project scope, the larger the SOW and funding required to obtain a positive financial ROI.

    a. **True**

    b. False

3. Why should an organization include part 1 of the UC pilot project requirements definition step in a UC proof-of-concept pilot project?

    a. It minimizes risk.

    b. Project budget is needed.

    c. A line-of-business champion needs to build a financial ROI model and obtain acceptance from the CFO if needed.

    d. **It forces a detailed analysis and solution for a unique business challenge that can be solved with UC enablement.**

    e. None of the above.

4. Which of the following steps is not included in part 2 of the UC pilot project implementation?

   a. **Map the solution to technology**

   b. Review and validate results of the financial ROI

   c. Define KPIs and metrics aligned to a financial ROI

   d. Build a financial ROI model with actual cost elements

   e. Define UC proof-of-concept project goals and objectives

5. A UC proof-of-concept pilot project does not need a line-of-business champion and can be driven by the IT organization.

   a. True

   b. **False**

6. _____ risk is an important task when an organization is deciding on whether or not to pursue a UC proof-of-concept pilot project.

   a. Studying

   b. Defining

   c. Maximizing

   d. **Minimizing**

   e. Understanding

7. A KPI or metric must be quantifiable and measurable to have validity in a proof-of-concept pilot project.

   a. **True**

   b. False

8. Which of the following is not an example of a measurable KPI or metric?

   a. Time

   b. Sales cycle time

   c. SG&A overhead

   d. Revenue per month

   e. **Productivity enhancement**

9. How do you fold the cost of a UC proof-of-concept pilot project into the budget if you do not have CAPEX to spend?

   a. Wait until next fiscal year but budget for it this year

   b. See if other cost centers are willing to help contribute to the project budget

   c. **Lease it and use OPEX to pay for the project based on a forecasted financial return**

   d. Convince the CFO to commit to the investment using CAPEX based on the projected financial ROI model

   e. None of the above

10. UC proof-of-concept pilot projects are easier to sell as a first step for organizations considering UC enablement.

    a. **True**

    b. False

Knowledge Check 11-1: Conducting Unified Communications Systems Integration

Answer the following questions. Answers to these Knowledge Check questions are located in *Appendix A: Answers to Knowledge Check Questions.*

1. What must be done before effective UC planning can occur?

   a. Purchase PBX licenses

   b. Survey the user community

   c. Purchase Microsoft licenses

   d. **Complete an assessment of the existing environment**

2. What can be integrated into the existing environment to allow non-IP-enabled PBXs to participate in UC?

   a. DSL modem

   b. **Gateway server**

   c. Network registration server

   d. Non-IP-enabled PBXs cannot participate in UC

A

Answers to Knowledge
Check Questions

3. Which role does the Office Communications Server 2007 Proxy server provide?

   a. Routing

   b. Authentication

   c. Header parsing

   d. State management

   e. Connection management

   f. All of the above

4. What must be configured to allow routing calls from the PBX to Office Communications Server 2007?

   a. Q-Sig

   b. Dialing plan

   c. SS7 signaling

   d. Emergency services

5. What is the purpose of personal call assistant on the PBX?

   a. Forward calls to voice mail

   b. Enable automated call distribution

   c. Forward fax messages to a multimedia mailbox

   d. Allow calls to be extended to the twinned Office Communicator 2007 client

6. What does a normalized phone number look like?

   a. 5613462348

   b. +15613472348

   c. (561) 3472348

   d. (561) 347-2348

7. Federation is a trust relationship between multiple SIP domains.

   a. True

   b. False

8. The Office Communications Server 2007 Web client can be used for enterprise voice services.

   a. True

   b. False

9. No configuration changes must be made to Active Directory to implement enterprise voice services with Office Communications Server 2007.

    a. True

    b. False

10. Which of the following is not a valid Office Communications Server 2007 server role?

    a. Telephony server

    b. Collaboration server

    c. IM conferencing server

    d. Web conferencing server

    e. A/V conferencing server

Knowledge Check 12-1: Applications Integration with Endpoint Devices

1. Which of the following are considered local endpoint devices?

    a. Tablet

    b. Laptop

    c. IP phone

    d. Desktop computer

    e. All of the above

2. Which of the following can be considered mobile endpoint devices?

    a. Tablet

    b. Laptop

    c. IP phone

    d. Smartphone

    e. Answers A and B

    f. Answers A, B, and D

3. Which is one goal for a unified endpoint device application?

   a. Use the same code base

   b. Restrict access to a single user

   c. **Have a consistent user interface**

   d. Work on only a select amount of devices

   e. None of the above

4. A PDA can support encrypted wireless VoIP sessions.

   a. **True**

   b. False

5. Which tracking system can be used to monitor a mobile device's location in a building?

   a. GPS

   b. **RFID**

   c. Asset tag

   d. Magnetic sensor

Answers to Knowledge Check Questions

A

Knowledge Check 13-1: VoIP Threats and Vulnerabilities

1. What is a black hat?

   a. A telco engineer

   b. A normal end user

   c. **A malicious hacker**

   d. A spy versus spy reference

2. What three things should be understood to make good security decisions?

   a. Network traffic flow

   b. The user-level experience

   c. **Vulnerabilities, risks, and threats**

   d. Authorization, authentication, and availability

3. Everything can be completely secured.

   a. True

   b. **False**

4. What can contain vulnerabilities in a VoIP deployment?

   a. End user

   b. Application

   c. Signaling protocol

   d. Hardware platform

   e. All of the above

5. What kind of vulnerability allows an attacker the ability to listen to calls?

   a. Phishing

   b. Link start

   c. Proxy DoS

   d. Man in the middle

Knowledge Check 14-1: Best Practices for VoIP Security

1. Privacy and confidentiality regulations do not apply to Voice over Internet Protocol (VoIP) and Unified Communications (UC) deployments.

   a. True

   b. False

2. When referencing the security standard called CIA, the A stands for:

   a. Auditing

   b. Availability

   c. Accessibility

   d. Authorization

   e. Authentication

3. A VoIP proxy should be used when:

   a. Access to voice mail is down

   b. An IP phone needs to be replaced

   c. VoIP protocols need to be translated

   d. User authentication through registration is deployed

   e. None of the above

4. What is the easiest way to reduce the chances that a VoIP signaling message cannot be intercepted and read?

   a. Reroute the message path through at least 15 hops

   b. Accelerate the packet speed to make it harder to capture

   c. Use encryption protocols such as Transport Layer Security (TLS)

   d. Obfuscate the message content so that a reader cannot understand the critical information being delivered

   e. None of the above

5. When a vulnerability is found that might affect deployed VoIP or UC applications for devices, the first step in the remediation process is to:

   a. Notify end users and customers of the issue

   b. Evaluate the risk the vulnerability might cause the enterprise

   c. Gather a list of devices that might be affected by the vulnerability

   d. Start deploying a new patch of code onto the affected devices or applications

Knowledge Check 15-1: SIP Threats and Vulnerabilities

1. Which transport protocols does SIP use? (Choose two.)

   a. TCP

   b. UDP

   c. ICMP

   d. SNMP

2. Which SIP request code is used when sending a call request?

   a. INVITE

   b. CANCEL

   c. CALLING

   d. REGISTER

   e. SUBSCRIBE

3. SIP is encrypted by default.

   a. True

   b. False

4. Which applications use SIP?

   a. Presence

   b. Video over IP

   c. Instant messaging

   d. Voice over Internet Protocol (VoIP)

   e. All of the above

5. Which is the most widely exploited vulnerability in SIP?

   a. Packet breakdown

   b. Social engineering

   c. Message manipulation

   d. Flooding denial of service

Knowledge Check 16-1: Best Practices for SIP Security

1. Which password encryption protocol is recommended for use with a SIP deployment?

   a. MD5

   b. SSL

   c. TLS

   d. 3DES

2. Which applications can be supported in a SIP deployment?

   a. Voice

   b. Video

   c. E-mail

   d. Messaging

   e. All of the above

3. Which protocol is used to signal SIP media sessions?

   a. H.264

   b. RTP

   c. SDP

   d. TCP

4. Which transport protocol is considered to have higher availability?

   a. SIP

   b. **TCP**

   c. UDP

   d. HTTP

   e. ICMP

5. Using SIP instead of H.323 as the signaling protocol allows an enterprise to ignore VoIP-based compliance laws and regulations.

   a. True

   b. **False**

Knowledge Check 17-1: Implementing a Multilayered VoIP and SIP Security Solution

1. A layered security design can be compared with a set of objects aligned back to back. What are these objects?

   a. Water

   b. **Walls**

   c. Buckets

   d. Shields

2. Which of the following is gained through using a layered security design over a flat design?

   a. Less deployed equipment

   b. Less cost for the initial deployment

   c. Less specific security measures for specific applications and devices, supporting generic measures to the whole network

   d. **More specific security measures for specific devices and applications, and still applying generic measures to the whole network**

   e. None of the above

3. End-user policies are not considered part of a layered security model.

   a. True

   b. **False**

4. Interoffice VoIP communications should be secured using what encryption scheme?

   a. SSL VPN

   b. TLS VPN

   c. IPsec VPN

   d. DES encryption

   e. Packet over Sonet

5. Hardening an application server should include which of the following?

   a. Reduced operating system footprint

   b. MD5 checksum validation for all binaries

   c. Authentication, authorization, and accounting schemes

   d. All of the above

Glossary

A

Acceptable use policy (AUP)
A policy statement, driven by human resources and IT, for all users who have access to organizational IT assets. AUPs define what is and is not acceptable when using organizational IT assets.

Access control
The ability to control a process, application, device, or user in accessing information data.

Active Directory directory services
Developed by Microsoft; the primary repository that stores user identity and access control information providing access to services throughout the environment. Active Directory acts as the organization's directory services listing, access control authentication keeper, and domain naming service.

Application convergence
The transformation of disparate applications from stand-alone islands of automation to a homogenous environment with a single end-user interface.

Applications-aware network
A quality of service (QoS)-aware network that can distinguish high-priority network traffic based on the application type and data that it carries.

Application layer gateway (ALG)
A security component that can be used for VoIP and UC protocols to allow them access through firewalls without a loss of services or features.

Application Module Link (AML)
Path across which control signals are delivered to the Nortel Communications Server 1000 from an application server.

Asset tag
A tag that identifies an object's ownership, tracking information, and use.

Associated Set Assignment (AST)
PBX extension number to which a particular feature applies.

Availability
System up-time, expressed as a percentage: total up-time divided by total amount of time.

B

Black hat
A hacker or malicious user whose intent is to use vulnerabilities to harm, steal, blackmail, or create chaos.

Business process reengineering
A management approach to solving inefficiencies in current business processes and functions.

C

Call detail records (CDR)
Computer record that contains activity associated with a communications session.

Capital expenditures (CAPEX)
The total amount of cash used to purchase assets for the business.

Cash flow
The amount of cash received and spent by a business during a defined period of time, often tied to a specific project.

CIA
Acronym for confidentiality, integrity, and availability, benchmarks for information system evaluation.

Coadaptation
The mutually beneficial process in which two companies modify their individual intellectual property to provide increased value to end users.

Codec
A device or program capable of encoding and/or decoding a digital data stream or signal.

Collaboration
Real-time multimedia communications that allow individuals to share resources such as applications, documents, and other resources where all individuals can control the shared desktop equally.

Communications-aware application
An application is built by developers knowing what communications medium or method is being used (for example, short message service [SMS] text messaging is an application built for short and concise text messaging using cell phones and personal digital assistant [PDA] devices, whereas a Web-enabled application is built for Web browsers as an end-user interface).

Communications channel
Any path through which one or more individuals interact with each other.

Conferencing
Real-time communication between two or more individuals.

Confidentiality
The requirement to protect and secure data or information, particularly privacy data or information.

Converged desktop
A method that enables users to control voice, video, and data communications directly from a desktop computer, including telephones on a PBX system.

Cost of goods sold
The aggregation of all cost elements, including labor, materials, overhead, and depreciation.

Co-Web browsing
Allows endpoints in a multimedia session to visit the same Web pages in nearly real time.

Critical success factor
A result or milestone that must be achieved in a project.

Customer acquisition
The process of developing new customers.

Customer experience management
The ongoing management of an organization's customers and their experience with the organization.

Customer lifetime value
The long-term financial returns that an organization can expect from a customer who brings repeat business.

Customer relationship management (CRM)
Part of an overall customer service–focused strategy in which CRM applications and tools allow sales, marketing, customer service, and other departments within an organization to analyze customers' buying and purchasing history.

Customer retention
The process of satisfying people who buy or use an organization's products or services.

Customer satisfaction (CSAT)
A metric used to measure and quantify customer satisfaction with the organization's goods or services.

Customer service (CS)
The act of assisting people who buy or use an organization's products or services in presales, sales, and postsales, and supporting resources that the organization provides to its customers.

Cycle time
The time it takes to perform a single task, function, or process.

D

Delivery, fulfillment, and logistics
The shipping of finished goods and products from the manufacturer to the customer.

Denial of service (DoS)
An attack on a device or application with the intent of disabling the device or one of its functions or services.

Disaster recovery plan (DRP)
A plan that complements a business continuity plan where the DRP focuses on the actual recovery and restoration of prioritized, mission-critical applications and services in a disaster or crisis situation (for example, flood, fire, and so on). Specific instructions and recovery procedures are typically defined in a DRP plan such that the disaster recovery team can recover mission-critical applications and processes within an acceptable amount of time.

Distribution network
The shipping and transportation infrastructure within an SCM infrastructure.

Dual tone multifrequency (DTMF)
Used for telephone signaling over the line in the voice frequency band to the PBX or carrier central office

E

Employee satisfaction (ESAT)
A metric used to measure and quantify employee satisfaction with the organization.

Endpoint device
Any device used by an end user to access the enterprise network.

Enterprise resource planning (ERP)
A fully integrated financial system and application that incorporates software modules for different functions and processes.

Enterprise transformation
Business analysis that identifies inefficiencies and replaces them with streamlined processes that include embedded people-to-people communication solutions within the overall solution.

F

Federation
A closed IP networking infrastructure that supports VoIP and SIP-enabled applications within a single domain.

Fixed mobile convergence
Provides the same connectivity to applications whether the user is located on the enterprise premise, or is connected to a mobile communications carrier.

Fully qualified domain name (FQDN)
An unambiguous name that specifies the exact location within the Domain Name System tree hierarchy through a top level and the root name server.

Functional requirements
Desired results (processes or procedures) determined by directly interviewing end users.

G

Gateway
A bridge between two divergent technologies or environments.

Generation Y or Echo Generation
Persons between the ages of 12 and 30 who were born in the United States.

Global Positioning System (GPS)
A satellite-based tracking system that can triangulate the location of any object that has, or is connected to, a GPS receiver.

Gray hat
A grey hat is a hacker that will eventually announce the vulnerability or exploit but will look to profit from the find before releasing it.

H

H.323
A signaling protocol initially designed for video over IP that was later adapted for Voice over IP. H.323 uses a binary message format that must be decompiled to read.

High-value customers
Customers who generate high-value revenue and profitability for an organization.

Hyperconnected
The state in which anything that can be IP connected will be, creating a virtual world of IP connectivity and communications.

I

Implementation plan
Tasks and deliverables that are mapped to a project plan. The implementation plan serves as the detailed project plan from start to finish.

Information system
A process, procedure, application, network, or environment that handles access to and use of information data.

Infrastructure convergence
The transportation of voice and data network traffic over the same physical media paths.

Innovative Communications Alliance (ICA)
A codevelopment and comarketing business relationship between the industry's two leaders in enterprise VoIP and business software applications, Nortel and Microsoft.

Integrity
Verification that data or information has not been tainted, modified, or altered.

Internal rate of return (IRR)
A financial key performance indicator that defines the efficiency of an investment. This differs from net present value, which is the calculated value of an investment.

J

Just-in-time (JIT) inventory
An SCM best practice reduction in purchasing and inventory holdings and minimization of warehousing.

Just-in-time (JIT) manufacturing
An SCM best practice production and workforce scheduling done in a timely fashion, thus minimizing inventory holdings and human resources.

L

Layered security
A security perimeter design that has multiple trap points that trigger as an attacker gets deeper into the network.

Line-of-business champion
The executive sponsor in a line of business different from the IT organization, who has a business challenge that can be solved with UC enablement.

Local endpoint device
An endpoint device that resides in the enterprise office or home office. The endpoint device rarely moves.

Location and presence status
Real-time services supported by Unified Communications. Linking location with presence status provides a unique, real-time location and time arrival status for critical processes and services that require mobility of end users and products. This service offering can uniquely solve business challenges that require real-time presence and location status updates such as emergency medical services, incident response to crises, real-time delivery services, and so on.

Low-value customers
Customers who do not generate high-value revenue and profitability for a business. Low-value customers can become high-value customers through appropriate sales and marketing campaigns and promotions.

M

Mapping the requirements to a solution
The conversion of functional and technical requirements into a technology and UC enablement solution.

Media Gateway Control Protocol (MGCP)
A signaling and control protocol that communicates between a Voice over IP gateway or soft switch and a media gateway with traditional telephony circuits, such as a DS1.

Mobile endpoint device
An endpoint device that is carried with the end user, either continuously or during trips.

Multimedia Convergence Manager (MCM)
A middleware software module that translates signaling between enterprise system elements and Nortel CS 1000.

Multimodal communications
The act of using multiple communication tools, including fax, e-mail, text messaging, voice call, IM chat, video conferencing, and audio conferencing.

N

Net present value (NPV)
A financial key performance indicator that defines the current monetary value of an investment. A positive NPV means that the investment's value is increasing.

Network-aware applications
Software that adapts to varying environments to achieve acceptable and predictable performance.

Network edge
The name commonly given to the part of the enterprise network that connects to the Internet. The edge is usually the last place in which an enterprise technician can control security for the network.

Network Routing Service (NRS)
Software that provides changes to existing network translations, allowing redirection of certain content.

O

Operational expenditures (OPEX)
Operating expenses and ongoing cost expenditure for a product, business, or system.

Operations
Back-office functions that support an SCM infrastructure.

Organization convergence
The creation of virtual entities that cross corporate boundaries to optimize productivity and produce increased levels of customer satisfaction.

P

Personal call assistant (PCA)
A telephone feature that allows programming of more than one device to ring simultaneously when a call is directed to a supported extension.

Phishing
A tactic used by malicious users to gain private or restricted information from an end user.

Private Branch Exchange (PBX)
A customer premise-based system that provides central management for telephone traffic.

Profit and loss (P&L)
A financial spreadsheet that tracks and monitors revenue, expenses, gross profit margin, and profit and loss.

Project milestone or checkpoint
A completed project task or deliverable that provides critical information to the project team about the project status. A project milestone usually coincides with a major decision point.

Project plan
Framework or schedule for a project's phases, tasks, deliverables, and milestones.

Public Switched Telephone Network (PSTN)
The traditional carrier-provided Public Switched Telephone Network.

R

Radio frequency identification (RFID)

A microchip tracking system with limited range. The RFID microchip can also hold a limited amount of information readable by an RFID antenna.

Remote call control (RCC)

A telephone feature that allows a software client to control the operation of an extension.

Remote device control

Allows a user not physically located at a device to control that device as if the user were local.

Requirements definition

The UC project's functional and technical requirements, mapped to achievable goals and objectives.

Return on investment (ROI)

A financial key performance indicator, expressed as a ratio, that shows the amount of money gained compared to the amount of money invested.

Risk

The probability of occurrence of an event with negative impact on an organization or business.

S

Sales force automation (SFA)

The integration of streamlined presales and sales processes in support of an outside or inside sales force.

Sales, general, and administrative overhead (SG&A)

A general accounting term that captures sales, general, and administrative overhead costs: Revenue minus costs of goods sold minus SG&A overhead equals profit.

Script kiddie

They are not real hackers. They are users that are out to break things because they can. Usually using scripts and applications created and leaked by the black hats, these users are out to truly harm, and usually don't have any idea what they have breached.

Secure Sockets Layer (SSL)

A communications protocol that encrypts its payload using a certificate-based solution.

Securities and Exchange Commission (SEC)

A governing body in the United States that oversees publicly traded companies' compliance with rules about disclosure of financial information to the general public.

Session border gateway (SBG)

A VoIP device that can act as a proxy and signal gateway as well as a way to convert one VoIP protocol to another, such as H.323 to Session Initiation Protocol (SIP). A session border gateway can also be used to inspect VoIP protocol signaling and media packets for malicious content.

Session Initiation Protocol (SIP)

A signaling protocol used primarily for Voice over Internet Protocol (VoIP) and Unified Communications (UC) sessions. SIP uses an HTML-like message format that is easy to read.

Shortened sales cycle
The result of streamlined processes in the sales process, which allows the organization to drive sales and revenue more quickly.

SIP-enabled application
Application that utilizes a simple text-based control protocol that creates, modifies, and terminates sessions with one or more participants.

SIP Proxy
A software application that provides call-routing services in a SIP telephony network.

Smartphones
Cell phones with an operating system that can use applications, including third-party applications.

Statement of work (SOW)
A document that describes all tasks and deliverables to be performed as part of the scope for a project.

Supplier network
The suppliers within an SCM infrastructure.

Supply chain management (SCM)
The incorporation of resources, manufacturing, operations, delivery, fulfillment, and logistics processes for commercial and custom products.

T

Technical requirements
The mapping of a functional requirement that requires technology to fulfill the process.

Threat
Capabilities, intentions, and attack methods of adversaries to exploit, damage, or alter information or an information system, or any circumstance or event with the potential to cause harm to information or to an information system.

Total cost of ownership (TCO)
A financial estimate or budget that shows the total cost of an investment.

Transport Layer Security (TLS)
The successor to SSL. Although there are some differences between the two communications protocols, SSL and TLS work the same way when deployed in a VoIP and UC environment.

Twinning
A method of moving telephone communication from a first device engaged in a call to a second device.

U

UC Business Value Tool v1.5
A financial ROI tool for Nortel voice and Microsoft software environments, developed by Forrester Consulting.

UC enablement
The act of implementing Unified Communications features and functions.

Unified Communications (UC)
An application foundation that enhances individual, workgroup, and organizational productivity by enabling and facilitating integrated control and management of communications channels, networks, systems, and business applications.

Unified Communications as a Service (UCAAS)
Offered by service providers who build and market outsourced VoIP, IP Centrex, and convergence communication solutions. Scalable Unified Communications (UC) service offerings and solutions will be bundled along with VoIP services allowing small and medium-sized businesses to consider an outsourced UC solution.

Unified Messaging (UM)
A messaging system that allows delivery of voice, e-mail, and fax messages to a common mailbox for later retrieval via voice or e-mail systems.

V

Value added server (VAS)
Any server software function that enhances the value of a given product.

View sharing
Sharing presence information of an individual in one organization with all subscribers to that information outside of that organization.

Virtual local area network (VLAN)
A broadcast domain that can be used to separate a network at layer 2 (the switching layer).

Voice mail
A messaging system that allows delivery of voice messages to a storage system for later retrieval.

Vulnerability
A known or unknown security exploit within an application, operating system, protocol, or hardware device.

W

White hat
A white hat is a hacker whose sole purpose is to find the exploit or vulnerability before the black hat so that they can notify the vendors and customers who use the device, application, etc.

Index

A

acceptable use policy (AUP), 224, 425
access control
    applications providing, 49
    business units, 311
    defined, 425
    designing VoIP and UC infrastructure and, 279
    devices, 301
    local vs. mobile devices, 257
    security best practices, 299–300
    tracking and monitoring access to endpoint devices, 261
    VoIP and UC service, 299–300
ack messages, SIP, 54
Active Directory
    defined, 425
    integration with Communications Server 2007, 243–244
    SIP proxies and SBCs and, 365
ADC (Analog to Digital conversion) chips, 270
address book, 240
address of record (AOR), 55
Advanced Encryption Standard (AES), 351–352
AES (Advanced Encryption Standard), 351–352
Alcatel, 75
ALGs (application layer gateways)
    defined, 425
    firewall risks and, 278
    NAT and, 364
    service restrictions and, 377
    SIP security best practices, 363–364
    VoIP security best practices, 308–309
American National Standards Institute (ANSI), 46
AML (Application Module Link)
    configuring, 237
    defined, 425

Analog to Digital conversion (ADC) chips, 270
ANSI (American National Standards Institute), 46
Answer Call function, converged desktop, 23
AOR (address of record), 55
application-based security layer
    designing layered security, 372
    endpoint devices and, 378–379
    VoIP and SIP security layers, 373
application convergence
    defined, 425
    overview of, 49–50
application layer gateways. See ALGs (application layer gateways)
Application Module Link (AML)
    configuring, 237
    defined, 425
applications
    authenticity of, 310
    critical business. See critical business applications
    data integrity and, 303
    dependencies, 387
    endpoint devices and, 253–254
    integrity (SIP), 353–354
    integrity (VoIP), 304
    mobile endpoint devices, 256
    SIP security best practices, 348–349
    SIP threats and vulnerabilities, 327–328
    UC decision makers, 173
    VoIP threats and vulnerabilities, 272
applications-aware network
    convergence and, 90
    defined, 425
application servers
    deploying Office Communication Server 2007 application server, 241–243
    layered security for UC application servers, 387–388

application-specific integrated chips (ASIC), 269
archiving, 240
ASIC (application-specific integrated chips), 269
asset tags
    defined, 425
    tracking endpoint device location, 262
Associated Set Assignment (AST)
    defined, 425
    VoIP/PBX integration and, 234
AST (Associated Set Assignment)
    defined, 425
    VoIP/PBX integration and, 234
attacks. See threats and vulnerabilities
attributes, in presence messages, 26
audio/visual conferencing, 239–240
audit policies
    enforcing enterprise security policies, 312
    software and images, 312–313
AUP (acceptable use policy), 224, 425
authentication
    access authentication, 351–352
    application-based security layer, 379
    availability authentication, 360–361
    endpoint devices, 259–260
    IP-PBX access, 386
    local vs. mobile devices, 257
    SIP threats and vulnerabilities, 337–338
    user authentication, 243, 304, 356–357
    VoIP threats and vulnerabilities, 300
authorization
    endpoint devices, 260
    IP-PBX access, 386
availability
    authentication and, 305
    core devices, 306

defined, 425
emergency services, 306
goals and objectives of, 305
network, 306
network availability best
practices, 360
overview of, 298
risks related to, 279
Avaya
drivers in UC market, 7
SMB market and, 75
telecommunications product
manufacturers, 14

B

B2B collaboration, 59
B2BUA (back-to-back user agent),
54
back-to-back user agent (B2BUA),
54
benefits net present value (BNPV),
188
black hat hackers
defined, 425
overview of, 269
vulnerabilities and, 268
BNPV (benefits net present value),
188
branch offices/remote locations
firewalls and, 380–381
interoffice communications, 382
layered security, 380
NAT (Network Address
Translation), 381
SIP proxies and, 381
breach laws, 307–308, 361
broad-based security layer
designing layered security, 371
VoIP and SIP security layers,
372–373
budgets
aligning project scope to, 222–
223
proof-of-concept pilot project,
207–208
business case, for UC enablement.
See also proof-of-concept pilot
projects
building, 186
cost elements, 175–176
cost savings, 175
decision makers, 173
drivers for UC enablement, 174
integrating UC enablement with
business processes, 177–178
measuring success of, 176

overview of, 173–174
pilot projects and, 199
review, 190–193
SFA example, 176–177, 179–182
UC Business Value Tool v1.5,
182–189
business challenges
aligning project scope to budget,
223
identifying for pilot projects,
215
milestones and checkpoints, 220
phases of UC enablement
projects, 200
solving, 216
business process optimization, 174
business process reengineering
defined, 425
enterprise transformation
compared with, 83
SCM and, 96
business rule sets, ERP systems, 100
business units, controlling access to,
311
bye message, SIP, 54

C

CALEA (Communications
Assistance for Law Enforcement
Act)
SIP compliance with, 361
VoIP compliance with, 307
call detail records. *See* CDR (call
detail records)
caller ID table, configuring, 236
Call Forwarding function,
converged desktop, 24
campus redundancy, SIP, 239
cancel message, SIP, 54
CAPEX (capital expenditures)
business case for UC enablement
and, 173
defined, 425
ROI and, 198
tracking KPIs and metrics for,
206–207
cash flow, 426
Cat 5 standard, ANSI, 46
CDR (call detail records)
Communications Server 2007
support for UC enablement,
240
defined, 426
RCC configuration and, 238
TDM-PBX system security and,
385

VoIP/PBX integration and, 236
cell phones
layered security, 378
as mobile endpoint device, 252
network access from, 380
central repository, standards based,
10
certificates, application-based
security layer, 379
CFO (chief financial officer)
building project team, 224
as UC decision makers, 173
change control policies, 305
change review policies, 312
chat, IM message types, 33
checkpoints and milestones,
220–222, 430
chief financial officer (CFO)
building project team, 224
as UC decision makers, 173
chief information officer (CIO)
building project team, 224
UC decision makers, 173
chips, hardware vulnerabilities, 269
CIA (confidentiality, integrity, and
availability)
availability. *See* availability
confidentiality. *See*
confidentiality
defined, 426
integrity. *See* integrity
overview of, 297–298
VoIP and SIP security and,
378–379
CIO (chief information officer)
building project team, 224
UC decision makers, 173
Cisco
drivers in UC market, 7
role in infrastructure
convergence, 47
Clear Connection function,
converged desktop, 24
CLECs (competitive local exchange
carriers), 339
CNPV (costs per present value), 188
coadaptation
defined, 426
forces driving UC enablement,
8–9
codecs
configuring G.711 codec, 234
defined, 426
vulnerabilities, 284
code vulnerabilities, 271–272
collaboration
defined, 426

tools, 36
UC enablement and, 7
view sharing and, 36–37
communication means, IM, 32
Communications Assistance for
Law Enforcement Act (CALEA)
SIP compliance with, 361
VoIP compliance with, 307
communications-aware
applications
business process integration
and, 66
defined, 426
UC solutions, 229
Vendor solutions, 12
communications channels
defined, 426
real-time exchange of
information, 5
Communication Server 2007. *See*
Office Communications Server
2007
communications, human
communications center, 3
communications, multimodal. *See*
multimodal communications
communication systems
integration, 229–247
Active Directory and, 243–244
assessing existing environment,
231–232
Communication Server 2007
application server
deployment, 241–243
Communications Server 2007
proxy with MCM, 235
normalization to TEL URI
format, 238
RCC configuration and, 237–238
review, 244–247
SIP routing and redundancy
configuration, 238–239
TDM-PBX, IP-PBX, and
softphone integration
requirements, 232–235
Telephony Gateway and
Services component, 235–236
UC enablement, 239–241
company-to-company
communication. *See* B2B
collaboration
compatibility issues, SIP, 350
competitive local exchange carriers
(CLECs), 339
compliance
breach laws, 307–308

CALEA (Communications
Assistance for Law
Enforcement Act), 307, 361
E911 services, 308, 362
HIPAA, 307, 361
ISO 17799/2005, 307, 361
privacy policies and corporate
regulations, 304
rules and regulations, 306
Sarbanes-Oxley (SOX), 307, 361
SIP security best practices,
361–362
Computer Supports
Telecommunications
Applications (CSTA), 11, 22
Conference Call function,
converged desktop, 23
conferencing
Communications Server 2007
support, 239–240
cost savings resulting from UC
enablement, 175
defined, 7, 426
overview of, 34
system requirements, 34–35
confidentiality. *See also* CIA
(confidentiality, integrity, and
availability)
access control, 299–300
authentication, 300
defined, 426
deploying network devices and,
301
overview of, 298–299
regulations and laws and, 302
signaling control, 300–301
SIP security best practices,
346–348
SIP threats and vulnerabilities,
326
connectivity models, SIP, 56–57
contact addresses, IM (instant
messaging), 32
content integrity, SIP, 354–355
content management, presence-
aware applications and, 31
converged clients, 5
converged desktop, 21–24
combining phone and computer,
21–22
defined, 426
key elements in, 22–24
convergence, of voice/data
networks, 43–62
application convergence, 49–50
B2B collaboration, 59

customer service and, 90
federations and company-to-
company communications,
57–58
infrastructure convergence,
46–47
organization convergence, 50–51
overview of, 43
protocol convergence, 47–49
SIP and, 52–57
stages of, 45
VoIP and, 51–52
what it is, 45
core devices
availability (SIP devices), 361
availability (VoIP devices), 306
corporations
regulations, 303–304
securing communications to
branch offices/remote
locations, 380–382
virtual, 57
cost elements
UC Business Value Tool v.1.5
and, 185
UC enablement, 175–176
cost of goods sold
defined, 426
SCM reducing, 96–97
costs
justifying project cost, 198–199
UC enablement-related savings,
175
costs per present value (CNPV), 188
Co-Web browsing, 37, 426
critical business applications
CRM (customer relationship
management), 90–92
CS (customer service), 87–90
enterprise transformation and,
83–84
ERP (enterprise resource
planning), 97–100
overview of, 81
SFA (sales force automation),
101–103
SOA (service-oriented
architecture), 84–87
SRM (supply chain
management), 93–97
critical success factors
budgeting as, 223
defined, 426
mapping solution to technology,
217
milestones and, 220

monitoring, 197
risk minimization and, 203
ROI modeling and, 221
time as, 129
CRM (customer relationship management), 90–92
applications and tools, 91
defined, 427
high-value vs. low-value customers, 92
overview of, 90
CSAT (customer satisfaction)
defined, 427
improved communication and, 176
CS (customer service), 87–90
challenges to, 87
defined, 427
elements in customer-focused strategy, 89–90
SOA and, 85, 87–88
tracking resolution of customer-related issues, 180–181
CSTA (Computer Supports Telecommunications Applications), 11, 22
customer acquisition
CRM and, 123
customer service challenges, 118
customer service driving, 81, 87, 90
defined, 426
strategies for, 91, 121
customer experience management
defined, 426
objectives for, 119
post-sale and ongoing customer service, 115
customer lifetime value
benefits of UC enablement, 174
calculating, 121
CRM and, 150–151
defined, 427
KPIs and metrics for calculating financial impact of, 181
profitability of, 123
customer relationship management. *See* CRM (customer relationship management)
customer retention
CRM and, 91
customized services and, 123
defined, 427
KPIs and metrics for, 181
mapping customer satisfaction to, 87

profitability of, 90, 118
SCM and, 96
SOA and, 86, 149
strategies for, 92, 121
streamlined communications and, 120
customers
high-value, 428
KPIs and metrics tracking resolution of customer-related issues, 180–181
low-value, 429
customer satisfaction (CSAT)
defined, 427
improved communication and, 176
customer service. *See* CS (customer service)
cycle time
defined, 427
of KPIs, 176
purposes of UC enablement, 198

D

DAC (Digital to Analog conversion) chips, 270
DARPA (Defense Advanced Research Projects Agency), 43
data communications
convergence with voice, 1, 45–46
defined, 45
FMC and, 37
history of, 43
multimedia conferencing and, 67
data integrity, 302–303
data networks
convergence with voice. *See* convergence, of voice/data networks
partitioning enterprise networks and, 384
UC decision makers, 173
data piggybacking, protocol vulnerabilities, 273
decision makers
linking project success to ROI, 195
selling project internally and, 218, 221
UC enablement, 173
Defense Advanced Research Projects Agency (DARPA), 43
Deflect Call function, converged desktop, 23

deliverables, project
defining, 202
milestones and checkpoints, 222
overview of, 215–217
delivery, fulfillment, and logistics
defined, 427
sales/revenues metrics and, 177
SCM and, 94
delivery rules, IM (instant messaging), 32
denial of service. *See* DoS (denial of service)
dependencies, application, 387
desktop computers, integration with laptops, 252
desktop interface, application convergence and, 50
desktop productivity vendors, 65–66
devices. *See also* endpoint devices
core device availability, 306
evaluating risks and, 313
IP-PBX authorized device list, 386
user communication, 3
VoIP and UC device deployment, 301
dialing plan, configuring, 234
Digital Signal Processors (DSP)
hardware vulnerabilities and, 269
VoIP and, 270
Digital to Analog conversion (DAC) chips, 270
directors
building project team, 224
UC decision makers, 173
directory services
Active Directory. *See* Active Directory
defined, 5
LDAP (Lightweight Directory Access Protocol), 49–50
disaster recovery plan (DRP)
defined, 427
in enterprise edition of Communication Server 2007, 427
distribution networks
defined, 427
delivery, fulfillment, and logistics, 126
end-to-end supply and delivery, 96
SCM and, 93, 127–128

DNS (Domain Name Server)
  servers
    RCC configuration and, 237
    VoIP/PBX integration and, 236
domain names, VoIP/PBX
  integration, 236
domains, Active Directory/
  Communications Server 2007
  integration, 244
DoS (denial of service)
  defined, 427
  network availability and, 306
  protocol vulnerabilities, 273
  SIP Internet accessibility, 327
  SIP threats and vulnerabilities,
    330–331
DRP (disaster recovery plan)
  defined, 427
  in enterprise edition of
    Communication Server 2007,
    427
DSP (Digital Signal Processors)
  hardware vulnerabilities and, 269
  VoIP and, 270
DTMF (dual tone multifrequency)
  defined, 427
  PBX loss plan and, 235
dual-mode devices, 255
dual tone multifrequency (DTMF)
  defined, 427
  PBX loss plan and, 235
Duet, Microsoft/SAP collaboration,
  12

E

E.164, INFO numbers, 236, 238
E911 services
  emergency services, 308
  SIP compliance with, 362
  SIP security best practices, 362
eavesdropping, SIP threats and
  vulnerabilities, 334–337
Echo Generation (Generation Y),
  120, 428
EDI (Electronic Data Interchange),
  57–58
EEPROM (erasable programmable
  read-only memory), 270
Electronic Data Interchange (EDI),
  57–58
e-mail
  functionality of, 1
  phishing and, 274
emergency services
  availability, 306

E911 services, 308
employees
  KPIs and metrics tracking
    resolution of employee
    retention, 182
  SOA-based applications
    improving employee services,
    85
employee satisfaction. *See* ESAT
  (employee satisfaction)
encryption
  application-based security layer,
    379
  corporate interbranch
    communication, 382
  data integrity and, 304
  endpoint devices, 257–259
  SIP, 350
  SIP best practices, 357–360, 365
  SIP threats and vulnerabilities,
    338
  VoIP best practices, 304, 310
endpoint devices, 249–264
  applications and services
    support, 253
  authentication, 259–260
  authorization, 260
  defined, 427
  desktop/laptop application and
    system integration and, 252
  dual-mode devices, 255
  encryption, 257–259
  layered security, 378
  local, 251, 429
  mobile, 251–252, 429
  mobile applications, 256
  mobile device application and
    system integration, 254
  overview of, 249, 251
  PDAs, 254–255
  project scope and, 199
  registering, 260
  review, 263–264
  security of local vs. mobile
    devices, 257
  SIP-enabled, 195
  smartphones, 255
  tablet computers, 254
  tracking and monitoring,
    260–262
  user interface, 252–253
end-user policy-based security
  layer
  endpoint devices, 380
  VoIP and SIP security layers,
    372–373

end users, building project team
  and, 224
engineers, building project team
  and, 224
enterprise application initiatives
  Microsoft/SAP collaboration,
    12–13
  PeopleSoft and Oracle and, 13
enterprise desktop productivity
  IBM Lotus Sametime, 71–73
  Microsoft Office and IBM Lotus
    Notes as dominant vendors,
    65–66
  Microsoft Office
    Communication Server 2007,
    66–71
enterprise IT consulting companies,
  15
enterprise networks
  accessing from PDAs/cell
    phones, 380
  LANs and WANs and, 251
  logging, 384
  partitioning, 383
  securing corporate
    communication to branch
    offices/remote locations,
    380–382
  SIP security best practices, 362
enterprise resource planning. *See*
  ERP (enterprise resource
  planning)
enterprise transformation, 83–84,
  427
equipment, compatibility issues,
  301
erasable programmable read-only
  memory (EEPROM), 270
ERP (enterprise resource planning),
  97–100
  business value of, 100
  challenges to, 97–98
  defined, 427
  key elements in, 98–99
error
  IM message types, 33
  presence attributes, 26
ESAT (employee satisfaction)
  defined, 427
  identifying business challenges
    and, 215
  improved communication and,
    176
  retaining employees, 177
Exchange Server, as UM solution,
  11

executives. *See also* decision makers
  linking project success to ROI, 195
  selling project internally and, 218, 221
Extensible Markup Language (XML)
  transporting XML messages over SIP sessions, 22
  vulnerabilities, 272
Extensible Messaging and Presence Protocol (XMPP), 58

F

federations
  Communications Server 2007 support, 240
  defined, 428
  overview of, 58–59
  securing between companies, 375–377
  SIP security best practices, 362
  SIP threats and vulnerabilities, 339
  of users into communities, 7
fetcher, presence personalities, 26
file transfer, view sharing and, 37
financial metrics. *See* metrics, financial
financial reports
  ERP systems providing real-time reporting, 100
  SFA and, 103
  UC Business Value Tool v1.5, 186–189
firewalls
  ALG and, 278, 308–309
  branch offices/remote locations and, 380–381
  IP-PBX system, 387
  SIP security best practices, 363
  VoIP security best practices, 308
fixed mobile convergence. *See* FMC (fixed mobile convergence)
fixes, certification of, 313
flooding DoS attacks, 334
FMC (fixed mobile convergence)
  defined, 428
  IMS (IP Multimedia Subsystem) and, 38
  overview of, 37
forests, Active Directory, 244
Forrester Consulting. *See* UC Business Value Tool v1.5

FQDNs (fully qualified domain names)
  defined, 428
  DNS server configuration and, 236
  SIP URI and, 322
fraudulent calls, 274
fulfillment. *See* delivery, fulfillment, and logistics
fully qualified domain names. *See* FQDNs (fully qualified domain names)
functional requirements
  defined, 428
  security and privacy issues and, 215

G

G.7xx codecs
  configuring, 234
  vulnerabilities, 284
Gartner Group, 75–77
gateways. *See also* ALGs (application layer gateways); H.323 protocol
  bridges to older voice platforms, 8
  Communication Server 2007 and, 241–243
  defined, 428
  function of, 4
  SCS 500, 74
  voice/data convergence and, 19
  Voice to Exchange, 267
  VoIP/PBX integration and, 232–233
general manager, UC decision makers, 173
Generate Digits feature, converged desktop, 24
Generation Y (Echo Generation), 120, 428
geographic redundancy, SIP, 239
Global Positioning System (GPS)
  defined, 428
  tracking endpoint device location, 262
goals and objectives
  aligning project scope to budget, 223
  aligning requirements, goals, objectives with PKIs and metrics, 205–206
  availability, 305
  confidentiality, 298–299

customer experience
  management, 119
  integrity, 302
  milestones and checkpoints, 221
  organizational, 84
  pilot projects, 202
  project, 203–205
GPM (gross profit margin), 97
GPS (Global Positioning System)
  defined, 428
  tracking endpoint device location, 262
graphical user interface (GUI)
  Java driving VoIP phone code, 271
  unified user interface for endpoint devices, 252–253
gray hat hackers
  defined, 428
  overview of, 269
gross profit margin (GPM), 97
groupchat, IM message types, 33
GUI (graphical user interface)
  Java driving VoIP phone code, 271
  unified user interface for endpoint devices, 252–253

H

H.225.0 protocol, 280–281
H.235 protocol, 283
H.239 protocol, 283
H.245 protocol, 282
H.26x protocol, 268, 284
H.323 Gatekeeper, 309
H.323 protocol
  communications standards and, 8
  convergence and, 48
  defined, 428
  overview of, 280
  SIP as replacement for, 345
  SIP confidentiality and, 348
  user registration and, 309
  vulnerabilities, 285–286
H.450 protocol, 282–283
H.460 protocol, 284
hackers
  black hat, 425
  gray hat, 428
  malicious users, 275–276
  types of, 269
  white hat, 433
HA (high availability), 306. *See also* availability

hardware
  cost savings resulting from UC enablement, 175
  unauthorized, 277–278
  vulnerabilities, 269–270
headline, IM message types, 33
Health Insurance Portability and Accountability Act (HIPAA), 307, 361
high availability (HA), 306. *See also* availability
high-value customers
  CRM and, 92
  defined, 428
HIPAA (Health Insurance Portability and Accountability Act), 307, 361
HLOC (Home Location), 236
Hold Call function, converged desktop, 24
Home Location (HLOC), 236
home offices
  access control, 300
  securing corporate communication to branch offices/remote locations, 381
HTTP (Hypertext Transfer Protocol), 350
human communications center, 3–4
human factor, threats, 278
human resources, building project team, 224
hyperconnected
  defined, 428
  virtual environment of connected devices, 120
Hypertext Transfer Protocol (HTTP), 350

I

IBM
  communications products of, 8
  IT infrastructure companies, 14
  Lotus product line, 8, 65–66, 71–73
  partner communities, 73
  role in infrastructure convergence, 47
  SMB solutions, 74
ICA (Innovative Communications Alliance), 13, 428
IETF (Internet Engineering Task Force), 345
images, audit policies, 312–313

IM (instant messaging)
  Communications Server 2007 support, 239–241
  defined, 5–6
  key terms, 32–33
  message types, 33
  SIP confidentiality and, 348
  white list and open federations, 58
implementation
  planning, 428
  project milestones and, 222
  selling project internally and, 218, 221
  steps in implementing pilot projects, 202
IMS (IP Multimedia Subsystem), 38
inbox user agent, IM (instant messaging), 33
industry
  risks, 279
  threats, 277
INFO (International Format), 236, 238
information flows, SCM and, 94–95
information, SOA applications for, 86
information systems
  defined, 428
  evaluating CIA for, 297
  threats and, 275
infrastructure convergence
  defined, 428
  overview of, 46–47
Innovative Communications Alliance (ICA), 13, 428
instant inbox, IM (instant messaging), 33
instant messages, 33
instant message service, 33
instant messaging. *See* IM (instant messaging)
instant messaging protocol, 33
Integrated Services Digital Network (ISDN), 232
integrity
  application integrity (SIP), 353–354
  application integrity (VoIP), 304
  change control, 305
  data integrity, 302–303
  defined, 429
  encryption, 304
  goals and objectives, 302
  message and content integrity (SIP), 354–355
  overview of, 298

privacy practices and corporate regulations and, 303
  SIP security best practices, 352–353
  user identity, 303
  validating operating systems, 388
internal rate of return (IRR), 188–189, 429
International Format (INFO), 236, 238
Internet
  infrastructure convergence and, 47
  layered security and, 381
  securing corporate communication to branch offices/remote locations, 381
  SIP threats and vulnerabilities and, 327
Internet Engineering Task Force (IETF), 345
Internet Protocol. *See* IP (Internet Protocol)
interoffice communications, layered security, 382
intrusion detection systems, 310
invite message, SIP, 54
IP backbone network, layered security, 383–384
IP (Internet Protocol)
  authentication of IP phone, 260
  managing TDM-PBX system through, 384–385
IP Multimedia Subsystem (IMS), 38
IP-PBX
  layered security, 385–387
  TDM-PBX, IP-PBX, and Softphone integration requirements, 232–235
IPsec (IP Security)
  securing corporate communication to branch offices/remote locations, 382
  SIP confidentiality and, 348
  VPNs and, 258
IRR (internal rate of return), 188–189, 429
ISDN (Integrated Services Digital Network), 232
ISO 17799/2005, 307, 361
IT administration, building project team, 224
IT (Information Technology)
  infrastructure companies, 14
  UC enablement and, 197

J

Java, VoIP phone code and, 271
JIT (just-in-time) inventory/
  manufacturing
  defined, 429
  operational efficiency and,
    114–115, 126, 130
  sales order system integration
    with, 133, 154
  SCM and, 93, 96
  SCM functional to technical
    requirements mapping,
    156–157
  time sensitivity in production
    scheduling, 126, 130

K

key performance indicators. See
  KPIs (key performance
  indicators)
known threats, 275
known vulnerabilities, 276
KPIs (key performance indicators)
  aligning project scope to budget,
    223
  aligning requirements, goals,
    objectives with PKIs and
    metrics, 205–206
  identifying for pilot projects, 202
  identifying for proof-of-concept
    pilot project, 206–207
  measuring success of UC
    enablement, 176
  milestones and checkpoints and,
    221
  project planning and, 197
  ROI assessment, 171
  SFA example, 176–177, 179–182
  tracking and monitoring, 178

L

LANs (local area networks)
  broad-based security layer, 371
  enterprise networks consisting
    of multiple, 251
laptop computers
  desktop/laptop application and
    system integration, 252
  as mobile endpoint device, 251
laws
  compliance with corporate, 304
  SIP security best practices, 352
  VoIP security best practices, 302

layered security, 369–391
  application-based security layer,
    378–379
  branch offices/remote locations
    and, 380
  CIA (confidentiality, integrity,
    and accessibility), 378–379
  defined, 429
  designing for VoIP and SIP
    infrastructures, 371–373
  endpoint devices and, 378
  end-user security layer, 380
  federations and, 375–377
  firewalls for, 380–381
  Internet and, 381
  interoffice communications and,
    382
  IP backbone networks and,
    383–384
  IP-PBX and VoIP system and,
    385–387
  NAT for, 381
  network access from PDAs/cell
    phones, 380
  overview of, 371
  review, 389–391
  SBCs (session border
    controllers), 382
  service-based security layer, 378
  SIP proxies for, 381
  SIP source restrictions in, 382
  TDM-PBX system and, 384–385
  transport protocols and, 378
  UC application servers and,
    387–388
  VoIP and SIP security policies,
    373–375
LDAP (Lightweight Directory
  Access Protocol), 49–50
lifecycle costs, 185
Lightweight Directory Access
  Protocol (LDAP), 49–50
line-of-business champions
  building project team, 224
  defined, 429
  identifying for pilot projects, 202
  identifying in SOW, 219
  milestones and checkpoints, 221
Live Communication Server 2005
  product line, 10–11
local area networks (LANs)
  broad-based security layer, 371
  enterprise networks consisting
    of multiple, 251
local endpoint devices

applications and services
  support, 253
defined, 429
desktop/laptop application and
  system integration, 252
encryption, 259
overview of, 251
security of local vs. mobile
  devices, 257
unified user interface, 252–253
location and presence status. See
  also presence status
  defined, 429
  for mobile users, 65
logging, enterprise networks, 384
logistics. See delivery, fulfillment,
  and logistics
loss plan, configuring PBX loss
  plan, 234
Lotus, 8
Lotus Notes, 65–66
Lotus Sametime, 71–73
low-value customers
  CRM (customer relationship
    management) and, 92
  defined, 429

M

MADN (Multiple Appearance
  Directory Number), 237
Magic Quadrant (MQ), Gartner
  Group, 75–77
Make Call function, converged
  desktop, 23
malicious users, 275–276
managers. See directors
manufacturing, SCM and, 94
mapping solutions to technologies
  aligning project scope to budget,
    223
  critical success factors, 217
  defined, 429
  milestones and checkpoints, 220
  UC enablement and, 144
MARP (Multiple Appearance
  Redirection Prime), 237
MCM (Multimedia Convergence
  Manager)
  defined, 429
  installing/configuring
    Communications Server 2007
    proxy with MCM, 235
MCS (Multimedia Communications
  Server), 7, 10
MCU (multipoint control unit), 53

MD5 (message digest 5)
application-based security layer, 378–379
authentication, 351–352
media content, data integrity and, 303
media control, SIP, 350–351
Media Gateway Control Protocol. See MGCP (Media Gateway Control Protocol)
Media Server Control Markup Language (MSCML), 35
message digest 5 (MD5)
application-based security layer, 378–379
authentication, 351–352
message formats, SIP threats and vulnerabilities, 337
message header rewriting, protocol vulnerabilities, 273
message integrity, SIP security best practices, 354–355
message tampering, SIP threats and vulnerabilities, 328
metrics, financial
aligning project scope to budget, 223
aligning requirements, goals, objectives with PKIs and metrics, 205–206
assigning to KPIs, 178
identifying for pilot projects, 202
identifying for proof-of-concept pilot project, 206–207
milestones and checkpoints, 221
project planning and, 197
SFA (sales force automation), 176–177, 179–182
tracking and monitoring UC KPIs, 178
MGCP (Media Gateway Control Protocol)
defined, 429
VoIP threats and vulnerabilities, 267, 290–291
Microsoft
communications products, 8
Communicator Web Access, 70
Exchange Server, as UM solution, 11
ICA (Innovative Communications Alliance), 13–14
as IT infrastructure company, 14
Live Communication Server 2005 product line, 10–11

Office, 65–66
Office Communications Server 2007. See Office Communications Server 2007
Office Outlook 2005, 29–31
SMB solutions, 74
UC Business Value Tool v.1.5 and, 183, 186
milestones and checkpoints, 220–222, 430
mobile communications
driving communications market, 7
FMC and, 37–38
mobile convergence, fixed. See FMC (fixed mobile convergence)
mobile endpoint devices
application and system integration, 254
applications, 256
defined, 429
encryption, 257–259
overview of, 251–252
PDAs, 254–255
protocol convergence and, 48
security of local vs. mobile devices, 257
smartphones, 255
tablet computers, 254
mobile users, access control, 300
mobility, SIP features, 53
modems, managing TDM-PBX systems, 384
money flows, SCM and, 94–95
monitoring
KPIs for, 178
VoIP and UC devices, 301
MPLS (Multi-Protocol Layer Switching), 47
MQ (Magic Quadrant), Gartner Group, 75–77
MSCML (Media Server Control Markup Language), 35
Multimedia Convergence Manager (MCM)
defined, 429
installing/configuring Communications Server 2007 proxy with MCM, 235
multimodal communications
consumers and, 120
customer service and, 87
defined, 429
security challenges, 4
VoIP and UC support for, 89

Multiple Appearance Directory Number (MADN), 237
Multiple Appearance Redirection Prime (MARP), 237
multipoint control unit (MCU), 53
Multi-Protocol Layer Switching (MPLS), 47

N

NAT (Network Address Translation), 362
branch offices/remote locations and, 381
SIP security best practices, 364
transport-protocol security layer, 371
net present value (NPV)
defined, 430
UC Business Value Tool v1.5 reports, 187–189
Network Address Translation. See NAT (Network Address Translation)
network availability, SIP security best practices, 360
network-aware applications
convergence and, 90
defined, 430
network edge
branch offices/remote locations and, 380
defined, 430
securing, 257
Network Routing Service. See NRS (Network Routing Service)
networks
accessing from PDAs/cell phones, 380
availability, 306
security of local vs. mobile devices, 257
SIP security best practices, 362
Network Voice Protocol (NVP), 51
normal, IM message types, 33
normalization, to TEL URI format, 238
Nortel
drivers in UC market, 7
ICA (Innovative Communications Alliance), 13–14
integration with Communication Server 2007, 69

MCS (Multimedia Communications Server), 7, 10
role in infrastructure convergence, 47
SCS (Software Communication System), 74–75
UC Business Value Tool v.1.5 and, 183, 185
in UC market, 10
notification, security enforcement, 313
NPA (Number Plan Areas), 236
NPV (net present value)
defined, 430
UC Business Value Tool v1.5 reports, 187–189
NRS (Network Routing Service)
defined, 430
RCC configuration and, 237
VoIP/PBX integration and, 236
Number Plan Areas (NPA), 236
NVP (Network Voice Protocol), 51

O

objectives. *See* goals and objectives
Office Communications Server 2007, 66–71
Active Directory and, 243–244
application server deployment, 241–243
background of, 66–67
Communicator Web Access, 70
configuration options, 69
features, 67
installing/configuring (with MCM), 235
Microsoft/SAP collaboration, 13
normalization to TEL URI format, 238
Office Communicator 2007, 69–70
platforms, 68
RCC configuration and, 237–238
SIP routing and redundancy configuration, 238
Telephony Gateway and Services component, 235–236
UC enablement, 239–241
Office Communicator 2007, 69–70
Office, Microsoft, 65–66
Office Outlook 2005, Microsoft, 29–31
one-time passwords, 379
open federations, IM (instant messaging), 58

operating costs, ERP lowering, 100
operating systems (OSs)
cost elements in UC enablement, 175
securing, 387–388
operational expenditures. *See* OPEX (operational expenditures)
operations, manufacturing, 115, 430
OPEX (operational expenditures)
business case for UC enablement and, 173
defined, 430
ROI and, 198
tracking KPIs and metrics for, 206–207
options message, SIP, 54
Oracle, 13
organizational convergence, 50–51, 430
organizations
enterprise transformation and, 83–84
goals and objectives of, 84
OSs (operating systems)
cost elements in UC enablement, 175
securing, 387–388

P

P&L (profit and loss)
defined, 430
UC Business Value Tool v1.5 reports, 189
partitioning enterprise networks, 383
passwords, application-based security layer, 379
patches, certification of, 313
PAT (Port Address Translation), 373
PBXs (Private Branch Exchanges)
comparing VoIP vs. SIP enablement of, 52
defined, 430
integration requirements, 232–235
IP-PBX. *See* IP-PBX
standards for interoperability, 47
TDM-PBX. *See* TDM-PBX system
voice conferencing and, 34
VoIP integration with, 232, 236
PCA (personal call assistant)
defined, 430
defining terminal number for, 235

VoIP/PBX integration and, 234
PDAs (personal digital assistants)
application and system integration and, 254–255
authentication, 259
layered security, 378
as mobile endpoint device, 252
monitoring endpoint device access, 261
network access from PDAs/cell phones, 380
PeopleSoft, 13
people-to-people communications, 86
performance
signaling control and, 301
SIP (Session Initiation Protocol), 350
personal call assistant. *See* PCA (personal call assistant)
personal digital assistants. *See* PDAs (personal digital assistants)
phases, project, 200–202, 215–217
phishing
defined, 430
vulnerabilities, 274–275
phone code vulnerabilities, 271–272
pilot projects. *See* proof-of-concept pilot projects
pinholing, ALG, 308–309
planning
pilot projects, 197, 202
projects, 430
policies
audit, 312–313
AUP (acceptable use policy), 224, 425
change control, 305
change review, 312
end-user policy-based security layer, 372–373, 380
layered security, 373–375
presence-aware applications and, 31
privacy, 304
usage, 310–311
poller, presence personalities, 26
Port Address Translation (PAT), 373
ports, restricting port access, 386
presence, 24–32
attributes in presence messages, 26
defined, 5
overview of, 24–25
personalities of, 26

presence-aware applications, 29–32

states and status notes, 27

state transitions, 28–29

what it is, 25–26

presence-aware applications, 29–32

presence status

content management and, 31

IM (instant messaging) and, 32–33, 239

MCS 51000, 27

for mobile users, 65

smart tags and, 7

presentity, presence personalities, 26

principals, IM (instant messaging), 32

privacy

compliance with privacy practices, 304

functional requirements and, 215

security best practices and, 303

Private Branch Exchanges. *See* PBXs (Private Branch Exchanges)

probe, presence attributes, 26

processes (workflows)

integrating UC enablement with business processes, 177–178

reducing sales process time, 102

SOA applications for, 86

product flows, SCM and, 94–95

productivity

business value drivers for, 177

drivers for UC enablement, 174

profit and loss (P&L)

defined, 430

UC Business Value Tool v1.5 reports, 189

project milestones and checkpoints, 220–222, 430

project plans

defined, 430

milestones and checkpoints, 221

project phases, tasks, and deliverables and, 215

projects

aligning project scope to budget, 222–223

KPIs and metrics tracking completion of, 180

phases, tasks, and deliverables, 215–217

pilot. *See* proof-of-concept pilot projects

proof-of-concept pilot projects, 195–211

aligning requirements, goals, objectives with PKIs and metrics, 205–206

budgeting, 207–208

goals and objectives, 203–205

justifying cost, 198–199

phases, 200–202

planning, 197

purpose of UC enablement, 198

review, 209–211

scope, 199

technical requirements and capabilities and, 199–200

UC Business Value Tool v1.5 KPIs and metrics, 206–207

protocols

compatibility issues, 301

convergence, 47–49

encryption, 258

SIP threats and vulnerabilities, 337

VoIP threats and vulnerabilities, 273–274, 280–286

proxies, SIP. *See* SIP proxies

PSTN (Public Switched Telephone Network)

defined, 430

E911 services and, 362

interoperability with PBX, 241

PBX loss plan and, 235

SIP gateway attached to, 23

VoIP gateway for connecting IP phones to, 53

public/private keys, application-based security layer, 379

Public Switched Telephone Network. *See* PSTN (Public Switched Telephone Network)

Q

Q.931 protocol, 284

QoS (quality of service)

network availability and, 306

QoS (quality of service)-aware networks, 425

R

radio frequency identification (RFID)

defined, 431

tracking endpoint device location, 262

RCC (remote call control)

configuring, 237–238

defined, 431

SIP CTI TR87 licenses and, 234

SIP routing and redundancy configuration and, 238–239

real estate, KPIs and metrics tracking costs of, 179

Real-Time Control Protocol (RTCP), 268, 284, 289–290

Real-Time Streaming Protocol (RTSP)

encryption, 358

VoIP threats and vulnerabilities, 268, 289

redirect servers, SIP roles, 54

redundancy, SIP, 238

registering endpoint devices, 260

register message, SIP, 54

registrar servers, SIP roles, 54

registration

hijacking, 328–329

user security and, 309

regulations

compliance with, 304, 306–308

corporate, 303

SIP security best practices, 352

VoIP security best practices, 302

remote call control. *See* RCC (remote call control)

remote device control

defined, 431

view sharing and, 36–37

remote locations, layered security, 380

reports, VoIP and UC devices, 301

request message codes, SIP, 322

requirements definition

aligning project scope to budget, 222–223

defined, 430

functional, 431

identifying for pilot projects, 200–201

mapping the requirements to a solution. *See* mapping solutions to technologies

project phases, tasks, and deliverables and, 215

technical, 432

response message codes, SIP, 323–325

review

milestones and checkpoints, 222

policies, 312

project results, 220

RFID (radio frequency identification)
defined, 431
tracking endpoint device location, 262
risk assessment team, 203
risks
accessibility and, 279
defined, 431
evaluating, 313
industry, 279
minimizing, 203
overview of, 278–279
product-related solutions, 279
technology investment and deployment, 197
ROI (return on investment)
aligning project scope to budget, 223
aligning requirements, goals, objectives with PKIs and metrics, 205–206
balancing improved communications with, 1
building ROI model, 202, 222
business case for UC enablement and, 173
defined, 431
integrating UC enablement with business processes, 177–178
linking project success to, 195
project scope and, 199
sales/revenues metrics and, 177
SOW (statement of work) and, 213
UC Business Value Tool v1.5 and, 182–186
UC enablement and, 198
routing, SIP, 238
RTCP (Real-Time Control Protocol), 268, 284, 289–290
RTP (Real-Time Protocol)
encryption, 358–359
as media transport protocol for SIP and VoIP systems, 377
RTP with H.323, 284
SIP message and content integrity and, 354
VoIP threats and vulnerabilities, 268, 289–290
RTSP (Real-Time Streaming Protocol)
encryption, 358
VoIP threats and vulnerabilities, 268, 289

S

sales cycles
KPI and metrics for sales cycle times, 176
KPIs and metrics tracking, 180
shortened, 111, 180, 205–206, 432
sales force automation. See SFA (sales force automation)
sales, general, and administrative overhead. See SG&A (sales, general, and administrative overhead)
sales, KPIs and metrics for, 206
sales users, access control, 300
Sarbanes-Oxley (SOX), 307, 361
SBCs (session border controllers)
Active Directory and, 365
defined, 431
layered security, 376, 382
securing corporate communication, 382
securing federations, 376
security best practices, 309–310
service-based security layer, 372, 373
SIP message and content integrity and, 354
SCADA (System Control and Data Acquisition), 251
schema, Active Directory, 244
SCM (supply chain management), 93–97
challenges to, 93
cost benefits of, 96–97
defined, 432
elements of, 94
illustration of SCM infrastructure, 94
information, money, and product flows, 94–96
scope, project
aligning to budget, 222–223
budgeting and, 207–208
goals and objectives, 203–205
overview of, 199
script kiddies
defined, 431
overview of, 269
SCS (Software Communication System), 74–75
SDP (Session Description Protocol), 36
SEC (Securities and Exchange Commission), 431

Secure Multipurpose Internet Mail Extensions (S/MIME), 350
Secure Sockets Layer (SSL)
defined, 431
SIP confidentiality and, 348
Securities and Exchange Commission (SEC), 431
security administration, building project team, 224
security best practices, SIP, 343–367
ALGs (application layer gateways), 363–364
application deployment, 348–349
application integrity, 353–354
authentication, 351–352
authentication availability, 360–361
availability, 360
compliance, 361–362
confidentiality, 346–348
core device availability, 361
E911 services, 362
encryption, 357–360, 365
for enterprises and federations, 362
firewalls, 363
integrity, 352–353
laws and regulations, 352
message and content integrity, 354–355
NAT, 364
need for security, 345–346
network availability, 360
network security, 362
review, 366–367
signaling control and media control, 350–351
user authentication, 356–357
user registration and proxies and, 364–365
VLANs, 365
security best practices, VoIP, 295–317
access control, 299–300
accessibility goals and objectives, 305
ALG (application layer gateway), 308–309
application authenticity, 309
application integrity, 304
audit policies, 312–313
authentication, 300
authentication availability, 305
change control, 305

CIA (confidentiality, integrity, and accessibility), 297–298
compliance with rules and regulations and, 306–308
confidentiality goals and objectives, 298–299
core device availability, 306
data integrity, 302–303
deploying network devices and, 301
emergency services availability, 306
encryption, 304, 310
firewalls and, 308
integrity goals and objectives, 302
intrusion detection systems, 310
need for security, 297
network availability, 306
privacy practices and corporate regulations and, 303
regulations and laws and, 302
review, 314–317
review policies, 312
session border controllers, 309–310
signaling control, 300–301
testing before deploying, 314
usage policies, 310–311
user identity, 303
user registration and proxies and, 309
validation of, 311–312
vendor solutions, 313–314
VoIP deployment and, 297
security, layered. See layered security
security policies
creating VoIP and SIP security policies, 373–375
end-user policy-based security layer, 372
servers, cost elements in UC enablement, 175
service-based security layer
designing layered security, 372
endpoint devices and, 378
VoIP and SIP security layers, 373
service-oriented architecture (SOA), 84–87
services
restrictions in layered security, 377
service provider initiatives, 14–15
support for local endpoint devices, 253

support for mobile endpoint devices, 254
session border controllers. See SBCs (session border controllers)
Session Description Protocol (SDP), 36
Session Initiation Protocol. See SIP (Session Initiation Protocol)
session registration, layered security, 376–377
SFA (sales force automation), 101–103
benefits of, 102–103
challenges to, 101
defined, 431
example business case for UC enablement, 176–177, 179–182
goals and objectives for pilot project, 204
key elements in, 101–102
SG&A (sales, general, and administrative overhead)
defined, 431
ERP systems providing real-time reporting, 100
tracking KPIs and metrics for, 206
UC KPIs, 179
shipping, 427
shortened sales cycle
defined, 432
KPIs and metrics and, 180
reviewing end of project results and, 205–206
UC benefits, 111
Siemens, 75
signaling control
SIP security best practices, 350–351
VoIP security best practices, 300–301
signaling server, RCC, 237
single-node redundancy, SIP, 238–239
SIP CTI TR87 standard, 234
SIP-enabled applications
customer service and, 118
defined, 432
SIP over TLS, 377
SIP ports, 233
SIP proxies
Active Directory and, 365
branch offices/remote locations and, 381
configuring proxy server, 235
defined, 432

proxy server role, 54
SBCs used as, 376
service-based security layer, 373, 378
SIP security best practices, 364–365
user registration and, 309
VoIP security best practices, 309
SIPS
application support for, 349
compatibility issues, 350
SIP (Session Initiation Protocol)
CIA (confidentiality, integrity, and accessibility) and, 378–379
conferencing, 34–35
connectivity models, 56–57
converged desktop and, 22
defined, 431
designing layered security for, 371–373
features, 53–54
as foundation for UC, 52–53
layered security, 372–373
Microsoft adopting, 8
overview of, 321–322
partitioning enterprise networks and, 384
protocol convergence and, 48–49
RCC configuration, 238
restricting SIP sources, 382
roles and messages, 54
routing and redundancy configuration, 238–239
security best practices. See security best practices, SIP
security policies, 373–375
status codes, 54–55
threats and vulnerabilities. See threats and vulnerabilities, SIP
URIs (Uniform Resource Identifiers), 322
VoIP as foundation for SIP enablement, 51–52
VoIP/PBX integration and, 236
VoIP threats and vulnerabilities, 267
vulnerabilities, 286–289
SIP trunks
configuring, 236
extensions of SIP threats and vulnerabilities, 339
securing federations, 375–376
smartphones
application and system integration and, 255
authentication, 259

defined, 432
as mobile endpoint device, 252
monitoring endpoint device
    access, 261
smart tags, 7
SMB, 74–75
S/MIME (Secure Multipurpose
    Internet Mail Extensions), 350
SOA (service-oriented architecture),
    84–87
social engineering
    SIP threats and vulnerabilities,
        328
    VoIP threats and vulnerabilities,
        274
social threats, 276
soft phones
    data security and, 297
    TDM-PBX, IP-PBX, and
        Softphone integration
        requirements, 232–235
software
    audit policies, 312–313
    cost savings resulting from UC
        enablement, 175
    unauthorized, 277–278
    vulnerabilities, 270–271
software administration, building
    project team, 224
Software Communication System
    (SCS), 74–75
SOW (statement of work), 213–227
    aligning project scope to budget,
        222–223
    defined, 432
    defining, 217–220
    milestones and checkpoints,
        220–222
    for pilot project, 202
    project phases, tasks, and
        deliverables, 215–217
    review, 225–227
    team building, 223–224
SOX (Sarbanes-Oxley), 307, 361
spam over Internet telephony
    (SPIT)
    SIP threats and vulnerabilities,
        328
    VoIP threats and vulnerabilities,
        273
SPIT (spam over Internet
    telephony)
    SIP threats and vulnerabilities,
        328
    VoIP threats and vulnerabilities,
        273

SSL (Secure Sockets Layer)
    defined, 431
    SIP confidentiality and, 348
standards documents, presence-
    aware applications and, 31
statement of work. See SOW
    (statement of work)
states, presence
    status notes and, 27
    transitions, 28–29
status notes, presence, 27
subscribe, presence attributes, 26
subscribed, presence attributes, 26
subscriber, presence personalities,
    26
supplier network
    defined, 432
    SCM and, 127
    UC enablement and, 126
supply chain management. See SCM
    (supply chain management)
system administration
    building project team, 224
    cost elements in UC enablement,
        175
System Control and Data
    Acquisition (SCADA), 251

T

T.120, 284
tablet computers
    application and system
        integration and, 254
    authentication, 260
tasks
    defining for pilot project, 202
    milestones and checkpoints, 222
    projects, 215–217
TCO (total cost of ownership)
    cost savings, 175
    defined, 432
    drivers for UC enablement, 174
TCP/IP (Transmission Control
    Protocol/Internet Protocol)
    infrastructure convergence and,
        46
    SIP and, 321
TCP (Transport Control Protocol)
    layered security. See transport-
        protocol security layer
    vs. UDP, 337
TDM-PBX system
    communication systems
        integration, 232–235
    layered security, 384–85

TDM (Time-Division Multiplexing)
    communication systems
        integration, 232–235
    infrastructure convergence and,
        46
    securing TDM side of IP-PBX
        system, 386
team building, 223–224
technical requirements
    defined, 432
    proof-of-concept pilot project
        and, 199–200
technology. See mapping solutions
    to technologies
TEI (Total Economic Impact) model,
    183–184
telecommunications
    product manufacturers, 13–14
    UC decision makers, 173
telephony
    securing telephony access in
        TDM-PBX system, 385
    SIP extension into traditional,
        339
    vendors, 75
Telephony Gateway and Services
    component, 235–236
TEL URI format, normalization to,
    238
termination DoS attacks, 331–333
tests, deployment and, 314
third-parties, controlling access, 300
threats and vulnerabilities, SIP,
    319–341
    application tampering, 327–328
    attacks, 338–339
    authentication, 337–338
    eavesdropping, 334–337
    encryption, 338
    extensions into other
        federations, 339
    flooding DoS, 334
    fuzzy DoS, 330–331
    Internet accessibility, 327
    message formats, 337
    message tampering, 328
    overview of SIP, 321–322
    protocol vulnerabilities, 337
    registration hijacking, 328–329
    review, 340–341
    risks, 326–327
    SIP request message codes, 322
    SIP response message codes,
        323–325
    social engineering, 328

termination DoS, 331–333
UDP vs. TCP and, 337
threats and vulnerabilities, VoIP
code, 271
defined, 432, 433
G.7xx codecs, 284
H.225.0, 280–281
H.235, 283
H.239, 283
H.245, 282
H.26x codecs, 284
H.323, 280, 284–286
H.450, 282–283
H.460, 284
hardware, 269–270
human factor, 278
industry, 277
known threats, 275
known vulnerabilities and, 276
malicious users, 275–276
MGCP, 290–291
overview of, 268–269, 275
phishing, 274–275
phone code, 271–272
protocol, 273–274
Q.931, 284
review, 292–293
RTCP, 284, 289–290
RTP, 284, 289–290
RTSP, 289
SIP (Session Initiation Protocol),
286–289
social, 276
social engineering, 274
software, 270–271
T.120, 284
UC applications and, 272
unauthorized hardware or
software, 277–278
UNISTIM, 289
unknown threats, 277
unknown vulnerabilities and,
277
VoIP protocols, 280
XML and, 272
Time-Division Multiplexing. *See*
TDM (Time-Division
Multiplexing)
TLS (Transport Layer Security)
defined, 432
encryption, 357
federation security and, 58–59
SIP confidentiality and, 348
SIP over TLS, 377
total cost of ownership. *See* TCO
(total cost of ownership)

Total Economic Impact (TEI) mode,
183–184
tracking and monitoring
endpoint devices, 260–262
KPIs (key performance
indicators), 178
training
cost savings resulting from UC
enablement, 175
KPIs and metrics tracking costs
of, 179
Transfer Call function, converged
desktop, 24
Transmission Control Protocol/
Internet Protocol (TCP/IP)
infrastructure convergence and,
46
SIP and, 321
Transport Control Protocol (TCP)
layered security. *See* transport-
protocol security layer
vs. UDP, 337
Transport Layer Security. *See* TLS
(Transport Layer Security)
transport-protocol security layer
designing layered security, 371
endpoint devices and, 378
VoIP and SIP security layers, 373
travel, KPIs and metrics tracking
costs of, 179
twinning
defined, 432
PCA trunks and, 234

U

uaCSTA (user agent CSTA), 22
UAC (user agent clients), 54
UAS (user agent servers), 54
UCAAS (Unified Communications
as a Service)
defined, 433
SMB market and, 74
UC Business Value Tool v1.5,
182–189
defined, 432
financial outputs from, 186–189
inputting data into, 184–186
intended uses, 183
KPIs and metrics for proof-of-
concept pilot project, 206–207
overview of, 182
TEI (Total Economic Impact)
model, 183–184
UC enablement
assessing, 77

communication systems
integration, 239–241
defined, 432
enterprise transformation and,
83
integrating with business
processes, 177–178
IT (Information Technology)
and, 197
purpose of, 198
real-time communications and,
102
SOA applications integrated
with, 86
UC (Unified Communications),
introduction to
basic elements in, 5–7
defined, 432
driving forces in, 7–9
enterprise application
initiatives, 12–13
enterprise IT consulting
companies, 15
IT infrastructure companies, 14
key market makers, 10–11
reasons for adopting, 9–10
review, 16–18
service provider initiatives,
14–15
telecommunications product
manufacturers, 13–14
vendor solutions, 12
what it is and benefits of, 4
UDP (User Datagram Protocol)
layered security. *See* transport-
protocol security layer
SIP and, 321
SIP and network availability
and, 360
vs. TCP, 337
UC applications and, 272
UM (Unified Messaging)
defined, 433
development and benefits of, 3–4
unavailable, presence attributes, 26
Unified Communications. *See* UC
(Unified Communications)
Unified Communications as a
Service (UCAAS)
defined, 433
SMB market and, 74
Unified Messaging (UM)
defined, 433
development and benefits of, 3–4

Uniform Resource Identifiers. *See* URIs (Uniform Resource Identifiers)

UNISTIM, 289

unknown threats, 277

unknown vulnerabilities, 277

unsubscribe, presence attributes, 26

URIs (Uniform Resource Identifiers)
  SIP, 322
  SIP AOR, 55
  VoIP/PBX integration and, 236

usage policies, VoIP, 310–311

user agent clients (UAC), 54

user agent CSTA (uaCSTA), 22

user agent servers (UAS), 54

User Datagram Protocol. *See* UDP (User Datagram Protocol)

users
  access control, 299–300
  authentication, 243, 304, 356–357
  designing VoIP and UC infrastructure and, 279
  identity, 303
  proxies, 309
  registration, 309, 364–365

V

validation
  milestones and checkpoints, 222
  operating system integrity, 388
  project results, 220
  security enforcement, 313
  security policies, 311–312

value added servers (VAS)
  configuring, 237
  defined, 433

VAS (value added servers)
  configuring, 237
  defined, 433

vendors
  enterprise desktop productivity. *See* enterprise desktop productivity
  ERP systems, 98
  SMB, 74–75
  solutions, 12
  UC, 65–66
  VoIP security solutions, 313–314

view sharing
  defined, 433
  file transfer and, 37
  remote manipulation and, 36–37

virtual corporations/communities, 57

virtual local area networks. *See* VLANs (virtual local area networks)

virtual private networks (VPNs)
  IPsec (IP Security) and, 258
  securing corporate communication to branch offices/remote locations, 382

visibility, controlling device visibility, 301

VLANs (virtual local area networks)
  partitioning enterprise networks and, 384
  SIP security best practices, 365
  transport-protocol security layer and, 373

voice conferencing, 34

voice mail
  defined, 433
  functionality of, 1

voice networks
  convergence with data. *See* convergence, of voice/data networks
  VoIP and, 47

VoIP (Voice over Internet Protocol)
  CIA (confidentiality, integrity, and accessibility) and, 378–379
  cost savings resulting from UC enablement, 175
  designing layered security for VoIP infrastructure, 371–373
  as foundation for SIP enablement, 51–52
  integration with PBX, 232
  layered security, 372–373, 385–387
  partitioning enterprise networks and, 384
  security best practices for deploying, 297
  security policies, 373–375
  threats and vulnerabilities. *See* threats and vulnerabilities, VoIP
  UC not dependent on, 4

VPNs (virtual private networks)
  IPsec (IP Security) and, 258
  securing corporate communication to branch offices/remote locations, 382

W

WANs (wide area networks)
  bandwidth costs, 175
  broad-based security layer, 371
  enterprise networks and, 251
  securing corporate communication to branch offices/remote locations, 381

watcher, presence personalities, 26

Web browsers, role in application convergence, 49

Web conferencing
  Communications Server 2007 support, 239
  SIP confidentiality and, 348

WEP (Wired Equivalent Privacy), 258

whiteboard function, view sharing and, 36

white hat hackers
  defined, 433
  overview of, 269

white list federations, 58

wide area networks. *See* WANs (wide area networks)

Wi-Fi Protected Access (WPA), 258

Wired Equivalent Privacy (WEP), 258

wireless local area networks (WLANs), 37

wireless networks
  layered security, 378
  protocol convergence and, 48

WLANs (wireless local area networks), 37

worms, phishing, 274

WPA (Wi-Fi Protected Access), 258

X

XML (Extensible Markup Language)
  transporting XML messages over SIP sessions, 22
  vulnerabilities, 272

XMPP (Extensible Messaging and Presence Protocol), 58

Y

Y-Generation (Echo Generation), 120, 428